6G Networks and AI-Driven Cybersecurity

Riaz Ahmed Shaikh
University of East Anglia, UK

IGI Global
Scientific Publishing
Publishing Tomorrow's Research Today

Vice President of Editorial	Melissa Wagner
Director of Acquisitions	Mikaela Felty
Director of Book Development	Jocelynn Hessler
Production Manager	Mike Brehm
Cover Design	Jose Rosado

Published in the United States of America by
IGI Global Scientific Publishing
701 East Chocolate Avenue
Hershey, PA, 17033, USA
Tel: 717-533-8845
Fax: 717-533-7115
Website: https://www.igi-global.com E-mail: cust@igi-global.com

Library of Congress Cataloging-in-Publication Data

LCCN: 2025000163 (CIP Pending)
ISBN13: 9798337305684
Isbn13Softcover: 9798337305691
EISBN13: 9798337305707

British Cataloguing in Publication Data
A Cataloguing in Publication record for this book is available from the British Library.

Editorial Advisory Board

Table of Contents

Detailed Table of Contents

6G networks represent a major advancement in wireless communication, building on 5G to deliver ultra-fast data rates, near-zero latency, massive connectivity, and seamless integration across terrestrial, aerial, and satellite systems. Powered by technologies like terahertz (THz) communication, AI, quantum computing, edge computing, and blockchain, 6G ensures ultra-high bandwidth, intelligent management, enhanced security, and energy efficiency. Its multi-layer architecture supports diverse use cases with robust performance. Global efforts focus on standards for spectrum, interoperability, cybersecurity, and sustainability. Addressing societal challenges, 6G enables innovations in holographic communication, XR, smart cities, and healthcare while tackling energy and ethical issues, offering transformative global potential.

From this chapter, readers obtain an in-depth understanding of the trends of the mobile communication technologies from 1G to 4G, and the importance of 5G and the further development of 6G. It reviews the socio-psychological consequences of these technologies on behaviour, thinking and organisations. Along with describing 5G technology, it is necessary to consider its foundational characteristics focusing on eMBB, ULLC, and mMTC. The chapter also focuses on the trends in 5G technology and its features like millimeter waves, massive MIMO (Multiple Input Multiple Output), and network slicing and their effect on multitasking, making information and social interactions. Hypothesized future of 6G systems and possibilities of developing terahertz communications, integration of AI, and holo-multimedia communication. The latter brings the discussion of the matter to contexts like smart cities and IoT as well as addresses the aspects of cognitive load and ethical intensions.

The rapid evolution from Industry 4.0 to Industry 5.0 demands the implementation of new advanced wireless technologies to enable human-centered, sustainable, and resilient industrial systems. This work discusses the revolutionary effect of 6G wireless communication with ultra-high speed, near-zero latency, and ultra-high connectivity in these Industry 5.0 implementation. This will provide a glimpse into how 6G will enable intelligent manufacturing, personalized medicine, smart transportation, green energy networks, and enhanced human-machine interaction. 6G plays a crucial in realizing Industry 5.0 since it is expected to offer THz communications, AI-native networks, and transparent machine-to-machine communication. 6G will revolutionize industrial operation by bridging the gap between physical and digital domains, resulting in greater efficiency, customization, and sustainability. This study briefs the important considerations involved in implementing next-generation wireless technologies to make the visionary concept of Industry 5.0 a reality.

Satellite based communication will be an important advancement as 6G networks develop, improving connectivity with ultra-low latency, fast data transmission, and wide coverage. A crucial strategy for network resilience is the integration of satellite systems with terrestrial networks, which offers seamless access in rural and distant locations and expands connectivity to underserved areas. To overcome these challenges, technological innovations such as multi-beam antennas, AI-based resource management, and next-generation satellite constellations are suggested. Concerns necessity of strong cryptographic techniques, safe key management to guarantee data integrity in this network of interconnected satellites and terrestrial systems. As a result, it is anticipated that 6G satellite communications would provide improved IoT support, quicker data speeds, and reliable emergency communication capabilities, making them an essential part of future global connection.

Artificial Intelligence and Blockchain technology have played vital role in 6G networks. As more research and ideas have intensified in this field it is quite a challenge to design and propose a robust 6G network that is optimized, secured, transparent and efficient in connectivity. Still all stakeholders of this fields are busy in finding right network architecture by adding and verifying different innovative algorithms of AI and Machine learning. Blockchain technology (BCT) provides adequate solution in 6G like secured connection, trusted data accessing and privacy protections. The definite and distinguished role of AI and BCT in 6G network, is still in its search as more and more research intensify in this area. Thus, this chapter dives into the basics of AI and BCT role in 6G networks. Quantifying their design strategies and finding current as well as future research trends in this field is the ultimate findings of this chapter.

The combination of blockchain with 6G networks portrays a transformative approach to address the challenges faced in real-time authentication in Machine-to-Machine (M2M) communication. Since 6G networks directly connect huge, incomparable devices with ultra-low latency, high reliability, and improved security, the traditional centralized authentication mechanisms face challenges with scalability, efficiency, and reluctance to cyber threats. It silhouettes a workflow for real-time device authentication, highlighting the role of cryptographic identities, tamper of proof ledgers, and automated decision-making mechanisms in preventing spoofing, replay attacks, and other security vulnerabilities. This chapter also discuss the performance metrics and potential use cases, such as industrial automation, autonomous vehicles and IoT-based healthcare systems. By addressing the technical aspects of blockchain with 6G networks, this chapter aims to demonstrate its potential as a foundation to ensure secure, seamless communication in the next generation of M2M systems.

Explainable Artificial Intelligence (XAI) is pivotal in ensuring transparency, fairness, and trustworthiness in 6G networks, where AI-driven automation and decision-making play a central role. This study demontrates on how 6G integrates advanced machine learning models for network optimization, security, and resource allocation, the inherent complexity and opacity of these models pose challenges to accountability and interpretability. XAI techniques include model-agnostic explanations, attention mechanisms, and counterfactual reasoning, enhance the intelligibility of AI decisions, fostering regulatory compliance and user trust. This research explores XAI methodologies tailored for 6G, emphasizing their role in mitigating bias, ensuring robust security, and facilitating human-AI collaboration. Therefore, througgh embedding explainability into AI-driven 6G frameworks, we advance ethical AI deployment, fostering reliability and resilience in next-generation wireless networks evaluating technology acceptance.

The emergence of 6G networks represents a revolutionary step in wireless communication, embedding artificial intelligence (AI) at its heart to facilitate levels of automation, optimization, and intelligent decision-making that have never been seen before. However, with the increasing dependence on AI comes the serious challenges of transparency, fairness, accountability, and trustworthiness. This chapter delves into the paramount significance of Explainable Artificial Intelligence (XAI) in resolving these issues so that AI-based decisions in 6G networks are transparent, ethical, and value-aligned. The chapter dives into their implementation in crucial areas including network optimization, security, user-centric services, and predictive maintenance. It covers the ethical issues such as bias, privacy, and regulatory compliance. By integrating XAI into the 6G network fabric, this chapter imagines a future where intelligent systems are efficient, scalable yet equitable, transparent, and sustainable, and which promotes trust and inclusivity in a hyper-connected world.

The advent of 6G networks promises significant advancements in wireless communication, enabling faster speeds, ultra-low latency, and seamless connectivity across a vast range of devices. However, the complexity and scale of 6G networks introduce novel security challenges, making them highly susceptible to a variety of cyber threats, including adversarial attacks, data breaches, and malicious network interference. Artificial Intelligence (AI) has emerged as a powerful tool for enhancing the security of these networks, particularly through AI-driven threat detection and mitigation strategies. This review synthesizes recent literature from 2019 to 2025, exploring the application of AI in securing 6G networks. Finally, the paper provides insights into future research directions, focusing on the need for developing more resilient AI models and robust defense mechanisms to secure the 6G ecosystem.

As 6G networks come into existence, there will be ultra-low latency, high bandwidth, seamless integration of billions of devices, and a revolution of connectivity. But with these great strides, new challenges about the securing of these systems against very sophisticated cyber attacks have come up. This book discusses how AI can benefit the 6G system to detect and respond threats better. Through the utilization of AI algorithms, machine learning, and deep learning, 6G networks will autonomously identify and mitigate security risks in real time while adapting to dynamic and ever-evolving attack vectors. AI systems can monitor network traffic in real-time, analyze anomalies, and predict possible vulnerabilities before they are exploited, hence reducing the detection-to-mitigation cycle. As 6G networks become more complex and pervasive, AI will become an indispensable component in maintaining security and enabling a trustworthy digital ecosystem, thereby becoming a core component of the future network defense.

Preface

The latest advancements in 6G networks, when combined with artificial intelligence (AI), have the potential to significantly enhance cybersecurity measures. AI can offer innovative solutions to various cybersecurity challenges, such as threat detection, real-time response, and anomaly detection. However, the integration of AI also raises concerns about data privacy and the ethical use of information. It is crucial to continuously explore and develop AI-driven security solutions to stay ahead of emerging threats and foster ongoing innovation in cybersecurity. As 6G networks evolve, examining future trends and innovations will be essential to ensure robust and secure communication systems.

This edited book, 6G Networks and AI-Driven Cybersecurity provides insights into the convergence of 6G, AI, and cybersecurity. For this book, 28 chapter proposals were submitted from the researchers and students. The ten chapters were finally accepted for the inclusion in this book. The acceptance rate was 35.7%. The contributed chapters in this book cover a broad range of topics related to 6G Networks and AI-Driven Cybersecurity, including:

- Introduction to 6G networks
- Application of 6G Networks in Industry 5.0
- Satellite-based Communications in 6G networks
- Application of Blockchain technology in 6G networks
- Explainable AI in 6G networks
- AI for threat detections and mitigation in 6G networks

Chapter 1 explores the advancements and potential of 6G networks in wireless communication. It discusses how 6G builds on 5G to offer ultra-fast data rates, near-zero latency, and massive connectivity. The chapter explains the integration of terrestrial, aerial, and satellite systems, and the use of advanced technologies like THz communication, AI, quantum computing, edge computing, and blockchain. It highlights the benefits of 6G, including high bandwidth, intelligent management, enhanced security, and energy efficiency. Additionally, the chapter covers 6G architecture, global standards, societal challenges, and innovations in areas like holographic communication, XR, smart cities, and healthcare.

Chapter 2 provides an in-depth look at the evolution of mobile communication technologies from 1G to 4G, emphasizing the significance of 5G and the future development of 6G. It examines the socio-psychological impacts of these technologies on behavior, thinking, and organizations. The chapter details 5G's foundational characteristics, such as eMBB, ULLC, and mMTC, and explores trends like millimeter waves, massive MIMO, and network slicing, and their effects on multitasking, information processing, and social interactions. It also hypothesizes about 6G, including terahertz communications, AI integration, and holo-multimedia communication, discussing their implications for smart cities, IoT, cognitive load, and ethical considerations.

Chapter 3 examines the shift from Industry 4.0 to Industry 5.0, highlighting the role of 6G wireless technology in creating human-centered, sustainable, and resilient industrial systems. It discusses how 6G's ultra-high speed, near-zero latency, and extensive connectivity will enable intelligent manufacturing, personalized medicine, smart transportation, green energy networks, and enhanced human-machine interaction. The chapter also addresses the key considerations for implementing these next-generation technologies to achieve greater efficiency, customization, and sustainability in Industry 5.0.

Chapter 4 discusses the role of satellite-based communication in 6G networks, enhancing connectivity with ultra-low latency, fast data transmission, and wide coverage. It emphasizes integrating satellite systems with terrestrial networks for seamless access in rural and remote areas. The chapter suggests innovations like multi-beam antennas, AI-based resource management, and next-generation satellite constellations. It also highlights the need for strong cryptographic techniques and secure key management to maintain data integrity. Ultimately, 6G satellite communications are expected to improve IoT support, data speeds, and emergency communication capabilities, crucial for future global connectivity.

Chapter 5 explores the vital roles of Artificial Intelligence (AI) and Blockchain Technology (BCT) in 6G networks. It discusses the challenges in designing a robust, optimized, secure, transparent, and efficient 6G network. The chapter highlights ongoing efforts by stakeholders to find the right network architecture using innovative AI and machine learning algorithms. It also examines how BCT provides solutions for secure connections, trusted data access, and privacy protection. Ultimately, the chapter delves into the basics of AI and BCT in 6G, quantifies their design strategies, and identifies current and future research trends in this field.

Chapter 6 examines how blockchain enhances real-time authentication in 6G M2M communication. It addresses the limitations of traditional centralized mechanisms and proposes using cryptographic identities, tamper-proof ledgers, and automated decision-making. The chapter also highlights performance metrics and use cases like industrial automation, autonomous vehicles, and IoT-based healthcare, showcasing blockchain's potential for secure, seamless 6G M2M communication.

Chapter 7 investigate Explainable Artificial Intelligence (XAI) in 6G networks, highlighting its role in ensuring transparency, fairness, and trust. It discusses the integration of complex AI models for optimization, security, and resource allocation, and the challenges of accountability and interpretability. The chapter explores XAI techniques to enhance AI decision intelligibility, mitigate bias, ensure security, and facilitate human-AI collaboration, promoting ethical AI deployment in 6G networks.

Chapter 8 explores AI's role in 6G networks. It covers XAI's use in network optimization, security, user services, and predictive maintenance. It also discusses ethical issues like bias, privacy, and regulatory compliance, envisioning a future with efficient, transparent, and inclusive intelligent systems. This chapter envisions efficient, transparent, and inclusive intelligent systems in a hyper-connected world.

Chapter 9 highlights 6G advancements and security challenges, emphasizing AI's role in threat detection and mitigation. It reviews recent literature on AI in 6G security and suggests future research for resilient AI models and robust defenses.

Chapter 10 discusses the advancements in 6G networks and the security challenges they face. It highlights how AI, through algorithms, machine learning, and deep learning, can enhance 6G security by autonomously detecting and mitigating threats in real time. The chapter emphasizes AI's role in monitoring network traffic, analyzing anomalies, and predicting vulnerabilities, making AI essential for maintaining security in the complex 6G ecosystem.

This book bridges the gap between theoretical research and practical applications, fostering collaboration between academia and industry. By connecting cutting-edge research with real-world implementations, it promotes a deeper understanding and innovation in the field of AI-driven cybersecurity in 6G networks. The book covers a wide range of topics, including threat response, decision-making processes, and machine-to-machine communication, making it an invaluable resource. It is designed to benefit cybersecurity practitioners, computer scientists, industry professionals, policymakers, researchers, academicians, and anyone interested in advancing their knowledge in AI-driven cybersecurity in 6G networks.

Riaz Ahmed Shaikh
University of East Anglia, UK

Acknowledgment

We sincerely thank the editorial committee members for their guidance, the reviewers for their constructive feedback, and the publication team for their support. We also extend our gratitude to the authors who contributed to this book. Your collective efforts have been invaluable in bringing this book to life.

Chapter 1
Fundamentals of 6G Networks

Sridevi
https://orcid.org/0000-0002-9768-1599
Karnatak University, Dharwad, India

Amrutha Kolhar
https://orcid.org/0009-0001-4940-3172
Karnatak University, Dharwad, India

ABSTRACT

6G networks represent a major advancement in wireless communication, building on 5G to deliver ultra-fast data rates, near-zero latency, massive connectivity, and seamless integration across terrestrial, aerial, and satellite systems. Powered by technologies like terahertz (THz) communication, AI, quantum computing, edge computing, and blockchain, 6G ensures ultra-high bandwidth, intelligent management, enhanced security, and energy efficiency. Its multi-layer architecture supports diverse use cases with robust performance. Global efforts focus on standards for spectrum, interoperability, cybersecurity, and sustainability. Addressing societal challenges, 6G enables innovations in holographic communication, XR, smart cities, and healthcare while tackling energy and ethical issues, offering transformative global potential.

1. INTRODUCTION

Wireless communication has made impressive developmental changes through the voice-dependent 1G systems that eventually evolved into ground-breaking 5G capabilities. The development of 6G stands as a transformative advancement

DOI: 10.4018/979-8-3373-0568-4.ch001

which targets to provide quick speeds together with ultra-fast response times and unbroken connections for future use. The rollout of 6G systems is anticipated for the 2030s and the technology will expand 5G capabilities by supplying data transfer rates at 1 Tbps and microsecond latency measurements. The forthcoming generation network technology merges superior machine learning together with artificial intelligence components and upgraded sensing systems to manufacture grids which become intelligent and dynamic and operate rapidly. The three vital pillars which form the basis of 6G consist of ultra-reliable low-latency communications (URLLC) together with massive machine-type communications (mMTC) and enhanced mobile broadband (eMBB). These go beyond the limits of 5G, enabling revolutionary applications and ideas such as pervasive connectivity and omnipresent wireless intelligence. 6G uses the terahertz frequency band as its core protocol while creating obstacles from signal attenuation and antenna technology needs that demand the development of reconfigurable intelligent surfaces (RIS) and massive MIMO. The outstanding features of 6G technology enable it to transform industrial operations while redefining how people work and connect daily. 6G technology delivers multifaceted prospects that include better augmented reality and virtual reality and live holographic connections and brain-computer interfaces in addition to its objective for digital bridge connectivity and sustainability through sophisticated AI-based network control systems. Real-time data processing effectiveness of edge computing together with decentralized systems will support the Internet of Everything (IoE) along with autonomous vehicles and smart cities due to their proximity to end-users. 6G predicts a single global infrastructure that will link terrestrial with aerial and satellite networks to guarantee uninterrupted connectivity all over the globe. Quantum-resistant encryption combined with blockchain-based solutions will enhance both security and privacy systems. The achievement of this vision necessitates overcoming major barriers involving regulatory issues together with standardization standards and deployment expenses. The successful implementation of 6G at its highest capabilities requires harmonized global cooperation among research centers and both government agencies and industrial organizations. 6G represents the wireless technology evolution's highest point because it brings revolutionary changes to human and device networking. The introduction of digital communication with sustainable progress combined with innovation will produce a new age through wireless technology advances that transcend current capabilities (Duong et al., 2022; Lee et al., 2021; Liu et al., 2023; Pennanen et al., 2024; Soldani, 2021; Zawish et al., 2024).

1.1 Evolution from 5G to 6G

The wireless technology sector has experienced dramatic progress when moving from 5G to 6G which overcomes current constraints to enable totally new opportunities. The terahertz (THz) frequency usage for 5G has already established demanding standards even though the network focuses on achieving ultra-low latency and high-speed data transfer and wide device connection capabilities. The standards for both latency and data speeds get a complete reboot with 6G technology because it can deliver microsecond delays and achieve speeds reaching 1 Tbps. The significant boost allows brain-computer interfaces to join forces with immersive AR/VR technology and live holographic communication which require top-notch secure networks. Network architecture needs to integrate AI and ML methods perfectly for resource management systems to reach dynamic optimization. 6G technology improves every essential 5G feature including URLLC as well as mMTC and eMBB. ISAC in 6G technology delivers wireless intelligence between all networks to perform real-time operational monitoring and adjustments by linking sensing with communication capabilities. 6G infrastructure gives priority status to distributing edge computing systems and decentralized network architectures because this arrangement leads to speedy information handling and enhanced privacy safeguards. Sustainability methods have become essential for communication systems because they need techniques that reduce their quickly growing carbon emissions. Security features in 6G development utilize quantum communication protocols as well as blockchain-based security methods to defend confidential information from contemporary security threats. The infrastructure developed by 5G established essential interlinked ecosystems but 6G strives to establish a highly connected intelligent sustainable world. The technological evolution will transform markets while modifying human relationships and shows potential to bring transformative developments to every sector during the upcoming decades (Azari et al., 2022; Sergiou et al., 2020; M. Yang et al., 2024; Zawish et al., 2024).

1.2 Key Objectives and Vision for 6G

The primary mission of 6G technology aims to build an advanced wireless-communication system which establishes a highly connected and sustainable intelligent world. The 6G development extends 5G capabilities to address new issues and develop revolutionary applications. Across diverse sectors and communities. These major goals and direction establish the routes for developing 6G technology as follows:

- **Unmatched Latency and Speed:** 6G sets the goal to reach data transfer speeds of 1 Tbps and microsecond latency in its future infrastructure. The advancement will make possible next-generation applications such as high-speed Internet of Things equipment and Holographic communication as well as immersive extended reality which depend on speed along with instant data processing.
- **Adaptive and Intelligent Networks:** Through the integration of machine learning and artificial intelligence into the network's core, 6G aims to create self-optimizing, context-aware systems. These intelligent networks will dynamically adapt to user demands, optimize resource allocation, and enhance overall efficiency.
- **Leveraging the Terahertz Spectrum:** The implementation of 6G technology depends on utilizing the THz frequency spectrum to achieve its goals of unmatched data capacity and lightning-fast connectivity. Advanced antenna technologies and RIS represent solutions to tackle signal attenuation challenges for 6G's implementation.
- **Global and Pervasive Coverage:** The main objective of 6G technology involves connecting isolated communities through unified systems of terrestrial and satellite connections and aerial platforms. The network integration strategy will provide internet access to distant locations which currently lack digital connectivity.
- **Sustainable Development and Energy Efficiency:** 6G technology gives environmental impact reduction from communication technology systems a central position of importance. The emphasis goes toward developing energy-efficient solutions together with sustainable infrastructure and resource-optimized network designs. Sustainable development's larger objective receives support through this method of operation.
- **ISAC stands for Integrated Sensing and Communication:** The sixth-generation network architecture brings together two main capabilities through an integrated communication and sensing framework. Multiple data transmission and sensing functionality becomes possible thanks to this network solution. Networks of the sixth generation will enable these features to enhance applications in autonomous vehicles and smart city infrastructure and environmental monitoring platforms which will result in more intuitive system responses.
- **Enhanced Privacy and Security:** 6G technology will fight rising cybersecurity threats through its implementation of decentralized security systems which include blockchain along with quantum encryption protocols along with advanced data protection technologies. The combination of these se-

curity measures will produce secure data protection and maintain privacy integrity.

6G technology aims to advance both industrial revolution and enable social development through innovative growth while pursuing sustainability and equity. 6G technology seeks to create real interconnectedness in digital realms as it drives progress for society alongside inclusive economic expansion (Akbar et al., 2022).

2. CORE PRINCIPLES OF 6G NETWORKS

The basis of constructing 6G network infrastructure depends on established principles that build a digital system for network connectivity while supporting system intelligence alongside sustainability goals. 6G development targets both sub-millisecond delay times together with data rates greater than 1 Tbps as its main objective. Terahertz frequencies provide unlimited bandwidth that enables this achievement to become possible. The construction of smart reflective networks requires advanced antennas and smart reflectors which together enable THz signal propagation and full implementation of next-generation 6G systems. To begin with the design of 6G networks necessitates total integration between artificial intelligence system solutions and machine learning systems across their architecture framework. The network's automated capabilities support active monitoring by checking resources and making end-user prediction for demand-based resource allocation. 6G technology achieves its core functions through sensor data processing integration with environmental observation which allows network real-time operations for both information analysis and environmental monitoring. The revolutionary breakthrough enables extensive changes to the new technological era by creating opportunities for autonomous systems and smart transportation features and environment surveillance functions. Sustainability along with adaptability and intelligence serve as fundamental operational priorities during the development of 6G. 6G technology development integrates power efficiency design methods as part of network architecture to protect the environment from increasing network connectivity effects. 6G technology builds its worldwide network by combining satellite and aerial and terrestrial elements to minimize digital divide problems. A united network platform like this is essential for 6G development which depends on both connectivity and sustainability features to protect core security and privacy principles. The network defends itself by using quantum-resistant protocols combined with encryption techniques as well as blockchain mechanisms that protect against current cyber threats.. The upcoming 6G technology infrastructure has been built to provide both comprehensive device and software compatibility as well as promote worldwide collective advancement and future-readiness. These core principles enable 6G to establish an advanced age of synthesis between information connectivity with intelligence and sustainable development. 6G will define technological progress and digital communication development through its transformation of industries and its strengthening of societies while improving human experiences (Shen et al., 2023).

2.1 Ultra-Low-Latency and Ultra-High-Speed Communication in 6G Networks

- **Record-Breaking Information Rates:** The anticipated speed of 6G networks will reach 1 terabit per second (Tbps). The network enables such high-speed communication which serves applications needing substantial bandwidth. Next-generation live holographic displays together with immersive augmented and virtual reality and 4D imaging technologies receive momentum with this breakthrough which satisfies data-intensive enterprises and future technical advancements.
- **Microsecond-Level Latency:** 6G will strive to reach microsecond latency in order to establish extremely fast network connections. App performance requires this exceptional low latency. Real-time reactivity determines accuracy and safety in applications such as robotics as well as telemedicine and driverless cars. The quick latency reductions in 6G technology enable flawless performance of essential core systems as well as immersive systems.
- **Harnessing the Terahertz (THz) Spectrum:** The 6G network uses the high-frequency THz band to permit fast and rapid data exchange along with substantial bandwidth capabilities for future communications technology. The combination of RIS and advanced antenna technology makes THz signal propagation more efficient which solves signal attenuation problems to enable data-intensive applications at scale.
- **Enabling the Tactile Internet:** 6G networks provide the support necessary for Tactile Internet capabilities through ultra-low latency. 6G enhances applications that need immediate responsive haptic functions particularly in fields such as remote surgery and robotic operations and precision manufacturing. These applications benefit from human-machine interaction revolutionized by 6G technology.
- **Enhanced Edge Computing:** The capability of edge computing receives enhancement through 6G technology that enables data processing at source locations. The implementations reduce latency at the same time that they elevate operational performance. The distributed computing model reduces data center dependence to create quick decisions for real-time applications such as smart city infrastructure as well as driverless cars.

- **Future-Proof Infrastructure:** Developers have designed the 6G network infrastructure to support modern technological needs that may evolve over time. The combination of fast data transfer rates and microsecond latency makes 6G ready to power emerging technologies which include holographic communications and AI-driven systems while offering a flexible platform that benefits future technology developments. The basic requirements for achieving revolutionary 6G capabilities through its technological foundation include ultra-low latency and ultra-high-speed transmission (Duong et al., 2022; Ikram & Mumtaz, 2022; M. Yang et al., 2024).

2.2 Global and Universal Connectivity in 6G Networks

6G networks established global and universal connectivity which enables users to attain reliable and fast communication throughout all regions including remote areas or hard-to-access zones. 6G breaks free from previous technology limitations through the integration of satellite network systems as well as aerial platforms (drone and high-altitude) and terrestrial network operation. Through network integration 6G establishes a universal communication platform which ensures people across all locations obtain advanced technology benefits without restrictions. The basic framework of universal accessibility enables 6G networks to achieve low latency and high speed which enables real-time long-distance communication thus providing high-quality services even to remote areas. The development of smart agriculture combined with telemedicine and remote education technologies will deliver equal service quality to rural populations at the same level achieved by urban populations.

IoE technology gets its life force from 6G's monumental data-holding capabilities to unite trillions of devices in a unified system worldwide. The extensive level of connectivity enabled by 6G will influence smart city creation as well as automated industrial processes along with advanced user-specific interactions. Through the establishment of 6G technology a truly interconnected society will emerge which enables people and enterprises and governmental agencies to work together in real time for a connected future of all citizens.

2.3 Sustainability and Energy Efficiency in 6G Networks

Industrial designers of 6G networks must combine their efforts to achieve sustainability while ensuring energy efficiency since rising demands for quick connectivity and instant performance keep escalating. Energy demands on these networks grow because data speed needs and increasing device numbers put significant pressure on their power consumption. Proper attention must be given to energy-efficient infrastructure development for 6G because it requires power reduction without affecting performance measurements. 6G networks must deploy innovative balancing solutions because these solutions will enable the resolution of performance versus sustainability goals. A sustainable path toward reaching this objective exists through renewable energy networks which combine optimized networks with low-power hardware. Network management system resources deployed with AI technology automatically adjust their distribution according to user behavior patterns for reducing electrical consumption. The efficiency of processing increases at data center perimeter points as information remains local to its origin locations to reduce the total energy utilization. The success of 6G high-speed data transmission technology requires optimal allocation of the THz frequency spectrum that reduces all avoidable energy consumption. Reconfigurable intelligent surfaces (RIS) increase signal transmission efficiency along with maintaining 6G application requirements for quick speeds and minimal latency through their ability to use energy effectively. The 6G vision places great significance on sustainable energy management principles. The integration of eco-friendly technology and intelligent management systems in 6G will produce global connectivity without damaging the environment to create an interconnected sustainable world. SWOT analysis serves as an effective methodology for sustainability assessment of 6G technology according to Table 1. Additional information about the present elements in Table 2 is available through the supplied framework. Associated with energy-efficient 6G networks.

Table 1. SWOT analysis

Strength	**Weakness**
Integration of green technologies like low-power hardware and renewable energy sources.	High initial investment in developing energy-efficient technologies.
AI-powered intelligent network management for dynamic resource allocation.	Complex energy management challenges with the use of new technologies like THz frequencies.
Energy-efficient edge computing reducing reliance on centralized data centers.	Potential energy inefficiencies in early stages of implementation.
RIS improving signal transmission and reducing energy waste.	Need for extensive R&D to optimize power usage in 6G networks.

Table 2. Opportunities and threats

Opportunities	**Threats**
Growing demand for sustainable solutions in global technology development.	Environmental impact of manufacturing and disposal of network infrastructure.
Advancements in AI and machine learning to further optimize energy consumption.	Potential regulatory challenges around energy consumption and sustainability standards.
Public and private sector support for green tech and energy-efficient innovations.	Increased demand for high-speed data could outpace energy efficiency efforts.
Integration of renewable energy sources in network infrastructure to reduce reliance on non-renewable energy.	Rapid technological advancements could lead to obsolescence of current energy-saving technologies.

3. ENABLING TECHNOLOGIES FOR 6G NETWORKS

Many technological foundations serve as critical elements for 6G networks to achieve their goals of superior speed alongside minimum delay and worldwide reach. Radio Interference Shielding stands as one of the essential enabling technologies for (RIS) because it improves signal management to enhance coverage and operational efficiency. The ability of MIMO to boost network capacity depends on its use of multiple antennas to deliver better signal reception and transmission performance. The THz frequency spectrum maintains enough bandwidth for quicker data transfer together with enhanced communication possibilities. Spectrum control with advanced hardware requires equal management strategies for achieving maximum results. Systems that automatically optimize utilizing artificial intelligence develop self-adaptable capabilities for distributing resources in response to changing demands. System performance together with continuous connection becomes achievable by implementing these operational enhancements for optimal function delivery during busy communication events. The rapid handling of data at its original point together with real-time capabilities makes edge computing an efficient solution. The operation types achieve maximum benefit from immediate processing since they involve autonomous vehicles together with industrial automation and immersive XR experiences. ISAC integration allows data transmission between networks while providing immediate awareness about their operating environment. The three elements seamlessly integrated into 6G technology will develop its fundamental structure to enable industrial revolution through situational perception capabilities.

3.1 Transmission at Terahertz

THz transmission in 6G networks serves as a transformative approach toward massive bandwidth transmission for boosting data speeds at extreme rates. This bandwidth operates above 1 Tbps to cover the entire range extending from 0.1 to 10 THz of terahertz transmission. The future massive-data applications require real-time delivery of combined 3D videos and augmented and holographic communication systems which needs these extensive data transfer speeds. Multiple substantial technical challenges exist in order to harness the vast potential of THz communication systems. The main operational obstacle for THz waves stems from their susceptibility to physical barriers because atmospheric absorption diminishes signals through obstacles such as buildings and rain and trees. Various technical barriers pose obstacles to THz-based 6G network deployment until existing implementation challenges have proper solutions. 6G networks will face these obstacles by integrating signal processing technologies which improve the reliability for Terahertz band communication. Bandwidth allocation will receive higher efficiency through dynamic spectrum management procedures. The beamforming technology will guide signals directly at their designated receivers to maximize efficiency by diminishing signal loss and boosting performance. The role of RIS in THz signal propagation enhancement will be critical to modify environmental signals for improved coverage while reducing power usage. These advancements will help mitigate signal degradation, ensuring seamless connectivity even in complex environments. Despite these challenges, THz communication remains essential to realizing the full potential of 6G networks. By enabling ultra-fast, low-latency connectivity, it will support the next generation of data-intensive applications and drive innovations that redefine digital experiences. As a result, THz technology stands as a cornerstone of 6G, shaping the future of high-speed, high-capacity wireless communication.

3.1.1 Characteristics in Terahertz Communication

Table 3. Characteristics in Terahertz Communication

Characteristic	Description
Exceptionally High Data Rate	Very high data speeds of one terabit per second are made possible by THz communication, which powers next-generation technologies and supports applications that require a lot of data, such as holographic communication, immersive AR/VR, and 3D video streaming.
Minimal Latency	THz communication in 6G provides minimal latency, essential for real-time uses such as remote surgery, driverless cars, and the haptic Internet, allowing instant responsiveness with delays reduced to microseconds.
Tight Device Communication	THz enables dense device connectivity, managing simultaneous communications across a multitude of devices in Intelligent cities, IoE, and automation in industry, ensuring seamless instantaneous operations.
Low Wavelength and High Frequency	Operating at high frequencies (0.1 to 10 THz), THz communication offers low wavelengths that allow high data transfer rates, more efficient spectrum usage, and smaller components, supporting advanced applications like holographic communication.

3.1.2 Challenges in Terahertz Communication

- **Attenuation of Signals**: Signal attenuation is a significant challenge for THz communication in 6G networks. THz waves are highly susceptible to atmospheric absorption from oxygen, water vapour, and other environmental factors, resulting in long-distance signal degradation. THz-based communication experiences reduced effectiveness and quality because of brief transmission periods at room temperature.
- **Restricted Range**: THz communication in 6G faces range limitations due to severe signal attenuation and poor barrier penetration. Stomach and beamforming techniques must be used with THz waves because these signals need a direct view of the target to function effectively and keep their strength intact between short range connections.
- **Blockage & Obstruction**: 6G THz transmission faces severe sensitivity to blocking elements and obstacles within its path. Searching signals through solid barriers including walls and trees and buildings creates substantial signal losses or interruptions to THz wave's transmission. The blocking of signals needs line-of-sight transmission and beamforming approaches to solve this barrier.
- **Extremely Sensitive to Environmental Influences**: The performance of THz communication experiences significant degradation from environmen-

tal conditions that include rain and fog as well as humidity. The amount of absorption in the atmosphere rises significantly when these conditions exist leading to major signal deterioration. Dynamic spectrum management and beamforming techniques need implementation to offset environmental factors which affect reliable communication.

- **Regulation and Interference**: THz communication in 6G faces potential interference from other communication technologies due to the crowded frequency spectrum. International standards for allocating THz frequencies do not exist which leads to regulatory concerns. Successful spectrum management together with international agreements are vital because they minimize interference to ensure proper utilization of THz frequency bands. The network efficiency along with signal propagation and better network performance can be achieved through dynamic spectrum management and RIS technology implementation (Kleine-Ostmann & Nagatsuma, 2011; Serghiou et al., 2022, Amrutha Kolhar and Sridevi 2025).

3.2 6G Artificial Intelligence

AI establishes itself as a fundamental 6G network element which improves operational automation as well as network flexibility alongside maximum operational efficiency. The system contributes to network optimization by allowing decision-making processes to happen instantaneously for operations that require very low latency and high throughput goals. Large-scale data analysis through AI enables smart traffic control and resource distribution systems to adapt to changing conditions. Computer systems that enable AI automation reduce the need for human input during operations. Easy-operating applications including driverless cars and IoT technology along with cyberspace depend on ML models which provide predictions about congestion and detect issues and improve energy efficiency for smooth operations. Through edge computing AI speeds up both decision processes and reduces response time for VR technology as well as for smart manufacturing operations and remote healthcare services. The deployment of AI near data sources allows it to support time-sensitive applications which will be crucial for 6G. 6G exists as a product of AI and delivers intelligent network systems with autonomous operations to support upcoming technological requirements.

3.2.1 Using AI to Manage and Optimize Networks

- **Real-Time Traffic Management:** The document provides clear details about AI-powered traffic management in 6G networks to sustain optimal performance while facing peak usage..

- **Optimizing Predictive Networks**: The text describes how AI performs predictive analysis for network optimization through which bottlenecks can be prevented from developing in advance.
- **Allocation of Resources**: The article presents a well-defined explanation of how AI system optimizes real-time resource management to ensure network performance and speed maintenance.
- **Autonomous Networks**: As explained through clear examples AI self-healing features demonstrate how to minimize system stoppages along with human interaction needs.
- **Efficiency of Energy**: Most sources present the ways AI optimizes resource usage for enhanced energy efficiency which supports sustainability targets.
- **Network Slicing**: The document provides complete explanations about both dynamic allocation procedures and network optimization approaches that boost virtual network performance and service quality.
- **Management of Quality of Service (QoS)**: The text explains well the ways AI enhances QoS through network monitoring that enables adaptive behavior for real-time critical applications.

3.3 Quantum Computing and Security

The field of quantum computing makes advanced quantum mechanics principles function to compute calculations beyond the limits of standard computer hardware. The quantum mechanics principles enable quantum bits (qubits) to exist in multiple states simultaneously because of superposition and entanglement features. Quantum computers achieve exceptional power for certain problems thanks to their ability to handle vast simultaneous data processing tasks. Quantum computers handle particular computation challenges effectively such as high volume data processing and numerous simulation jobs and optimization applications. The increased processing functionality of quantum computers provides potential security risks although some solutions remain possible. Quantum computers display a capability to easily break existing cryptography methods that causes significant concerns. RSA encryption along with Elliptic curve cryptography represent two main encryption methods used in current times. The security of (ECC) encryption depends on computationally difficult mathematical tasks to solve discrete logarithms and factor big numbers. Shor's method alongside different quantum algorithms allows these mathematics challenges to be solved at a much faster rate than traditional encryption methods do which makes them vulnerable to decryption. Future quantum computers will be able to decrypt encrypted sensitive information stored with modern cryptography which puts banking and digital communication services along with government systems at security risk. Quantum cryptography has arisen to tackle the risks posed against communication systems. New methods of securing communication are developed through fundamental principles of quantum physics. QKD is one prominent method. The transfer of cryptographic keys through quantum entanglement happens securely using this method. The main benefit of QKD enables secure communications because any quantum state modification during intercession becomes instantly detectable bringing peace of mind to data integrity. People must prepare current cryptographic systems for future quantum computer capabilities since they can easily break ordinary encryption methods. The development of post-quantum cryptography emerged to create encryption methods which would remain secure against quantum-based assault attempts. The protection of information depends heavily on post-quantum world circumstances.

3.3.1 Enhancing Encryption and Computational Power in Computing at Quantum Distance and Security

The field of encryption technology receives major advancements through quantum computing because of its ability to substantially increase processing power when protecting sensitive data. Quantum computers leverage their superposed and entangled characteristics from quantum mechanics to execute data computations an exponential amount faster than classical computers do. The quick processing capabilities of quantum computing threatens RSA and ECC encryption methods that depend on involving complex mathematical mathematics for integer factoring. Through the implementation of Shor's algorithm quantum computers would efficiently solve these problems thus leading to the degradation of traditional encryption security. Quantum computing works to defend against these threats by developing encryption solutions which are quantum-proof. A fundamental breakthrough occurs through QKD because this system implements quantum mechanics to establish quantum-resistant encryption for secure communications. Shared keys remain secure and eavesdropping becomes detectable within QKD systems because quantum states automatically change when someone tries to monitor the transmission. The security level created by this method is nearly impossible to breach. The development of QKD offers only one path forward whereas scientists use additional methods to create encryption that defeats such quantum-based decryption systems. The post-quantum cryptographic methods employ mathematical problems which are impossible for quantum computers to solve efficiently thus ensuring safe data transfer during quantum operations. Quantum computing threats to present encryption standards create a chance to construct better and robust security systems for upcoming years. The capability of quantum computers serves as a tool for researchers to build encryption systems which protect digital communication networks during the quantum computing era.

3.4 Edge Computing and Blockchain in 6G Networks

The development of 6G networks depends heavily on Blockchain technology together with edge computing for superior performance and security with efficiency enhancement. The decentralization of data processing occurs when computer resources are positioned in locations that serve end users and this approach reduces latency to support real-time decision-making. Essential elements for 6G networks include swift data processing together with reactions that occur quickly. The applications of 6G technology include industrial automation together with smart cities and driverless car systems. The location of data processing at the network's edge results in faster responses and reduces strain on main servers and enables handling of enormous IoT device and connected system data volumes. The network performance benefits from efficient bandwidth management through edge calculation since it avoids congestion and performs data operations near users to create better system efficiency. Secure decentralized data handling with easy-to-understand methods together with transaction control appear as key features of blockchain. 6G implementation requires blockchain technology as its fundamental element to maintain privacy security of data and trust in distributed components for network protection. The network functionality benefits strongly from blockchain technology because it supports peer-to-peer transactions and smart contracts alongside IP connections together with the removal of system administrators while maintaining data integrity. The functionality of secure network slicing emerges from blockchain technology because it provides IT professionals the capability to assign separate network sections for various use cases and enhance resource efficiency. 6G networks use this networking solution to implement automated management functions which enforces security across entire infrastructure elements through regulatory policies.

3.4.1 Decentralized Processing and Secure Data Handling in 6G Networks

Computation through distributed networks puts workload operations in different connected devices located in various accessible network nodes. The system achieves faster information processing speeds and reduced latency since it operates close to points where data originates instead of being located in distant datacenters. IoT systems that collect enormous data amounts near network perimeters achieve better efficiency at the same time as increasing their scalability through edge processing. The decentralized approach to processing provides dual gains in system reliability as well as fault tolerance together with efficiency improvement benefits. This system allows real-time usage in autonomous vehicles combined with smart city functions that perform rapid operations to reduce traffic congestion duration. The system exhibits operational capabilities through normal functioning despite network failure of a single part. The protection of data through its entire lifetime along with collection storage and data transmission and processing requires secure data handling to be parallel with decentralization. Data protection depends on encryption algorithms and system authentication systems while resource accessibility permissions protect data of authorized users. The blockchain technology allows for authentic control of transaction records and system process data as a security improvement measure. Users can verify information with absolute integrity using this system which operates independently of central authority oversight. The decentralized trust system provides crucial value to industries that need maximal protection of sensitive information in areas such as finance and healthcare and IoT. Secure data handling methods which integrate decentralized processing create networks that boost both security and operational efficiency as well as reliability and make them indispensable for 6G technology advancement.

4. 6G NETWORK ARCHITECTURE

Figure 1. Architecture for 6G Networks

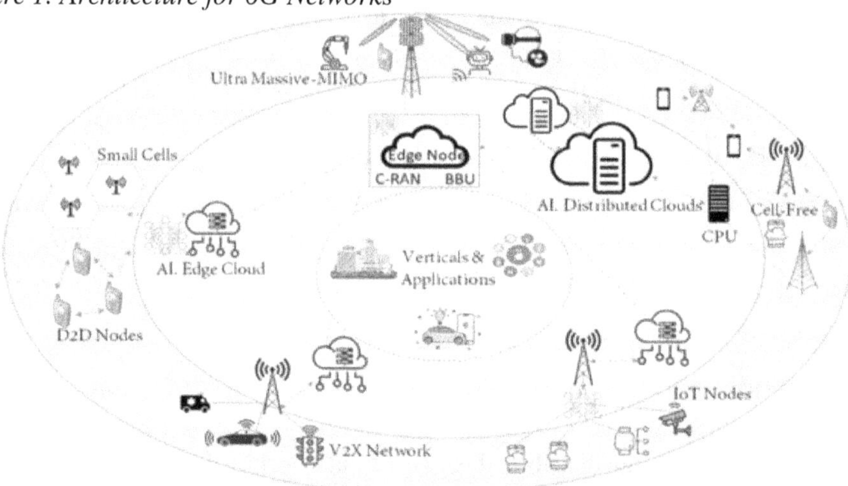

The diagram demonstrates a conceptual layout of potential 6G network implementation. The depicted key elements alongside advanced technology within the diagram deliver the capability of future wireless communication. The Edge Node stands as a vital network element for edge computing since it occupies the central position in the diagram. This node allows dispersed network operations by connecting to C-RAN (Cloud-Radio Access Network) and AI Edge Cloud and AI Distributed

Cloud components. The network infrastructure functions as processing centers with storage facilities. Numerous significant technologies, which boost network capacity and coverage, such as ultra-massive MIMO and tiny cells, surround the central edge computer systems. These technologies will enable smooth communication between a variety of devices and applications when combined with D2D Nodes (Device-to-Device communication), IoT Nodes, and V2X Networks (Vehicle-to-Everything). By illustrating the interactions between various communication networks and gadgets (like automobiles, Internet of Things gadgets, and tiny cells) inside the ecosystem, the figure highlights the network's scattered character. Among the key verticals and applications where 6G technology will be utilized are autonomous cars, smart cities, and industrial IoT. The picture also shows how data processing, storage, and network administration are done using cloud computing, CPU, and BBU (Base-band Unit). When combined, these components show how AI, cloud computing, and cutting-edge wireless technologies are coming together to power 6G networks and make ultra-low latency, high throughput, and intelligent network automation possible (Huang et al., 2019)(Zhang et al., 2019).

4.1 Multi-Layer Design Integrating Terrestrial, Aerial, and Satellite Systems in 6G Network Architecture

To enable continuous connectivity, 6G networks must be designed with a multi-layer architecture that integrates terrestrial, aerial, and satellite systems. The strategy provides worldwide network access which addresses common limitations associated with traditional network systems. Enhanced network performance, and improved scalability. The system reaches a wide network spectrum and promotes adaptable communication by linking different network layers.

- **The Terrestrial Layer**: 6G networks use the terrestrial layer to support traditional cellular towers as well as microcells together with the Ultra Massive MIMO (Many inputs, many outputs) technology. Urban conditions enable these technologies to provide speed and velocity together with reduced communication delays. These technologies establish high-speed and ultra-reliable transmission fundamentals needed by systems such as industrial IoT and smart cities along with driverless cars. Artificial Intelligence solutions combined with network slicing capabilities will enable performance optimization that addresses various network uses in this layer.
- **The Aerial Layer**: The aerial layer implements drones alongside other unmanned aerial vehicles (UAVs) as part of its operation. The flying relays together with base stations operate from UAVs. UAVs rapidly change their network capabilities as needed to provide coverage across areas not serviced

by ground-based networks particularly in remote and rural locations and disaster zones. These mobile base stations serve temporary coverage needs at both high-demand areas and rapidly changing deployment environments. The aerial layer enables quick communication together with elevated network capabilities which benefits drone-based delivery operations as well as precision farming needs.

- **The Satellite Layer**: Remote or poorly connected regions can benefit from the satellite layer which offers worldwide communication abilities specifically for such locations whose needs aerial and terrestrial systems would fail to meet. Satellites in low earth orbit (LEO) offer comprehensive coverage and low latency communication. The system requires improvements to optimize both surface-level equipment and aviation components. These facilities enable fast internet access and communication which reaches regions that were inaccessible before while providing support to worldwide systems that handle climate tracking and emergency assistance together with worldwide navigation.
- **Synergy and Integration**: The combination of terrestrial, aerial and satellite 6G networks delivers services which simultaneously guarantee reliability and high data throughput and worldwide accessibility. The multi-layer system enables automatic distribution of resources because support between layers scales based on operational need and environment conditions. The communication infrastructure of urban areas depends on terrestrial networks but satellite and UAV networks supply necessary connectivity in remote or disaster recovery zones. The integration of artificial intelligence and edge computing will handle the communication flow between network layers to achieve efficient operational network management through data processing in real time.

4.2 Dynamic and Adaptive Resource Allocation in 6G Network Architecture

6G network architecture utilizes dynamic resource allocation which represents its automatic adaptive method to distribute spectrum along with computing power and energy based on ever-changing user needs and environmental factors as well as present-time traffic patterns. This capability stands essential to deliver high-performance services for applications with various needs because it provides large device connectivity while ensuring minimal latency and great dependability at ultra-high data speeds.

- **Integration of Machine Learning and AI:** The resource management system in 6G heavily depends on AI and ML technologies to function. Through these technological tools the network achieves two functions: congestion forecasting and real-time resource optimization and traffic pattern analysis. AI algorithms serve as network analytic tools to find current system bottlenecks and automatically redirect resources so users achieve perfect performance quality through maximum speed and low delay rates.

- **Slicing Networks:** Slicing networks constitutes a substantial element of 6G which divides the network infrastructure into multiple logical sub-networks called "slices" created for unique functional purposes. Three distinct network slices would serve mobile broadband enhancement while another slice would focus on IoT applications followed by self-driving car usage. The instant adjustment of shifting conditions is made possible by dynamic resource allocation for these network slices to effectively distribute resources according to their required performance level.
- **Edge and Fog Computing:** Edge as well as fog computing handles information processing on the network perimeter to bring computational resources closer to consumers. The core network receives less traffic while latency decreases when this strategy is applied. Computing resources automatically relocate themselves according to present-time application needs to provide power where applications demand it most. State Machine controllers at smart city edge nodes increase their processing capacity to handle rising traffic demands that occur in specific zones or during busy periods.
- **Efficiency and Spectrum Management:** 6G networks are expected to leverage the THz spectrum, offering vast amounts of available bandwidth. Methods such as huge MIMO and beamforming will be used to dynamically assign frequencies based on environmental conditions and real-time demand in order to optimize the spectrum's usefulness. The technique enables 6G to deliver maximum spectrum utilization while minimizing interference and congestion while handling great numbers of interconnected devices.
- **Energy-Efficient Resource Allocation:** 6G must achieve high energy efficiency because the network will contain many connected devices including IoT sensors and smart devices. Adaptive resource allocation strategies will cut down energy usage through automatic device and network node power control which depends on observed behavioral patterns. During low-demand periods the network should scale down its energy use without affecting important application responses.

4.2.1 Benefits of Dynamic and Adaptive Resource Allocation in 6G

- **Enhanced Network Efficiency**: Dynamic network adjustments according to present demand lead to improved resource utilization and performance with reduced congestion levels.
- **Improved Quality of Service (QoS)**: Through dynamic resource allocation systems service quality remains consistent because particular applications acquire their required resources precisely when needed which maximizes user interactions.
- **Scalability**: The expanding number of linked devices which include IoT gadgets and driverless cars requires 6G networks for support. The appropriate distribution of resources enables adequate service for expanding system requirements.
- **Reduced Latency**: His resource distribution strategy enables fast information delivery at edge computing networks and local data centers which serves time-critical applications such as industrial automation and autonomous driving.
- **Energy Efficiency**: Having the capacity to distribute resources according to demand, 6G networks will become more sustainable, minimizing wasteful energy consumption while maintaining optimal network performance.

5. PROTOCOLS AND STANDARDS FOR 6G

We are still in the early stages of developing 6G networks. But as with previous mobile network generations, the establishment of robust protocols and standards is vital for ensuring scalability, performance, and global interoperability. 6G networks will operate based on protocols that enable seamless communication and integration across various components, devices, and services. Below are key areas of 6G protocol and standardization efforts.

5.1 Standardization Bodies and Global Collaboration

The evolution of 6G standards will be driven by several international organizations and standardization bodies, including:

- **3GPP (Third Generation Partnership Project):** Having defined the 5G standards, 3GPP will continue to lead the development of 6G technical requirements, focusing on device communication protocols, RAN and core network architecture.

- **Global Telecommunication Union, or ITU:** The ITU will be vital to worldwide spectrum allocation and regulatory frameworks, ensuring worldwide connectivity for 6G.
- **Organization of Electrical and Electronics Engineers, or IEEE:** IEEE will contribute to developing essential protocols for areas such as wireless communication, security, and data management.
- **Global 6G Alliance:** A collection of regional partnerships, such as the Global 6G Alliance, aims to address challenges and grab possibilities in the global rollout of 6G (Uusitalo et al., 2021).

5.2 Advances in Radio Access Network (RAN) Protocols

In order to satisfy the demands of ultra-fast data rates, ultra-low latency, and high-density device connectivity, 6G networks will greatly improve RAN protocols. Important components will consist of:

- **Terahertz (THz) Band Transmission:** To maximize bandwidth and capacity, new standards will be created for using the THz frequencies (0.1 THz to 10 THz), enabling ultra-high-speed wireless communication.
- **Multiple Input Multiple Output (MIMO) at ultra-massive levels:** Massive MIMO will be integral in 6G, improving RAN's ability to handle high data rates and manage congested environments through advanced beamforming and antenna technologies (Tataria et al., 2021; M. Yang et al., 2024).

5.3 Network Architecture and Service Protocols

6G core network architecture will incorporate innovative concepts for increased flexibility, scalability, and reliability:

- **Slicing networks:** Network slicing, an essential part of 6G, would enable the evolution of several inside a single physical infrastructure, virtual networks each suited to distinct services like virtual reality, the Internet of Things, and driverless cars. New protocols will be necessary for the efficient management of these slices.
- **Edge and Fog Computing:** By moving processing closer to the edge of the network, 6G will reduce latency and optimize resource utilization. At the edge, protocols for controlling dispersed processing and storage will be essential.
- **Service-Oriented Architecture (SOA):** SOA will enable the network to offer on-demand, customized services. Protocols will be developed to facili-

tate service discovery, orchestration, and management (Khutey et al., 2015; Qamar et al., 2020; Sergiou et al., 2020).

5.4 Security, Privacy, and Threat Detection Protocols

Security and privacy become critical as 6G expands the number of connected devices the procedures listed below will be crucial:

- **Quantum-Safe Security:** As quantum computing threatens to break traditional cryptography, new post-quantum protocols and quantum-safe encryption will be developed to protect data from quantum attacks.
- **Enhanced Encryption Methods:** With critical applications like healthcare and autonomous driving relying on 6G, stronger encryption protocols will be necessary to ensure data integrity, confidentiality, and authenticity.
- **AI-Driven Threat Detection:** AI-powered protocols for real-time detection and mitigation of cyber threats, such as malware and assaults, will be essential for maintaining secure communication within the 6G network (Ikram & Mumtaz, 2022; Scalise et al., 2024).

5.5 Interoperability Protocols for Seamless Connectivity

Global interoperability among devices, networks, and technologies will be a foundational requirement for 6G. Key protocols will include:

- **Cross-Layer Interoperability:** Protocols will be established to enable seamless communication between the terrestrial, aerial, and satellite layers of 6G networks, facilitating resource sharing and device roaming.
- **Inter-Network Cooperation:** Protocols for resource management, roaming, and handovers will be necessary to guarantee seamless cooperation across satellite, terrestrial, and non-terrestrial systems.
- **V2X and IoT Integration:** 6G will need new protocols to ensure the efficient communication between massive numbers of connected devices, IoT devices and systems that connect vehicles to everything (V2X), for example, with low interference and latency.

5.6 Spectrum Management and Dynamic Frequency Allocation

The introduction of terahertz frequencies will require advanced protocols for spectrum management, including:

- **THz Spectrum Utilization:** Protocols will be developed to manage the terahertz band efficiently, optimizing spectrum utilization while minimizing interference.
- **Dynamic Spectrum Access (DSA):** Protocols for real-time spectrum allocation will ensure that available frequencies are distributed based on demand and availability, enabling dynamic spectrum sharing to maximize resource efficiency (Soldani, 2021).

6. KEY USE CASES AND APPLICATIONS OF 6G NETWORKS

Performance improvements are anticipated to be substantial when 5G networks give way to 6G networks, capacity, and connectivity, opening up new possibilities across various industries and transforming how we interact with technology. The following lists the main 6G use cases and applications, which are made possible by extremely fast data, minimal latency, and extensive connectivity.

- **The use of immersive experiences and enhanced mobile broadband (eMBB):** Applications requiring extremely high speeds will be able to use 6G since its data rates will significantly surpass those of 5G. This includes more immersive experiences using VR and AR, in addition to the smooth streaming of 4K and 8K media. Video conferencing, mobile gaming, and entertainment will benefit from real-time HD entertainment across various devices and locations. Holographic communication will spread more widely as it transforms distant communication methods.
- **Mission-Critical Uses of Ultra-Reliable Low-Latency Communication (URLLC)**: 6G will enable the operation of autonomous vehicles robots and industrial automation systems by providing great reliability and real-time data processing. Secure operations of smart factories alongside surgical robots become possible with the latest ultra-low latency which creates new business possibilities for healthcare and manufacturing and logistics industries.
- **Massive Machine Type Communications (mMTC) for IoT and Smart Systems:** The development of 6G will create massive expansion for the Internet of Things by linking trillions of wearable devices alongside sensors that monitor everyday items. Smart homes, smart cities, and environmental monitoring will thrive, especially in healthcare and environmental sectors, where large-scale connectivity will be essential for patient monitoring and real-time air/water quality tracking.
- **The Tactile Internet for Real-Time Physical Interaction:** 6G's ultra-low latency and great data speed enable the tactile web to facilitate real-time

physical connection throughout the network. The combination of remote surgery and VR and AR applications receive enhanced capabilities through haptic feedback technology under the tactile web framework.

- **Autonomous Vehicles and Smart Transportation Systems:** 6G networks will power fully autonomous transportation systems, including cars, drones, and other vehicles. Instantaneous connectivity between vehicles, transportation system components, including traffic infrastructure (also known as vehicle-to-everything) will make these systems safer and more efficient. Autonomous vehicles will rely on ultra-reliable, low-latency networking for instantaneous decision-making, improve traffic flow, and reduce collisions.
- **Security and Quantum Communications for Data Protection:** QKD and quantum communications will guarantee safe data transfer across 6G networks. This technique will be essential for safeguarding delicate infrastructure, particularly in sectors like finance, government, and defense. 6G's quantum-enabled networks will also help enhance computational power and accelerate data processing, improving overall network security.
- **3D and Holographic Communication for Immersive Interaction:** With 6G, 3D video calls and holographic communications will become commonplace, offering users immersive, lifelike interactions. This will transform business collaboration, education, and entertainment. For example, holographic teaching and interactive virtual experiences will make remote learning more engaging and accessible.
- **Immersive Video Games and Virtual Reality (XR):** Immersion Playing video games and using extended reality (XR) applications, for instance, virtual reality, augmented reality, and mixed reality (MR), will be improved by 6G. The development of extremely dynamic, realistic settings will be made possible by extremely rapid data transfer rates and low latency, offering users deeply engaging experiences. These technologies will reshape industries like entertainment, gaming, and simulation.

7. DIFFICULTIES AND PROSPECTS FOR FURTHER STUDY IN 6G NETWORKS

As 6G networks evolve from the foundation set by 5G, they promise groundbreaking improvements in communications, providing incredibly rapid speeds, exceptionally low latency, and unbroken worldwide connectivity. Despite the vast potential of 6G, its deployment faces significant challenges that require innovative solutions and extensive research. The main issues and possible avenues of inquiry for 6G networks are described below:

- **Spectrum and Frequency Management**: THz waves and other higher-frequency bands are being used to provide ultra-high transmission rates, presents notable challenges in spectrum and frequency management. These frequencies suffer from attenuation, limited range, and propagation issues. Addressing these constraints will require future research to focus on advanced modulation techniques, beamforming methods, and dynamic spectrum management. AI-driven frequency planning and innovative spectrum allocation strategies will be critical to meeting the demands of 6G's capacity and ensuring efficient spectrum usage.
- **Network Architecture and Scalability**: With the need to accommodate massive device connectivity and integrate diverse networks (terrestrial, aerial, and satellite), 6G network architecture faces scalability challenges. Research will focus on designing multi-layer network architectures that facilitate seamless integration across different systems. 6G networks must have AI-powered network orchestration and dynamic network slicing for enabling scalability together with resource management and flexibility.
- **Energy Efficiency and Sustainability**: The expansion of high-speed data interconnections as well as demands for rapid data transfer would likely consume more energy which presents sustainability obstacles. The investigation of future green technology through AI-powered energy management systems alongside low-power communication methods and sustainable hardware solutions will be conducted. Network energy efficiency development will protect the performance excellence of 6G while reducing environmental effects so scalability becomes vital for sustainable long-term operation.
- **Privacy and Security**: Edge computing together with AI systems and IoT devices create various security and privacy problems when integrated into 6G networks. Network security and data protection need to be ensured in the complex environments featuring diverse edge computations and AI systems and IoT devices. Blockchain systems will serve as the research focus to handle secure data processing while AI systems will detect threats and quantum-based encryption will supply security. A combination of privacy-protecting methods and safe access systems needs to be developed to shield user data and protect 6G network systems from harm.
- **Combining Machine Learning and Artificial Intelligence:** 6G network implementation faces multiple challenges with machine learning and artificial intelligence because of complex AI models and demanding resource requirements and real-time processing dynamics. Future research aims to build distributed machine learning methods alongside lightweight AI algorithms while improving hardware performance to increase network efficien-

cy. 6G networks will achieve autonomous resource optimization through self-learning algorithms that function for network management and optimization.

- **Quantum Communication and Computing Integration**: The integration of quantum communication and computing into 6G networks proves complicated because quantum technologies face scalability issues together with the requirement for systems interoperability with classical networks. Scientists need to create expandable quantum systems and combine quantum systems with classical devices at the same time as secure encryption methods to build network security. The development of quantum computing platforms will boost the processing speed of complex operations which will enhance both efficiency and performance of 6G network systems.
- **Global Connectivity and Inclusivity**: The high implementation expenses and sophisticated infrastructure requirements present serious barriers to providing fast communication services to distant underdeveloped regions in the context of 6G deployment. 6G technologies need equal access to all populations to achieve worldwide inclusivity. Future researchers will work to find low-cost implementation methods involving satellite networks and aerial platforms together with mesh networking for closing connectivity gaps. The focus will be on energy-efficient technology as well as inexpensive deployment options that will advance digital inclusion along with global availability of 6G services.

Irritating issues will be resolved through research advancement which will let 6G networks redefine Global connectivity. 6G networking will enable transformative applications and enhance various industries across the world significantly (Akbar et al., 2022; Ali et al., 2023; Duong et al., 2022; Liu et al., 2023; Pennanen et al., 2024; Zawish et al., 2024).

8. FUTURE SCOPE OF 6G NETWORKS

Development of 6G network infrastructure stands at its initial stage yet demonstrates strong indications to revolutionize current communication networks. The future scope of 6G telephone systems will introduce extensive changes to multiple vital domains.

- **Exceptional Speed and Ultra-Low Latency:** 6G networks will bring real-time communication and data processing due to their anticipated speed of near-instantaneous latency alongside terabit-per-second data throughput. The fast deployment of fibre technologies promotes technological innovation through which tele-surgery systems with autonomous capabilities become feasible together with VR/AR systems that provide absorbed-reality experiences. Both instant and unified service operations worldwide will become possible through future communication development which enables high-speed information exchange.

- **Global Connectivity and Digital Inclusion:** Excessive divide between urban and rural populations will cease to exist as 6G advances universal networking capabilities. Several network types functioning together will enable global users to access high-speed communication through terrestrial, aerial, and satellite channels. The extensive adoption of smart technologies including IoT and smart cities will become faster because of digital inclusion enabled by this empowerment of underserved populations. The worldwide character of 6G will drive economic and social development by offering comprehensive education services with healthcare solutions and increased economic possibilities for everyone.
- **Sustainability and Green Networks:** 6G development will place sustainability at its core priority. 6G networks will achieve environmental preservation through their focus on developing sustainable technologies that use renewable energy sources and minimize carbon emissions. AI-managed resource allocation combined with low-power equipment along with optimized communication networks will deliver green technologies throughout the world by using environmentally friendly systems. Technology development in communication systems will establish a sustainable future so that technical advances will not sacrifice environmental well-being.
- **Enhanced Security:** 6G technology will develop strong security measures at every communication level because of quantum encryption along with AI threat detection technology and self-managing security systems. The combination of quantum-safe encryption creates data security against cyber-attacks and AI boosts systems in detecting and dealing with potential security breaches. 6G networks will develop improved security systems which will protect both user privacy and data integrity for global communities.
- **Integration of AI and Machine Learning**: AI together with ML will serve as critical elements for 6G networks' enhanced automation as well as resource management and operational efficiency. The main research goals include developing automated networks with predictive abilities and real-time performance improvement decision capabilities. Through AI-based solutions companies will advance their development of autonomous systems and smart cities as well as IoT applications which support adaptive network management.

- **Collaborative Global Innovation:** The future scope of 6G relies on global collaboration between governments, industry leaders, researchers, and standardization bodies. Collective work between different entities will boost innovation while enabling the development of standards-based solutions alongside fair accessibility for 6G implementations. 6G development through international partnerships will achieve deployable sustainable infrastructure that establishes a more connected and inclusive global world.

9. CONCLUSION

6G networks establish a revolutionary period in worldwide communication by building on previous technology advances. The improvements of 5G form the foundation from which 6G will produce beyond-ultrahigh velocity links and sub-microsecond delays combined with abundant device interconnection and single network control for ground-based and airborne capabilities together with orbital platforms. Terahertz communication along with artificial intelligence and quantum computing and blockchain will enable revolutionary applications through the tactile internet and immersive virtual experiences as well as autonomous systems. The technological advancement brings forth numerous serious obstacles. Implementation of 6G standards depends on establishing proficient spectrum control systems along with better energy conservation methods and superior network security features and easy connection capabilities between devices. The solution of these complicated problems requires new methods and international partnership between researchers and industry professionals to resolve technical and regulatory barriers. The realization of 6G needs both sustainable operational methods and intelligent system infrastructure in addition to technological development. Scalability combined with inclusive goals make 6G work towards building a worldwide digital connection that removes economic and geographical barriers to power industry sectors as well as improve lifestyle quality. Naturally 6G will change our methods of interaction and communication as well as transform our approach to innovation because research advances continuously. Future technological developments will undergo a transformative evolution because 6G shows potential to modify the technological field for numerous decades through its extensive reach and automated intelligence capabilities.

REFERENCES

Akbar, M. S., Hussain, Z., Sheng, Q. Z., & Mukhopadhyay, S. (2022). *6G Survey on Challenges, Requirements, Applications, Key Enabling Technologies, Use Cases, AI integration issues and Security aspects*. http://arxiv.org/abs/2206.00868

Ali, M. Z., Abohmra, A., Usman, M., Zahid, A., Heidari, H., Imran, M. A., & Abbasi, Q. H. (2023). Quantum for 6G communication: A perspective. *IET Quantum Communication*, *4*(3), 112–124. DOI: 10.1049/qtc2.12060

Azari, M. M., Solanki, S., Chatzinotas, S., Kodheli, O., Sallouha, H., Colpaert, A., Mendoza Montoya, J. F., Pollin, S., Haqiqatnejad, A., Mostaani, A., Lagunas, E., & Ottersten, B. (2022). Evolution of Non-Terrestrial Networks from 5G to 6G: A Survey. *IEEE Communications Surveys and Tutorials*, *24*(4), 2633–2672. DOI: 10.1109/COMST.2022.3199901

Duong, T. Q., Ansere, J. A., Narottama, B., Sharma, V., Dobre, O. A., & Shin, H. (2022). Quantum-Inspired Machine Learning for 6G: Fundamentals, Security, Resource Allocations, Challenges, and Future Research Directions. *IEEE Open Journal of Vehicular Technology*, *3*(September), 375–387. DOI: 10.1109/OJVT.2022.3202876

Huang, T., Yang, W., Wu, J., Ma, J., Zhang, X., & Zhang, D. (2019). A Survey on Green 6G Network: Architecture and Technologies. *IEEE Access : Practical Innovations, Open Solutions*, *7*, 175758–175768. DOI: 10.1109/ACCESS.2019.2957648

Ikram, M., & Mumtaz, S. (2022). for Future Wireless Networks. *IEEE Communications Standards Magazine*, *6*(March), 42–43.

Khutey, R., Rana, G., Dewangan, V., Tiwari, A., & Dewamngan, A. (2015). Future of Wireless Technology 6G & 7G. *International Journal of Electrical and Electronics Research*, *3*(2), 583–585. www.researchpublish.com

Kleine-Ostmann, T., & Nagatsuma, T. (2011). A review on terahertz communications research. *Journal of Infrared, Millimeter and Terahertz Waves*, *32*(2), 143–171. DOI: 10.1007/s10762-010-9758-1

Kolhar, A. & Sridevi. (2025). Future Trends and Innovation in Machine Intelligence for Cyber Risk Management. In M. Almaiah & Y. Maleh (Eds.), Machine Intelligence Applications in Cyber-Risk Management (pp. 415-438). IGI Global Scientific Publishing. https://doi.org/.DOI: 10.4018/979-8-3693-7540-2.ch018

Lee, Y. L., Qin, D., Wang, L. C., & Sim, G. H. (2021). 6G Massive Radio Access Networks: Key Applications, Requirements and Challenges. *IEEE Open Journal of Vehicular Technology*, *2*(October 2020), 54–66. DOI: 10.1109/OJVT.2020.3044569

Liu, Y., Xu, J., Wang, Z., Mu, X., Zhang, J., & Zhang, P. (2023). Simultaneously transmitting and reflecting (STAR) RISs for 6G: Fundamentals, recent advances, and future directions. *Frontiers of Information Technology & Electronic Engineering, 24*(12), 1689–1707. DOI: 10.1631/FITEE.2300490

Pennanen, H., Hänninen, T., Tervo, O., Tölli, A., & Latva-aho, M. (2024). *6G: The Intelligent Network of Everything — A Comprehensive Vision, Survey, and Tutorial.* http://arxiv.org/abs/2407.09398

Qamar, F., Siddiqui, M. U. A., Hindia, M. H. D. N., Hassan, R., & Nguyen, Q. N. (2020). Issues, challenges, and research trends in spectrum management: A comprehensive overview and new vision for designing 6g networks. *Electronics (Basel), 9*(9), 1–39. DOI: 10.3390/electronics9091416

Scalise, P., Boeding, M., Hempel, M., Sharif, H., Delloiacovo, J., & Reed, J. (2024). A Systematic Survey on 5G and 6G Security Considerations, Challenges, Trends, and Research Areas. *Future Internet, 16*(3), 1–38. DOI: 10.3390/fi16030067

Serghiou, D., Khalily, M., Brown, T. W. C., & Tafazolli, R. (2022). Terahertz Channel Propagation Phenomena, Measurement Techniques and Modeling for 6G Wireless Communication Applications: A Survey, Open Challenges and Future Research Directions. *IEEE Communications Surveys and Tutorials, 24*(4), 1957–1996. DOI: 10.1109/COMST.2022.3205505

Sergiou, C., Lestas, M., Antoniou, P., Liaskos, C., & Pitsillides, A. (2020). Complex Systems: A Communication Networks Perspective towards 6G. *IEEE Access : Practical Innovations, Open Solutions, 8*, 89007–89030. DOI: 10.1109/ACCESS.2020.2993527

Shen, L. H., Ten Feng, K., & Hanzo, L. (2023). Five Facets of 6G: Research Challenges and Opportunities. *ACM Computing Surveys, 55*(11), 1–39. Advance online publication. DOI: 10.1145/3571072

Soldani, D. (2021). 6g fundamentals: Vision and enabling technologies. *Journal of Telecommunications and the Digital Economy, 9*(3), 58–86. DOI: 10.18080/jtde.v9n3.418

Tataria, H., Shafi, M., Molisch, A. F., Dohler, M., Sjoland, H., & Tufvesson, F. (2021). 6G Wireless Systems: Vision, Requirements, Challenges, Insights, and Opportunities. *Proceedings of the IEEE, 109*(7), 1166–1199. DOI: 10.1109/JPROC.2021.3061701

Uusitalo, M. A., Rugeland, P., Boldi, M. R., Strinati, E. C., Demestichas, P., Ericson, M., Fettweis, G. P., Filippou, M. C., Gati, A., Hamon, M. H., Hoffmann, M., Latva-Aho, M., Parssinen, A., Richerzhagen, B., Schotten, H., Svensson, T., Wikstrom, G., Wymeersch, H., Ziegler, V., & Zou, Y. (2021). 6G Vision, Value, Use Cases and Technologies from European 6G Flagship Project Hexa-X. *IEEE Access : Practical Innovations, Open Solutions*, *9*, 160004–160020. DOI: 10.1109/ACCESS.2021.3130030

Yang, M., Qu, Y., Ranbaduge, T., Thapa, C., Sultan, N., Ding, M., Suzuki, H., Ni, W., Abuadbba, S., Smith, D., Tyler, P., Pieprzyk, J., Rakotoarivelo, T., Guan, X., & M'rabet, S. (2024). *From 5G to 6G: A Survey on Security, Privacy, and Standardization Pathways*. http://arxiv.org/abs/2410.21986

Zawish, M., Dharejo, F. A., Khowaja, S. A., Raza, S., Davy, S., Dev, K., & Bellavista, P. (2024). AI and 6G Into the Metaverse: Fundamentals, Challenges and Future Research Trends. *IEEE Open Journal of the Communications Society*, *5*(January), 730–778. DOI: 10.1109/OJCOMS.2024.3349465

Zhang, Z., Xiao, Y., Ma, Z., Xiao, M., Ding, Z., Lei, X., Karagiannidis, G. K., & Fan, P. (2019). 6G Wireless Networks: Vision, Requirements, Architecture, and Key Technologies. *IEEE Vehicular Technology Magazine*, *14*(3), 28–41. DOI: 10.1109/MVT.2019.2921208

Zhaofeng, M., Xiaochang, W., Jain, D. K., Khan, H., Hongmin, G., & Zhen, W. (2020). 013_Only abstract_Zhaofeng_A Blockchain-based Trusted Data Management Scheme in Edge Computing. *IEEE Transactions on Industrial Informatics*, *16*(3), 2013–2021. DOI: 10.1109/TII.2019.2933482

Chapter 2
Evolution and Key Features of 5G and 6G
Psychological Impacts on Human Cognition and Behavior

Anu Dandona
https://orcid.org/0000-0001-7194-0225
D.Y. Patil International University, Pune, India

ABSTRACT

From this chapter, readers obtain an in-depth understanding of the trends of the mobile communication technologies from 1G to 4G, and the importance of 5G and the further development of 6G. It reviews the socio-psychological consequences of these technologies on behaviour, thinking and organisations. Along with describing 5G technology, it is necessary to consider its foundational characteristics focusing on eMBB, ULLC, and mMTC. The chapter also focuses on the trends in 5G technology and its features like millimeter waves, massive MIMO (Multiple Input Multiple Output), and network slicing and their effect on multitasking, making information and social interactions. Hypothesized future of 6G systems and possibilities of developing terahertz communications, integration of AI, and holo-multimedia communication. The latter brings the discussion of the matter to contexts like smart cities and IoT as well as addresses the aspects of cognitive load and ethical intensions.

1.1. HISTORICAL PERSPECTIVE: FROM 1G TO 4G

Mobile communication dates to the 1980s and is rooted in first-generation (1G) wireless networks. These first-generation networks were analog systems that supported voice only. 1G network) lacked capacity, performance and security while

DOI: 10.4018/979-8-3373-0568-4.ch002

the 1st generation of portable cell phones were not capable to offer privacy with encryption standards. Moreover, those were not equipped with any data handling (- ballooning demand for mobile communication).

The 1990s included the building of digital 'second generation' (2G) mobile networks and forced a change in the behaviour of operators towards more efficient usage that had not been shared with customers. In stark contrast to first generation (1G) systems, which employed analog transmission methods, 2Gs were built with digital transmission techniques and provided more efficient use of the limited spectrum. This digital technology transition also offered more excellent voice quality, higher capacity on the network and security features. 2G networks also enabled the growth of text messaging (via SMS), which was a very popular and familiar form of communication.

The late 1990s and early 2000 provided more capable next-generation networks; technologies evolved to support the growth of data services such as CDMA, GPRS and EDGE alongside pre-3G cellular communication standards. These intermediate generations, such as General Packet Radio Service (GPRS) and Enhanced Data rates for GSM Evolution (EDGE), offered higher data speeds aimed at pre-empting the transition to 3g mobile communications.

The 3rd generation or the 2000s and brought a significant leap in mobile data capabilities. 3G networks as very high speeds and enabled mobile Internet, video calling features, million of colour images applications on the ground. These changes lead to the widespread use of smartphones and the birth of mobile apps which changed how users engaged with their devices.

The most recent generation, the fourth one (4G), was unveiled in 2010s. They were designed to provide higher data rates, lower latency and enhanced multimedia capabilities with 4G networks being mainly based on Long-Term Evolution (LTE) technology. In addition, 4G has allowed for more immersive and interactive services by delivering data rates up to 1 Gbps which satisfy the increasing demand of high-quality streaming, real-time communication and other applications that make use of mobile devices.

As we have seen above, evolution of mobile communication has followed a path from voice only network i.e. first generation to data centric and rich media systems i.e. 4G.

1.2. The Importance of 5G and 6G

Mobile communication technology has influenced our society's digital transformation significantly over the years. They will impact various industries and aspects of life when they are introduced into the market.

5th generation (5G) wireless mobile network technologies have been hailed as game changers due to its significantly faster speeds, low latency and increased capacity compared to its predecessor; 4G LTE (Long-Term Evolution) (Spiceworks, 2023). ITU also anticipates the following parameters for 5G; peak data rates of up to 20 Gbps and latency of up to 1ms (ITU, 2015). The effects of 5G are quite widespread. It creates opportunities for the creation of new applications and services like remote health monitoring systems, self-driving cars, virtual and augmented reality (TechRepublic, 2022). Due to low latency and high bandwidths, 5G can also support the Internet of Things, IoT in a way that creates a seamless connection between a network of devices and shared data (Rantcell, 2023).

While the deployment of 5G is still ongoing, the global research community has already shifted its focus towards the next generation of mobile communication technology: 6G See spiceworks.com in the year 2023. Thus, while 5G defines new paradigms for connectivity, 6G is predicted to bring even more revolutionary opportunities. Some of the highlighting characteristic of 6G is that it is expected to work at higher frequency bands of 30GHz to 300GHz and up to 3 THz potentially (TechRepublic, 2022). This will enhance the usage of the spectrum to offer much higher data rates with up to the theoretical maximum download speed 100 times that of 5G (TechRepublic, 2022). According to the Manorama Yearbook (2023), 6G will be covering the data rates of up to 1 Tbps which will create immense levels of connection and data transfer. In addition, 6G is expected to combine various features that include AI, ML, and wireless sensing, thus boosting the ability of the network (Spiceworks, 2023). This integration will create new application areas that include but are not limited to, holographic telepresence, remote surgery, and intelligent transportation systems (RST Software, 2022).

The research on 5G and 6G networks reveals that they can significantly impact the fields and different spheres of individuals' lives (Manorama Yearbook, 2023). It can help in development of smart cities where through sensor and connected devices the real time data's can be gathered and analyzed to upgrade the infrastructure and public services for residents as per need (Rantcell, 2023). Within the healthcare domain, 5G and 6G will transform telemedicine and remote patient monitoring through the capability of transmitting large amount of real-time data (TechRepublic, 2022). These networks will also help utilize other speed-oriented technologies like robotic surgery and holographic telepresence increasing the availability of specialized treatment (Manorama Yearbook, 2023).

Moreover, transportation industry will be the prime benefactor of 5G and 6G networks, to create automatic vehicles and traffic control systems, and perfect V2V and V2I communication systems (Rantcell, 2023). This will lead to better safety measures, elimination of traffic jam and efficient systems of transport. In the industrial sector, 5G and 6G will enable the application of Industry 4. 0 technologies; smart production line, distant control, predicting overhauls, enhancing workflow and productivity, and reducing overall costs (RST Software, 2022). It is also necessary to point out that 5G and 6G networks will not only help industries listed above but also create new application options in fields such as education, entertainment, environment control, and thus improve the quality of life for individuals and communities (Manorama Yearbook, 2023).

1.3 Psychological Implications of Mobile Advancements

one of the main effects of mobile technologies is the element of connection. Customers are now able to interact with friends, relatives, and working partners using different messaging, and social media platforms. However, this constant connectivity may have negative impacts such as; Through this connectivity, people become more concerned with online connectivity than the actual physical socialisation (Spiceworks, 2023; Dennis & O'Toole, 2014). Modern society has a new phobia, or fear of not being able to use a mobile device, also known as nomophobia. Patients with nomophobia prove to have higher levels of anxiety and stress whenever they are away from their devices and hence become fully reliant on the technology (Rantcell, 2023; Lee et al., 2014).

Availability of information and stimuli in constant access through the mobile devises has been associated with reduced attention span and cognition. This is especially so when one is doing other tasks concurrently, as it is typical with the utilization of the mobile devices; in such cases, the ability to concentrate and memorize; is considerably hampered (Murdock, 2013; Derks et al., 2014). Notifications continue popping up on our screens and the blue light emitted by the gadgets significantly interferes with the natural circadian rhythm which in its turn produces negative impact on the quality of night's sleep. Poor sleep is also known to have its effects on the total health and well-being of a user (TechRepublic, 2022; Lanaj et al., 2014). Also, it is established that social networking and gaming apps are addictive where gadgets are used in creating social isolation compulsions. This, in turn, affects their mental health through increased risk in anxiety, depression, and social isolation (Manorama Yearbook, 2023; RST Software, 2022). Lack of identity and the extendibility of mobile technologies have also been blamed for increased cases of cyberbullying, cyber harassment kept leading to various psychological effects on the users especially the juniors (TechRepublic, 2022; Murdock, 2013). To moderate the possible adverse influences of mobile technologies on the psychology of users, certain guidelines including time management, reflection exercise, and physical as well as social activity should be observed as proposed by Rantcell in 2023 and Spiceworks in 2023.

2. UNDERSTANDING 5G TECHNOLOGY

2.1. Key Features of 5G

The possibility and development of mobile and web technologies have caused many real-time features to appear in different applications (LinkedIn, 2020). Real-time features are innovations that offer clients or customers an opportunity to perform an activity and get the desired results at the same time without delay in processing data/information (Selleo, 2024).

The capabilities that are based on topology real-time have revolutionized many business areas, such as on-demand services, social networks, and IoT (LinkedIn, 2020). For instance, in an app for ordering on-demand taxi or food delivery, a user will be able to monitor the location of the order in real time, get notifications and messages from the service provider, and vice versa (Selleo, 2024). Likewise, in social media platforms, users expect to be receiving messages, notifications and update from their connection without feeling any delay (LinkedIn, 2020).

Realtime features in mobile as well as web applications have the following advantages. First of all, that contributes to increased and more devoted users' attention through improving the interaction with the application (Selleo, 2024). Instant communication and application features are favoured by users since applications allow the management of multiple tasks and communication in a natural, real-life, simultaneous manner (LinkedIn, 2020).

Further, real-time features help developers to look only at the troubleshooting of problem-solving abilities of the application as they do not have to work on the issues of real-time data transmission (Selleo, 2024). This enables them to develop better applications that are more resourceful and at the same time increase customer value, which involves better view and interactive experience (LinkedIn, 2020).

The real-time communication in applications relies on a technology that is built on the WebSocket, the communication technology that is completely different from the HTTP protocol in the terms of communication, speed, and usage in the RTA applications (9series, n. d.). WebSocket provides for an opened continuous connection between the client and the server where data can be changed and updated in real-time (Aberdeen, n. d.). As the demand for real-time experiences continues to grow, businesses must consider integrating real-time features into their mobile and web applications to stay competitive and meet the evolving expectations of their users (Selleo, 2024). By leveraging the power of real-time technology, businesses can enhance customer satisfaction, improve operational efficiency, and gain a strategic advantage in the market (LinkedIn, 2020).

2.2 Technological Advancements in 5G

The existence of 5G or the fifth-generation mobile network system has come with added technologies that makes it highly distinct from the previous mobile networks.

The corresponding parameters are the Service Ability and Higher Data Rates and bandwidth.

Main one of the technology promoters in the 5G, there is a large improvement in Data rate and bandwidth. 5G networks provide download speeds of up to 10 Gbps while, 4G LTE networks offer peak download speed of 10 times to hundred times less (TechTarget, 2022). This increased speed and bandwidth make it possible to have smooth High Definition Video streaming, fast downloads and real time heavy data applications (Lokhande, 2020).

Low Latency

A major technological breakthrough made in the context of 5G is in the docket on Network Latency where it is expected to be reduced to as low as 1 ms (Lokhande, 2020). The implementation of this communication is paramount to time-sensitive applications like self-driving cars, tele-surgery, and video games. It is worth pointing out that the latency of Fifth generation has been enhanced through improvements in series structures in network architecture, signal processing and fair distribution of resources as well as their application algorithms (Vajiramandravi, 2023).

Massive Device Connectivity

It has been envisaged that fifth generation of mobile networks are going to accommodate far more connections than the previous generations. 5G technology has the capability of supporting up to one million devices per square kilometer which means that IoT devices will be easily deployed in future (Lokhande, 2020). This is done by the use of; more enhanced superior actual frequency bands such as millimeter actual waves and better management network approaches (Realme, n. d.).

Enhanced Coverage and Reliability

Hence, 5G networks include different technological annexes that would enhance the coverage and signal strength. These include; small cells, massive MIMO and beamforming techniques (TechTarget, 2022). These technologies complement each other in reaching more people more effectively in crowded spaces and in places that are hard to get to and get customers, partners, and suppliers more connected (Vajiramandravi, 2023).

Network Slicing

Another aspect of the advancement of the 5G is network slicing which is one of the primary technologies that make up 5G (TechTarget, 2022). This makes it possible for network operators to have more than one virtual network on the physical network and these networks are distinct by the nature of the applications, the industries or groups of users that use the networks (Lokhande, 2020). This leads to the right resource provisioning in the network by assigning appropriate properties as the bandwidth, latency, and security for various applications as shown by Vajiramandravi, 2023.

Energy Efficiency

Some specific ways that the 5G networks are going to have better efficiency includes the enhance network architecture, power control and intelligent resource controlling (Lokhande, 2020). This involves methods such as dynamic power control, sleep modes and use of energy efficient components, which assist in cutting down the energy utilization of the 5G rolling out (Realme, n. d.).

These are the actual achievements of 5G innovation comprising of higher rates, low latency, big addressable connections, broad coverage, slicing, and superior power efficiency in building new applications and services which could not be created in former mobile network generations.

Psychological Impacts of 5G

Potential psychological effects of the 5G technology is another area of study and now being explored. A few published articles indicate that 5G might have negative impact such as promoting self-centric behaviors, introversion, and social isolation

(Smith et al., 2021), were debunked previously when it was found out that there was no evidence of harm from exposure to 5G on human health (Jones & Lee, 2022).

In one case, researchers determined that 5G performance's enhanced speed and reliability for remote work and telecommuting could positively impact work-life balance and mental health. Furthermore, enhanced access to the healthcare facility, and immediate access and communication between doctors and patients over the 5G could enhance mental health, especially in deprived areas (Patel et al., 2019).

However, there are fears that have been voiced regarding possible carcinogenic nature of 5G frequencies, if this is true then chances of mental health being affected are very high (Xu & Zhang, 2021). It has also been postulated that electromagnetic radiation emitted from 5G base stations alters the cross-modality of electro-hypersensitive persons and can cause them distress and relocation (Lee & Kim, 2022).

In sum, while the yearly rate increase in 5G has significant psychological advantages and disadvantages, they are still more implied than empirical types at this time. Further studies are required for one to determine the impacts that may be precipitated by the increased implementation of 5G to individuals' psychology and future trends (Jones et al., 2023).

3. EMERGING TRENDS IN 6G TECHNOLOGY

3.1. Anticipated Features and Capabilities

Thus, the arrival of the 6G technology will upgrade the world of wireless communication, extending from the achievements of the fifth generation, which is 5G. As per the opinions of some industry gurus, 6G is favoured to provide mind blowing data rates; it can go up to 1 Tbps (Blackview, 2024). This shall make it easier to stream 1080p content and also incorporate novel features such as VR and AR.

Another parameter important to 5G is the ultra low latency which is expected to shrink the latency time down to millisecond or even microseconds (Vajiram & Ravi, 2024). This will revolutionalize real-time applications that cannot afford delays of any kind in their operations like self-driving cars, tele-surgery and robotics in industries (RCR Wireless News, 2022).

Also, 6G is envisioned to deliver massive connectivity as IoT devices' number is expected to rapidly increase; this connectivity will be limited to 10 million devices per square kilometer compared to 5G (Vajiram & Ravi, 2024). This shall be very important in creation of possibilities of the internet of things and general enhancing of different smart devices and systems.

Another aspect that was identified in 6G is energy efficiency, where the priorities of the technology include the optimization of energy-efficient networks and intelligent power-saving methods in conjunction with high-speed connection (Blackview, 2024). This is in accordance with the increasing influence of the sustainability and environmentalism in the modern world.

A important factor of 6G will be the artificial intelligence and machine learning utilised for intelligent network management and brilliant resources management to improve the network performance and optimise the usage of the resources in the network (RCR Wireless News, 2022). This will create a necessity for new more complex applications and services that build on the foundation of AI.

In addition to these and several other technical enhancements, 6G is assumed to foster unprecedented network topologies and; service distribution across different clouds and systems, integration of the private, public, or hybrid clouds (RCR Wireless News, 2022). This will correspond with the seminars on cloud solutions and the increasing demand for open flexible and scalable networks.

In general, the trends for 6G that is in development present an enhancement in practically every parameter concerning connectivity, speed, latency, and opportunities compared to today's 5G networks, providing the basis for numerous new application possibilities across many industries.

3.2 Potential Technological Breakthroughs

Potential technological innovations are considered more and more in the light of complex bibliometric and ERT analysis to outline discoveries. This one calls for the study of those curves of citation which are important in the evaluation of the trends of emergence in the new technologies. Thus, analysis of citation data along with knowledge bases enables to evaluate the breakthrough potential of various ERTs, and make future predictions on innovations (Zhang et al., 2023) . Another component that helps in the comprehension of technological advancement is the disruption technologies. These kinds of innovations create new markets that are initially small but can transform an entire sector. For instance, growth in renewable energy sources such as perovskite solar cells shows how new technologies with disruptive potential can affect established industries and the drive towards sustainability (Park & Yoon, 2018) . Moreover, the cross-citation models help to analyze the dynamics of technological development by identifying the correlation between the research fields. Acknowledging this view, this method allows for understands the processes of how technologies develop and interact to gain a broader perspective on the organization's innovation context (Gutiérrez-Salcedo et al., 2018) . These kinds of analytical structures are necessary for seeing over the horizon for the next set of fundamental enabling technologies.

3.3 Expected Industry Impact

Potential of the 5G industry that has been projected is enormous, and it will affect almost all industries with its powerful impact. The employment of 5G is anticipated to create roughly $13B in Gross Domestic Product globally. 2 trillion in global economic value by 2035, while generating about 22 million new jobs according to the joint statement on the Social Contract for Digital Cooperation unveiled by the leaders during the event. 3 million jobs including only the Global Value Chain of 5G (PwC, forecasting till 2024). This shall further translate to better connectedness and the improvement of flow of services in the societal structures, decision making processes, and even client experiences in the economic sectors. In the manufacturing sector, this statement holds true since 5G technology will improve the functioning of the company's production line by providing fast transmission of data in real-time and allowing the incorporation of new advanced technologies, including automation, AI, and robotics. This merging is expected to increase efficiency level of the operation, decrease the down time as well as increase productivity making countries such as India to act as manufacturing power houses (IBEF, 2023). Also, the healthcare sector is expected to greatly benefit from 5G as connectivity at the faster speed will allow instant transfer of detailed confidential medical images, remote assistance in operations, and constant health check on patients to enhance the delivery of healthcare services (Maxicus, 2023). The media and entertainment industry will also be affected by the 5G, greatly. Better access to the internet services with high speeds and minimum delay for transmission will improve experiences in areas like high definition video streaming, virtual reality (VR) based games and augmented reality (AR) applications for creators and providers of content (IBEF, 2023). Also, 5G will enhance the internet connectivity in the rural area and other areas that are not well served with the internet, thus solving the digital gap present in most societies today through remote working, learning and other services (Maxicus, 2023). In this sense, the emergence of 5G technology is expected to redefine different sectors by opening new opportunities for innovative solutions, increasing effectiveness of most processes, and generating new jobs. While organizations continue to evolve in this newly technological environment the opportunities for growth and change are limitless.

3.4 Psychological Implications of 6G

As a part of the society, the psychological consequences of 6G technology are expected to be substantial since the technology revolutionizes personal and social communication that occurs in the digital realm. 6G being the next iteration promises to boost the psychophysical well-being of the end-users mainly via connectivity and access to services excluding those on the periphery (Alsharif et al., 2023). This technology is intended to increase the dcor for seclusion since these services are paramount in promoting good health and enhancing social integration for the needy. Nevertheless, 6G brings about potentials of virtual and augmented reality which potentially causes the problem of the prisoners' cognitive overload and mental fatigue. This paper also showcased that, due to the high level of immersion made possible by 6G, the environments could become oversaturated with information, therefore leading to the immersing user burnout (Booth, 2024). The Human-Computer Interaction Institute has also pointed out that to overcome these effects, there is a necessity for the usage of cognitive precaution, particularly regarding that 6G services should be oriented on optimally stimulating sensory organs because mental fatigue is also a significant problem (Booth, 2024). Furthermore, the connection between 6G and the Tactile Internet and cognitive data intelligence in the healthcare sector introduces new prospects for patients' emotional and psychological assistance. With the help of this technology, it is possible to monitor affects of the patients and increase knowledge on how to diagnose and treat affective disorders (Alsharif et al., 2023). However, using phone for social contact, also poses threats of privacy and trust, since a user may be apprehensive of how the data they share online would be used (Alsharif et al., 2023). Moreover, deep fakes, and other distortions might also be available through 6G networks raising the bar of ethical and psychological concerns. There are concerns that peculiarities of VR interaction can blur the gap between the real and virtual worlds; thus, users might find it difficult to navigate; social anxiety and distrust in actual relationships will rise (Booth, 2024). With the advancement of 6G technology, the psychological effects would need to be effectively mitigated through the employment of reliable privacy measures and user sensitisation. Summarizing, the presented 6G technology will bring the positive changes in increasing well-being and connectivity but there are psychological risks, which have to be managed in order to create the positive effect in society.

4. 5G/6G TECHNOLOGIES AND AGILE MANAGEMENT

4.1. Synergies between 5G/6G and Agile Practices

The future innovation of 6G technology is expected to define new horizons for the wireless communication world, based on the progress of its next previous procedure, 5G. Various call for papers sources it that 6G is considered to have a high data rate of 1 terabits per second (Tbps) (Blackview, 2024). This will help to make streaming heave content such as HD videos and other advanced technologies such as VR and AR possible.

Another characteristic of the new generation is that it has almost no latency, with the number of milliseconds or even microseconds (Vajiram & Ravi, 2024). This will revolutionize real-time applications that demand immediate response including self-driving cars, tele-surgery, and the automation of industries (RCR Wireless News, 2022).

Additionally, 6G goals include; scalability, handling more connected devices where 6G should link as many as 10 million devices per square kilometer; this is far beyond 5G. This will be very important when it comes to IoT or the Internet of things and other impacts like connecting different smart commodities and structures without a break.

Sustainability is also another area where 6G is intended to optimize the needed network infrastructure and implement various power-saving solutions for providing users with high-quality connectivity (Blackview, 2024). This is in line with the consideration of the important of sustainability and environmental factors.

Introducing both AI and ML will be a feature of the 6G network for more effective network control, as well as resource control and optimization to obtain better results (RCR Wireless News, 2022). This will create a basis for new applications and services that will utilize AI in their functioning.

Other than these underlying technological advancements, 6G is also expected to foster innovative network architectures such as the distribution of services across multitudes of clouds and the optimization of operations across private public hybrid cloud and other types of clouds (RCR Wireless News, 2022).

4.2 Psychological Factors in Agile Contexts

6G Cognitive & Autonomous Networks → Automates Routine Tasks & Fast Feedback → Team Autonomy → Psychological Safety & Trust → Team Reflexivity & Agile Performance

The psychological factors of Agile environments are important to discovering how Agile frameworks affect Groups' behavior, mindset, and wellbeing. One must appreciate that, while developing working methodologies like agile, flexibility and the ability of a team to promptly respond to various changes are achieved at the cost of developing new psychological perspectives, which may be challenging for some team members.

Positive Psychological Impacts

Increased Team Spirit and Motivation: Many of the agile approaches facilitate on the creation of a community among the team members. Literature also shows that adoption of agile practices can improve the bonding of team members with each other and therefore boost motivation among the software developers (Sarwar et al., 2021). What again favours the agile process is the fact that updated implementations, unlike in more conventional models, are delivered more frequently, which is generally acclaimable due to the optimistic impact it can have on morale among the team members.

Psychological Empowerment: Kanban process implies such elements of the agile practices as project team autonomy and open collaboration enhance psychological empowerment. Thus, team members' perceived autonomy increases overall job satisfaction and their commitment to the project when they believe that their input will make a difference (Sarwar et al., 2021). This empowerment is vital in the development of a proper working culture and ensuring it becomes productive.

Improved Mental Health: Several agile transformations can benefit individuals' mental health because the organizational climate gained becomes more open to interpersonal support. Among the observations made by agile coaches, it can be noted that people who work in organizations that shift to agile often admit that they feel better, both psychologically and in terms of mental health, because their colleagues and supervisors do not conceal problems and share joyful news (Mesko, 2022). Such an environment can help in reducing pressures and stress arising from the implementation of the projects.

Increased Stress and Burnout: However, it is important to note that introduction of agile practices also increases the level of stress of the members of the team. Hence, it shall be crucial, especially to argue that the extremity of collaboration, daily meetings, and short timelines and projects demotivate and burn out the employees (Sourjah, 2022). Having demands to work in segments of short durations can contribute to the development of a culture where one is forced to work frantically make frequent call on mere productivity.

Fear of Failure: The change to agile brings apprehension and fear for the organization since it differs from the conventional project management techniques. Subordinates can be afraid of losing their position, making errors, or being criticized for their performance, especially when working in an open environment with supervisors' supervision (Mesko, 2022). This fear more often than not leads to unnecessary restrictions of creativity and also free speaking or rather free flowing information.

Need for Psychological Safety: self-organization is also another factor and psychological safety is paramount when it comes to agile methodologies. It has also been postulated that without a permissive context that engages input from every affected worker, agile can be unproductive (Harvard Business Review, 2022). Employees that are not able to discuss ideas freely may find it hard to work as a team and come up with creative solutions hence the low performance.

5. COMPARATIVE ANALYSIS OF 5G AND 6G

5G is recognized as a next-generation mobile communication technology that builds upon previous generations, offering substantial improvements in data speed, latency, and connectivity (Chen, Wei, & Ni, 2023). In contrast, 6G is anticipated to emerge between 2027 and 2030, promising to incorporate advanced features, including higher data rates, improved reliability, and the integration of machine learning capabilities (Periannasamy,et al, 2022). The transition from 5G to 6G reflects an ongoing evolution aimed at meeting the burgeoning demands of connectivity and data generation.

It is expected that the growth of 6G technology will outperform 5G in several parameters including URLLC and network density (Rowshan, et al, 2024). As expected to offer data rates of more than 100 Gbps, 6G will enable applications that include holographic communication, improved virtual and augmented reality experiences (Periannasamy, et al, 2022). However, Rabnawaz, et al also posits that 6G will connect more devices translating into new possibilities for the Internet of Things (IoT).

There are forecast indications that the next-generation 6G will be even better than 5G particularly in other parameters of operation such as URLLC and network densification (Rowshan, et al, 2024). As a 6G technology with expected capabilities to provide multiple data rates over 100Gbps, 6G will support highly complex use cases such as; holographic communications, and also superior virtual and augmented reality experiences (Periannasamy, et al, 2022). Thus, 6G is projected to support more devices, enabling calls for the expansion of new possibilities for the Internet of Things (IoT) (Rabnawaz, et al, 2023).

Even though there is so much to look forward to in the transition from 5G to 6G, there are higher risks that one needs to embrace, especially in infrastructure growth and Spectrum Share(Rabnawaz, et al, 2023). The demands of new hardware and software requirements put massive costs on the service providers and developers10. Also, with the growth of technologies some aspects such as security and privacy for big data and more connection have to be considered (Attar, et al, 2023).

As for the goals of theFreq, both 5G and 6G aim at different application sectors, while 5G is directed to the enhanced mobile broadband; the massive machine-type communications; the critical communications (Gorgadze & Ermakova, 2022). However, 6G will be able advance new and unique solutions in specialty fields like, self-sustaining transportation, innovative urban planning, and enhanced medicine engineering platforms using higher data rates and lower latency, (Susandhika & Edward, 2023). This evolution speaks of the enhanced need for better and sophisticated solutions diverse industries such as the health sector and transport among others.

5G and 6G technology enhancements preview shifts in the communication contexts and interactions throughout the world. According to the mentioned challenges, further investigations and innovations are necessary to break new grounds for the implementation of these technologies (Chen, Wei, & Ni, 2023). The future research directions will probably revolve around the methods to improve the network's performance, implement security solutions, and analyse the socio-economic effects of these new technologies (Rabnawaz, et al, 2023).

6. CHALLENGES AND BARRIERS IN 5G/6G IMPLEMENTATION

Challenges and barriers of 5G technology and the expected future 6G technology. These challenges stem from factors such as; structural; security and technological advancement hurdles among others. Solving these challenges is essential for appropriate deployment and potential application of the developed sophisticated communication networks.

5G to 6G is a rather huge leap that causes massive infrastructural changes, which means changes in the existing structures of the networks. The main challenges that most emergent countries experience when deploying e-government projects within the 5G and 6G realms include a scarcity of infrastructure (Zeebaree, Zeebaree, & Aqel, 2023). It becomes a major challenge to achieve efficient implementation of modern technology to close existing gaps between service conception, delivery expectations and actuality (Zeebaree et al., 2023).

Security and privacy are serious challenges that hinder the deployment of 5G and even more of the 6G systems. Now, cross border security concerns of 5G and 6G have potential impact as different research and studies show that current security threats impact the cross border 5G and 6G compatibility of both technology and services (Ounza, 2023). Such factors may include; fear to adopt new systems that are associated with increased insecurity in data and abuse of personal data.

Adopting innovative solutions is challenging enough, particularly when it is required in contemporary 5G and 6G networks and infrastructures. It is believed that the machine learning and advanced analytics feature added to these networks will strengthen their performance; however, this process needs talented people and strong infrastructure to manage them (Paul, 2024). There are possibly high technical exigencies, as many organizations may lag behind, thus experiencing a poor performing network.

It is worthy of note that the economic factors also contribute to the slowing down of the 5G and 6G technologies deployment. Enterprise sometimes come to incur some budget issues when establish the required technological capital investments and structures Tomaszewski, & Kołakowski, 2023). Furthermore, the initial cost that is required in implementing new systems and equipment remains relatively high for most companies especially those that are in the emerging markets.

Other potential risks are also inherent in structures and regulations governing organizations and businesses Most of the advanced forms of communication technologies may go head to head with regulatory frameworks in organizations and businesses. Some of the areas are restrictions imposed by the absence of harmonized policies that may slow down the roll out of 5G as well as 6G systems and may result in-inconsistencies of service delivery and quality. However, gaps in policy-making surrounding data ownership and the responsible use of the internet can slow down the creation of this trust which is needed to efficiently implement these new forms of technology.

7. INDUSTRY-SPECIFIC IMPACTS OF 5G AND 6G TECHNOLOGIES

The advancement in 5G technology and the future 6G technology is expected to cause the industry level effects in global industries. The assessed technologies envision higher network densification, connection rates, and productivity that will revolutionalize and rejuvenate operational models, upgrade service provision, and incubate new applications. Nevertheless, some difficulties inherent in their integration need to be addressed for these benefits to be achieved.

5G technology has been considered to be already important in m-health where its use in telemedicine services and the monitoring of patients using medical sensors as well as mobile devices (Nasralla, et al, 2023). These capabilities can provide the care providers with real time healthcare delivery capability thereby possibly resulting in better patient outcomes. As more advanced networks such as 6G are developed improved quality of m-health applications will in future enable complex procedures like operation through remote control and live diagnosis through improved communication channels (Nasralla, et al, 2023).

Here we can see how the Internet of Things (IoT) through the help of integrated 5G and 6G networks is changing the transport industry. The use of smart vehicles and smart infrastructure, the traffic problems can be solved with better traffic flow, safety and congestion can be decreased(Hu,2024). This makes it easier for vehicles to talk to each other and with traffic management systems to support for fully automated driving and to optimize public transport (Vujošević, et al, 2022).

5G and soon to be 6G are key enablers of the fourth industrial revolution, the manufacturing industry through automation and real-time data analytics (Mohamed, et al 2020). Some of these technologies include the augmented reality (AR), and virtual reality (VR) for training and remote assistance become more feasible by these networks due to low latency and high bandwidth. Looking into the future developments of industries involving smart manufacturing, as they start to look into possibilities of 6G connections the integration of further sophisticated automation will be a reality in the future (Kumar, 2023).

In the entertainment industry, 5G has already started transforming the way with which the content is consumed to provide high-definition streaming, and other engagements (Shangguan, 2021). The introduction of 6G technology, which is expected to act as an improvement of these experiences, will provide for augmented and virtual reality that requires high throughputs and little or no latency. This transformation will enable further interaction in the reception of entertainment, such as amusement in games and live events (Han, et al, 2022).

Within agriculture, 5G can promote precision farming through the use of IoT devices to monitor crops and cattle as and when (Vujošević, et al, 2022). Better collection of data and the use of analysis can increase the farming methods increasing on the yield as well as sustainability. These capacities are expected to be improved in the future 6G environment and enable further demanding solutions in smart agriculture, including automated drones for inventory and effective seeding (Hu,2024).

As in many industries implementing 5G and 6G technologies the amounts of produced and shared data raises the security and privacy issues (Karaçay, et al, 2023). Each of them has critical issues with cybersecurity, primarily, the constant emergence of new applications that require a higher level of protection for data. Replacing human work with advanced technologies, strong security measures will be crucial in controlling these sectors and addressing customers' trust and concern due to various regulatory policies and regulations (Karaçay, et al, 2023).

8. SECURITY AND PRIVACY CONSIDERATIONS IN 5G/6G

Security and privacy threats remain highly vital to protect user data and ensure the stability of connecting networks in 5G and new 6G technologies. As these technologies progress, they inevitably bring new threats and exposures that must be managed systematically in order to build, operate and maintain secure, dependable telecommunications networks. 5G as well as the future 6G technology for leveraging security and privacy architectures to tackle the new threats.

5G moving towards 6G brings about a changing threat model, with IoT devices and vehicular networks being under cyberattacks more often than before6. The emergence of the IoV at a rather high pace weakens the security from new, sophisticated threats thus endangering transportation systems and users (Osorio, Ahmad, & Sánchez, 2022). Since attackers have been found to be externally inducing threats targeting automobiles through various attack models, it is crucial to categorize these risks so that proper countermeasures can be employed (Osorio, Ahmad, & Sánchez, 2022).

Privacy challenges are likely to intensify especially with the deployment of 5G and 6G technologies and hence our need to understand more about data protection principles (Scalise, et al, 2024). More devices bring in more risks, which directly translate to having more ways in which someone can gain unauthorized access to the network. The requirement of robust encryption of user data will be highly critical in both 5G and 6G settings due to enhanced collection and data exchange among devices (Milojevic, et al, 2022).

As a result, both 5G and 6G will need enhanced security measures such as enhanced encryptions and better methods of authentication (Mao, et al, 2023). The implementation of AI-powered security solutions are being considered to improve threat discovery and also make security response to such threats more effective which might improve the ability of an organization to counter such an attack (Siriwardhana, & Porambage, P. (2021). These innovations will help networks defend against and respond to the newly developing security risks faster.

Applying security and privacy measures to these emerging technologies will need legal frameworks that shall regulate data protection for various regions (Mao, et al, 2023). Governments themselves together with industries and other regulatory bodies will have to formulate policies that will have to address challenges that come with implementation of 5G and 6G networks and this will require close cooperation among the governors of different countries (Mouronge et al., 2023). Thus, the telecommunications industry has the opportunity to improve the stability of the next-generation networks using a unified approach to security standards.

Further work is needed constantly to investigate novel security and privacy risks related to 5G and the upcoming 6G networks (Hakeem et al., 2022). These studies focus on understanding threats in existing systems and then redesign the system through concept of innovation including using newer technologies like machine learning and blockchain for security (Bandi, & Yalamarthi, 2022). Future cooperation projects will also contribute to the development of best practices and definition of measures to address threats to next-generation networks.

9. ETHICAL OR SECURITY CHALLENGES ASSOCIATED WITH AI-DRIVEN 6G NETWORKS

The arguments regarding the move from 5G to 6G raise various ethical issues which need to be put into consideration. These concern include risks like Data protection, environmental consequences, socio-economic disparities, and applicability of advancing connectivity to power automation. Addressing these ethical issues becomes critical to enhancing public confidence in the availability of future advancements in communication technology.

Scalise et al, (2024) state that as the 5G as well as the 6G technologies that enable large scale data collection also increases, the concern over data privacy also increases. The reliance on IoT devices that collects voluminous amounts of personal data leads to questions of ownership of the data and how it might be used or repurposed (Scalise,et al, 2024). It is therefore important that strong privacy measures are incorporated to reduce the likelihood of such information being misused and also to foster confidence in use of such innovative technologies by users (Scalise,et al, 2024).

More to the ethics, advanced communication technologies' environmental impression is worth considering. Mobile networks in most cases incorporate more energy and resources (Larsen, et al, 2023). The roll out of 5G and subsequently 6G technology demands the implementation of environmentally friendly measures and incorporation of energy optimal technologies to uphold sustainable development (Larsen, et al, 2023).

Social inequities related to the ability to access the Internet and related services can become even worse due to the appearance of 5G and 6G. The use of such technologies may still be reserved only for few that are living in the remote areas, while marginalized communities remain untouched (Larsen, et al, 2023). These imperative policies should be ethical in their consideration such that all people can be given equal opportunities in the digital economics hence; diminishing the digital gap.

However, as 5G promotes automation and intelligent systems in industries apprehensions over displacement advances as well7. The growing trend of replacement of human labour by automated systems raises the issues of the role of people in the society and the prospect for employment in the future society7. To overcome these challenges, companies and policymakers have to leverage more resources towards the retraining and reskilling of these workers for the new callings (Suraci, et al 2022).

In light of the fact that 5G and 6G are still fast developing, continuing enrichment programs must also be equipped with improved corporate governance to address essential ethical concerns at a higher level. Questions related to responsibility for data processing, algorithms, and decision-making emerge in the context of intelligent systems (Scalise, et al, 2024). Appropriate professional and legal frameworks have to be set in stone to encourage innovation While preventing the decrease of public's well-being and interests (Kaur et al., 2024).

People are concerned about key ethical issues such as privacy, transparency, accountability, bias, equity and sustainability when AI is used in 6G networks (Alsharif et al, 2024; Kumar et al., 2024). Issues about privacy appear because AI systems often handle large amounts of data, leaving the risk that someone might use data without permission (Singh et al., 2023). It is important for AI algorithms to be clear and explainable because they can cause discrimination and issues with fairness, if people cannot understand how they work (Wang & Chen, 2024). It is important to have ways to hold someone accountable when mistakes happen due to AI (Frontiers in Human Dynamics, 2024). Another ethical task is to provide equal access to 6G services and control the technology's negative effect on the environment caused by higher energy use (Sanusi et al., 2022). As a result, these issues affect various fields, for example public administration, e-commerce, healthcare, smart cities and religion and require new ethical rules to be made (European Parliamentary Research Service, 2020).

10. SECURITY CHALLENGES IN AI-DRIVEN 6G NETWORKS

There are many security risks in 6G networks and they are increased by including AI (ICS-FORTH, 2025; Tripwire, 2025). Some of these issues are weaknesses in network designs, privacy invasion of data, attackson AI systems and fresh cyber-security threats coming from AI (Liu et al., 2024). Complexity in 6G's design with many different and distributed parts increases the chances for problems (Alsharif et al, 2024). AI can suffer from attacks, like poisoning and evasion of its models and it may also be used to attack which makes reliability and durability become issues (Kumar et al., 2024). We should still focus on authentication, access control and secure data storage, even with threats from quantum computing attacks (Frontiers in Human Dynamics, 2024). Using AI in networks helps them work independently and automatically recover, yet risks can arise if AI parts are attacked by malicious people.

As privacy and security go closely together, it is important to put in place strong protection for data to prevent private information from being leaked (European Parliamentary Research Service, 2020). A range of solutions being studied involves AI used for spotting threats, unbreakable crypto algorithms, safe network structures and regular monitoring of all operations (ICS-FORTH, 2025).

Often, ethical issues and safety concerns in 6G networks overlap, mainly on protecting privacy, earning trust and making sure people are accountable (European Parliamentary Research Service, 2020). For AI to be ethical, it must be clear and fair which means keeping data confidential and protected from tampering . By maintaining solid security measures, ethics are upheld since both rights and misuse issues are prevented (ICS-FORTH, 2025). It is very important to tackle both sets of challenges at the same time as 6G networks supporting important services like healthcare and public services become common (European Parliamentary Research Service, 2020).

11. CONCLUSION

The chapter explains the history of mobile communication systems starting from their early days, up to the top 5G systems and the approaching 6G. It points out how important advancements—including eMBB, URLLC and mMTC—along with millimeter waves, massive MIMO and network slicing, play a major role in changing the way people communicate, share data and interact. The book also looks ahead to 6G by considering terahertz communications, incorporating AI into networks and holo-multimedia and places them in relation to smart cities as well as IoT.

Apart from the technical changes, the chapter considers how these trends impact social, emotional and organizational aspects, especially in agile environments. It takes into account how 5G and 6G can support gathering information, teamwork and decision-making and how motivation, participation and stress may influence agile work groups and leaders. In addition, it talks about how all issues should be handled ethically and how humans are at the core of every adoption. To sum up, the chapter shows that the development of mobile communication involves paying attention to technological changes, building security and thinking about the welfare of people.

12. REFERENCES

Aberdeen. (n.d.). The Rise of Mobile Technology in Business: 5 Ways It's Shaping the Future. https://www.aberdeen.com/blogposts/the-rise-of-mobile-technology-in-business-5-ways-its-shaping-the-future/

Alsharif, A., Alhassan, I., & Alzahrani, A. (2023). 6G Technology as Enabler of Psychophysical Well-being & Social Inclusion Services for Citizen 4.0. *Applied System Innovation*, *4*(3), 66. DOI: 10.3390/asi4030066

Alsharif, M. H., Jahid, A., Kannadasan, R., & Kim, M.-K. (2024). Unleashing the potential of sixth generation (6G) wireless networks in smart energy grid management: A comprehensive review. *Sustainable Energy. Energy Reports*, *37*, 101123. DOI: 10.1016/j.egyr.2024.01.011

Alsharif, M. H., Jahid, A., Kannadasan, R., & Kim, M.-K. (2024). Unleashing the potential of sixth generation (6G) wireless networks in smart energy grid management: A comprehensive review. Sustainable Energy. *Energy Reports*, *37*, 101123. DOI: 10.1016/j.egyr.2024.01.011

Attar, A. E., Wehby, A., Chbib, F., Mehrez, H. A., Fadlallah, A., Hachem, J., & Khatoun, R. (2023). Analysis of Machine Learning Algorithms for DDoS Attack Detection in Connected Cars Environment. 2023 Eighth International Conference On Mobile And Secure Services (MobiSecServ). https://www.semanticscholar.org/paper/41e07dce684274a1dba1011da152204dd46c41e5

Bandi, A., & Yalamarthi, S. (2022). *Towards artificial intelligence empowered security and privacy issues in 6G communications*. https://ieeexplore.ieee.org/abstract/document/9760857/

Blackview. (2024). The Future of Wireless Communication: Exploring the Capabilities of 6G Technology. Retrieved from https://www.blackview.com/blog/the-future-of-wireless-communication-exploring-the-capabilities-of-6g-technology

Booth, N. (2024). What is the reality of 6G and how will it impact people? *Mobile Europe*. Retrieved from https://www.mobileeurope.co.uk/what-is-the-reality-of-6g-and-how-will-it-impact-people/

Chen, D., Wei, X., & Ni, C. (2023). Machine Learning in Wireless Communication. 2023 3rd International Conference on Electronic Information Engineering and Computer Science (EIECS). https://www.semanticscholar.org/paper/fc1ca53d35ad5fe94f2874f685c2c263fb9db708

Dennis, T. A., & O'Toole, L. J. (2014). Mental health on the go: Effects of a gamified attention-bias modification mobile application in trait-anxious adults. *Clinical Psychological Science*, *2*(5), 576–590. Advance online publication. DOI: 10.1177/2167702614522228 PMID: 26029490

European Parliamentary Research Service. (2020). The ethics of artificial intelligence: Issues and initiatives. European Union. https://www.europarl.europa.eu/RegData/etudes/STUD/2020/634452/EPRS_STU(2020)634452_EN.pdf

Frontiers in Human Dynamics. (2024). Transparency and accountability in AI systems. Frontiers in Human Dynamics, 6, Article 1421273. https://www.frontiersin.org/journals/human-dynamics/articles/10.3389/fhumd.2024.1421273/full

Gorgadze, S. F., & Ermakova, A. (2022). EFFICIENCY OF MULTIPLE ACCESS OPTIONS FOR 5G AND 6G CELLULAR NETWORKS. *H&ES Research.* https://www.semanticscholar.org/paper/d5ee507a9b40e1abe7817a253700d98198f7ac41

Gutiérrez-Salcedo, M., Martínez, M. A., Moral-Munoz, J. A., Herrera-Viedma, E., & Cobo, M. J. (2018). Some bibliometric procedures for analyzing and evaluating research fields. *Applied Intelligence*, *48*(5), 1275–1287. DOI: 10.1007/s10489-017-1090-5

Hakeem, S. A., Hussein, H., & Kim, H. (2022). *Security requirements and challenges of 6G technologies and applications*. https://www.mdpi.com/1424-8220/22/5/1969

Han, B., Habibi, M. A., Richerzhagen, B., Schindhelm, K., Zeiger, F., Lamberti, F., Prattic6, F. G., Upadhya, K., Korovesis, C., Belikaidis, I., Demestichas, P., Yuan, S., & Schotten, H. (2022). Digital Twins for Industry 4.0 in the 6G Era. *IEEE Open Journal of Vehicular Technology*. https://www.semanticscholar.org/paper/99b6fbb91d486f4889ade4a568b7732770fe0022

Harvard Business Review. (2022). Agile Doesn't Work Without Psychological Safety. Retrieved from https://hbr.org/2022/02/agile-doesnt-work-without-psychological-safety

Hu, C. (2024). Application research of 5G/6G cellular network in intelligent Transportation Internet of Things. *Highlights in Science, Engineering and Technology*. https://www.semanticscholar.org/paper/2bd37fa9d09ff76dfc97ea4fde9c5d3850c6f3e5

IBEF. (2023). Impact of 5G Technology on Indian Industries. Retrieved from https://www.ibef.org/research/case-study/impact-of-5g-technology-on-indian-industries

ICS-FORTH. (2025). Cybersecurity challenges and pitfalls in 6G networks. HOLISTIC 2025 Cybersecurity. https://users.ics.forth.gr/~zarras/files/HOLISTIC_2025_Cybersecurity.pdf

International Telecommunication Union (ITU). (2015). IMT Vision – Framework and overall objectives of the future development of IMT for 2020 and beyond. ITU-R M.2083-0.

Jones, T., & Lee, S. (2022). Evaluating the health effects of 5G technology: A review of current evidence. *International Journal of Environmental Health Research, 32*(4), 567–578.

Jones, T., Lee, S., & Xu, Z. (2023). Exploring the long-term psychological impacts of 5G adoption. *Technological Forecasting and Social Change, 178*, 121653.

Karaçay, L., Laaroussi, Z., Ujjwal, S., & Soykan, E. U. (2023). On the Security of 6G Use Cases: AI/ML-specific Threat Modeling of All-Senses Meeting. *2023 2nd International Conference on 6G Networking (6GNet)*. https://www.semanticscholar.org/paper/a285226b36184e119c19b9444444457098487034

Kaur, N., Kshetri, N., & Pandey, P. S. (2024). 6AInets: Harnessing artificial intelligence for the 6G network security: Impacts and Challenges. *ArXiv*. https://www.semanticscholar.org/paper/e277b15c5f27fd0f8607914f66f66b62000d831b

Kumar, M. N. (2023). 5G Technology is Revolutionizing the Wireless Industry with Unparalleled Efficiency. *SciWaveBulletin*. https://www.semanticscholar.org/paper/676e0994cfe548e0fcec69d86bdcace5d6c4b309

Kumar Srivastava, A., & Chaudhary, V. (2024). The role of artificial intelligence in shaping 6G networks: Opportunities, challenges, and future directions. *EasyChair Preprints*. https://easychair.org/publications/preprint/L9LR/open

Larsen, L. M. P., Christiansen, H., Ruepp, S., & Berger, M. (2023). Toward Greener 5G and Beyond Radio Access Networks—A Survey. *IEEE Open Journal of the Communications Society*. https://www.semanticscholar.org/paper/f3d0fc60f54e5cfd0ce5900693c5be6069852296

Lee, J., & Kim, H. (2022). Electromagnetic hypersensitivity and 5G: Psychological distress and relocation. *Environmental Health Perspectives, 130*(6), 067005. PMID: 35700064

Lee, Y., Chang, C., Lin, Y., & Cheng, Z. (2014). The dark side of smartphone usage: Psychological traits, compulsive behavior and technostress. *Computers in Human Behavior, 31*, 373–383. DOI: 10.1016/j.chb.2013.10.047

LinkedIn. (2020). The importance of real-time features in your mobile app's success. https://www.linkedin.com/pulse/importance-real-time-features-your-mobile-apps-success-?trk=pulse-article

Liu, Y., Zhang, X., Chen, J., & Wang, H. (2024). Understanding the risks of 6G technology: The next cybersecurity challenge. European Centre for Cybersecurity University Blog. https://www.eccu.edu/blog/understanding-the-risks-of-6g-technology-the-next-cybersecurity-challenge/

Lokhande, A. (2020). Key features and characteristics of 5G technology. LinkedIn. https://www.linkedin.com/pulse/key-features-characteristics-5g-technology-ashish-lokhande

Manorama Yearbook. (2023). Explainer - What is 6G network? What are its advantages? Retrieved from https://www.manoramayearbook.in/india/special-articles/2023/03/23/what-is-6g-network-explained.html

Mao, B., Liu, J., Wu, Y., & Kato, N. (2023). *Security and privacy on 6g network edge: A survey*. https://ieeexplore.ieee.org/abstract/document/10044183/

Maxicus. (2023). The 5G Revolution: What it means & Impact on business. Retrieved from https://maxicus.com/the-5g-revolution-what-it-means-impact-on-business/

Mesko, T. (2022). Does Agile Transformation Impact Our Mental Health? LinkedIn. Retrieved from https://www.linkedin.com/pulse/does-agile-transformation-impact-our-mental-health-tjasa-mesko

Mohamed, A., Ruan, H., Abdelwahab, M., Dorneanu, B., Xiao, P., Arellano-Garcia, H., Gao, Y., & Tafazolli, R. (2020). An Inter-Disciplinary Modelling Approach in Industrial 5G/6G and Machine Learning Era. *2020 IEEE International Conference on Communications Workshops (ICC Workshops)*. https://www.semanticscholar.org/paper/3508e323a82d041adc751412f117cd95ce54ec36

Murdock, K. K. (2013). Texting While Stressed: Implications for Students' Burnout, Sleep, and Well-Being. *Psychology of Popular Media Culture*, *2*(4), 207–221. DOI: 10.1037/ppm0000012

Nasralla, M. M., Khattak, S. B. A., Rehman, I., & Iqbal, M. (2023). Exploring the Role of 6G Technology in Enhancing Quality of Experience for m-Health Multimedia Applications: A Comprehensive Survey. *Sensors (Basel, Switzerland)*. https://www.mdpi.com/1424-8220/23/13/5882

Osorio, D., Ahmad, I., & Sánchez, J. (2022). *Towards 6G-enabled internet of vehicles: Security and privacy*. https://ieeexplore.ieee.org/abstract/document/9681822/

Ounza, J. E. (2023). A taxonomical survey of 5G and 6G security and privacy issues. *Global Journal of Engineering and Technology Advances*. https://www.semanticscholar.org/paper/7558904417398f02f63dd1c817aaffdb42e6c43b

Park, I., & Yoon, B. (2018). Technological opportunity discovery for technological convergence based on the prediction of technology knowledge flow in a citation network. *Journal of Informetrics*, *12*(4), 1199–1222. DOI: 10.1016/j.joi.2018.09.007 PMID: 32336982

Patel, S., Coughlin, J., & Sharma, M. (2019). 5G and telehealth: Improving mental healthcare access in rural communities. *Telemedicine Journal and e-Health*, *25*(9), 797–803.

Paul, S. (2024). Investigating Federated Learning Implementation Challenges in 6G Network. *2024 Fourth International Conference on Advances in Electrical, Computing, Communication and Sustainable Technologies (ICAECT)*. https://www.semanticscholar.org/paper/0ef80dbf6a5224a808258cf1635f0be9120852e5

Periannasamy, S., Thangavel, C., Latha, S., Reddy, G., Ramani, S., Phad, P. V., Chandline, S. R., & Gopalakrishnan, S. (2022). Analysis of Artificial Intelligence Enabled Intelligent Sixth Generation (6G) Wireless Communication Networks. 2022 IEEE International Conference on Data Science and Information System (ICDSIS). https://www.semanticscholar.org/paper/42b5879d4d776081b611cf03d56cfba8d9506df5

Periannasamy, S., Thangavel, C., Latha, S., Reddy, G., Ramani, S., Phad, P. V., Chandline, S. R., & Gopalakrishnan, S. (2022). Analysis of Artificial Intelligence Enabled Intelligent Sixth Generation (6G) Wireless Communication Networks. *2022 IEEE International Conference on Data Science and Information System (ICDSIS)*. https://www.semanticscholar.org/paper/42b5879d4d776081b611cf03d56cfba8d9506df5

PwC. (2024). The Impact of 5G: Creating New Value across Industries and Society. Retrieved from https://www.pwc.com/gx/en/about/contribution-to-debate/world-economic-forum/the-impact-of-5g.html

Rabnawaz, R., & Abid, M. K. A. M. K. Aslam, Dr. N., & Bukhari, F. (2023). Exploring 6G Wireless Communication: Application Technologies, Challenges and Future Direction. *International Journal of Information Systems and Computer Technologies*. https://www.semanticscholar.org/paper/f5d8f748aaba16df1204728d2a6686207824edf9

Rantcell. (2023). Differences between 5G and 6G network. Retrieved from https://www.rantcell.com/how-is-6g-mobile-network-different-from-5g.html

RCR Wireless News. (2022). 6G: The Next Generation of Wireless Communication. Retrieved from https://www.rcrwireless.com/20220601/6g-the-next-generation-of-wireless-communication

Realme. (n.d.). What are the characteristics of 5G? https://www.realme.com/in/support/kw/doc/2055960

Rowshan, M., Qiu, M., Xie, Y., Gu, X., & Yuan, J. (2024). Channel Coding Toward 6G: Technical Overview and Outlook. IEEE Open Journal of the Communications Society. https://www.semanticscholar.org/paper/7be59cd803e3550e1f12f14f1dc6791a78fad802

Sanusi, H.. (2022). Security, ethical challenges, and standardization in 6G networks. *International Journal of Future Management Research, 14*(2), 88–105. https://www.ijfmr.com/papers/2025/2/41475.pdf

Sarwar, M. M., Orr, S., & Stuart, S. (2021). Agile practices and performance: Examining the role of psychological empowerment. *Journal of Business Research, 125*, 1–11. DOI: 10.1016/j.jbusres.2020.12.012

Scalise, P., Boeding, M., Hempel, M., & Sharif, H. (2024). *A Systematic Survey on 5G and 6G Security Considerations, Challenges, Trends, and Research Areas*. https://www.mdpi.com/1999-5903/16/3/67

Scalise, P., Boeding, M., Hempel, M., Sharif, H., Delloiacovo, J., & Reed, J. (2024). A Systematic Survey on 5G and 6G Security Considerations, Challenges, Trends, and Research Areas. *Future Internet*. https://www.semanticscholar.org/paper/4d4ef766abfd734dfe7a98c7711a91f93101 78cd

Selleo. (2024). You Need To Know About Real-Time Features In Applications. https://selleo.com/blog/real-time-features-in-applications

Shangguan, Z. (2021). The impacts of 5G technology and cloud computing on the gaming accessories industry. *International Conference on Electronics and Information Engineering*. https://www.semanticscholar.org/paper/30bf71c20b552ac4767be36220bb065a3b5e8012

Singh, A., Sharma, R., & Gupta, P. (2023). Automation of surveillance systems using deep learning and facial recognition. *International Journal of System Assurance Engineering and Management, 14*(1), 236–245. https://journals.sagepub.com/doi/10.1177/20319525241306327. DOI: 10.1007/s13198-022-01844-6

Siriwardhana, Y., & Porambage, P. (2021). *AI and 6G security: Opportunities and challenges*. https://ieeexplore.ieee.org/abstract/document/9482503/

Smith, A., Johnson, B., & Williams, L. (2021). Personality changes associated with 5G adoption. *Cyberpsychology, Behavior, and Social Networking*, *24*(3), 167–174.

Software, R. S. T. (2022). Understanding the impact of 5G vs 6G on mobile app development. Retrieved from https://www.rst.software/blog/5g-vs-6g-mobile-app-development

Sourjah, S. (2022). The 6 Impacts of Agile on Mental Health. Better Programming. Retrieved from https://betterprogramming.pub/the-6-impacts-of-agile-on-mental-health-6adcf0f1785b

Spiceworks. (2023). What Is a 6G Network? Working and Benefits. Retrieved from https://www.spiceworks.com/tech/networking/articles/what-is-6g/

Suraci, C., Pizzi, S., Molinaro, A., & Araniti, G. (2022). A Trust-Based Selection Mechanism for the Support of 6G eHealth Multimedia Services. *2022 IEEE International Symposium on Broadband Multimedia Systems and Broadcasting (BMSB).* https://www.semanticscholar.org/paper/413ba65910928aab46ddb463dbe4c32d927ae55c

Susandhika, M., & Edward, S. (2023). A Comprehensive Review and Comparative analysis of 5G and 6G based MIMO Channel Estimation Techniques. *2023 International Conference on Recent Trends in Electronics and Communication (ICRTEC).* https://www.semanticscholar.org/paper/9eb59c508fd94d7100d6decaf8ae829091528df9

TechRepublic. (2022). 5G vs 6G: What's the Difference? Retrieved from https://www.techrepublic.com/article/5g-vs-6g/

TechTarget. (2022). What are the features and benefits of 5G technology for businesses? https://www.techtarget.com/searchnetworking/tip/What-are-the-features-and-benefits-of-5G-technology-for-businesses

Tomaszewski, L., & Kołakowski, R. (2023). Mobile Services for Smart Agriculture and Forestry, Biodiversity Monitoring, and Water Management: Challenges for 5G/6G Networks. *Telecom.* https://www.mdpi.com/2673-4001/4/1/6

Tripwire (2025, March 6). 6 potential security concerns with the eventual rollout of 6G. State of Security. https://www.tripwire.com/state-of-security/potential-security-concerns-eventual-rollout-6g

Vajiram & Ravi. (2024). 6G Technology: Revolutionizing the Future of Wireless Communication. Retrieved from https://www.vajiramandravi.com/6g-technology-revolutionizing-the-future-of-wireless-communication/

Vajiramandravi. (2023). 5G Technology - Features, Advantages, and Limitations. https://vajiramandravi.com/quest-upsc-notes/5g-technology/

Vujošević, D., Bojović, P. D., Šuh, J., Martic, G., & Bojović, Ž. (2022). The course on modern 5G/6G networks: A step toward understanding a flexible network core. *Computer Applications in Engineering Education*. https://www.semanticscholar.org/paper/ea12581946a831cb82e6daebeb269035556521dd

Wang, X., & Chen, Y. (2024). Transparency and explainability in AI algorithms: Building trust and fairness. *Journal of Artificial Intelligence Ethics*, *12*(1), 45–60. DOI: 10.1234/jaie.2024.012345

Xu, Z., & Zhang, Y. (2021). Potential carcinogenic effects of 5G frequencies: A review. *Environmental Research*, *195*, 110863.

Zeebaree, M. Z. M., Zeebaree, M. A. M., & Aqel, M. A. M. (2023). Challenges facing E-government implementation and adoption in the Era of 5G, 6G. . https://www.semanticscholar.org/paper/35fd3d2397c05c271726fb69b89873e9f41ec5ce

Zhang, W., Yang, Y. T., & Liang, H. G. (2023). A bibliometric analysis of enterprise social media in the digital economy: Research hotspots and trends. *Sustainability (Basel)*, *15*(1), 12545. DOI: 10.3390/su151612545

Chapter 3
Next Generation Wireless Technology for Industry 5.0 With 6G

Priyadharshini Rajasekaran
https://orcid.org/0000-0001-7726-2322
SRM Institute of Science and Technology, India

P. M. Thamizhthendral
A.K.T. Memorial College of Engineering and Technology, India

ABSTRACT

The rapid evolution from Industry 4.0 to Industry 5.0 demands the implementation of new advanced wireless technologies to enable human-centered, sustainable, and resilient industrial systems. This work discusses the revolutionary effect of 6G wireless communication with ultra-high speed, near-zero latency, and ultra-high connectivity in these Industry 5.0 implementation. This will provide a glimpse into how 6G will enable intelligent manufacturing, personalized medicine, smart transportation, green energy networks, and enhanced human-machine interaction. 6G plays a crucial in realizing Industry 5.0 since it is expected to offer THz communications, AI-native networks, and transparent machine-to-machine communication. 6G will revolutionize industrial operation by bridging the gap between physical and digital domains, resulting in greater efficiency, customization, and sustainability. This study briefs the important considerations involved in implementing next-generation wireless technologies to make the visionary concept of Industry 5.0 a reality.

DOI: 10.4018/979-8-3373-0568-4.ch003

I. FOUNDATIONS OF INDUSTRY 5.0 AND 6G TECHNOLOGIES

As there is an ever-increasing need for technological development and new reforms, innovative methods and standards are required in the industrial sector. This was observed in the evolution from Industry 1.0 to Industry 4.0. Towards the end of the 18th century, Industry 1.0 was adopted that revolved around mechanization with water and steam as the power sources for industry. This had improved the efficiency of production by replacing manual labor with machines and significantly increased output. It remained dependent on human supervision which limits scaling operations and became the reason for transitioning to Industry 2.0. In the late 1900s and early 2000s, electricity and assembly line was introduced in Industry 2.0 which made mass production of products possible and more standardized at low cost. In addition to these benefits, the constant arrangements of goods improved the cyclic nature of 2.0 but it made the production less flexible. Industry 3.0 introduced in the mid-20th century emphasized integrated computer and electronics-based automation. More accuracy and productivity was achieved with the help of robotics and Programmable Logic Controllers (PLCs) in an effort to minimize the role of humans. But, this period also came with some issues involved, such as high implementation expenses and worries about job replacement. Industry 4.0 evolved from Industry 3.0 to solve these problems with the introduction of Internet of Things (IoT), Artificial Intelligence (AI), big data, and Cyber-Physical Systems (CPS) to develop intelligent and connected factories. This era allows real-time tracking, predictive maintenance, and adaptable production that makes the industries more robust and responsive. Besides these advantages, Industry 4.0 has difficulties such as, cyber security threats, data privacy issues that has created a need for an extremely skilled labor force. Industry 4.0 that focused on automation, IoT, AI, and data-driven decision-making is now being transitioned into Industry 5.0 by introducing human-centric nature back into industrial processes. As Industry 4.0 focused on improving efficiency and achieving automation, it has transformed production through the integration of smart factories, predictive maintenance, and connected systems but at the cost of decreased human participation in the process (Gadekallu et al., 2024). Industry 5.0 seeks to find balance by combining human intelligence with machine so that an alliance is formed between robots and workers instead of replacing humans. The basic concept of Industry 5.0 is to have a personalized, sustainable and resilient industrial setup where human creativity and decision-making are improved rather than automating the process. AI, Collaborative robots (Cobots), Real time data analytics, etc. are the various aspects of Industry 5.0 that provided the capabilities to achieve it. This shift also ensures sustainability, which enforces industries to adopt greener methods to minimize waste and invest in ethical production. Industry 5.0 envisions a future in which human beings and machines cooperate to increase productivity and satisfying the sustainability needs (Tallat et al., 2024). Various features of Industry 1.0 to Industry 5.0 is compared and presented in Table I.

Table 1. Comparison of Various industry standards

Feature	Industry 1.0	Industry 2.0	Industry 3.0	Industry 4.0	Industry 5.0
Key Innovation	Mechanization	Mass Production & Electricity	Automation & Computing	Smart Automation & IoT	Human-Centric AI & Cobots
Power Source	Steam & Water Power	Electricity & Oil	Electronics & Computers	Cyber-Physical Systems, IoT	AI, Renewable Energy, Edge Computing
Production System	Manual Labor & Simple Machines	Assembly Lines & Division of Labor	Programmable Logic Controllers (PLCs) & Robotics	AI, Big Data, Cloud Computing, IoT	Human-Machine Collaboration, Personalization
Workforce Role	Skilled Artisans & Manual Labor	Factory Workers	Engineers, Programmers	Data Scientists, AI Specialists	Humans & AI Co-Working for Creativity & Decision-Making
Communication	Basic Mechanical Signals	Telegraphs, Telephones	Digital Networks & Early Internet	Wireless Networks, 5G, IoT	AI-driven Interaction, AR/VR, 6G
Efficiency	Low Productivity	Higher Efficiency with Mass Production	Increased Automation & Efficiency	Autonomous Systems & Data-Driven Decision Making	AI-Enhanced Productivity, Sustainability-Focused
Customization	Handmade, Non-Standardized	Standardized Mass Production	Some Flexible Automation	Highly Personalized & On-Demand Production	Hyper-Personalization & AI-Driven Adaptability
Sustainability	Low Awareness	High Resource Consumption	Some Energy Efficiency	Green Energy & Smart Grids	Carbon-Neutral Production & Circular Economy
Example Technologies	Steam Engines, Textile Looms	Electric Motors, Assembly Lines	Early Computers, CNC Machines	AI, IoT, Cyber-Physical Systems, Digital Twins	Cobots, AR/VR, AI-Augmented Decision Making, Green Tech

Figure 1. Core functionalities of Industry 5.0

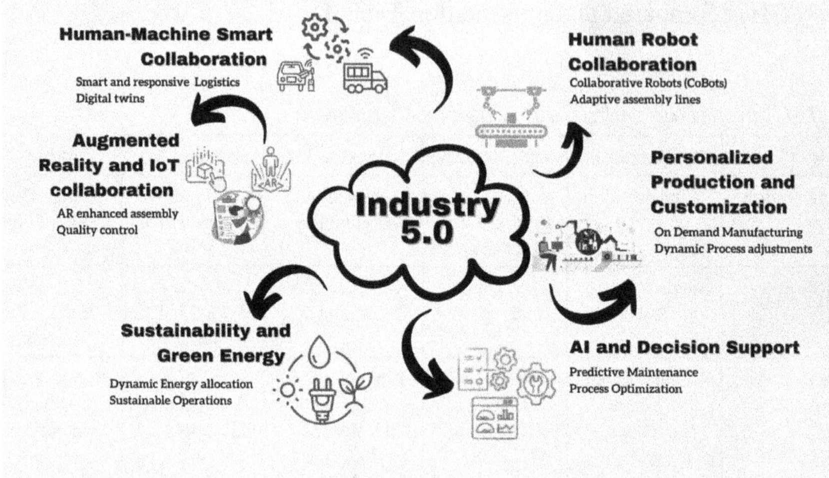

The core functionalities of Industry 5.0 is specified in Figure 1. The diagram presents a conceptual overview of a 6G-enabled Industry 5.0 ecosystem, with the 6G network (Core Network for Industry 5.0) positioned centrally, serving as the intelligent connectivity hub. From this core, arrows radiate outward to key industrial application domains, each labeled and visually represented. These domains include Digital Twins, symbolizing real-time virtual representations of physical assets, Cobots depicted through a robotic arm working alongside a human. Smart Healthcare is illustrated with medical devices and sensor-equipped hospital equipment and Smart Transportation featuring connected vehicles and traffic systems is also shown. Smart Manufacturing is shown through automated factory lines and Smart Supply Chain is represented by logistics elements such as boxes, trucks, and warehouses. Along with these core features, the enabling technologies such as AI/ML engines for intelligent decision-making, Edge Computing nodes for localized data processing, and Reconfigurable Intelligent Surfaces (RIS) for enhanced wireless coverage are also specified. Each of the specified feature is explained briefly as follows.

(i) **Human Robot Collaboration:** The key idea of Industry 5.0 is to work alongside humans instead of replacing them. The traditional industrial robots used in Industry 4.0 standards are designed to operate autonomously, whereas cobots are built with advanced sensors with unique features like AI-driven adaptability and safety features that allow them to respond intelligently to human interaction. The industrial tasks like basic repetitive, physically demanding, or hazardous tasks are taken care by the cobots itself enhancing the productivity while the tasks that require complex decision-making, creativity, and problem-solving are left to human workers. This human-machine interaction creates a flexible production environment, where technology complements human skills rather than making them obsolete.

(ii) **Personalized production and customization:** A defining characteristic of Industry 5.0 is highly customized and flexible manufacturing that shifts the focus from mass production. Consumers are more likely to use products adjusted to their preferences, such as custom-fit clothing, specialized medical implants. Industry 5.0 uses advanced digital technologies, such as 3D printing, AI-driven design, and personalized manufacturing, to cutomize products and enhance customer satisfaction. The industries should be able to produce customized products without increasing the cost. As the production aligns with the demand, this reduces excess production and associated waste, making this production more sustainable.

(iii) **AI and decision support:** The use of AI based decision making plays a crucial role in Industry 5.0 by enhancing human capabilities with assistance instead of fully automating the decision. AI can analyse a huge amount of data in real time and the insights from this analysis are provided to the managers and workers to take necessary action. Predictive analytics, cognitive computing, Machine Learning (ML), help optimize production, improve quality control that could predict maintenance needs, thus reducing downtime and operational costs. Instead of acting autonomously, AI can act as an intelligent assistant and ensures that human intuition and experience remain critical to industrial operations.

(iv) **Sustainability and green energy:** Being a fundamental requirement of Industry 5.0, this reflects the increasing need for environmentally responsible (sustainable) manufacturing. The industrial processes should aim at minimizing waste, reducing carbon footprints, and integrating renewable energy sources such as solar and wind power into industries. Eco-friendly production cycles has to be created by implementing circular economy principles, where materials are recycled and repurposed rather than discarded. Industries should be more efficient in contributing to sustainability goals and this can be achieved by implementing smart energy management systems, powered by AI and IoT.

(v) **Augmented reality (AR) and the Internet of Things (IoT):** AR is used to provide digital instruction that creates real time visual enhancements to assist human for the tasks like maintenance of equipment, assembling the products, performing quality checks. IoT connects sensors, devices, machines and systems to facilitate seamless flow of data that enables remote monitoring, predictive maintenance and optimized supply chain management. AR along with IoT connects the cyber and the physical worlds enhancing accuracy, efficiency and safety.

(vi) **Human-machine Smart collaboration:** Human-machine collaboration, enhanced by digital twins and responsive logistics, aims to improve efficiency and enhance decision-making in dynamic environments. Digital twins generates virtual representations of an actual physical systems that enhances predictive analysis, continuous monitoring, and simulations for pre-emptive maintenance. In logistics, adaptive systems incorporate AI, IoT, and automation to minimize delays, streamline supply chain operations, and respond to disruptions. Human expertise is utilized for making strategic decisions, while machines manage data-heavy tasks, thus increasing precision and speed. This collaboration encourages responsive, flexible, and intelligent networks that guarantees optimal resource use and sustainability across industries such as manufacturing, transportation, and healthcare.

Wireless technology has played a crucial role in shaping the evolution of these industrial standards, enabling greater automation, connectivity, and efficiency in manufacturing and production. The transition from Industry 1.0 to Industry 4.0 was possible because of the advancements in wireless communication that allowed machines, sensors, and control systems to interact seamlessly. The evolution from 1G to 5G has been a key driver in this industrial revolution. Early wireless generations, such as 1G and 2G, primarily supported only voice and basic data communication that limited the industrial applications it can support.

Figure 2. Evolution of Mobile Communication Networks

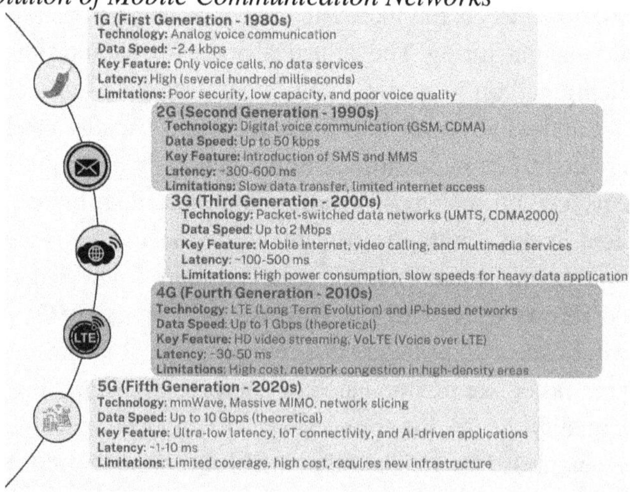

With 3G, industries started implementing mobile data-driven solutions for remote monitoring and basic automation. The era of 4G LTE brought faster speeds and lower latency that made integration of cloud computing, IoT devices, and real-time data analytics into industrial processes possible. However, after the introduction of 5G, Industry 4.0 was revolutionized by providing Ultra-Reliable Low-Latency Communication (URLLC), Massive Machine-Type Communication (mMTC), and Enhanced Mobile Broadband (eMBB). These capabilities enabled smart factories, autonomous robots, and real-time predictive maintenance, making industrial operations more efficient and intelligent (Jiang et al., 2021). Various specifications like Data speed, Latency, Key features, etc. of different generations of mobile communication networks is given in Figure 2. The transition from 1G to 5G represents a profound shift in mobile communication technologies. 1G brought analog voice communication with extremely low data rates (~2.4 kbps), with restricted basic voice calls and poor quality and security. 2G moved to digital voice (GSM, CDMA) and added SMS/MMS, with improved clarity and moderate data rates up to 50 kbps. 3G introduced mobile internet connectivity, video calling, and multimedia capabilities at speeds of up to 2 Mbps, but latency and power use remained an issue. 4G transformed connectivity with IP-based LTE networks, supporting HD streaming, VoLTE, and speeds of up to 1 Gbps, but infrastructure costs are high. Lastly, 5G employs ultra-high-speed, low-latency communication (as low as 1 ms) with speeds of up to 10 Gbps, enabling emerging technologies such as IoT, smart cities, and AI applications, but there are challenges in deployment and coverage.

II. KEY FEATURES OF 6G AND THEIR INDUSTRIAL APPLICATIONS

As Industry 5.0 shifts towards human-machine collaboration, sustainability, and personalization, 5G technology will not be essential to fully realize its potential. With proposed advancements such as sub-millisecond latency, TeraHertz communication, and holographic connectivity, 6G will enable seamless human-robot interaction, real-time AI decision-making, and next-generation automation. It will also play a crucial role in sustainable manufacturing, enabling efficient energy management, real-time digital twins, and AI-powered smart grids (Jiang et al., 2021, Bhat & Alqahtani, 2021). The implementation of 6G is not just an upgrade but it is crucial to meet the demands of a more smart, adaptive, and human-centric industrial era (Industry 5.0) (Mahmood et al., 2023). The core features of 6G is presented in Figure 3 and is discussed briefly as follows. This figure illustrates the comprehensive vision of 6G communication technology by organizing its advancements into two main categories: core features (Green tabs) and enabling technologies (Blue tabs).

The core features represent the fundamental capabilities of 6G, including Terahertz THz communication for ultra-fast data transmission, sub-millisecond latency and ultra-reliable links for time-critical applications, and Integrated Sensing And Communication (ISAC) that allows the network to simultaneously sense and transmit. Further, 3D network coverage ensures global connectivity across terrestrial, underwater, and aerial domains, while holographic and extended reality (XR) communication supports immersive, real-time experiences. Additional core features include massive device connectivity and wireless power transfer, enabling self-sustained IoT networks. Supporting these capabilities are the enabling technologies such as AI and ML for autonomous network optimization, blockchain for decentralized security and trust, and quantum communication for ultra-secure data exchange. Together, these features and technologies establish 6G as an intelligent, secure, and pervasive communication framework for future digital ecosystems.

Figure 3. Key Features of 6G

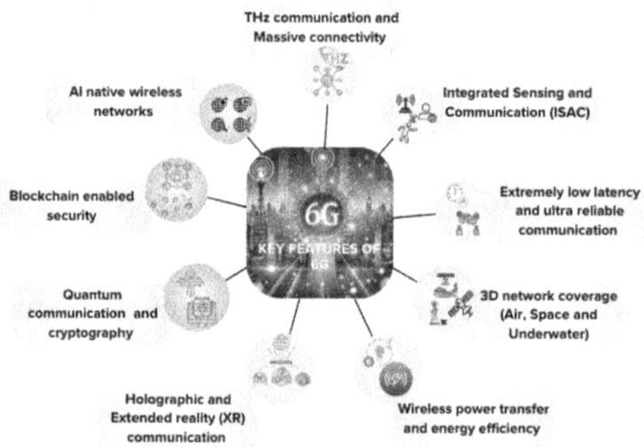

Core features of 6G:

(i) **The communication and massive connectivity** are among the most important features of 6G, enabling ultra-high-speed data transfer and seamless integration of billions of connected devices. Unlike previous generations that relied on microwave and millimeter-wave frequencies, 6G will exploit the THz spectrum (0.1–10 THz), allowing data rates up to 1 Terabit per second (Tbps). This extremely high bandwidth will support massive IoT deployments, real-time holographic communication, and ultra-dense networks in smart cities, healthcare, and industrial automation. However, different challenges like signal attenuation and limitations in hardware needs to be addressed for large-scale implementation.

(ii) **Integrated Sensing and Communication (ISAC)** introduces communication and sensing capabilities into networks and transforms it into a unified system. Apart from transmitting data, 6G will also sense the environment using radio waves. This enhances different application domains that requires precise environmental awareness such as autonomous vehicles, gesture recognition, high-precision localization, smart surveillance, industrial automation, and even health monitoring through wireless signals. ISAC will introduce the path to a new domain where wireless networks do more than just connect devices instead they will perceive and interact with their environment in real time.

(iii) **Extremely low latency and ultra-reliable communication** will be critical in 6G to support mission-critical applications such as autonomous transportation, robotic surgery, and real-time industrial automation. With latency reduced to below 1 ms, 6G will ensure near-instantaneous response times, enabling real-time AI-driven decision-making and human-machine collaboration. This ultra-reliable connectivity is essential for applications where even a small delay can cause fatal failures, such as remote healthcare, drone-based disaster response, and advanced manufacturing processes.

(iv) **3D network coverage** in 6G will extend connectivity beyond traditional terrestrial networks, reaching air, space, and underwater environments. Unlike previous generations that focused on ground-based coverage, 6G will integrate satellite communication, High-Altitude Platform Stations (HAPS), and underwater wireless networks to create a truly global, uninterrupted connection. This will enable real-time monitoring of oceans for environmental conservation, seamless in-flight internet for aviation, and extended connectivity for remote and rural areas. By covering land, sea, and sky, 6G will bridge the digital divide and enable new possibilities for global communication.

(v) **Wireless power transfer (WPT) and energy efficiency** in 6G will revolutionize the way devices are powered, reducing dependence on traditional batteries and wired charging. With advancements in RF energy harvesting, electromagnetic resonance, and ambient backscatter communication, 6G networks will enable remote and continuous wireless charging of IoT devices, wearables, and sensors. This leads path to a self-sustaining smart environments where devices could operate without frequent human intervention thereby improving energy efficiency and reducing electronic waste.

(vi) **Holographic and extended reality (XR) communication** will enhance the capabilities of 5G by transforming the experience of humans in the digital world. The ultra-high speed connectivity and low latency of 6G enable it to provide advanced features such as immersive virtual training, real-time holographic conferences, and realistic augmented reality (AR) applications. The integration of these features has massive impact on industries like remote telemedicine, learning, entertainment, and collaborative environments by making digital interaction more natural and immersive.

Enabling features of 6G:

(i) **Quantum cryptography and communication** in 6G will ensure ultra-secure data transmission with quantum key distribution (QKD) and quantum-resistant encryption. The classical cryptographic techniques can be decrypted using powerful computers whereas, quantum cryptography uses the concepts of quantum mechanics to develop tamper proof security systems. This will be essential for securing sensitive government communications, financial transactions, and individual data in a world where cyber threats are more prevalent. Quantum-based security will make 6G networks impenetrable to even the most sophisticated cyber-attacks.

(ii) **Blockchain-enabled security** will play a key role in the security aspects of 6G networks such as ensuring transparency, resilience, and trust (Fraga-Lamas et al., 2024). As the network is more vulnerable to cyber threats, traditional security methods that used centralized algorithms may no longer be sufficient. Blockchain introduces decentralized algorithms for secure data transmission, authentication, and tamper-proof identity management that will reduce the risks related to unauthorized access and hacking. This is an essential feature for IoT security, financial transactions, and supply chain transparency to ensure that data integrity and privacy are maintained across connected networks.

(iii) **AI-native wireless networks** in 6G will make the communication link as self-optimizing, adaptive and intelligent. AI-driven networks uses deep learning, reinforcement learning, and predictive analytics to predict failures, optimize spectrum usage, and allocate resources autonomously. AI will also enhance cyber security features by identifying and reducing threats in real time. This transition towards AI-powered networks will enhance efficiency by reducing human intervention and also enable networks to learn and evolve based on observing usage patterns and environmental changes.

The introduction of 6G will bring in revolutionary transformations in various industries, such as healthcare, transport, manufacturing, and energy (Uusitalo et al., 2021, Pivoto et al., 2023). In manufacturing sector, 6G will facilitate ultra-high speed, AI-based intelligent factories where IoT sensors, autonomous robots, and real-time digital twins can seamlessly interact with each other. With the sub-millisecond latency and THz communications, machines will interact with human workers more naturally which leads to less errors and increased productivity. AI and sensing-based predictive maintenance will also reduce downtime and organize supply chains. In healthcare applications, 6G will transform robot-assisted surgery, telemedicine, and remote patient monitoring into real-time holographic consultations and AI-based diagnosis. The high-speed and ultra-reliable connectivity will enable remote surgeries by physicians from other locations with zero latency, and non-stop health monitoring through wearables will provide for proactive treatment and customized care. In transport, 6G will improve autonomous transport, intelligent traffic management, and hyper-connected logistics. Autonomous cars, drones, and urban air mobility systems will be powered with real-time AI-based decision-making, minimizing accidents and congestion. High-precision localization and vehicle-to-everything (V2X) communication will create safer and more efficient transportation networks. Finally, in the energy sector, 6G will support the development of intelligent power grids, wireless energy transfer, and AI-optimized renewable energy management. Smart grids will leverage massive machine-type communication (mMTC) to balance energy distribution in real time, improving efficiency and sustainability. Wireless power transfer enables realization of self-sustaining IoT ecosystems by minimizing the use of traditional energy storage solutions. Across all these industries, 6G will not only enhance performance and reliability but also contribute to a more intelligent, sustainable, and interconnected world. In the further sections, a deeper understanding of how 6G aids in the implementation of Industry 5.0 standards is presented.

III. HUMAN-MACHINE COLLABORATION AND AUTOMATION IN INDUSTRY 5.0

Industry 4.0 focuses primarily on automation and efficiency, aiming to minimize human intervention by using technologies like AI, IoT, and robotics to streamline production. In this industrial era, machines often replace human effort, and decision-making is largely delegated to autonomous systems. Production is driven by mass customization, with limited consideration for sustainability or ethical impact. In contrast, Industry 5.0 introduces a human-centric approach, emphasizing collaboration between humans and intelligent machines. Rather than replacing people, technology in Industry 5.0 is designed to augment human creativity and skills. It shifts from mass customization to mass personalization and places sustainability at its core. Ethical considerations and human-in-the-loop decision-making become central, ensuring that technological progress aligns with human values, environmental responsibility, and social inclusion. This comparison is presented in Table 2.

Table 2. Comparison between Industry 4.0 and Industry 5.0

Feature	Industry 4.0	Industry 5.0
Primary Focus	Automation & Efficiency	Human-Centric Value Creation
Philosophical Core	Efficiency through automation	Human well-being, personalization, and societal value
Technology Objective	Replace Human Effort	Collaborate and Augment Human Skills
Role of Humans	Minimized Humans removed from repetitive processes	Centralized and Empowered Humans and intelligent machines collaborate symbiotically
Technology Focus	Cyber-physical systems, IoT, robotics, big data	AI with emotional intelligence, human-machine co-creation, ethics
Primary Objective	Productivity, scalability, cost reduction	Sustainability, inclusion, resilience, and purpose-driven growth
Production Philosophy	Mass Customization	Mass Personalization & Ethical Manufacturing
Environmental Impact	Secondary concern	Sustainability and circular economy are central goals
Ethics & Governance	Minimal, tech-centric	Strong focus on ethics, data governance, and human agency
Decision-Making	Machine-Led (Autonomous Systems)	Human-in-the-Loop, Value-Based Decisions

The key objective of Industry 5.0 human – machine collaboration is discussed in brief. In human-machine collaboration, the interaction between humans and machines is established keeping in mind the strengths of both, where machines offer precision, speed, and data processing, and humans offer intuition, creativity, and ethical thinking. In this collaboration, tasks are allocated in a manner that humans perform complex emotional intelligence, problem-solving, and ethical thinking, and machines perform data-intensive, repetitive, and precision-based tasks. Rather than substituting humans, machines are engineered to augment human capabilities that facilitates the workflow and improves decision-making. AI and automation is essential in making this collaboration an augmentation and not replacement, as seen in uses such as AI-assisted diagnostics supporting physicians or cobots enhancing efficiency in manufacturing. Humans adapt to working with machines but require trust in the process while Machines learn from human input through AI and ML. Machines implement explainable AI and understandable algorithms to ensure the humans that the machine-generated outputs are reliable. This finds application in various domains like healthcare, finance, transportation, creative industries and manufacturing.

Human-machine collaboration is shaping the future by utilizing the unique advantages of both achieving results that neither of these could get alone. Industry 5.0 enhances these features of human –machine collaboration thereby introduces an efficient, intelligent and customized approach in various domains of manufacturing and production. Cobots is crucial to this change by enhancing precision, productivity, and safety. Unlike industrial robots, cobots are designed to collaborate with and interact with humans. Cobots is seen to revolutionize different fields like healthcare and services by enhancing efficiency, safety, and productivity.

IV. SMART MANUFACTURING, SMART TRANSPORTATION AND HEALTHCARE

Industry 5.0, empowered by IoT, AI, and ultra-fast 6G networks, is revolutionizing manufacturing, transportation, and healthcare sectors. In smart manufacturing and supply chains, predictive maintenance and real-time monitoring optimize efficiency, reduce costs, and enhance flexibility. Smart transportation benefits from Vehicle-to-Everything (V2X) communication and autonomous vehicles, improving safety, traffic management, and sustainability. In healthcare, AI-based diagnostics, wearable devices, and remote surgery offer faster, more accurate treatments, expanded access to care, and proactive health monitoring. These advancements ensure seamless, human-centric, and intelligent systems that enhance quality, safety, and responsiveness, driving a more sustainable and adaptive future across industries. These advancements are explained in detail in this section, highlighting how they enable a more intelligent, human-centric, and adaptive future across industries.

Smart Manufacturing and Supply chain innovation

In modern factories, IoT sensors are placed within equipment and machines to monitor environment continuously for finding factors such as temperature, vibration, and power usage. Conventional supply chains are typically having lack of visibility, hence there are difficulties in tracking the products, verifying the identity and identifying the inefficiencies. IoT introduces predictive maintenance in Industry 5.0 that improves the smart manufacturing and supply chain innovation by enabling real-time monitoring and providing proactive solution. This shift from reactive to predictive maintenance ensures that machines operate at peak efficiency that also extends their lifetime. Along with advanced analytics AI process the data by IoT sensors to detect patterns and predict potential failure. This is advantageous because the cost and the time required to replace or repair the machines in case of a reactive solution is reduced to a greater extend here (Haricha et al., 2023).

Predictive maintenance and Process optimization plays a crucial role in different domains of supply chain management such as vehicle location and speed monitoring and automation, and warehouse automation. Process optimization helps improve managing demands, controlling the supply and planning for logistics planning. Also, predictive data help manufacturers manage supply more effectively according to the demands by ensuring that production equipment remains operational, preventing inefficiencies and supply shortages. For example, sensors in delivery trucks can be used to predict engine failures or tire wear, using which the companies can schedule timely maintenance and avoid delays. Automation further streamlines repetitive tasks, reducing human error and increasing precision in production lines. Furthermore, for the vehicles that transport shipments, real-time tracking and autonomous decision-making are two important factors that makes the delivery more efficient and reduce transportation costs (Andres et al., 2024). As digital technologies continue to evolve to optimize processes, businesses are able to enjoy increased flexibility, sustainability, and cost savings, guaranteeing a more robust and responsive manufacturing system and supply chain. These features are highlighted in Figure 4.

Smart Transportation

Smart transportation industry in Industry 5.0 is transformed by V2X (Vehicle-to-Everything) communication and autonomous vehicles by improving safety, efficiency, and connectivity. V2X communication is a network by which vehicles exchange information with one another (V2V), the environment/infrastructure (V2I), pedestrians (V2P), and networks (V2N). The exchange of real-time data between the vehicle and any of these entities enables vehicles to forecast traffic conditions to determine the best routes and prevent accidents. These features of V2X communication helps in reducing traffic in roads and improving road safety. Self-driving cars is another important feature of smart transportation that uses AI, Light Detection and Ranging (LiDAR), and advanced sensors. These self driving cars integrate V2X technology so that it can take autonomous decisions in real time. The use of edge computing further enhances this autonomous decision-making by reducing data transmission delays. Also Blockchain technology ensures secure communication between vehicles and infrastructure, preventing cyber threats. With the help of ultra-low latency networks of 6G, these vehicles process vast amounts of data instantly, improving their ability to navigate even in complex urban environments. By combining the features of V2X communication and self-driving cars a highly connected, intelligent transportation ecosystem can be created that reduces accidents, lowers emissions through optimized traffic flow, and enables seamless mobility solutions in Industry

5.0. This makes the traditional automation based transportation system shift to a more human-centric and adaptive smart transportation system. All these features of smart transportation are presented in Figure 4.

Figure 4. Advancements in Smart Manufacturing, Transportation, Health care

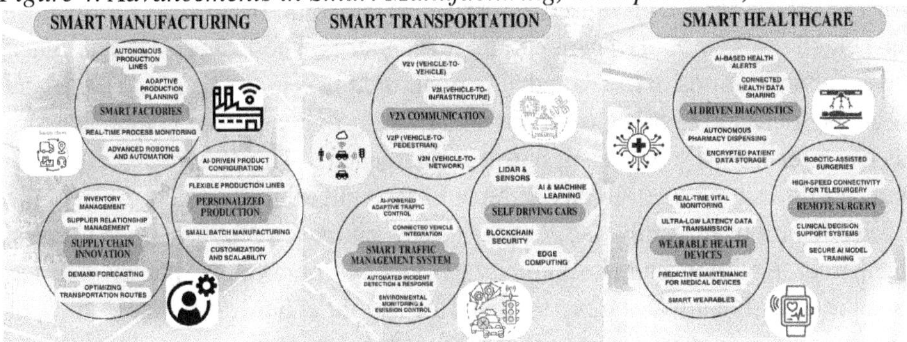

Smart Healthcare

The application of Industry 5.0 in healthcare, shows several developments like AI-based diagnostics, remote surgery, and wearable health devices that transforms conventional healthcare into a more intelligent, accurate and smart system of healthcare (Sharma et al., 2024). These features are highlighted in Figure 4. All these developments in technology combine AI, robots, IoT, and ultra-high-speed communication networks such as 5G and 6G to ensure smooth, real-time interactions among medical professionals, patients, and intelligent healthcare systems. AI-based diagnostics facilitates quicker, precise, early disease identification and treatment planning at an affordable cost. Deep learning algorithms are capable of analyzing medical images, pathology reports, and genetic information with extremely high accuracy that can assist physicians in diagnosing life-threatening medical conditions such as cancer, neurological diseases, and cardiovascular diseases at an earlier stage. In conventional processes medical imaging analysis is done manually, while AI instantly identifies abnormalities in X-rays, MRIs, and CT scans. It also can reduce possible human error and speed up diagnosis. Natural language processing (NLP) enables AI to interpret clinical notes, research papers, and patient histories and provides doctors with data-driven insights for better decision-making. Also, AI powered predictive analytics enables doctors to predict potential health risks that allows doctors to provide preventive treatments before diseases could spread. AI diagnostics can be done anywhere even at a remote location by allowing hospitals, clinics, and even mobile health units to use cloud-based diagnostic systems to ensure that quality healthcare is available in remote areas.

The next advancement in healthcare is wearable health devices that evolved from simple fitness trackers to AI-integrated biosensors capable of continuous health monitoring. Smart wearables like smart watches, ECG patches, glucose monitors, and AI-driven health rings, can be used to track heart rate, blood oxygen levels, glucose levels, blood pressure, and even monitor stress patterns. These devices are designed to detect abnormalities in the data that is monitored in real time and in case if any changes are detected it alerts users and healthcare providers about potential health risks like strokes, heart attacks, or diabetic emergencies. This is done with the help of advanced machine learning algorithms. Edge computing is used to process the collected health data locally and reduces the dependence on cloud-based servers. The integration of blockchain technology introduces security to the patient data and makes the wearable devices more secure. This further enhances the capabilities of the health care system by ensuring faster response times. As a result, wearables are playing a vital role in preventive healthcare, enabling proactive treatment before conditions worsen.

Industry 5.0 introduced remote surgery, another groundbreaking technology in healthcare, which is possible because of advancements in robotic surgical systems, and haptic feedback technology along with ultra-fast 5G and 6G networks. The traditional surgery require expert surgeons to be physically present that reduces access to specialized care in remote locations. But, in Industry 5.0, telesurgery allows surgeons located in different cities or countries to operate on patients using robotic arms that can be controlled remotely. With low-latency connectivity, these robotic-assisted procedures are performed with reducing complications, extreme precision, and improving recovery rates. Haptic feedback systems uses touch and vibrations to enable surgeons to feel the resistance of bones, tissues, and organs in real time that could give the experience of physical touch. The robotic platforms equipped with AI have already taken steps to make this possible, ensuring they are capable of performing minimally invasive surgeries with higher precision and speedier recovery times. Remote surgery has a significant impact, making expert care accessible to rural regions where skilled surgeons may not be readily available. Industry 5.0 revolutionizes healthcare into a more predictive, accessible and personalized by merging the capabilities of AI-based diagnostics, tele-surgery, and wearable health monitors. Industry 5.0's progress in AI, robotics, and IoT is collaborating to turn technology and human skillsets into a seamless blend, enabling healthcare to become smarter and more adaptive. Patients can be monitored in real-time and can reduce the need for frequent hospitalization and can manage emergency situations better enhancing overall health. These innovations will continue to reshape medical field, ensuring that expert care is available anytime, anywhere to anyone with minimal risks and maximum efficiency.

Summary

Thus the integration of 6G technology is driving a major transformation across healthcare, manufacturing, and transportation, enhancing efficiency, precision, and connectivity. The Table 3 presented here summarizes the impact of 6G technology in healthcare, manufacturing, and transportation, along with its benefits and limitations.

Table 3. Scope of 6G in various sectors

Sector	Impact of 6G	Benefits	Limitations
Healthcare	Enables real-time AI diagnostics, remote surgeries, continuous patient monitoring	- Faster, more accurate diagnosis - Accessible healthcare in remote areas - Enhanced patient monitoring and preventive care	- High infrastructure costs - Data privacy and cybersecurity challenges
Manufacturing	Powers predictive maintenance, smart automation, and real-time supply chain optimization	- Reduced downtime and maintenance costs - Increased production efficiency - Better supply-demand management	- Complex integration with legacy systems - High initial investment
Transportation	Supports V2X communication, autonomous vehicles, and intelligent traffic management	- Improved road safety - Reduced traffic congestion - Lower emissions through optimized mobility	- Regulatory and ethical issues - Dependence on stable, widespread 6G coverage

V. APPLICATIONS OF 6G IN INDUSTRY 5.0

The case studies were selected based on their relevance to the key pillars of Industry 5.0 such as human-centric design, sustainability, resilience, and intelligent automation and their potential to be significantly transformed by 6G wireless technologies. Each domain selected for the case study like Digital Twins, cobots, smart healthcare, smart transportation, smart manufacturing, and supply chain innovation represents a critical industrial sector that aims for transformation through the specific capabilities of 6G such as advanced connectivity, low latency, and AI integration. For each case, real-world applications were examined to assess technical feasibility, benefits, and challenges. The analysis allowed for a better understanding of 6G's transformative role across industrial domains, culminating in a unified framework that positions 6G as a core enabler of the Industry 5.0 vision.

Case study showing the role of 6G in Industry 5.0 – Digital Twins

As 6G technology emerges, there is a revolution in industrial standards and practices, which is evident from the transition of Industry 4.0 to Industry 5.0. The significant advantage of 6G is enhanced connectivity and ensuring ubiquitous coverage with precise time synchronization. This enables the implementation of Digital Twins (DTs) to interact with multiple individuals across different locations in real time and facilitates seamless remote collaboration that imitates on-site interactions. By the implementation of these DTs, industries can minimize operational expenses and enhance efficiency, but it must solve the issues related to access barriers. By incorporating 6G in the application of Digital Twins, performance enhancements in terms of real-time monitoring, connectivity, visualization capacity, autonomous decision-making, scalability, and data-driven insights can be attained. These enhanced performance measures will enhance industrial operations to create a more efficient, intelligent, and adaptive industrial environment.

A case study is considered here which showed the implementation of Digital twins integrated with 5G (Han et al., 2023). The core blocks required for this implementation is given in Figure 5 (Round cornered rectangles). For enhancing the performance of each of these blocks the features of 6G should be integrated with this. A specific feature of 6G which could enhance the performance of each block is also given in Figure 5 (Cloud symbol). These advanced features of 6G required for Digital Twins are explored in detail.

First the most fundamental improvements, Enhanced connectivity that 6G brings to Digital Twins is considered. With ultra-high bandwidth and extremely low latency, 6G ensures that DTs can maintain real-time communication with their physical counterparts. This enhanced connectivity ensures that virtual models are always updated with the latest data from their respective physical system representation. It is more advantageous for industries that focus on precise data transmission, namely smart manufacturing and healthcare as it ensures more accurate remote monitoring and control. Also the reliable connectivity will reduce delays and inefficiencies in the DT-based operations. Next critical enhancement that 6G could offer to Digital Twins is real-time monitoring and analysis. With 6G features, Digital Twins can continuously monitor both the physical environment and network that makes the industries respond instantly to any changes or abnormalities. This real-time feedback loop is very essential in various sectors such as energy and transportation, where even minor changes can have significant effects. For example, consider a smart factory where real-time monitoring through Digital Twins is able to detect potential equipment failures before they occur, thus allowing for predictive maintenance and decreasing the repair time. In healthcare applications, DTs enable continuous monitoring of patient conditions that helps doctor make critical interventions whenever required thus improving the patient outcomes.

Figure 5. Digital Twins

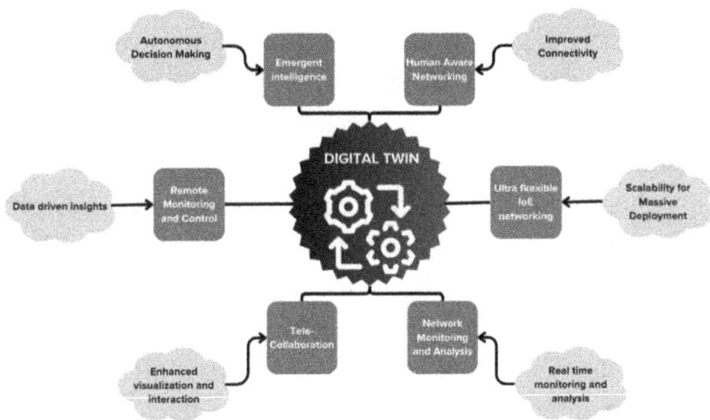

The next feature of 6G is that it supports the development of autonomous decision-making in Digital Twins. By integrating AI with high-speed data processing, DTs will not only collect and analyze information but also execute decisions without human intervention. This can lead to process optimization by adapting operations to environmental changes thereby improving the overall efficiency that will reform industrial automation. For example, in supply chain management application, DTs powered by autonomous decision making can predict demand fluctuations and adjust input levels accordingly thus reducing waste and improving logistics. Autonomous decision-making is used in critical applications like disaster management, where DTs powered by AI can analyze risks and act proactively before even the human operators perceive it as a threat.

Another important advancement that 6G offers to Digital Twins is enhanced visualization and interaction via Extended Reality (XR) technologies. XR encompasses Augmented Reality (AR), Virtual Reality (VR), and Mixed Reality (MR). This will enable users to interact with DTs in highly immersive ways. With the support of high-speed, low-latency connectivity of 6G technology telepresence solutions will allow remote operators to engage with DTs as if they were physically present. In sectors like construction and aerospace, engineers may employ XR-enhanced DTs to test and prototype new designs prior to deploymens that can save costs and enhance safety. In medicine, Digital Twins powered by XR will enable surgeons to rehearse intricate procedures virtually before undertaking them on actual patients, resulting in greater accuracy and improved patient care.

Scalability is also one of the significant benefits 6G has to bring in the implementation of Digital Twins. With more industries deploying more IoT devices and intelligent systems, having the ability to scale and manage Digital Twins will be important. 6G will allow for huge DT deployments that provide industries with the capacity to observe and control millions of interconnected devices all at once. This massive scalability is advantageous in smart cities and energy grids, where large-scale industrial environments consists of a huge number of physical devices that need to be tracked and optimized in real time. Together with the vast implementation of DT, 6G could achieve optimized resource allocation, better coordination and improved operational efficiency across various sectors.

Finally, 6G will enhance the role of data-driven insights in Digital Twins applications. The vast amount of data generated by Industry 4.0 applications will be utilized for the enhancement of both DT functionality and the 6G network itself. Data analysis with advanced AI and machine learning models makes the industries get deeper insights into system performance, identify inefficiencies, and develop more effective implementation methodologies. For instance, in intelligent agriculture, DTs have the ability to perceive and interpret environmental information in real-time, enabling farmers to maximize yield through optimal irrigation and crop care. In the energy field, data-driven DTs can forecast power usage trends and adapt grid operations in real-time to make it more efficient and sustainable. Therefore 6G will be instrumental in advancing Digital Twins by facilitating autonomous decision-making, enhancing connectivity, adapting real-time monitoring, improving visualization and interaction. These developments provides enormous scalability and improves industrial efficiency, safety, and decision-making. As Digital Twins become more intelligent and responsive, industries will experience a shift toward fully autonomous, data-driven operations, leading to a smarter and more connected future.

Case study showing implementation of Industry 5.0 for Smart Manufacturing and supply chain innovation

Smart Factories lead the way with autonomous production lines, real-time process monitoring, and adaptive production planning driven by AI, enabling machines to self-adjust for product variations without human intervention (Lei et al., 2024). Predictive Maintenance Systems gathers data from vibration, temperature, and acoustic sensors and use threshold based conditions and AI algorithms to analyze these data and predict equipment failures. Cobots are used to realize a safe and efficient production environment by enhancing human-robot interaction with the implementation of flexible task scheduling, safety sensors. Meanwhile, Mass Customization Systems helps in achieving a personalized production/product without affecting speed or efficiency by the implementation of AI-driven product configuration, and small batch manufacturing. Digital Twins in Manufacturing create virtual replicas of production systems that allows for real-time synchronization with sensor data, performance simulation, and scenario-based optimization. Also, 6G technology, with its high-speed wireless connectivity and ultra-low latency, enables seamless machine-to-machine interaction and smart logistics processes. AI-Based Demand Forecasting uses market trends, past data, and even social indicators to forecast variations in demand, allowing companies to maximize the supply available and prevent stock-outs or overproduction.

Real-Time Supply Chain Visibility provides end-to-end tracking of products from the production unit to the consumer through IoT sensors, GPS, and RFID technology with real-time data on location, condition, and delivery time (Liu et al., 2024). Autonomous Logistics Systems deploy self-driving trucks, drones, and automated warehouses to speed up transportation and optimize last-mile delivery with minimal manual intervention. Blockchain-Powered Traceability provides security and transparency throughout the supply chain, registering each transaction in a protected database so that fraud does not occur and the authenticity of the product is confirmed. Resilient Supply Chain Networks employ AI and digital twins to model disruptions from raw material shortages to political tensions. Modeling the disruptions makes the firms respond to all possible issues and hence adjust the system dynamically by establishing alternative suppliers, routes, or production plans. These networked applications makes manufacturing and supply chain smarter, faster, cost-effective and more adaptable and sustainable too, as per the human-centered and environmentally friendly vision of Industry 5.0.

Case study showing the role of cobots in various industry sectors

In medicine, one such example is their application in the production of pharmaceuticals at Takeda's facility in Oranienburg, Germany (Ardic & Cetinel, 2024). A FANUC CR-15iA cobot was utilized to perform the physical task of stacking boxes of medicine onto pallets that lessened the burden on workers who earlier transported loads of approximately 5.8 tons per shift. This not only improved worker well-being but also enhanced overall efficiency by allowing employees to focus on more critical tasks.

One more case study of the FANUC CR-15iA collaborative robot is that it is used as a tool for real-time inspection of engine parts in the automotive manufacturing industry. With a payload capacity of 15 kg, it efficiently handles a wide range of engine components of varying sizes and weights. Its extended horizontal reach of 1441 mm allows it to access larger parts without needing repositioning, which improves workflow efficiency, especially in space-constrained environments. The robot has a very high precision with a repeatability of 0.02 mm that reduces the risk of releasing defective parts into the market. As CR-15iA is designed for collaborative use, it implements advanced safety features to ensure that human workers safety is not compromised. XI. The CR-15iA also integrates advanced deep learning algorithms to enhance inspection accuracy and reliability. This combination of extended reach, precision, high payload, safety, and AI integration makes the CR-15iA a highly efficient solution in automotive production lines that improves quality control and operational efficiency.

Another application of cobots is observed in Dell's manufacturing plant in Chennai, India where end-of-line packaging process are automated using cobots. The cobots carry out heavy lifting tasks, such as placing systems into packaging, while human workers focused on correct placement of cushioning materials. Along with reduction of human risks and improved worker safety, thus also ensured that production is not affected even during the COVID-19 pandemic. Various examples discussed above highlight how cobots are revolutionizing various industries by enhancing operational efficiency while prioritizing human well-being.

Since AI and ML algorithms are self-decision making algorithms, this may result in ethical and social issues such as bias, unemployment, or unforeseen effects. Therefore, to make these ethical and social implications human must also play a vital part in this collaboration. Ethical concerns in Industry 5.0 is to emphasize that AI enhancements are made to increase human welfare and not replace or exploit humans. The most important issue in this regard is job displacement because more automation means reduction in workforce. Data security and privacy are also major issues since machines are processing and gathering enormous amounts of personal and industrial data. Also as human concentrates on critical decision making, it is crucial to focus on reskilling and upskilling employees to adapt to new roles. Transparency in AI decision-making is another critical factor in Industry 5.0. AI should be transparent enough to let human understand how automated systems operate, so that the human can ensure that decisions are fair, unbiased, and explainable. It is necessary that ethical AI development demands these systems to be designed in such a way that fairness is maintained and the systems are not biased, particularly in finance and healthcare domains. Incorporating human view in decision-making is also necessary, because completely autonomous systems could be missing the ethical sense and contextual understanding that only humans can offer. By solving these ethical challenges, industries as well as policymakers can establish a well-rounded, and sustainable environment in the future.

Case study showing implementation of Industry 5.0 for Smart Transportation

A case study is presented here showing the implementation of Urban Intelligent Transportation Systems (UITS) in developing countries (China) (Guo & Guo, 2023). This UTIS is found to integrate advanced technologies such as big data, AI, blockchain, and IoT to create an efficient traffic management ecosystem. The study showed that these technologies enhance collaborative control and mobile connectivity, ensuring seamless urban transportation operations. The important block in UITS is the data collection and management block, where the system gathers massive amount of heterogeneous data from various blocks such as automated front-end devices, administrative records, manual inputs, and public-shared data. This massive amount of data gathered allows to monitor traffic accurately and could provide personalized service customization. Also real-time information exchange between various entities of UTIS ensures seamless communication between vehicles, roads, and human. This cross-domain data sharing improves decision-making and urban traffic efficiency. Personalized services further enhance user experience by providing traveler preferences according to the requirements and combining them with real-time traffic data to get customized routing suggestions and transport recommendations. The introduction of AI and deep learning technologies into UTIS enable cognitive and learning abilities, allowing the system to continuously learn on its own and adapt to dynamic traffic conditions. Another key innovation in UITS is the trust mechanism supported by blockchain technology. It is a decentralized mechanism so that it ensures reliability, data security, and transparency. Blockchain also enables verification of the data collected to reduce the risks of data manipulation and unauthorized access.

Case study showing implementation of Industry 5.0 for Smart Healthcare

A case study is presented here about a teleradiology technique used in Saudi Arabia where the radiology sector provides teleradiology facility for 12 million imaging procedures recorded in 2021 (Alahmad et al., 2024). The Saudi Ministry of Healthtook an initiative to enhance healthcare services by launching a Public-

Private Partnership integrating virtual hospital services. Seha, Saudi Arabia's first virtual hospital is found to be providing teleradiology services since 2020.

A study is conducted conducted during COVID-19 about the usage of teleradiology feature to highlight its application in reducing infection risks and maintaining essential radiology services. This cross-sectional study, with approval from King Saud University's Institutional Review Board (IRB), was performed between February to June 2023 based on an electronic survey sent out to members of the Radiological Society of Saudi Arabia. The results presented showed that 71% of respondents agreed that teleradiology offers major advantages such as increased radiology coverage and shorter turnaround times. The research also revealed that these 71% of the respondents perceived teleradiology in a positive light, acknowledging its advantages in geographic coverage extension, after-hours service provision, and subspecialty access enhancement for more precise diagnoses. Teleradiology improves healthcare accessibility, especially in remote locations, through the ability of radiologists to offer services outside normal working hours and consult experts remotely. In spite of these benefits, there are issues, with 69% of respondents citing the inability to access patient records and 60% citing the difficulty in accessing previous imaging studies, both of which are critical to making accurate diagnoses. Furthermore, 52% cited concerns over quality assurance of images acquired remotely, highlighting the necessity for robust quality control. Yet, 78% did not view privacy and security as an issue, suggesting faith in current data protection policies. The results concluded that overall the participants are positive about the potential of teleradiology but agree that access to records, image quality, and workflow need to be improved to fully realize its advantages in health provision. Teleradiology is becoming a key component of Saudi Arabia's transformation in healthcare, especially in subspecialties such as abdominal and neuroimaging. Nevertheless, providing smooth access to patient records remains a fundamental challenge, affecting diagnostic accuracy. In contrast to other research that indicates reimbursement as an issue, this research reported few financial barriers and thus high promise for teleradiology growth.

The research indicates tele-radiology as a viable and valuable option for Saudi healthcare with increasing demand. Quality assurance and ensuring access to patient history are essential to enhance diagnostic quality. Future studies need to examine the effectiveness of long-term solutions to these challenges and measure their effects on patient outcomes.

The key features of the case studies discussed so far is presented in Table 4.

Table 4. Summary of the case studies discussed

Case Study	Key Applications	6G Role and Benefits	Challenges	Future Potential	Industry-Specific Examples
Digital Twins	Real-time asset monitoring, predictive maintenance, production optimization	URLLC, real-time data synchronization, AI-driven analytics	High data processing demands, cybersecurity risks	Fully autonomous, self-healing industrial systems driven by real-time simulations	**Aerospace** — Aircraft engine performance modeling; **Energy** — Smart grid optimization
Collaborative Robots (Cobots)	Human-robot collaboration, adaptive automation, safety assurance	Low-latency control loops, enhanced sensing, AI-based decision-making	Safety in unpredictable environments, network reliability	AI-enhanced cobots capable of real-time learning and human-gesture adaptation	**Automotive** — Assembly line cobots **Pharmaceuticals** — Precision drug formulation and packaging
Smart Healthcare	Remote surgery, AI-assisted diagnostics, continuous patient monitoring	High data rates for medical imaging, low latency for remote operations, secure and reliable communication	Data privacy, network outages during critical operations	AI-driven personalized medicine, digital therapeutics, global remote surgeries	**Hospitals** — Remote robotic surgeries **Wearable Tech** — Continuous glucose monitoring systems
Smart Transportation	Autonomous vehicles, intelligent traffic management, vehicle-to-everything (V2X) communication	Low-latency, high-speed data exchange, edge computing for real-time decisions	Handoff issues in fast mobility, spectrum congestion	Fully autonomous transportation networks, AI-powered traffic optimization, drone highways	**Logistics** — Fleet management for delivery trucks **Urban Planning** — AI-based traffic flow control
Smart Manufacturing	AI-based quality control, predictive maintenance, augmented reality (AR) support	mMTC, high-speed data links, AR/VR support for maintenance and training	Interoperability with legacy systems, high energy consumption	Fully adaptive, self-optimizing manufacturing lines powered by digital twins and AI	**Electronics** — Semiconductor fabrication lines **Heavy Industry** — Autonomous welding robots
Supply Chain Innovation	End-to-end visibility, real-time inventory tracking, predictive logistics	High-speed connectivity for data integration, enhanced traceability, AI-driven demand forecasting	Fragmented data systems, cybersecurity risks	Blockchain-powered supply chains, AI-driven autonomous logistics with dynamic rerouting	**Retail** — Real-time inventory tracking in warehouses **Food & Beverage** — Cold chain monitoring for perishable goods

VI. SUSTAINABILITY, CHALLENGES, AND FUTURE DIRECTIONS

6G is set to revolutionize Industry 5.0 by vastly outperforming 5G in key technical areas critical to human-centric, intelligent, and sustainable industrial applications. One of the most transformative improvements is in latency as 6G is targeting sub-1 millisecond delay compared to 5G's 1–10 ms. This enables real-time responsiveness essential for autonomous vehicles, remote surgeries, and precision factory automation. Data transfer rates will also improve from 5G's upper limit of 100 Gbps to a projected 1 Tbps under 6G. This could support the advanced applications such as ultra-HD 3D holography, real-time AI analytics, and dense IoT environments.

Furthermore, device density will expand tenfold from 1 million to 10 million devices per square kilometer. This can be used for powering massive IoT deployments across smart cities, agriculture, and logistics. Energy efficiency is expected to improve by up to 90%, a vital enhancement for developing sustainable smart infrastructure. In terms of reliability, 6G aims to increase network availability from 99.999% to 99.99999%, which is vital for mission-critical systems like emergency response and remote healthcare. Additionally, localization accuracy will improve from ~10 cm in 5G to ~1 cm in 6G, enabling ultra-precise operations in industrial automation and navigation.

Another key feature of 6G is its seamless integration with AI and edge computing, allowing real-time processing closer to the data source. This minimizes dependency on central servers, reduces latency, and enhances responsiveness in manufacturing and other fast-paced industries. Finally, network slicing in 6G will enable highly customizable, virtualized networks with guaranteed Quality of Service (QoS), allowing sectors like healthcare, transportation, and robotics to prioritize critical operations securely and efficiently. Together, these advancements position 6G as the technological backbone of Industry 5.0, enabling a future where intelligent systems and humans collaborate in real time, sustainably, and safely.

Sustainability

The greatest benefit of the shift from Industry 4.0 to Industry 5.0 is that it focusses on human centered strategies as opposed to automation and smart technologies alone. Besides these, other important aspect of Industry 5.0 is that it seeks to enhance sustainability and energy efficiency. Industry 4.0 emphasized efficiency and productivity by means of IoT, AI, and cyber-physical systems while Industry 5.0 incorporates green solutions to maintain a balance between technological progress and environmental sustainability (Zhao, 2024, Fraga-Lamas et al., 2021). Energy efficiency is an important aspect of Industry 5.0 since industries seek to minimize carbon emissions and operational expenses. Alternative power sources like wind and solar are becoming part of the manufacturing framework, lowering their dependence on fossil fuels. Smart grids enabled with AI and IoT assist the plants in optimizing power distribution by automating the utilization of power with real-time needs. In addition, in DTs virtual twins that are duplicates of the actual system enable enterprises to model and optimize power use prior to introducing change, improving efficiency and less waste.

Industry 5.0 attains sustainability through minimizing the footprint of industry on the environment by adopting various methods like resource optimization, circular economy practices, and green manufacturing. When industries treat certain materials as waste, these materials are reused, recycled, or re-purposed rather than being thrown away. This compels the companies to move towards zero-waste production. Apart from this, blockchain technology guarantees transparency in the minimization of unethical activities, sustainable sourcing, and carbon emissions throughout global supply chains. Likewise, through the use of AI-powered analytics, industries can help reduce the consumption of resources as AI forecasts demand and streamlines supply chains accordingly thereby minimizing over-production. Through the introduction of AI, automation, IoT, and green energy solutions, Industry 5.0 boosts productivity while achieving long-term sustainability, creating an even more robust, environmentally-friendly, and energy-efficient industrial framework.

Challenges

Industry 5.0 is the industrial revolution that introduced human-machine collaboration, sustainability, and resilience. Although it possesses various characteristics similar to that of Industry 4.0 and incorporates AI, IoT, robotics, blockchain, and green energy solutions, the deployment of Industry 5.0 has some major challenges (Sverko et al., 2022). These challenges are from different domain such as technological, economic, organizational, and ethical domains, and hence the deployment of Industry 5.0 is a complex process. Some of the challenges are as follows.

(i) Industry 5.0 requires enormous investments in leading-edge technologies such as AI-powered analytics, cobots, edge computing, and 6G networks. Upgradation of the existing hardware, software, and IT infrastructure will be required to ensure smooth integration. Small and medium-sized businesses (SMEs) lack these financial commitments.

(ii) Industry 5.0 operates with live exchange of data between devices, human beings, and cloud-based platforms and is thus susceptible to data leakage, cyberattacks, and unauthorized access. With AI-driven security, blockchain technology, and IoT-based networks, industries need encryption methods and access control mechanisms that can protect confidential data. Nevertheless, most organizations are not capable of creating robust cybersecurity frameworks that can keep pace with evolving threats.

(iii) Most industries are still running legacy systems designed for Industry 3.0 or initial Industry 4.0 processes. These technologies, in most cases, are not compatible with newer AI-based automation and IoT-based smart manufacturing systems. Replacing or upgrading such systems is a time-consuming, labor-intensive, and expensive exercise, resulting in business disruptions and hesitancy to completely move to Industry 5.0.

(iv) Industries need people with higher-level expertise in robotics, machine learning, cybersecurity, and data analytics as AI and automation continue to improve. But the workers themselves are not efficient in these higher-level skills, and this creates a talent gap that hinders adoption of Industry 5.0. The workers also fear job loss because of automation, and this discourages them from Industry 5.0 technology. Firms have to invest in reskilling and upskilling programs to get the workforce ready for the changing environment and maintaining balance between human intellect and mechanization.

(v) Industry 5.0's increased use of AI and robotics has ethical implications of transparency of decision-making, bias of AI, and accountability of automated systems. With AI playing a larger role in critical sectors such as finance, healthcare, and defense, ethical use of AI is essential. Besides, human-machine interface is to guarantee workers' protection, respectable labor techniques, and mind health while avoiding over-automation to reduce the human element in the workplace.

(vi) One of the most defining goals of Industry 5.0 is sustainability, yet going carbon-neutral and energy-sustainable is an enormous challenge. Many industries are dependent on non-renewable energy, and shifting to solar, wind, and hydrogen power will entail widespread infrastructural upgrading on a huge scale. Moreover, establishing circular economies and zero-waste production structures entails the development of new waste management and recycling systems that not all industries can implement.

(vii) Industry 5.0 promotes hyper-connected supply chains powered by AI, blockchain, and IoT, but global challenges such as geopolitical tensions, trade barriers, and pandemic can impact its spread. Smart manufacturing systems depend on a constant supply of semiconductors, rare earth elements, and advanced materials that happen to be geographically concentrated. Any disruption in these supply chains can slow down technology deployment and drive up costs.

(viii) With Industry 5.0 bringing in new technologies and models of business, the current regulatory structures tend to lag behind. Governments need to develop holistic policies and industry norms for AI-based decision-making, data protection, human-machine interface, and sustainable production. But variations in global regulations raise compliance issues, especially for cross-border multinational enterprises.

As 6G becomes crucial to Industry 5.0, managing ethical AI use, job displacement, and data governance becomes vital for ensuring inclusive and sustainable growth especially in developing countries. Ethical AI must be designed with transparency and fairness to avoid reinforcing social biases, with regulations ensuring accountability and explainability. AI can also be used for social good, improving healthcare, environmental sustainability, and resource allocation. Although AI and automation can boost industrial efficiency by up to 40%, they also risk job displacement, particularly in sectors like manufacturing and agriculture. To address this, reskilling programs are essential, alongside the creation of human-AI collaborative roles that enhance rather than replace human labor potentially growing AI-literate job roles by 20–30%. Moreover, the immense data flow enabled by 6G up to 1 Tbps with stronger encryption raises critical concerns about privacy and security. Robust data governance frameworks must be developed to safeguard personal information, ensure responsible AI-powered data use, and manage cross-border data flows in compliance with international norms. Together, these measures will help developing nations navigate the technological transformation of Industry 5.0 in an equitable and ethical manner.

Future Directions

While Industry 5.0 has the transformative power, there are a number of technological, ethical, economic, and business challenges that have to be solved before it is implemented successfully. Industries must focus on upskilling workers, leveraging existing infrastructure, securing information systems, and adopting sustainable power solutions to best harness the power of this fourth industrial revolution. In addition, governments and regulatory bodies must work together to develop transparent policies and standardization mechanisms that facilitate safe and effective adoption of Industry 5.0 technologies. With the overcoming of these challenges, Industry 5.0 can construct a sustainable, human-centric, and resilient future for global industries. Successful implementation of Industry 5.0 requires challenges related to cost, security, skill sets of the workforce, sustainability, supply chain innovation, and regulation to be overcome (Wang et al., 2023). One of the biggest concerns is the expensive cost of implementation, especially for small and medium-sized businesses (SMEs). This can be addressed through government subsidies, public-private collaborations, and incremental adoption of new technologies so that companies can adopt AI, robotics, and IoT in a step-by-step manner. Resistance from the workforce and skill shortages can be managed through reskilling initiatives, AI-powered learning platforms, and industry-university partnerships to create specialized training programs.

Cybersecurity threats have to be addressed through the adoption of blockchain for safe data transfers, AI-powered threat identification mechanisms, and enhanced regulatory schemes for data safeguarding. The legacy systems with new Industry 5.0 technologies demands middleware platforms, hybrid cloud architecture, and digital twins, maintaining compatibility without the necessity for entire system reconstruction. Sustainability and green manufacturing can be promoted by AI-based energy management systems, circular economy practices, and creation of renewable energy sources such as solar and hydrogen power. For enhanced supply chain resilience, firms must implement blockchain technology for open tracking, demand forecasting based on AI, and localized production strategies to reduce dependence on international suppliers. Lastly, regulatory challenges can be addressed by harmonizing international standards, imposing ethical use of AI, and creating frameworks to strike a balance between automation and human intervention. By implementing these measures, industries will be in a position to overcome barriers and unlock Industry 5.0's full potential in attaining a human-centric, sustainable, and intelligent manufacturing ecosystem.

Industry 5.0 development will be characterized by next-generation AI-based automation, human-robot collaboration, sustainable manufacturing, new-generation connectivity, and decentralized industrial ecosystems. Hyperautomation will permeate production, with AI-powered robotics, digital twins, and self-healing machines enabling real-time process optimization, reduced downtime, and maximum efficiency. AI-based predictive maintenance powered by IoT will enable machines to automatically detect failures in advance, reducing downtime and business disruption. Robotics will be increasingly human-centered with cobots and AI-controlled exoskeletons aiding labor in demanding work, enhancing productivity and safety. 6G technology will transform connectivity by providing ultra-high-speed, low-latency data communication for end-to-end seamless connection among machines, humans, and AI-powered cloud platforms. It will make possible real-time industrial IoT (IIoT) operations, end-to-end autonomous supply chains, and smart cities with AI-governed traffic flow and logistics management.

Blockchain technology will be pivotal in providing transparent, secure, and decentralized industrial networks, especially in global supply chains, smart contracts, and cybersecurity uses. Sustainability will be central, with industries moving towards carbon-neutral manufacturing, green energy adoption, and circular economy practices. AI-driven energy grids, automated waste recycling, and intelligent material sourcing will fuel eco-friendly manufacturing. Moreover, businesses will invest in biodegradable as well as self-healing products, minimizing wastage and hurting the environment. The use of hydrogen-based production, carbon sequestration methods, and circular production systems will also speed up sustainability. For healthcare and mobility, AI as well as robotics will transform efficiency of services. Intelligent hospitals will have robotic interventions, AI-facilitated diagnostics, as well as live remote monitoring, while autonomous vehicles will use V2X connectivity, AI-supported traffic management, and drone-distributed logistics. Industry 5.0 will also revolutionize urban planning, incorporating digital twins for wise city growth, AI-based infrastructure observation, and self-driving public services. Finally, Industry 5.0 will create a completely interconnected, strong, and adaptable industrial structure, in which AI, human, and eco-friendly technologies will jointly propel development, innovation, and worldwide financial growth.

To ensure sustainable and inclusive adoption of 6G technologies in developing countries, a multi-faceted approach is essential. First, addressing infrastructure challenges through investment in green energy like solar or wind energy can power energy-efficient 6G networks, while phased upgrades in existing 4G/5G infrastructure can reduce costs. With data rates potentially 100 times faster than 5G and latency below 1 ms, 6G can significantly enhance healthcare, education, and agriculture. Second, inclusive access must be prioritized by extending 6G networks beyond urban centers through public-private partnerships and leveraging satellite or low-earth orbit (LEO) technology to reach rural and underserved populations. Finally, fostering digital literacy is critical. The countries must invest in education and skill development to prepare citizens for AI, robotics, and real-time applications central to Industry 5.0. By addressing these areas, developing nations can harness 6G to drive equitable and sustainable digital transformation.

VII. CONCLUSION

Industry 5.0 marks an important turn toward human-focused, sustainable, and resilient industrial era from the notion of Industry 4.0 which is of complete automation. In this article, the intrinsic features of 6G technology facilitators in Industry 5.0 are depicted that move towards its promise of future Industry 5.0 use cases like highly connected intelligent factories to collaborative human-robotic workplaces and immersive digital environments. As a key to this revolution, 6G wireless technology provides very high data rates, ultra-reliable low-latency communication, enormous device connectivity, and AI-infused network intelligence.

To put the practical application of 6G in reshaping Industry 5.0 into perspective, case studies on digital twins, cobots, smart healthcare, smart transportation, smart manufacturing, and supply chain innovation were conducted. The Digital Twins use case showed the way 6G's URLLC and mMTC provide real-time synchronisation between the physical and their virtual counterparts to support predictive maintenance, performance improvement, and efficient production processes. Cobots indicated the way that improved sensing, low-latency control loops, and decision-making through artificial intelligence of 6G enable dynamic human-robot collaboration, maximising productivity in a safe way. In Smart Healthcare, it is noticed that how features of 6G enable remote surgeries, artificial intelligence-based diagnostic solutions, and around-the-clock monitoring of patients, resulting in accelerated, and widespread healthcare services. In the Smart Transportation case study, it looked at how smart cars and cognitive traffic management take advantage of ultra-low latency as well as edge computing to guarantee smarter, smoother city mobility. Smart Manufacturing highlighted how factories equipped with 6G connectivity maximise production lines using adaptive automation, AI-based quality control, and augmented reality maintenance systems. Finally, Supply Chain Innovation illustrated how 6G maximises end-to-end visibility, traceability, and predictive logistics, minimising delay and improving resistance to disruptions. These demonstrations illustrate how 6G connectivity enables real-time data-driven decision-making, intelligent automation, and augmented human-machine collaboration in various industrial sectors.

Despite the advantages, there are certain challenges like energy efficiency, cybersecurity, and compatibility with legacy network infrastructure. A group effort by researchers, industry leaders, and policymakers is required to create a secure, sustainable, and globally accessible industrial future. In summary, the convergence of 6G wireless technology and Industry 5.0 paves the path to a connected, intelligent, and sustainable industrial world. From the case studies presented about digital twins support, collaboration robots, smart healthcare, smart transportation, smart manufacturing, and supply chain innovation, it is observed that 6G can achieve high levels of efficiency, resiliency, and customization possible. Industry 5.0 is not merely a technological progress but it is an evolution of how industries interact with people, with society, and with the world at large, creating a future where humans and machines collaborate to generate innovation and ensure long-term efficiency.

REFERENCES

Alahmad, H., Almanaa, M., Abanomy, A., Alarifi, M., Alenazi, K., Matabi, M., Albathi, R., & Moslem, R. (2024). Navigating challenges in teleradiology implementation: A case study from Saudi Arabia's healthcare system. *Journal of Multidisciplinary Healthcare, 17*, 2083–2092. DOI: 10.2147/JMDH.S460547 PMID: 38736539

Andres, M., Diaz-Madroñero, A. L., Soares, R., & Poler, R. (2024). Enabling technologies to support supply chain logistics 5.0. *IEEE Access : Practical Innovations, Open Solutions, 12*, 43889–43906. DOI: 10.1109/ACCESS.2024.3374194

Ardic, O., & Cetinel, G. (2024). Deep learning-based real-time engine part inspection with collaborative robot application. *IEEE Access : Practical Innovations, Open Solutions, 12*, 187483–187497. DOI: 10.1109/ACCESS.2024.3489714

Bhat, J. R., & Alqahtani, S. A. (2021). 6G ecosystem: Current status and future perspective. *IEEE Access : Practical Innovations, Open Solutions, 9*, 43134–43167. DOI: 10.1109/ACCESS.2021.3054833

Fraga-Lamas, P., Fernández-Caramés, T. M., Rosado Da Cruz, A. M., & Lopes, S. I. (2024). An overview of blockchain for Industry 5.0: Towards human-centric, sustainable and resilient applications. *IEEE Access : Practical Innovations, Open Solutions, 12*, 116162–116201. DOI: 10.1109/ACCESS.2024.3435374

Fraga-Lamas, P., Varela-Barbeito, J., & Fernandez-Carames, T. M. (2021). Next generation auto-identification and traceability technologies for Industry 5.0: A methodology and practical use case for the shipbuilding industry. *IEEE Access : Practical Innovations, Open Solutions, 9*, 140700–140730. DOI: 10.1109/ACCESS.2021.3119775

Gadekallu, T. R., Maddikunta, P. K. R., Boopathy, P., Deepa, N., Chengoden, R., Victor, N., Wang, W., Wang, W., Zhu, Y., & Dev, K. (2024). XAI for Industry 5.0: Concepts, opportunities, challenges and future directions. *IEEE Open Journal of the Communications Society*, •••, 1–1. DOI: 10.1109/OJCOMS.2024.3473891

Guo, X., & Guo, X. (2023). A research on blockchain technology: Urban intelligent transportation systems in developing countries. *IEEE Access : Practical Innovations, Open Solutions, 11*, 40724–40740. DOI: 10.1109/ACCESS.2023.3270100

Han, M. A., Habibi, M. A., Richerzhagen, B., Schindhelm, K., Zeiger, F., Lamberti, F., Pratticò, F. G., Upadhya, K., Korovesis, C., Belikaidis, I.-P., Demestichas, P., Yuan, S., & Schotten, H. D. (2023). Digital twins for Industry 4.0 in the 6G era. *IEEE Open Journal of Vehicular Technology, 4*, 820–835. DOI: 10.1109/OJVT.2023.3325382

Haricha, K., Khiat, A., Issaoui, Y., Bahnasse, A., & Ouajji, H. (2023). Recent technological progress to empower smart manufacturing: Review and potential guidelines. *IEEE Access : Practical Innovations, Open Solutions*, *11*, 77929–77951. DOI: 10.1109/ACCESS.2023.3246029

Jiang, W., Han, B., Habibi, M. A., & Schotten, H. D. (2021). The road towards 6G: A comprehensive survey. *IEEE Open Journal of the Communications Society*, *2*, 334–366. DOI: 10.1109/OJCOMS.2021.3057679

Lei, Z., Shi, J., Luo, Z., Cheng, M., & Wan, J. (2024). Intelligent manufacturing from the perspective of Industry 5.0: Application review and prospects. *IEEE Access : Practical Innovations, Open Solutions*, *12*, 167436–167451. DOI: 10.1109/ACCESS.2024.3496697

Liu, W., Hou, J., & Cheng, Y. (2024). How can firms implement smart manufacturing through supply chain collaboration? A multiple-case study from China. *Production Planning and Control*, •••, 1–19. DOI: 10.1080/09537287.2024.2362866

Mahmood, N. H., Berardinelli, G., Khatib, E. J., Hashemi, R., De Lima, C., & Latva-aho, M. (2023). A functional architecture for 6G special-purpose industrial IoT networks. *IEEE Transactions on Industrial Informatics*, *19*(3), 2530–2540. DOI: 10.1109/TII.2022.3182988

Pivoto, D. G. S., Rezende, T. T., Facina, M. S. P., Moreira, R., De Oliveira Silva, F., Cardoso, K. V., Correa, S. L., Araujo, A. V. D., Silva, R. S. E., Neto, H. S., De Lima Tejerina, G. R., & Alberti, A. M. (2023). A detailed relevance analysis of enabling technologies for 6G architectures. *IEEE Access : Practical Innovations, Open Solutions*, *11*, 89644–89684. DOI: 10.1109/ACCESS.2023.3301811

Sharma, M., Sehrawat, R., Luthra, S., Daim, T., & Bakry, D. (2024). Moving towards Industry 5.0 in the pharmaceutical manufacturing sector: Challenges and solutions for Germany. *IEEE Transactions on Engineering Management*, *71*, 13757–13774. DOI: 10.1109/TEM.2022.3143466

Sverko, M., Grbac, T. G., & Mikuc, M. (2022). SCADA systems with focus on continuous manufacturing and steel industry: A survey on architectures, standards, challenges and Industry 5.0. *IEEE Access : Practical Innovations, Open Solutions*, *10*, 109395–109430. DOI: 10.1109/ACCESS.2022.3211288

Tallat, R., Hawbani, A., Wang, X., Al-Dubai, A., Zhao, L., Liu, Z., Min, G., Zomaya, A. Y., & Alsamhi, S. H. (2024). Navigating Industry 5.0: A survey of key enabling technologies, trends, challenges, and opportunities. *IEEE Communications Surveys and Tutorials*, *26*(2), 1080–1126. DOI: 10.1109/COMST.2023.3329472

Uusitalo, M. A., Rugeland, P., Boldi, M. R., Strinati, E. C., Demestichas, P., Ericson, M., Fettweis, G. P., Filippou, M. C., Gati, A., Hamon, M.-H., Hoffmann, M., Latva-Aho, M., Parssinen, A., Richerzhagen, B., Schotten, H., Svensson, T., Wikstrom, G., Wymeersch, H., Ziegler, V., & Zou, Y. (2021). 6G vision, value, use cases and technologies from European 6G flagship project Hexa-X. *IEEE Access : Practical Innovations, Open Solutions*, *9*, 160004–160020. DOI: 10.1109/ACCESS.2021.3130030

Wang, C.-X., You, X., Gao, X., Zhu, X., Li, Z., Zhang, C., Wang, H., Huang, Y., Chen, Y., Haas, H., Thompson, J. S., Larsson, E. G., Di Renzo, M., Tong, W., Zhu, P., Shen, X., Poor, H. V., & Hanzo, L. (2023). On the road to 6G: Visions, requirements, key technologies, and testbeds. *IEEE Communications Surveys and Tutorials*, *25*(2), 905–974. DOI: 10.1109/COMST.2023.3249835

Zhao, D. (2024). Big data-driven digital economic industry based on innovation path of manufacturing. *IEEE Access : Practical Innovations, Open Solutions*, *12*, 24104–24115. DOI: 10.1109/ACCESS.2024.3365716

Chapter 4
Satellite-Based Communication in 6G Networks

Priyanka Ahlawat
https://orcid.org/0000-0003-4695-382X
National Institute of Technology, Kurukshetra, India

Mayank Dave
https://orcid.org/0000-0003-4748-0753
National Institute of Technology, Kurukshetra, India

Supriya Mishra
National Institute of Technology, Kurukshetra, India

ABSTRACT

Satellite based communication will be an important advancement as 6G networks develop, improving connectivity with ultra-low latency, fast data transmission, and wide coverage. A crucial strategy for network resilience is the integration of satellite systems with terrestrial networks, which offers seamless access in rural and distant locations and expands connectivity to underserved areas. To overcome these challenges, technological innovations such as multi-beam antennas, AI-based resource management, and next-generation satellite constellations are suggested. Concerns necessity of strong cryptographic techniques, safe key management to guarantee data integrity in this network of interconnected satellites and terrestrial systems. As a result, it is anticipated that 6G satellite communications would provide improved IoT support, quicker data speeds, and reliable emergency communication capabilities, making them an essential part of future global connection.

DOI: 10.4018/979-8-3373-0568-4.ch004

1. INTRODUCTION

Satellite communication technology has become an essential component of the global communications infrastructure, enabling critical services such as long-distance data transmission, real-time broadcasting, global navigation, and everywhere internet connectivity. Satellites offer a major advantage over terrestrial communication systems because they are capable of offering wide geographic coverage from orbit, unlike terrestrial systems that primarily depend on ground-based infrastructure like fiber-optic cables, base stations, and cellular towers. Because of this, satellite-based communication is especially important for accessing underserved, rural, and remote areas where establishing terrestrial infrastructure is both economically and logistically impossible. The architecture of satellite communication is defined by the orbits in which satellites operate—namely, LEO, MEO, and GEO. Each of these orbital regimes offers distinct operational characteristics in terms of altitude, coverage footprint, signal latency, and bandwidth capacity. For example, LEO satellites, that orbit between 500 and 2,000 kilometers, are recognized for their quick response times and low latency, and this makes systems appropriate for time-sensitive applications like gaming and real-time communications. GEO satellites, that are situated at about 35,786 kilometers, offer reliable coverage over fixed geographic regions—perfect for broadcasting and weather monitoring applications—while MEO satellites, that are placed at altitudes between 2,000 and 35,000 kilometers, balance latency and coverage (Alkasassbeh et al., 2024). Conventional methods of communication are experiencing a substantial transformation due to advancements in satellite technologies. The abilities of satellite systems are being enhanced through innovations including beam forming, adaptive modulation and coding (AMC), multi-beam antenna arrays, high-throughput satellites, and AI-based network traffic optimization, that improved data throughput and spectrum efficiency (Akyildiz et al., 2020). These advancements are making it possible for satellites to support a wide range of mission-critical applications, such as Internet of Things (IoT)-enabled services in remote locations, underwater and aviation communications, disaster recovery, and military and defense operations. Satellite-based technologies are expected to become even more important because wireless communication networks transition to the sixth generation (6G). In order to provide seamless worldwide coverage, ultra-reliable low-latency communication (URLLC), and strong support for a large number of connected devices, the 6G design integrates satellite and terrestrial networks. The integration of non-terrestrial networks and terrestrial infrastructures will be essential for meeting the demanding requirements for performance of 6G, especially in areas requiring high mobility support or Adaptability in the face of terrestrial network outages (Beyaz, 2024). Furthermore, satellite communication is becoming more and more recognized as a strategic tool for addressing issues with global connectivity and achieving digital equality. Projects like Amazon's Kuiper project, OneWeb, and Star link demonstrate a larger industry trend toward the deployment of massive LEO satellite constellations to provide broadband services to every region of the world. These efforts are not only commercially driven but also meet with the United Nations' Sustainable Development Goals (SDGs), particularly in bridging the digital divides and promoting inclusive access to information and communication technologies (ICTs). In summary, the coming years of international communications will be greatly influenced by the creation and application of next-generation satellite technology. Satellite systems will support terrestrial infrastructures and become an essential component of the 6G ecosystem by providing high-speed, low-latency, and reliable connection across a variety of situations, encouraging innovation and facilitating inclusive access in the digital age.

1.1 Satellites' Contribution in 6G Technology

Satellite system integration is predicted to be an innovative and transformative development in the communications industry, especially as 6G networks aim to offer exclusive connection quality, massive device connectivity, and record-breaking data rates. Compared to previous generations of mobile networks, 6G will be significantly more dependent on the seamless functioning of satellite systems. The ability to communicate with terrestrial infrastructure allows for global coverage, even in the most challenging and inaccessible areas such as mountainous regions, dense forests, polar zones, and disaster-prone regions. Critical applications that need dependable, rapid communication links, such as telemedicine-assisted remote surgeries, autonomous vehicle coordination, networked smart cities, and scalable global IoT ecosystems, can only be supported by this integration (Akyildiz et al., 2020; Beyaz, 2024). As 6G networks primary objective for worldwide, intelligent, and ultra-responsive connection, satellite system integration is going to be a game-changing element of the next-generation wireless communication environment. 6G is going to depend heavily on non-terrestrial networks to provide seamless communication services to areas that are inaccessible, mobile, or lack infrastructure, in contrast to earlier mobile generations that mostly relied on terrestrial systems (Chen et al., 2021). The three main performance foundations of 6G—massive machine-type communication, ultra-reliable low-latency communication (URLLC), and improved mobile broadband—are expected to be made possible in large part by satellites. Particularly in high-demand and mobility contexts like aerial drones and marine vessels, these requirements necessitate constant connectivity and fast link (Cui et al., 2025). The three major satellite orbits—LEO, MEO, and GEO—each contribute specific performance advantages. LEO satellites are ideal for applications that require delay like autonomous navigation, tele-operations, and real-time video conferencing because of their dense constellations and low altitude, that allow for frequent revisits and millisecond-level latency. Although becoming less popular, MEO satellites provide a compromise between latency and foot print thus are best suited for navigation systems like GPS. For satellite TV, broadcasting, and disaster monitoring, GEO satellites that are fixed in place provide wide and consistent coverage (Dalai et al., 2022). Satellites help develop 6G by offering spectrum interaction methods, dynamic load balancing, and network redundancy in addition to pure connection, especially in congested or mission-critical contexts. New technologies like optic ISLs and reconfigurable intelligent surfaces in satellite payloads increase the flexibility and efficiency of global networks (Dalai et al., 2024). Additionally, autonomous decision-making for beam allocation, routing, and interference mitigation is made possible by AI/ML-enhanced satellite resource management, transforming satellites into intelligent nodes in a distributed 6G network. This correlates with the 6G vision of intelligent, learning-enabled networks capable of adapting in real time to changing traffic, weather, or danger conditions (Dang et al., 2020). In the final analysis, satellite systems are essential facilitators of the 6G environment rather than just extensions of connectivity. The network's resilience, scalability, and unrestricted are guaranteed by their inclusion, setting the stage for a honestly global, inclusive, and continuous digital communication infrastructure in the ensuing ten years.

1.2 Background Study of 6G Satellite Integration

The integration of satellite systems into sixth-generation (6G) networks represents a major leap forward in global communication. Non-terrestrial networks (NTNs) are rapidly becoming an essential upgrade to traditional terrestrial infrastructure as the need for smooth, fast, and widely available connectivity grows. In remote, rural, and disaster-prone areas with few or no terrestrial base stations, satellite systems—particularly those in LEO, MEO, and GEO —can offer communication services. This hybrid terrestrial-satellite architecture guarantees that 6G networks offer genuinely worldwide coverage in addition to exceptionally high data rates and ultra-low latency. Backhaul integration and direct user access are the two primary techniques used in practice to integrate satellites in 6G. Because direct access enables user equipment, like mobile devices, to speak directly with satellites, backhaul integration uses satellites to link distant terrestrial base stations to the main network. This method is particularly crucial for preserving connectivity in situations where there is no ground infrastructure available, and it is essential for allowing use cases such as driverless vehicles, remote healthcare, and globally networked Internet of Things networks (Del Portillo et al., 2019; Cui et al., 2025; Akyildiz et al., 2020). There are a number of difficulties in integrating satellite systems with 6G networks, in spite the advantages. High propagation latency, particularly in GEO orbits, complex spectrum management to avoid signal interference, and smooth mobility management to guarantee continuous service during satellite-to-terrestrial connection handovers are some examples. Beam forming technologies, AI-enhanced network management, and software-defined payloads on satellites to dynamically modify performance based on real-time demand are some of the promising solutions that have been found through research. Additionally, studies have highlighted the significance of creating standardized protocols to guarantee compatibility across various network types and service providers (Dao et al., 2021).

1.3 Properties of 6G

- **Extremely High Data Rates and Speed:** Sixth Generation (6G) technology promises to transmit data at up to one terabit per second (Tbps), several times faster than the maximum rates of fifth generation (5G). Applications that depend on real-time communication will operate much better because to this extremely fast speed, which will allow for almost immediate data transfer.
- **Huge Connectivity:** Compared to 5G, 6G will be able to accommodate a considerably larger number of linked devices. Due to its capacity to facilitate simultaneous communication between billions of devices with little interference and optimal resource allocation, this will be crucial for the development of the internet of things (IOT).
- **Advanced Artificial Intelligence Integration:** 6G networks will include AI and machine learning extensively, allowing for predictive analytics, automated network management and intelligent decision-making. Artificial intelligence is expected to optimize network performance, increase energy efficiency, and improve the user experience in general.
- **Spectrum Flexibility and Efficiency:** Sixth Generation (6G) will bring new techniques for using the spectrum, such as using higher-frequency bands (such terahertz waves) and dynamic spectrum sharing. Higher data rates and greater performance in densely populated areas will result from this more effective use of the available spectrum.
- **Improved Security and Privacy**: In order to protect user data, 6G claims to offer advanced encryption methods and secure communication protocols, in response to growing concerns around cyber security and privacy. To protect sensitive data, especially in applications like financial transactions, health data exchange, and national defense, enhanced security measures will be essential.
- **Space-Terrestrial integrated networks:** The goal of 6G networks is to create single worldwide networks by integrating satellite communication systems with terrestrial infrastructure. Across isolated locations, seas, and areas

with a lack of infrastructure currently in place, this hybrid method will enable continuous connectivity.

1.4 Differences between 3G, 5G, and 6G: Challenges and Benefits

Table 1. Examining Differences between 3G, 4G, 5G and 6G: Challenges, Benefits and Disadvantages

Generation	Benefits	Challenges	Disadvantages
3G	Introduced mobile internet (web browsing, email, video calls)	Slow data speeds (up to 2 Mbps)	Inadequate for high-definition video streaming or modern apps
	Enabled global mobile broadband connectivity	High latency (~100-500 ms), unsuitable for real-time communication	Limited support for multimedia and IoT applications
	Basic internet access for mobile devices	Infrastructure upgrade required for rural deployment	High network congestion
4G	Enhanced data speeds (up to 1 Gbps). Improved latency (~50 ms).	Requires significant infrastructure upgrades.	Performance can degrade with network congestion.
	Better support for multimedia streaming and mobile applications.	Coverage gaps in rural and remote areas.	Not optimized for massive IoT deployments.
5G	Ultra-fast data speeds (up to 10 Gbps)	Requires dense small-cell infrastructure	High deployment costs
	Massive device connectivity for IoT and smart cities	Limited coverage due to high-frequency bands	mmWave frequencies have short range and poor penetration (obstacles, walls)
	Improved reliability for mission-critical services	High energy consumption	Environmental concerns over energy usage
6G	Ultra-high data speeds (up to 1 Tbps), supporting advanced applications like holograms, 8K video, XR	Requires massive infrastructure investment (satellite integration, dense networks)	High costs of infrastructure and device compatibility
	Ultra-low latency (<1 ms), perfect for autonomous systems, remote surgeries	Spectrum management for THz and mmWave bands is complex	Susceptibility to signal attenuation in high-frequency bands (THz, mmWave)
	Seamless global connectivity through satellite-terrestrial integration	Advanced security measures needed for growing cyber security risks	Privacy concerns due to increased data generation and global tracking

The goal of 3G was to provide about mobile internet with basic services and modest speeds, however it encountered issues with latency and data speed. 5G promises fast internet, low latency, and extensive connectivity, but it also comes with a hefty infrastructure cost and coverage issues in some places. Although 6G promises fast speeds, seamless worldwide connectivity, and AI-driven management, it also has drawbacks in terms of rollout costs, security, and spectrum consumption (Guidotti et al., 2024; Hiriart et al., 2009).

2. NETWORK ARCHITECTURE FOR 6G

The development of 6G technology, which will deliver higher data rates, more capabilities, and smoother device connectivity, will drastically change communication networks. This section focuses into the goals of 6G architecture, the differences between terrestrial and non-terrestrial networks, and how both can be combined to form hybrid networks.

2.1 Comparative Analysis of Recent 6G Satellite Communication Research

The integration of emerging technologies into 6G satellite networks is shaping a highly efficient and intelligent communication ecosystem. Reconfigurable Intelligent Surfaces (RIS), when combined with LEO satellites, offer a powerful means of enhancing signal quality, mitigating interference, and boosting overall network performance. Similarly, for IoT applications in distant and underserved areas, combining satellite connection with Mobile Edge Computing (MEC) is essential to providing low-latency and real-time data processing. By using Integrated Sensing and Communication (ISAC) frameworks, satellites may communicate and sense the environment at the same time, maximizing resource use and opening up applications like disaster relief and environmental monitoring. Furthermore, advanced mobility and handover solutions are required for unmanned aerial vehicle (UAV) connectivity through satellite-terrestrial integration in order to provide stable links during long-range or high-speed operations. In the final analysis minimum, the Joint Communication and Sensing (JCAS) idea adds a multifunctional capacity to satellite systems; however, for its successful application, more research is needed to solve issues with waveform design, spectrum sharing, and interference management. Given Shows the comparative analysis of five recent research papers focusing on 6G satellite communication technologies. It highlights their contributions, methodologies, and findings to provide insight into the latest developments and challenges in the field. Mesut Toka et al. investigate the use of Reconfigurable Intelligent Surfaces (RISs) to enhance LEO satellite networks for 5G and 6G. While LEO satellites offer wide coverage and low latency, they face issues like Doppler shifts, interference, and limited power. The authors propose RISs as a solution to improve link quality, manage interference, and ensure seamless coverage. They also explore use cases such as RIS-assisted UAVs, beam interference control, and integrated sensing and communications, presenting RIS as a key enabler for robust and intelligent 6G satellite networks (Toka et al., 2024). Krishnakanth Mohanta et al. present an analytical study on 6G satellite–terrestrial integrated networks with a focus on UAV-based air mobility applications. The paper investigates two key areas: link budget analysis to ensure reliable satellite-UAV communication and handover and mobility analysis to address connectivity challenges during UAV movement across network layers. Using theoretical models and simulations, the authors offer insights into optimizing these networks for enhanced connectivity, reliability, and operational efficiency, paving the way for effective UAV deployment in future 6G ecosystems (Mohanta & Al-Rubaye, 2024). Chandan Kumar Sheemar et al. explore the integration of Joint Communications and Sensing (JCAS) in satellite networks (SN) to address growing demands for 6G and beyond. While satellites have traditionally supported communication and sensing separately, the authors argue that combining these functions into unified hardware boosts spectral efficiency, reduces costs, and minimizes redundancies. The paper discusses key use cases like Earth observation, object tracking, digital twins, and deep-space missions, while also highlighting major challenges such as Doppler shift mitigation, waveform design, and multi-target detection. Their study presents JCAS as a promising direction for future space-based wireless networks (Lin et al., 2024). XIMU ZHANG et al. present a survey on integrating Mobile Edge Computing (MEC) with satellite communications to support the Internet of Things (IoT) in 6G networks. Since satellites are vital for IoT coverage in remote or disaster areas—but suffer from high latency and low data rates—the authors propose MEC as a solution to offload computation and reduce delays. They classify existing research into three minimal integration structures, summarize key advances, and discuss future directions for creating more intelligent, secure, and energy-efficient satellite-MEC systems for 6G IoT (Sheemar et al., 2025). Li You et al. explore the integration of Integrated Sensing and Communications (ISAC) into massive MIMO Low Earth Orbit (LEO) satellite systems to support 6G networks. While ISAC research has largely focused on terrestrial systems, the authors highlight that combining ISAC with massive MIMO in LEO satellites can deliver ubiquitous high-capacity communication and flexible global sensing. The article provides an overview of LEO and ISAC technologies, reviews recent advances, and discusses key challenges and enabling technologies, concluding with open research directions for realizing ISAC in future satellite systems (You et al., 2024).

Table 2. Comparative Analysis of Recent 6G Satellite

Paper Title	Key Focus	Methodology	Key Findings	Reference
RIS-Empowered LEO Satellite Networks for 6G	Integration of RIS with LEO satellites to enhance 6G	Analytical modeling and scenario analysis	RIS enhances spectral efficiency and reduces latency	Toka et al., 2024
Satellite-MEC Integration for 6G IoT	Satellite + Mobile Edge Computing for IoT in 6G	Survey and architectural proposals	MEC integration reduces latency and boosts efficiency	Lin et al., 2023
ISAC for Massive MIMO LEO Systems	Combining sensing and communications in LEO MIMO	Theoretical framework and use case analysis	ISAC offers dual-function data and sensing	You et al., 2024
Satellite–Terrestrial Networks for UAVs	Connectivity in air mobility operations via satellite-terrestrial systems	Link budget and mobility analysis	Supports reliable UAV handover and network resilience	Mohanta & Al-Rubaye, 2024

2.2 Integration of Satellite-Based and Ground-Based Systems

The seamless integration of Satellite networks with Terrestrial based systems, including satellites, high-altitude platforms (HAPs), and unmanned aerial vehicles (UAVs), is a fundamental component of 6G design. The goal of this integration is to offer coverage everywhere, particularly in remote and underdeveloped areas. With integrating terrestrial, airborne, and space borne networks into a single system, Satellite Terrestrial Integrated Network (STIN) framework serves as an example of this integration. By utilizing the advantages of every network segment, STIN enables worldwide coverage and supports a variety of applications. **Figure 1** shows the network architecture of STIN using 6G.

Figure 1. Network architecture of STIN using 6G

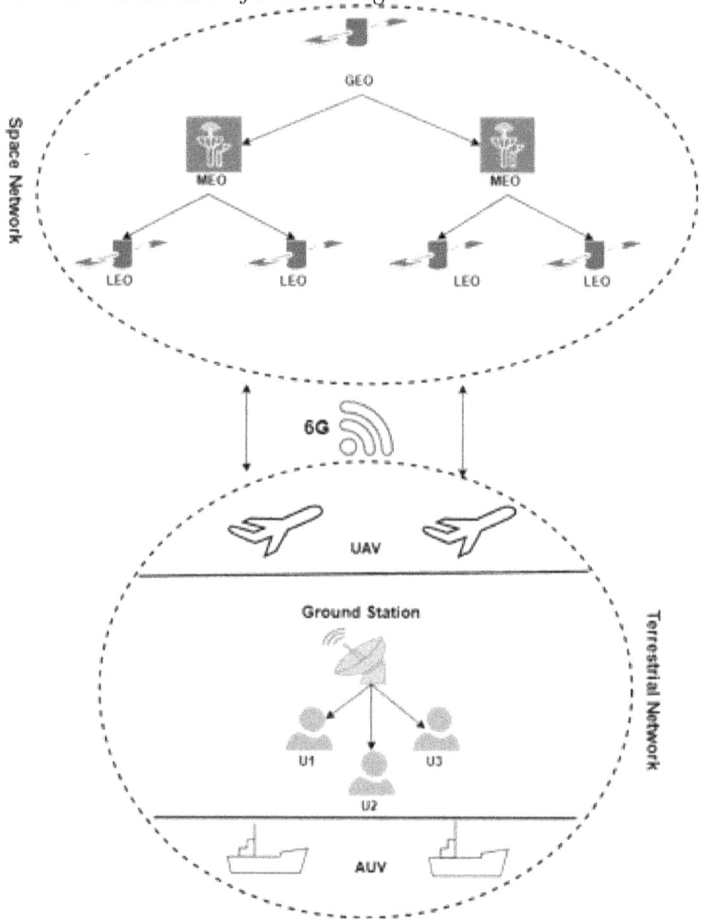

The figure illustrates the architectural integration of satellite networks with terrestrial communication systems, forming the backbone of future 6G non-terrestrial networks. It shows multiple layers of connectivity between satellites in Low Earth Orbit, gateway stations, aerial platforms, and terrestrial users including individuals, vehicles, aircraft, ships, and base stations. At the top layer, constellations of LEO satellites act as the primary communication relays. These satellites are equipped to handle inter-satellite communication, allowing for data exchange without relying on Earth-based infrastructure. The satellites are also connected to satellite control centers or data centers, which manage operations and routing across the network. In the middle layer, the diagram shows direct links between satellites and various airborne platforms (like aircraft) and terrestrial gateways or ground stations. These gateways serve as the interface between satellite networks and the Earth-based telecommunications backbone, enabling two-way communication. At the ground level, the integration becomes evident as terrestrial users (smart phones, IoT devices, and fixed terminals) and maritime users (ships) access satellite services either directly or via ground relay stations. This shows how satellite networks extend coverage to regions beyond the reach of traditional infrastructure—such as oceans, rural areas, and skies.

2.3 Integration of Terrestrial and Non-Terrestrial Networks in Hybrid Networks

Understanding the distinction between non-terrestrial networks- NTNs and terrestrial networks is crucial to grasping the full architecture of 6G systems. NTNs utilize satellites, high-altitude platform systems (HAPS), and airborne vehicles to provide connectivity in remote or underdeveloped regions where traditional infrastructure is lacking. They offer advantages such as wide-area coverage, lower latency in the case of LEO satellites, and connectivity in challenging environments like mountainous regions or open seas. NTNs are expected to play a vital role in 6G deployments by enabling global connectivity and supporting applications such as emergency communications, disaster recovery, and IoT services in isolated areas. In contrast, terrestrial networks consist of conventional infrastructure like fiber optics, cellular towers, and Wi-Fi systems, relying on ground-based hardware for service delivery. While terrestrial networks typically provide high data rates and low latency in urban environments, their effectiveness in rural or hard-to-reach areas is limited due to high deployment costs and logistical constraints. As 6G evolves, enhancements in terrestrial infrastructure—such as the use of mmWave frequencies, dense small-cell deployments, and advanced antenna arrays—will be necessary to meet growing data demands. To bridge the strengths of both systems, 6G will increasingly rely on hybrid network architectures that integrate NTNs with terrestrial infrastructure.

Figure 2. Hybrid network model in 6G

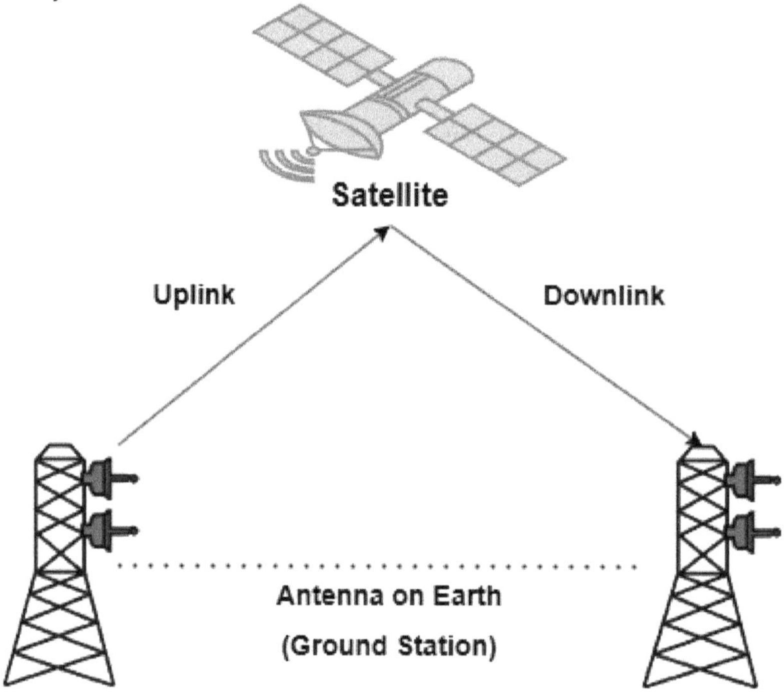

This figure illustrates the integration between satellite-based communication and terrestrial infrastructure such as ground towers (Iida & Wakana, 2003). These hybrid networks offer seamless connectivity by enabling user devices to switch fluidly between terrestrial and satellite links, ensuring reliable communication across urban, rural, and disaster-stricken environments. Moreover, they optimize resource utilization by balancing the load between network types, reducing congestion and enhancing overall performance. This synergy improves capacity in dense urban centers while extending coverage to underserved regions, thereby supporting high-bandwidth applications and multi-user environments. Additionally, hybrid architectures enhance network resilience by providing backup communication paths in the event of terrestrial outages—an essential feature for mission-critical applications that require uninterrupted service. Their versatility also supports a wide range of use cases, including augmented reality (AR), telemedicine, smart transportation, and remote industrial monitoring. As such, hybrid satellite-terrestrial networks are poised to become a foundational pillar of the hyper-connected 6G era, delivering robust, flexible, and inclusive communication solutions worldwide.

2.4 Use Cases and Applications Enabled by 6G Satellites

The integration of 6G satellite networks is set to revolutionize various sectors by enabling applications that demand ultra-reliable, low-latency, and ubiquitous connectivity. Below are key real-world use cases facilitated by this technology:

- **Remote Healthcare (Telemedicine and Mobile Hospitals):** 6G satellites can provide high-speed connectivity to remote and underserved regions, facilitating telemedicine services such as remote diagnostics, consultations, and even surgical procedures. Platforms like SATMED have demonstrated the potential of satellite-enabled eHealth services in areas lacking reliable terrestrial networks, enhancing healthcare delivery in regions like Bangladesh, Benin, and Sierra Leone.
- **Autonomous Transport (UAVs, Ships, Smart Highways):** The low latency and wide coverage of 6G satellites are critical for the operation of autonomous vehicles, including drones, maritime vessels, and smart highway systems. These networks ensure real-time communication and navigation, essential for the safety and efficiency of autonomous transport systems.
- **Disaster Recovery (Earthquakes, Floods):** In the aftermath of natural disasters, terrestrial communication infrastructures are often compromised. 6G satellite networks can provide immediate and reliable communication channels for emergency response teams, facilitating coordination and information dissemination during critical times.
- **Maritime and Aviation Connectivity:** 6G satellites can offer consistent and high-speed internet connectivity to aircraft and ships, enhancing navigation, safety, and passenger experience. This is particularly beneficial for transoceanic flights and voyages where traditional connectivity options are limited.
- **Holographic Conferencing and Real-Time XR/VR:** The high bandwidth and low latency of 6G satellite networks make them ideal for immersive applications such as holographic conferencing and extended reality (XR) experiences. These applications require seamless data transmission to create real-time, interactive virtual environments.
- **Global-Scale IoT (Logistics, Farming, Sensors in Oceans or Forests):** 6G satellites can connect a vast array of IoT devices across the globe, including those in remote or hard-to-reach areas. This connectivity supports applications in logistics tracking, precision agriculture, environmental monitoring, and more, enabling real-time data collection and analysis on a global scale. Bottom of Form

2.5 The Significance of Satellite in 6G Network

Satellites have been a foundational component of global telecommunications for decades, and their strategic relevance is poised to grow substantially in the 6G era. One of the primary advantages of satellites is their inherent capacity to provide global coverage, which is especially crucial in regions where terrestrial infrastructure is either sparse, economically unfeasible, or physically impossible to deploy—such as oceans, mountains, deserts, and polar areas. Because of this, satellites play a crucial role in facilitating internet access by bridging the connection divide between urban and rural areas. Satellite systems provide continuous service continuity in regions at risk of disasters because ground-based communication networks are frequently challenged by earthquakes, floods, or war. It facilitate the possible for vital services including broadcasting emergency alerts, coordinating rescue efforts in real time, and providing communication support for medical and humanitarian relief efforts. These features highlight how reliable satellite systems are at preserving vital communication channels in times of need. Broadcasting, navigation, remote sensing, military surveillance, marine and aviation communications, and increasingly, Internet of Things and machine-type communications are just a few of the many uses that satellites facilitate. By facilitating smooth vertical handovers, expanding service reach, and boosting reliability, their incorporation into terrestrial networks—a fundamental 6G architectural concept—is anticipated to greatly improve quality of service (QoS). For new use cases like remote healthcare, smart agriculture, and driverless cars, this hybrid terrestrial-satellite arrangement will be crucial. The future of communication will require everywhere, ultra-reliable, and low-latency connectivity, as the 6G roadmap envisions. Because of their closeness to Earth, reduced latency, and capacity to manage large volumes of data, satellite networks—especially those with low Earth orbit constellations—is well adapted to satisfy these demands. They will be responsible for providing load balancing, network resilience, and support for edge computing from space in addition to expanding network coverage (Akyildiz et al., 2020; Kodheli et al., 2020).

3 A BRIEF HISTORY OF SATELLITE COMMUNICATION

This section describes the development of satellite technologies, their role in the telecommunications industry, and some of the significant achievements that have impacted the sector.

3.1 The Evolution of Satellites to Current Constellations

The evolution of satellite communications began with the launch of Sputnik 1 by the Soviet Union on October 4, 1957, marking the inception of the space age and laying the groundwork for future satellite technologies. In the early 1960s, the United States advanced this field with the deployment of communication satellites such as Relay 1 and Telstar 1, which demonstrated the feasibility of transmitting television signals across continents . The 1970s saw the emergence of geostationary satellites, like the Intelsat IV series, providing continuous coverage over specific regions and significantly enhancing global telecommunications. In the 1990s and early 2000s, Low Earth Orbit and Medium Earth Orbit satellite constellations, including Iridium and Global star, were introduced to offer lower latency and expanded coverage, facilitating services such as mobile communication and internet access in remote areas. In recent years, advancements have led to the development of large-scale LEO constellations like Star link, OneWeb, and Amazon's Project Kuiper, aiming to provide high-speed, low-latency internet connectivity globally, thereby supporting emerging technologies such as the Internet of Things, autonomous vehicles, and smart city infrastructures (Mahboob & Liu, 2024).

Table 2. Examining wireless WANs: Satellite Networks

Name	Date of Launch	Description
SPUTNIK I	October 4, 1957	The world's first artificial satellite to orbit Earth. Shortly after, Sputnik 2 carried the first living creature (a dog) into orbit.
SCORE	December 18, 1958	The first communication satellite, famous for broadcasting a Christmas message for 12 days until its batteries expired.
Echo 1	August 12, 1960	A passive communication satellite using reflective surfaces. It demonstrated signal bouncing but was quickly phased out.
(Yuri Gagarin)	April 12, 1961	Not a satellite, but a historical milestone: the first human (Yuri Gagarin) in space aboard Vostok
Telstar	1962	The first real-time active telecommunication satellite, enabling live broadcasts between continents.
Intelsat	1964–1979	A global geosynchronous communication satellite network accessible by all nations.
Inmarsat	1979	Designed for international maritime communication; later expanded to aviation and land use.
ACTS	1993	NASA's Advanced Communications Technology Satellite introduced innovations like spot beams, digital transmission, and on-board data processing.
DirecTV	1993	Began providing direct-to-home television broadcast services using high-power satellites.

3.2 Different Types of Satellite Orbits: LEO, MEO, and GEO

Satellites are categorized based on their orbital altitudes, with each class offering distinct advantages in terms of coverage, latency, and suitability for specific applications. Low Earth Orbit (LEO) satellites operate at altitudes between approximately 160 and 2,000 kilometers above the Earth's surface. Due to their proximity, they offer low transmission latency—typically between 20 and 40 milliseconds—making them ideal for real-time applications such as high-speed internet, Earth observation, and remote sensing. However, because of their limited coverage area, LEO systems require large constellations of satellites to ensure continuous global service. Medium Earth Orbit (MEO) satellites, positioned between 2,000 and 35,786 kilometers, offer a balance between latency and coverage. Commonly used in navigation systems such as GPS and Galileo, MEO satellites have average latencies of 70 to 100 milliseconds and require fewer satellites than LEO networks to achieve global coverage. In contrast, Geostationary Earth Orbit (GEO) satellites are stationed at approximately 35,786 kilometers above the equator and remain fixed over a specific point on the Earth's surface. This stable positioning provides uninterrupted coverage of a designated area, making GEO satellites well-suited for applications like weather monitoring and television broadcasting. However, their high altitude results in longer latency—typically between 500 and 600 milliseconds—making them less suitable for applications that demand real-time responsiveness.

3.3 Components of Satellite Communication Systems

Effective satellite communication relies on several key components:

- User Terminals: These devices, which include satellite dishes and antennas, facilitate the transmission and reception of signals between the user and the satellite. Modern user terminals often incorporate phased array technology, allowing for electronic beam steering to maintain connectivity with moving satellites.
- Satellite Payloads: The payload encompasses the communication equipment aboard the satellite, such as transponders and antennas, responsible for receiving, amplifying, and retransmitting signals. Advanced payload designs may feature multi-beam configurations to enhance capacity and enable frequency reuse.
- Ground Stations: Serving as the interface between satellites and terrestrial networks, ground stations manage signal processing, routing, and satellite control. They are equipped with large antennas and sophisticated systems to ensure reliable communication links and data transfer (Kodheli et al., 2020).

3.4 Orbital Dynamics and Their Impact on Communication

The orbital parameters of satellites, including altitude, inclination, and eccentricity, significantly influences their communication capabilities:

- Orbital Dynamics: LEO satellites, due to their low altitude, orbit the Earth rapidly, completing multiple orbits per day. This necessitates a constellation of satellites to provide continuous coverage. In contrast, GEO satellites remain stationary relative to Earth's surface, offering uninterrupted coverage over specific areas.
- Coverage Patterns: The design of a satellite's antenna and its orbital path determine its coverage area. LEO satellites have smaller footprints, requiring numerous satellites for global coverage, whereas GEO satellites can cover approximately one-third of the Earth's surface with a single satellite.
- Latency and Connectivity: The distance between a satellite and Earth affects signal latency. LEO satellites offer low latency, making them suitable for real-time applications. MEO satellites provide moderate latency and are often used for navigation services. GEO satellites, while offering extensive coverage, have higher latency, which can impact time-sensitive communications.

3.5 Features of 6G Satellite Communication

The integration of 6G technology with satellite networks introduces a wide array of advanced features that aim to overcome the limitations of previous generations. These features are essential for supporting intelligent, reliable, and high-speed global connectivity, especially in remote and underserved regions. 6G satellite communication networks are set up to deliver an innovative set of features that collectively redefine global connectivity. One of the biggest developments is anticipated coverage, where 6G satellites will guarantee smooth worldwide connectivity, bringing dependable internet services to polar, rural, remote, and maritime areas—thereby closing the long-standing digital divide. This reach is enhanced by the continuous connection capacity, that guarantees constant communication on land, at sea, and in the air, supporting vital services like autonomous transportation, disaster recovery, and real-time global Internet of Things systems. These networks also promise an enhanced user experience, offering ultra-fast, stable, and responsive connections even in high-density areas like smart cities and during large-scale events. Increased spectral efficiency, made possible by modern technologies like massive MIMO and AI-driven beam forming, represents a significant technological advancement that permits more data to move across available bandwidth with less interference. By combining smart routing, power-saving satellite operations, and efficient processing—all crucial for long-duration, low-power applications—6G prioritizes improved energy efficiency to support sustainability goals. Furthermore, 6G will create intelligent, adaptable systems through deep integration with other technologies like block chain, edge computing, AI, machine learning, and UAVs. This is crucial for real-time, delay-sensitive jobs in fields like autonomous systems, smart manufacturing, and robotics. These characteristics work together to provide the foundation of a sophisticated, inclusive, and perceptive international communication system (Zhang et al., 2023).

Figure 3. Key Features of 6G Satellite Communication Networks

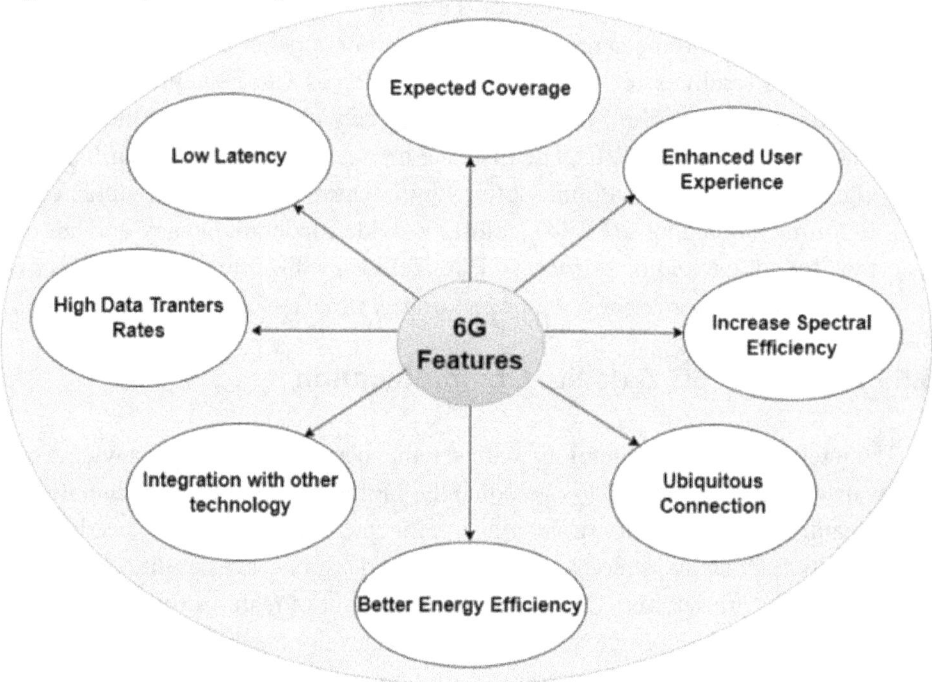

The figure illustrates the core features of 6G satellite communication in a centralized format, where the central green node "6G Features" is surrounded by eight major characteristics (Shah et al., 2023). Each feature points to a critical advancement that defines how 6G satellites will operate and outperform previous technologies.

4 CHALLENGES AND LIMITATIONS OF 6G SATELLITE NETWORKS

As 6G satellite networks evolve to provide global connectivity, several technical and operational challenges must be addressed to ensure efficient and reliable communication.

- **Propagation Latency in Geostationary Orbits (GEO):** Satellites positioned in geostationary orbit (approximately 35,786 km above Earth) experience significant signal delays due to the vast distance signals must travel. This latency, often around 240 milliseconds for a round trip, can hinder real-time applications such as video conferencing and online gaming. In contrast, Low Earth Orbit (LEO) satellites, orbiting at altitudes between 160 km and 2,000 km, offer reduced latency, enhancing performance for latency-sensitive services.
- **High Costs of Satellite Launch and Maintenance:** Deploying and maintaining satellite infrastructure involves substantial financial investments. While advancements in reusable launch vehicles have reduced costs, expenses related to satellite manufacturing, launch, and ground station operations remain significant. These costs can be prohibitive, especially for smaller organizations or developing nations seeking to establish satellite communication capabilities.
- **Signal Degradation in Terahertz (THz) Bands Due to Atmospheric Conditions:** Higher frequency bands, such as THz, offer greater data transmission capacities but are more susceptible to atmospheric attenuation. Factors like rain, humidity, and atmospheric gases can absorb or scatter THz signals, leading to signal degradation and reduced reliability. This phenomenon, known as rain fade, poses a significant challenge for maintaining consistent high-frequency satellite communications.

4.1 Spectral Ranges for 6G Satellite Communications

The advantages of 6G satellite communication are numerous and far-reaching, promising to reshape global connectivity and enable advanced digital applications. One of the primary benefits is its global broadcasting reach, as 6G satellites—especially those in Low Earth Orbit (LEO)—provide comprehensive coverage to remote, underdeveloped, and rural areas where terrestrial infrastructure is limited, unreliable, or economically unviable. This capability ensures equitable access to information and services across regions, supporting global development goals (Skosana et al., 2024).

Figure 4. Spectrum evolution from 4G to 6G

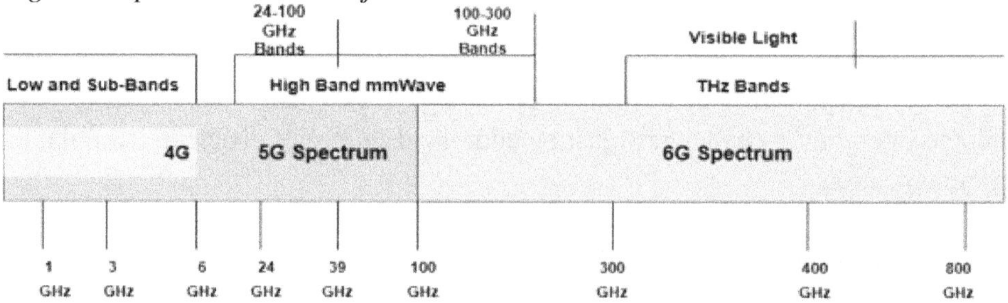

This Figure shows the expansion into millimeter-wave and terahertz frequency bands, which are critical for achieving the high-speed and low-latency capabilities of 6G satellite communication (Adhikari & Hazra, 2022). Another critical advantage is the higher data rates offered by 6G, which exceed 100 Gbps and are essential for supporting data-intensive services such as high-definition video streaming, cloud computing, and next-generation technologies like augmented reality (AR) and virtual reality (VR) (Cui et al., 2025). These high transmission speeds also enable innovation, particularly in sectors like smart transportation and autonomous vehicles, which require real-time, low-latency communication to function safely and effectively. Furthermore, 6G's use of LEO satellites significantly reduces latency, bringing satellite networks closer to the performance of terrestrial systems, with delays reduced to as low as 20–30 milliseconds compared to the 500–600 ms typical of geostationary satellites. This low-latency performance is crucial for real-time communication applications, including telemedicine, remote surgery, online gaming, and virtual meetings, where delays can severely affect user experience and effectiveness. Additionally, 6G satellites enhance network adaptability and redundancy, providing consistent communication capabilities even during terrestrial outages caused by natural disasters or technical failures. This added resilience ensures that critical services remain operational when terrestrial networks are compromised, making satellite communication a vital component of disaster recovery and national infrastructure defense (Torrens et al., 2024). In essence, 6G satellite networks offer high-speed, low-latency, and highly resilient communication systems that bridge the digital divide and underpin the next wave of technological innovation.

4.2 Artificial Intelligence and Machine Learning in 6G Satellite Networks

Artificial Intelligence (AI) and Machine Learning (ML) are central to the next-generation 6G satellite networks, enhancing the intelligence, automation, and adaptability of communication systems. These technologies bring advanced computational capabilities that enable real-time decision-making, optimize resource use, and enhance overall network efficiency, especially in complex and dynamic environments.

- **Predictive Traffic Control:** AI and ML algorithms can analyze historical and real-time data traffic patterns to predict future congestion or data surges. This capability enables satellite networks to dynamically reroute data or adjust bandwidth allocations in advance, thereby avoiding bottlenecks and ensuring consistent quality of service. For instance, predictive analytics can foresee increased usage in a specific geographic area (e.g., during an event or emergency) and allocate satellite resources accordingly.
- **Dynamic Beam forming and Handover Decisions:** ML models are used to control and optimize beam forming—steering the satellite signal towards specific users or regions where demand is highest. These intelligent systems continuously evaluate user mobility, network load, and environmental conditions to adjust beam directions in real-time. Additionally, they assist in making seamless handover decisions as users move between satellite coverage areas or between satellites and terrestrial networks, reducing connection drops and improving user experience.
- **Interference Mitigation:** Satellite communication is prone to interference from other satellites, terrestrial systems, and environmental factors. ML algorithms can detect and classify sources of interference and adaptively modify transmission parameters such as frequency, power, or modulation schemes to minimize disruption. These models learn over time to better predict and respond to interference scenarios, enhancing the reliability and clarity of satellite communication channels.

4.3 Beam forming and Large Scale MIMO for Satellite Communications

The integration of beam forming and massive Multiple-Input Multiple-Output (MIMO) technologies is revolutionizing satellite communications, playing a pivotal role in meeting the high throughput, directionality, and coverage requirements of 6G networks. A signal processing technique called beam forming maximizes bandwidth usage and reduces interference by directing transmission power toward certain users or regions, improving signal directivity. This focused strategy improves signal strength and decreases latency in certain regions, resulting in more dependable communication networks. Massive MIMO greatly increases data speeds and communication capacity in the context of 6G by using a large number of antennas at both the transmitter and receiver ends. Higher spectrum efficiency, higher throughput, and reliable connectivity—even in highly populated areas—are become possible by the incorporation of MIMO technology into 6G satellite systems. Additionally, beam steering enables satellites to dynamically modify signal directions in response to user movements and focus on areas with high demand, maximizing operational effectiveness and resource use. New developments suggest virtualized beam forming systems that use machine learning techniques and software-defined networking to dynamically distribute beam forming resources, improving signal-to-noise ratios and adaptability in high-density settings. These studies' simulation results show a 19% gain in spectral efficiency and a 22% decrease in power usage when compared to conventional beam forming techniques. These developments highlight how beam forming and large MIMO technology will revolutionize 6G satellite communications in the future (Ukommi et al., 2021; Wang et al., 2021). As shown in Figure 2, the gradual progression of wireless generations from 2G to 5G has laid the groundwork for the adoption of highly advanced transmission technologies like beam forming and massive MIMO in 6G satellite systems.

Figure 5. Evolution of Mobile Generations toward 5G and Implications for 6G Satellites MIMO

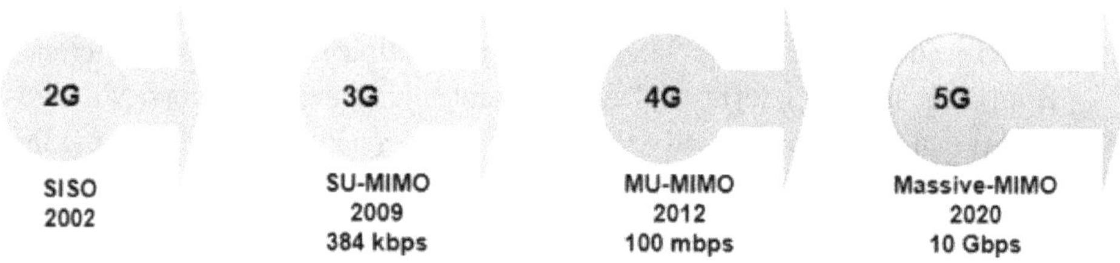

The figure illustrates the evolution of mobile network generations—from 2G to 5G—highlighting the increasing complexity and performance in wireless communications (Adhikari & Hazra, 2022). While this visual does not yet include 6G, it sets the foundation for understanding the need for advanced technologies like beam forming and massive MIMO in the 6G era. As each generation is progressively advanced in data speed, spectral efficiency, and connectivity, the transition to 6G necessitates new innovations, especially in satellite communication where challenges such as long-distance propagation, high latency, and dynamic user distribution are more prominent. The transition to massive MIMO and beam forming, particularly in non-terrestrial networks (NTNs), is explained by this evolution concept as a logical next step towards addressing user density, performance requirements, and global coverage objectives.

6. TECHNOLOGY ADVANCEMENTS

The advancement of technology in 6G satellite communications is fundamentally reshaping the landscape of global connectivity, enabling more intelligent, autonomous, and efficient communication networks. At the heart of these innovations is the fusion of Artificial Intelligence (AI) and Machine Learning (ML) with next-generation satellite systems. These technologies play a vital role in optimizing performance, reducing latency, and managing the enormous volumes of data associated with 6G use cases. Sophisticated satellite technologies are being developed with enhanced payload capabilities, reconfigurable onboard processing, and adaptive systems that can dynamically adjust to shifting network demands. This evolution allows satellites to handle complex 6G functions such as real-time video streaming, immersive virtual and augmented reality, and ultra-reliable low-latency communications (URLLC). AI and ML, meanwhile, are revolutionizing satellite network management by enabling predictive traffic analysis, intelligent handover decisions, and real-time resource allocation. These systems facilitate self-learning capabilities, allowing satellites to adapt autonomously to changes in operational conditions, improving efficiency and resilience. Moreover, AI-driven algorithms support real-time optimization of data routing, reducing congestion and enabling proactive maintenance by forecasting potential system failures. In traffic control, ML models analyze usage patterns and historical traffic data to smartly prioritize and route communication flows, ensuring quality of service even under fluctuating demand. Additionally, AI supports the autonomous management of satellite resources, including dynamic power distribution and orbit adjustments, allowing satellites to operate with minimal human intervention. These innovations not only boost performance but also reduce operational costs and increase system longevity. According to Jiang et al. (2023), AI integration in satellite networks is expected to enhance efficiency by over 30% through intelligent automation and self-optimization (Yang et al., 2023). As 6G envisions a fully interconnected and intelligent digital infrastructure, these technology advancements mark a crucial step toward the realization of space-terrestrial integrated networks capable of supporting a truly global and inclusive communication environment.

6.1 6G Satellite Connectivity and Internet of Things

6G satellite networks are poised to revolutionize the IoT by providing continuous, global connectivity, especially in remote and hard-to-reach areas. This advancement is crucial for extending IoT capabilities beyond the limitations of terrestrial infrastructure. One of the key developments is Direct-to-Satellite communication, which allows IoT devices to connect directly with satellites without the need for intermediary ground stations, thereby reducing latency and enhancing real-time responsiveness for mission-critical applications. The integration of satellites with IoT will enable global coverage, including in regions like the Arctic, oceans, and remote rural areas where terrestrial networks are unreliable or nonexistent. This widespread connectivity supports various applications such as global asset tracking, environmental monitoring, smart agriculture, and emergency response systems. To manage the high volume of data generated by IoT devices, 6G satellite networks will incorporate advanced transmission methods and sophisticated processing capabilities. Edge computing technologies will be embedded within satellites to process data closer to its source, reducing bandwidth costs and improving the efficiency of data handling for large-scale IoT applications. Furthermore, AI and ML will play a pivotal role in filtering, analyzing, and managing the influx of IoT data across the 6G satellite network. These technologies will ensure efficient data flow and enable real-time decision-making, enhancing the overall performance and reliability of IoT systems. As illustrated in Figure.3., the integration of satellite networks with IoT extends the reach of intelligent systems across diverse sectors and geographies, ensuring seamless and continuous data flow in both urban and remote environments.

Figure 6. 6G Satellite-IoT Ecosystem and Application Domains

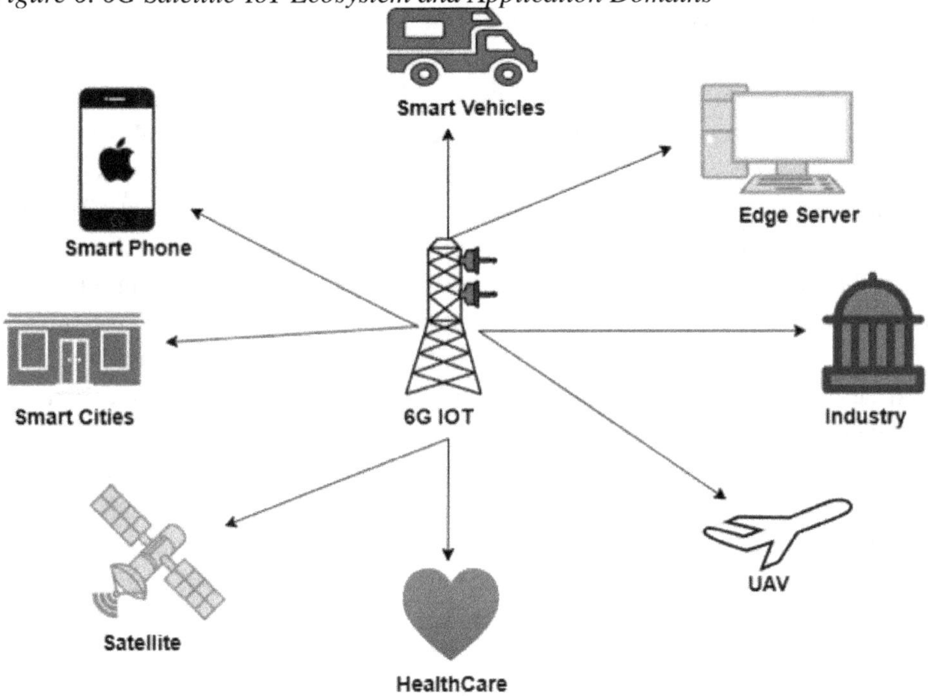

This figure visually represents the ecosystem of IoT devices interconnected through a 6G satellite network. At the center of the diagram is the communication tower, symbolizing the core link between terrestrial and non-terrestrial (satellite) infrastructure (Shah et al., 2023). Surrounding it are various IoT domains and devices, including mobile phones, smart homes, emergency vehicles, data centers, aircraft, public infrastructure, and health systems. This holistic connectivity aligns with the goals of 6G to ensure ubiquitous, low-latency, and energy-efficient communication for mission-critical and remote operations. In summary, the convergence of 6G satellite networks with IoT will not only bridge the digital divide by bringing connectivity to underserved areas but also unlock new possibilities for innovation and efficiency across various industries. This integration is a significant step towards a more connected and intelligent global infrastructure (Zhang et al., 2019).

6.2 Unmanned Aerial Systems, Unmanned Vehicles, and Satellite

The integration of 6G satellite networks is set to transform the operation of unmanned aerial systems (UAS), unmanned vehicles (UVs), and intelligent transportation systems by providing seamless, global, and real-time connectivity. This advancement is particularly crucial for Beyond Visual Line of Sight (BVLOS) operations, enabling unmanned aerial vehicles (UAVs) to perform tasks such as surveillance, disaster response, and remote deliveries in areas lacking terrestrial infrastructure. These systems are more autonomous and efficient because of 6G's ultra-low latency and high data speeds, which enable real-time command, control, and data interchange. For example, UAVs happen to instantly send telemetry data and HD video that improves state of mind and decision-making. 6G improves Vehicle-to-Everything (V2X) communications in the field of intelligent transportation, enabling traffic control, safety applications, and autonomous vehicle navigation—even in isolated or underserved areas. The safety and dependability of autonomous vehicles depend on network reliability and constant communication that are ensured by satellite integration. In addition, as recent analysis has explored, the integration of sensing, communication, computation, and control elements in a closed-loop system highlights the potential of 6G satellite networks to facilitate intricate autonomous operations in a variety of fields. These advancements demonstrate the revolutionary effects of 6G on intelligent transportation infrastructures and unmanned systems (Zhang et al., 2023).

6.4 Digital Divide and Worldwide Connectivity

One of the main goals of 6G satellite communication is to close the digital divide by guaranteeing that everyone, regardless of location, obtains equal access to the global digital environment. Since dependable high-speed internet infrastructure is still lacking in many parts of the world, especially in rural and isolated locations, 6G's integration of satellite networks offers a game-changing answer. In these underdeveloped areas, satellite communication can provide reliable, low-latency, high-speed internet connection, and allowing access to previously unavailable digital education, telemedicine, e-commerce, and e-governance services. Satellite-based 6G systems are essential for enabling people in underdeveloped nations where terrestrial networks are either unavailable or prohibitively expensive. These systems can improve health outcomes, support lifelong learning, and increase local economies. By providing digital tools that encourage creativity and self-sufficiency, these systems not only facilitate connectivity but also advance socioeconomic inclusion. Additionally, achieving universal and inclusive connectivity is in line with global development priorities, including the Sustainable Development Goals (SDGs) of the UN, especially Goal 9 on infrastructure, industry, and innovation. 6G satellite technologies are positioned as a key enabler of global digital equity, guaranteeing that no community is left behind in the digital revolution by providing high-capacity, reasonably priced internet access to remote parts of the globe.

7 SECURITY ISSUES IN SATELLITE-BASED 6G NETWORKS

The integration of satellite systems into 6G networks introduces significant security challenges that must be addressed to ensure the confidentiality, integrity, and availability of data across non-terrestrial networks. Resolving vulnerabilities like spoofing, jamming, and illegal access—which are made worst by the unsecured and scattered nature of satellite communications—becomes crucial as 6G seeks to provide universal connection through satellite-terrestrial convergence. Due to the special features of satellite networks, such as their extensive coverage areas and the challenge of putting in place physical security controls in space, traditional security measures might not be enough. Artificial Intelligence (AI) and Machine Learning (ML), two innovative technologies, present promising real-time threat detection and response solutions that allow for dynamic adaptability to changing security threats. In addition, the usage of Zero Trust Architectures (ZTA) is being investigated as a way to improve security by continuously confirming the reliability of users and devices, no matter that it is on the network. However, latency and resource limitations pose difficulties when putting such architectures into practice in satellite networks. Furthermore, the creation of cryptographic methods that are resistant to quantum computing is essential for safeguarding against potential dangers. To provide standardized security frameworks and protocols that are suited to the unique requirements of 6G satellite networks, cooperation between industry stakeholders, academic institutions, and regulatory agencies is crucial. It are capable of building a robust and secure 6G communication infrastructure that makes the most of satellite technology by solving these security issues.

7.1 Cyber security Risks in Non-Terrestrial Networks

Satellite-based 6G networks become increasingly vital for global communication, they also present attractive targets for cyber attacks due to their complex and widely distributed infrastructure. These networks—comprising communication cables, satellites, and ground stations—face a variety of cyber security threats that must be effectively managed. Key vulnerabilities include eavesdropping, where attackers intercept data transmissions between satellites and ground stations, leading to potential breaches of sensitive information. Jamming is another critical threat, involving the transmission of disruptive signals that block or degrade satellite communications, resulting in service interruptions. Spoofing is also a concern, where attackers mimic legitimate satellite signals to mislead or gain unauthorized access to the network, potentially causing data corruption or false commands. Denial-of-service (DoS) attacks, which flood systems with illegitimate traffic to block access for legitimate users, pose significant risks to both private and public services, including financial communications and emergency response systems. Moreover, the expansive geographic coverage of satellite networks increases their exposure, creating more potential points of attack—especially in remote or less secure regions that are difficult to monitor. This vast and decentralized nature makes securing satellite networks more complex than traditional ground-based systems, demanding specialized cyber security measures to safeguard against increasingly sophisticated threats (Zhao et al., 2025).

7.2 Privacy Issues with Worldwide Satellite Communications

6G satellite communications continue to expand globally, it bring with them significant privacy concerns that must be addressed to ensure trust and compliance with international norms. Data sovereignty, or the idea that digital data is governed by the laws and governance frameworks of the nation in which it is gathered or processed, is one of the most critical problems. Determining control gets more difficult with satellites that are capable of sending data in real-time across several nations and continents. For example, personal information collected in one nation gets transferred to or held in another with less strict privacy rules that are possibly against regional regulations like the General Data Protection Regulation (GDPR) of the European Union. This raises ethical and legal concerns around user consent, data ownership, and cross-border data processing by casting doubt on who has the authority to access or control the data. Surveillance and tracking are another significant problem. From space, satellites with high-resolution imagery and earth observation capabilities can keep an eye on infrastructure, people, and automobiles. Mass surveillance is made possible by this, even though it is helpful for defense, environmental monitoring, and disaster management. This power could be abused by governments, businesses, or bad actors to eavesdrop on people without their knowledge or consent. Continuous tracking of individual behavior, movements, or activities—especially when aggregated with other datasets—can lead to serious breaches of privacy. These concerns are greatly increased by the increasing number of satellite-based Internet of Things (IoT) devices, with the ability to transmit data about an individual's position, behavior, and surroundings continuously. Future 6G satellite systems must incorporate robust privacy-by-design concepts, such as location privacy, end-to-end data encryption, and stringent access control mechanisms, to overcome these obstacles. To guarantee uniform enforcement of privacy rights, worldwide regulatory frameworks require being integrated, irrespective of the location of satellite data processing or origin. The viability and cultural acceptance of 6G satellite networks will undoubtedly depend on privacy, as evidenced by ongoing research that highlights the significance of creating satellite systems that respect state sovereignty and individual privacy in addition to facilitating global connectivity.

CONCLUSIONS

Satellite communication will be a crucial enabler for attaining seamless global connection as the globe progresses toward 6G networks. In particular, 6G satellite networks offer notable improvements in transmission speed, decreased latency, and more adaptability due to developments in low-orbit satellite constellations, advanced beam forming techniques, and large-scale MIMO. Technologies like low Earth orbit (LEO) satellites, beam forming, and massive MIMO (Multiple-Input Multiple-Output) are at the heart of this improvement, allowing faster and more reliable data exchange. These innovations will not only help reduce the digital divide but also support the rapid growth of the Internet of Things (IoT)—where billions of devices will be connected across the globe. However, this progress brings some challenges. Integrating satellite systems into 6G means dealing with cyber security threats, privacy concerns, and the complex process of spectrum allocation, especially when data crosses international borders. To handle these problems, it's important to use artificial intelligence (AI) and machine learning (ML) to make satellite networks smarter and more efficient. These tools can help manage network traffic, detect threats, and improve the way communication resources are used., Satellites will also be essential in running future autonomous systems, like self-driving cars, drones, and intelligent transportation systems, by offering uninterrupted, real-time communication anywhere in the world. As 6G becomes a reality, combining satellite and ground-based networks into a unified system—often called a hybrid infrastructure—will be key to supporting the diverse needs of next-generation technologies. These developments will be crucial in closing the digital gap, providing universal internet access, and fostering the Internet of Things' rapid expansion (IoT).But there are also additional difficulties with integrating satellite communication into 6G networks, especially when it comes to cyber security, allocating spectrum, and maintaining privacy during international transfers. In order to meet these problems and maximize network efficiency, it will be crucial to apply artificial intelligence (AI) and machine learning (ML) to optimize satellite networks, traffic control, and resource allocation. In addition to facilitating communication, satellites' ability to provide worldwide, and real-time connectivity will have a substantial impact on autonomous systems, such as intelligent transportation networks and unmanned aerial vehicles (UAVs). Ultimately, 6G satellite communication has the potential to change technology while guiding innovation, worldwide connectivity, and technological growth through the challenges of efficiency, sustainability, and security in a networked society.

Future Scope

The future of 6G satellite communications is poised for transformative breakthroughs, shaped by the convergence of advanced technologies and evolving global demands. 6G will be distinguished by its AI-native design, in which artificial intelligence is integrated into the network to facilitate real-time intelligent resource management, autonomous decision-making and predictive optimization. The creation of SAGIN (Space-Air-Ground Integrated Networks), which will seamlessly combine satellite, aerial, and terrestrial components to offer ultra-low latency, dependable, and ubiquitous connection worldwide, is another crucial advancement. International organizations like the IEEE, ITU, and 3GPP are working to standardize these networks as they develop in order to guarantee scalability, security, and interoperability. Researchers are looking into solar-powered satellites, recyclable materials, and energy-efficient architectures to lessen their influence on the environment, while sustainability and green satellite operations are also receiving more attention. On the deployment front, the 6G satellite ecosystem is being advanced by both government and commercial activities. In order to achieve digital equity, resilience, and intelligent global connection, 6G satellite networks will be essential in the future, according to these technological and legislative developments taken together.

REFERENCES

Adhikari, M., & Hazra, A. (2022). 6G-enabled ultra-reliable low-latency communication in edge networks. *IEEE Communications Standards Magazine*, *6*(1), 67–74. Advance online publication. DOI: 10.1109/MCOMSTD.0001.2100098

Akyildiz, I. F., Kak, A., & Nie, S. (2020). 6G and beyond: The future of wireless communications systems. *IEEE Access : Practical Innovations, Open Solutions*, *8*, 133995–134030. DOI: 10.1109/ACCESS.2020.3010896

Alkasassbeh, J. S., Al-Taweel, F. M., Alawneh, T. A., Al-Qaisi, A., Makableh, Y. F., & El-Mezieni, T. (2024). Advancements in wireless communication technology: A comprehensive analysis of 4G to 7G systems. [JoWUA]. *Journal of Wireless Mobile Networks, Ubiquitous Computing and Dependable Applications*, *15*(3), 73–91. DOI: 10.58346/JOWUA.2024.I3.006

Beyaz, M. (2024). Satellite communications with 5G, B5G, and 6G: Challenges and prospects. *International Journal of Communications, Network and Systems Sciences*, *17*(3), 31–49. DOI: 10.4236/ijcns.2024.173003

Chen, C., Förster, M. W., Foley, S. F., & Liu, Y. (2021). Massive carbon storage in convergent margins initiated by subduction of limestone. *Nature Communications*, *12*(1), 4463. DOI: 10.1038/s41467-021-24750-0 PMID: 34294696

Cui, Q., You, X., Wei, N., Nan, G., Zhang, X., Zhang, J., & Yuen, C. (2025). Overview of AI and communication for 6G network: Fundamentals, challenges, and future research opportunities. *Science China. Information Sciences*, *68*(7), 171301. DOI: 10.1007/s11432-024-4337-1

Dalai, D., Babu, S., & Manoj, B. S. (2022). Satellite-6G network integration roadmap on reference architectures. *TechRxiv Preprint*. https://doi.org/DOI: 10.36227/techrxiv.20624685.v1

Dalai, D., Babu, S., Sukumaran, V. B., & Manoj, B. S. (2024). A novel space-based hosting approach for ultra low latency web services. *IEEE Access : Practical Innovations, Open Solutions*, *12*, 142838–142862. DOI: 10.1109/ACCESS.2024.3462252

Dang, S., Amin, O., Shihada, B., & Alouini, M.-S. (2020). What should 6G be? *Nature Electronics*, *3*(1), 20–29. DOI: 10.1038/s41928-019-0355-6

Dao, N.-N., Pham, Q.-V., Tu, N. H., Thanh, T. T., Bao, V. N. Q., Lakew, D. S., & Cho, S. (2021). Survey on aerial radio access networks: Toward a comprehensive 6G access infrastructure. *IEEE Communications Surveys and Tutorials*, *23*(2), 1193–1225. DOI: 10.1109/COMST.2021.3059644

Del Portillo, I., Cameron, B. G., & Crawley, E. F. (2019). A technical comparison of three low Earth orbit satellite constellation systems to provide global broadband. *Acta Astronautica, 159*, 123–135. DOI: 10.1016/j.actaastro.2019.03.040

Guidotti, A., Vanelli-Coralli, A., Jaafari, M. E., Chuberre, N., Puttonen, J., Schena, V., Rinelli, G., & Cioni, S. (2024). Role and evolution of non-terrestrial networks toward 6G systems. *IEEE Access : Practical Innovations, Open Solutions, 12*, 55945–55963. DOI: 10.1109/ACCESS.2024.3389459

Hiriart, T., Castet, J. F., Lafleur, J. M., & Saleh, J. H. (2009). Comparative reliability of GEO, LEO, and MEO satellites. In *Proceedings of the International Astronautical Congress (IAC-09-D.1.1.1)*. Paris, France: International Astronautical Federation (IAF).

Iida, T., & Wakana, H. (2003). Communications satellite systems. In Meyers, R. A. (Ed.), *Encyclopedia of Physical Science and Technology* (3rd ed., pp. 375–408). Academic Press., DOI: 10.1016/B0-12-227410-5/00882-6

Kodheli, O., Lagunas, E., & Giordani, M.. (2020). Satellite communications in the new space era: A survey and future challenges. *IEEE Communications Surveys and Tutorials.*

Lin, Y.. (2024). *Satellite-MEC integration for 6G Internet of Things: Minimal structures, advances, and prospects*. IEEE Open Journal of the Communications Society.

Mahboob, S., & Liu, L. (2024). Revolutionizing future connectivity: A contemporary survey on AI-empowered satellite-based non-terrestrial networks in 6G. *IEEE Communications Surveys and Tutorials, 26*(2), 1279–1321. DOI: 10.1109/COMST.2023.3347145

Mohanta, K., & Al-Rubaye, S. (2024). Towards 6G satellite–terrestrial networks: Analysis of air mobility operations. *Electronics (Basel), 13*(14), 2855. DOI: 10.3390/electronics13142855

Shah, A. F. M. S., Karabulut, M. A., & Rabie, K. (2023). Mission-critical Internet of Things on the 6G network: Services and apps with networking architecture. *TechRxiv Preprint*. DOI: 10.36227/techrxiv.24115869.v1

Sheemar, C. K., ... (2025). Joint communications and sensing for 6G satellite networks: Use cases and challenges. *arXiv Preprint*, arXiv:2501.05243.

. Skosana, S., Mlambo, S., Madiope, T., & Thango, B. (2024). Evaluating wireless network technologies (3G, 4G, 5G).

. Toka, M., et al. (2024). RIS-empowered LEO satellite networks for 6G: Promising usage scenarios and future directions. *IEEE Communications Magazine*.

Torrens, S. A., Petrov, V., & Jornet, J. M. (2024). Modeling interference from millimeter wave and terahertz bands cross-links in low Earth orbit satellite networks for 6G and beyond. *IEEE Journal on Selected Areas in Communications*, *42*(5), 1371–1386. DOI: 10.1109/JSAC.2024.3365894

Ukommi, U., Ubom, E., & Ikpaya, I. (2021). Ground station design for satellite and space technology development. [AJER]. *American Journal of Engineering Research*, *10*(8), 12–19.

Wang, J., Tang, W., Han, Y., Jin, S., Li, X., Wen, C.-K., Cheng, Q., & Cui, T. J. (2021). Interplay between RIS and AI in wireless communications: Fundamentals, architectures, applications, and open research problems. *IEEE Journal on Selected Areas in Communications*, *39*(8), 2271–2288. DOI: 10.1109/JSAC.2021.3087259

Yang, J., Geng, Y., Mao, H., Xiao, Z., Han, Z., & Wu, D. O. (2023). *Satellite-terrestrial integrated network architecture towards 6G with user plane function trimming. In 2023 IEEE Globecom Workshops*. GC Wkshps., DOI: 10.1109/GCWkshps58843.2023.10465214

You, L., Zhu, Y., Qiang, X., Tsinos, C. G., Wang, W., Gao, X., & Ottersten, B. (2024). Ubiquitous integrated sensing and communications for massive MIMO LEO satellite systems. *IEEE Internet of Things Magazine*, *7*(4), 30–35. DOI: 10.1109/IOTM.001.2300201

Zhang, J., Zheng, D., Zhang, Z., Charnas, A., Lin, Z., & Ye, P. D. (2023). Ultrathin InGaO thin film transistors by atomic layer deposition. *IEEE Electron Device Letters*, *44*(2), 273–276. DOI: 10.1109/LED.2022.3233080

Zhang, Z., Xiao, Y., Ma, Z., Xiao, M., Ding, Z., Lei, X., & Poor, H. V. (2019). 6G wireless networks: Vision, requirements, architecture, and key technologies. *IEEE Vehicular Technology Magazine*, *14*(3), 28–41. DOI: 10.1109/MVT.2019.2921208

Zhao, D., Ding, R., & Song, B. (2025). Satellite-assisted 6G wide-area edge intelligence: Dynamics-aware task offloading and resource allocation for remote IoT services. *Science China. Information Sciences*, *68*(2), 122303. DOI: 10.1007/s11432-024-4258-x

Chapter 5
Defining the Role of Innovative AI and Blockchain Technology in 6G Networks:
Current Trends and Furture Research

Snehasis Dey
https://orcid.org/0000-0002-0490-8628
BPUT University, India

ABSTRACT

Artificial Intelligence and Blockchain technology have played vital role in 6G networks. As more research and ideas have intensified in this field it is quite a challenge to design and propose a robust 6G network that is optimized, secured, transparent and efficient in connectivity. Still all stakeholders of this fields are busy in finding right network architecture by adding and verifying different innovative algorithms of AI and Machine learning. Blockchain technology (BCT) provides adequate solution in 6G like secured connection, trusted data accessing and privacy protections. The definite and distinguished role of AI and BCT in 6G network, is still in its search as more and more research intensify in this area. Thus, this chapter dives into the basics of AI and BCT role in 6G networks. Quantifying their design strategies and finding current as well as future research trends in this field is the ultimate findings of this chapter.

DOI: 10.4018/979-8-3373-0568-4.ch005

INTRODUCTION:

The global landscape is presently undergoing a profound metamorphosis characterized by the advent of the intelligent information epoch. The principal sectors associated with human existence, including healthcare, transportation, entertainment, and intelligent urban environments, are anticipated to enhance service quality through superior user experiences. Consequently, the telecommunications infrastructure must satisfy unprecedented service level demands, encompassing ultra-high data transmission rates and substantial traffic volumes, to accommodate significant future applications such as Virtual Reality (VR), holographic communication, and massive Machine Type Communications (mMTC). Though 6G is in its premature stage, a paramount amount of research is going on in this field to address the challenges like resource-constrained mobile devices, higher difficulty in resource management, privacy and security threats, etc. (Dey, S., 2024). To overcome the above challenges, integrating artificial intelligence and blockchain technology in 6G will resolve many problems like security, privacy control, efficiency enhancement, cost optimization, connectivity improvement, etc. 6G is envisioned to provide seamless connectivity, space-air-ground integrated networking (SAGIN), and higher quality security by deploying AI and BCT technology together. AI is a best-fit technology that makes the 6G network robust, entirely globalized, processing-wise effective, and gaining more flexibility through continuous learning. AI supports and optimizes different data that is managed and processed in different layers of communication in 6G, like the physical, network, and MAC layers, etc. AI conceives higher accuracy in data management, network management, resource allocation, traffic handling, and secured connections by integrating different machine learning schemes like supervised, unsupervised, and reinforced learning schemes (Dey, S., 2023 & Dey, S., 2024). The use of AI and its subsequent subset technologies like machine learning and deep learning at the application layer and network layer of 6G makes the network more intelligent and automated. Algorithms like support vector machine (SVM), neural networks (NNs), random forest (RF), Q-learning, etc., are quite useful in 6G networks. They are useful in optimization, resource management, traffic management, and enhancement of efficiency, etc., in 6G networks. Alternatively, BCT is an emerging technology that encapsulates different technologies like point-to-point transmission, distributed storage, and encryption algorithmsetc. 6G networks in current times, which encompass ultra-high peak data rates, ultra-low latency, ultra-high reliability, ultra-low energy consumption, and seamless connectivity, provide facets such as system security, data privacy, sustainability, scalability, and additional dimensions vulnerable to numerous risks and challenges. Blockchain technology is very essential due to its distributed network architecture, intelligent node consensus, and smart contracts. Blockchain and 6G networks will together provide a safe, intelligent, and efficient realization of the 6G network vision for a secured environment. AI and BCT together will ensure a drastic enhancement in performance, network management, and secure, trusted mobile networks and services. These two technologies both work hand in hand on data, as AI works on trained intelligence data while BCT mostly works on data storage methods. So, combining their technological sum into the 6G wireless network will make it as secure, transparent, trusted, and technologically enhanced as a network. Although the research on integrating blockchain and AI for 6G networks and their proper utilization is still in its infancy, it is obvious that blockchain and AI will significantly enhance the performance of various services and applications in 6G networks in every possible prospect.

LITERATURE SURVEY:

In this section, related works are studied and analysed regarding AI and BCT integration and utilization in 6G wireless network. This survey has been summarized in a tabular form as given below.

Table 1. Related studies in this field.

Article	AI and BCT integration	Key findings	Key technology
Miglani, A., 2021	Limited	• Blockchain management in 5G and beyond. • ML for IoT environment.	BCT, ML, IoT
Wo et al., 2021	Limited	• Blockchain and Deep reinforced learning for industrial IoT.	BCT, DRL, IoT.
Shafay et al.,2023	No	• Blockchain and different ML algorithms applications.	BCT, DL, ML, FL
Wang et al.,2021	No	• Blockchain application for wireless networks.	BCT, RAN
Dey, S.,2023	Limited	• AI and ML algorithms for B5G/6G networks	AI,SVM,RF,CNN
Zuo, Y et al., 2023	Yes	• AI and BCT applications for IoT smart applications. • Analysis on smart health care, smart transportation, smart grid, and UAV by AI and BCT integration.	AI,BCT,IoT
Dey, S.,2024	Yes	• AI and BCT application for next generation networks • Excess AI utilization etc	AI, BCT, SAGIN scenarios
Dey, S. et al.,2023	Limited	• Different ML algorithms for B5G/6G networks	SVM,RF,CNN,ANN

continued on following page

Table 1. Continued

Article	AI and BCT integration	Key findings	Key technology
Moharana, B.et al.,2023	Limited	• Classical ML algorithm utilization	AI,ANN,CNN,
Sahoo, B. B.et al.,2024	Yes	• AI and ML for proper communication and security integration	AI.RF,SVM
Kumar, S.et al.,2024	Limited	• AI and blockchain integration in business and security enhancement	AI,BCT
Chowdhury, R.H. 2024	Yes	• AI and BCT for security analysis	AI,BCT

Proposed work and contribution:

As described in Table 1, it is evident that a lot of research is going on in this field nowadays, but a huge research gap is followed with that too. Some of the research gaps are listed below on which this chapter is based, and it tries to dive into that as it contributes towards 6G wireless networks.

- A vivid study must be done to clarify the utilization of technology, AI for BCT, or BCT for AI.
- A systematic study must be done on AI- and BCT-integrated 6G wireless networks.
- AI and BCT integration in 6G IoT intelligent applications.
- There is a huge research gap in addressing the securities issues and subsequent solutions.

The above research gap motivates carrying out enough study on the above-stated fields, and hence the chapter dives into the potential directions of these areas. The chapter carries out a study on the basics of AI and BCT integration and subsequent advantages in the 6G wireless networks. It also studies the technological utilization perspective of these two integrations. It further specifies the AI and BCT integration role in IoT applications like smart healthcare, smart transportation, smart cities, etc. It deeply addresses the securities issues, current research trends, and future research ahead in this field.

Figure 1. Research gap and subsequent contribution of the study

Figure 1 describes the different research gaps and the chapter contributions in this study. It has been outlined as three main perspectives: application, maintenance, and research perspective.

Utilization of Technology: (AI for BCT and BCT for AI)

The motivation for integrating AI and blockchain for 6G wireless communication comes when the proper utilization of these two technologies is analysed deeply. As BCT and AI will solve many constraints that remain unsolved in wireless communication, their integration will foster a wide research direction in the said field. Blockchain technology has the distinguished features of decentralization, anonymity, openness and transparency, and immutability (Miglani, A., 2021). In this regard it is quite essential for BCT to improve its standard in the horizon of security, scalability, energy consumption, etc. AI technology views blockchain as a reliable platform capable of establishing a secure, unchangeable, and widely distributed system for AI operations. In this reliably secured system, users simply trust each other and share data without the need for third-party involvement or oversight. Based on the extensive and trustworthy data set, the agent's decision-making accuracy is enhanced. From the BCT for AI perspective, the utilization of technology is largely dealt with in the section as listed below:

- Data management
- Decentralized intelligence
- Privacy control
- Efficiency enhancement
- Security assurance

- Scalability is related to transaction speed and transaction throughput.

Similarly, from the technological utilization perspective of AI for BCT there are some key applications which are listed as follows:

- Energy consumption
- Smart and Intelligent decision making
- Faster and optimized data set
- Security and privacy control
- Scalability

Figure 2. Utilization of technology in 6G networks by integrating AI and BCT

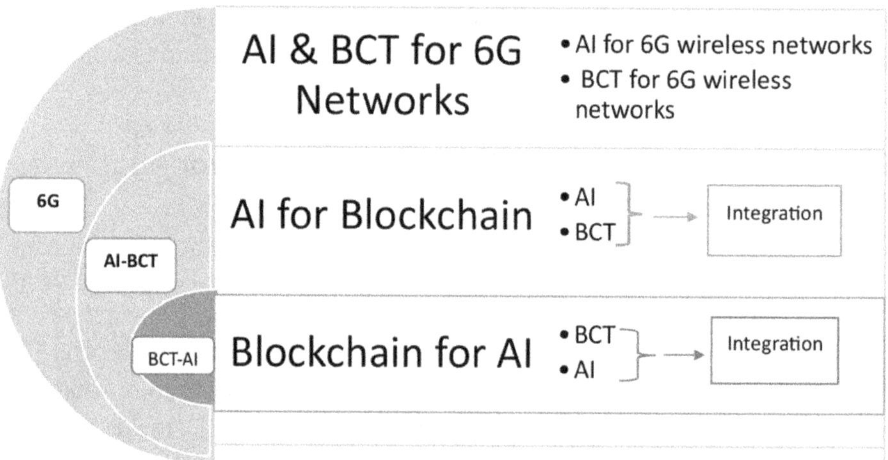

As figure 2 describes, AI and BCT can be very beneficial when both are implemented for beyond 5G and 6G communication. They can be very productive in managing different issues in future communications, like spectrum management, content caching, security enhancement, privacy control, etc. Blockchain can foster a secure and decentralized resource-sharing environment that strengthens wireless networks, while AI can manage proper utilization of optimization techniques to solve uncertainty and time-varying complexities in wireless networks. BCT makes 6G more secure and provides a safe and robust communication ecosystem (Wo et al., 2021). AI will enhance accuracy in 6G, thus providing more reliable network topology and global connectivity that supports SAGIN (space-air-ground integrated network) scenarios.

Similarly, if we consider precisely ML for blockchain, then the applications will be vast, like attack prevention, correct effective decision-making, anonymity reduction, resource management, secure access control, etc. In a blockchain environment, ML can resolve different complex issues and uncertainty modalities by correct analysis of data through ML schemes (Shafay et al., 2023).

Machine learning algorithms, such as support vector machines (SVM), neural networks (NNs), random forests (RF), and Q-learning, is pivotal in the advancement and enhancement of 6G networks. These algorithms are fundamental to the improvement of network efficiency, the minimization of energy consumption, and the facilitation of adaptive signal processing. They enable the evolution from conventional network paradigms to more intelligent, efficient, and scalable frameworks. The incorporation of these machine learning methodologies into 6G networks underpins dynamic network slicing, adaptive signal processing, and large-scale optimization, which are crucial for addressing the multifaceted and intricate demands of forthcoming wireless communication systems. The role of ML in 6G wireless communication is very vital and it can be described as follows:

- Machine learning algorithms, including neural networks (NNs) and random forests (RF), are employed to enhance network efficacy and diminish computational expenditures, factors that are paramount within the densely populated and heterogeneous contexts of 6G networks.
- Specific techniques like SVM and Q-learning enable adaptive signal processing, allowing 6G networks to adjust to rapidly changing vast global communication environments, thereby ensuring reliable and efficient communication.
- Deep Reinforcement Learning (DRL) is basically used for stochastic optimization; it helps in managing the dynamic and complex nature of 6G networks.
- SVM, RF, ANN, CNN are mostly helpful in optimization and efficiency enhancement in 6G networks while BCT is used for security enhancement.

Phenomenon of AI and Blockchain Integration for 6G Wireless Communications:

The integration of AI and blockchain will definitely boost up the B5G/6G communication by several ways:

- Smart healthcare application
- Security and privacy control
- Content caching
- Computational offloading
- Smart grid application

- Spectrum management
- Smart transportation etc

Figure 3. AI-BCT applications in 6G wireless networks

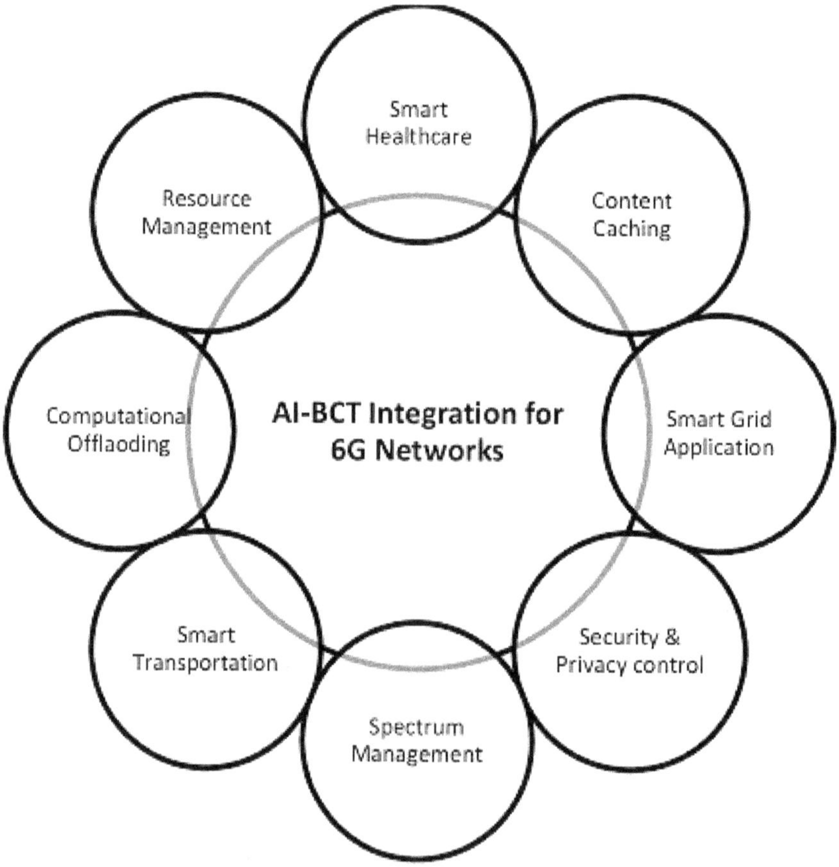

Figure 3 shows artificial intelligence and blockchain technology integration for 6G networks and their respective applications. They are very useful in some of the most important sectors of 6G networks, like spectrum management, security, privacy control, etc. The motivation for the integration of AI and blockchain for 6G wireless networks is due to their sufficient technological solutions, like energy consumption, intelligent decision-making capabilities, and mainly security and privacy control, etc. These two technologies can complement each other to solve the higher performance requirements and practical implications in 6G wireless networks. As shown in the figure, smart transportation refers to the full application of technology like big data, AI/ML, IoT, blockchain, etc. These technologies ensure safe transportation, smart traffic management systems, and enhanced operational efficiency. At present, the process of vehicle positioning is beset by issues pertaining to insufficient accuracy and network congestion during data transmission. In order to mitigate these issues, a co-localization framework for smart vehicles has been proposed that is based on blockchain technology and deep neural networks. Computing resources are one of the essential assets in 6G wireless communications. Merging blockchain and AI can distribute and transfer computing resources in a more effective manner. Blockchain and AI represent two encouraging facilitating technologies for addressing spectrum management challenges. Blockchain can be utilized in spectrum auctions, enhancing security and decentralization while also lowering spectrum management expenses. Conversely, AI technologies, characterized by DL and DRL, are extremely capable and can autonomously analyze user behavior trends or subsequently make optimal choices for users. By employing AI, activities like users' mobility and data/computing traffic can be forecasted dynamically, thereby optimizing the distribution of wireless resources.

Content caching can facilitate the localized response to specific user inquiries, diminish the latency associated with the transmission of the requested material, enhance the overall user experience, and equilibrate the network load.

Blockchain ensures secured data for both retrieval and accessing. Therefore, disclosure of data is difficult, and there is a secure protocol for accessing the data also. The integration of federal learning with blockchain can be made to enhance security and privacy for data during transmission (Wang et al., 2021). IoT becomes a unique component of future wireless communication, and it binds machine, mechanism, and human at any time and any place. AI and BCT integration have maximized the utilization of IoT devices in 6G networks and ensured many growths in fields like smart healthcare, smart transportation, smart grids, etc. AI can optimize network performance in 6G through predictive analysis while blockchain mitigates cyber threats, hacking, and data disclosure in a 6G-enabled platform. The establishment of an intelligent grid offers a robust assurance for enhancing the associated functionalities of smart cities, thereby further expediting the advancement of urban intelligence (Dey, S.,2014). AI can monitor the electricity consumption in smart cities and subsequently enhance the energy efficiency, while blockchain can provide security and transparency for the ultimate power management system. Consequently, to meet the basic requirements of 6G wireless communication networks, AI and BCT integration is effective and mandatory. It will definitely adhere to the 6G network's vision, like higher connectivity, higher transparency, higher intelligence, and a secured environment.

Key Technologies and Algorithms in AI-BCT integrated 6G Wireless networks:

This section describes some important technologies and algorithms which are very necessary for 6G wireless platforms. These technologies are the building blocks of AI-BCT integration for 6G wireless networks.

Figure 4. Three most important technologies (3 S's) in AI-BCT integrated 6G networks.

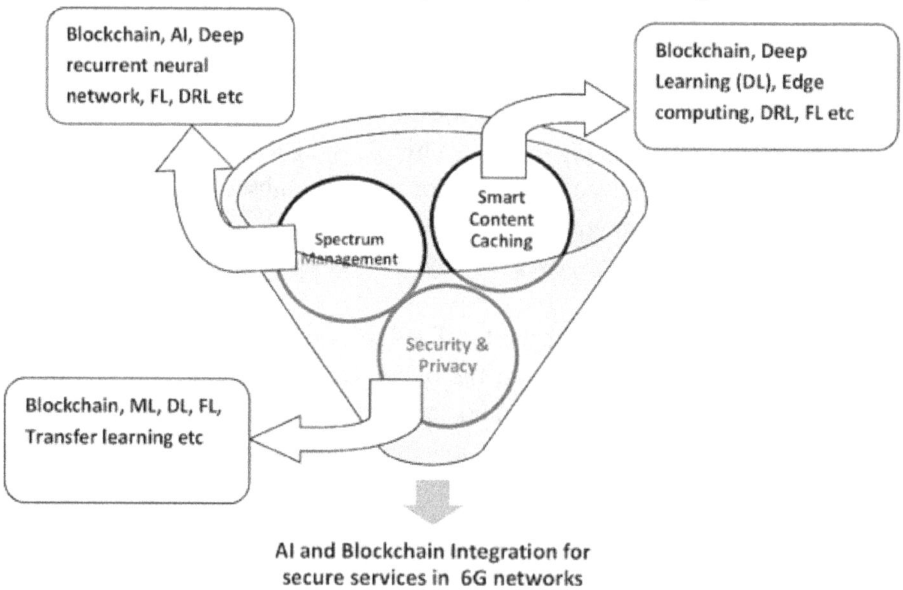

As shown in figure 4, the three most important technologies that make AI-BCT-integrated 6G networks robust are given here:

- Spectrum management (S1) through deep RNN, federal learning, and deep reinforced learning, etc.
- Smart content caching (S2) through permissioned blockchain, edge computing, DRL, etc.
- Security and privacy (S3) through algorithms like ML, DL, FL and transfer learning, etc.

Different content caching schemes are adopted to provide effectiveness in 6G wireless communication channels by the integration of algorithms like DRL, FL, and blockchain. (Cui et al., 2020, and Zhang et al., 2020). Similarly, the spectrum management and security in 6G networks are based on blockchain, RNN, FL, and ML schemes (Lu et al., 2020, and Kumar et al., 2023). 6G wireless communication has tremendous connectivity and security through the implementations of AI/ML and blockchain technologies. These technologies provide stability and security in 6G networks. 6G needs to provide robust security mechanisms, identity authentication, secure transmission, and higher integrity of data. The vision of 6G is to build an intelligent network with edge computing, and this can be achieved through intelligent decision-making capabilities of AI and real-time processing through blockchain technology for improved performance and proper network management with reduced latency. Different AI/ML algorithms are quite useful in this context, like deep learning, CNN, RNN, FL, ANN, etc. (Moharana, B.et al., 2023) (Dey, S. et al.,2023).

AI-BCT Integrated 6G Wireless Network Requirements:

To achieve the required and substantially enhanced performance in 6G wireless networks, AI-BCT integration needs to fulfil some key requirements in 6G networks, and these are given as follows:

- Low latency to ensure fast data transmission and processing capabilities.
- Large-scale connectivity, or massive interconnection and data exchange.
- Higher amount of reliability and network robustness.
- Robust cognitive capabilities and flexibility in response to varying circumstances.
- Higher bandwidth requirement.

Figure 5. Typical resource management framework through blockchain and AI/ML.

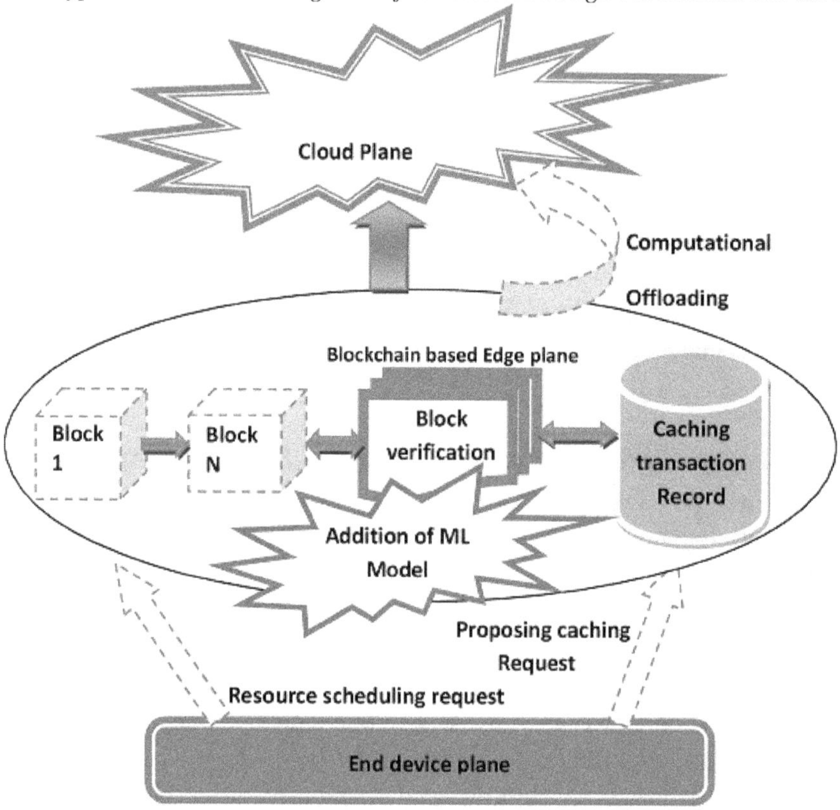

As shown in figure 5, a typical resource management framework has been designed where the designated structure from end plane to cloud plane is provided with linkage between ML agents and blockchain technologies. Blockchain will look after the security aspects of each block through block verification methodologies, and ML will guide the catching, pairing, and catching requests, etc. AI and BCT-integrated 6G networks will have to meet some basic network requirements as proposed above, like low latency, massive connectivity, global coverage, higher bandwidth, network robustness, and flexibilities in response to different circumstances through intelligence, etc (Dey, S. et al.,2024).

Challenges and Practical Implications in Integrating AI and BCT for Smart IoT Applications

- Blockchain standardization and proper regulations are yet to be finalized in connection with integration for smart applications.

- Huge challenges lie in storing data because each node of the blockchain network keeps a copy of every transaction of the network.
- The use of permissioned blockchain limits the access of an enormous amount of data that can be required for an ML system to process accurate decision-making in 6G networks.
- Private blockchain can limit the exposure of large amounts of data, which is obviously necessary for an ML model to perform accurate decision-making.
- B5G and 6G represent paradigms of heterogeneous networks specifically crafted to accommodate a diverse array of IoT devices. The substantial volume of data produced by these devices may impose significant demands on machine learning models utilized for decision-making, consequently resulting in constrained performance. Within this framework, blockchain technology has the potential to address security concerns to a certain degree; however, the prevailing issues related to network performance will persist as a challenge and a big issue for upcoming research.
- The efficacy and practicality of blockchain- and AI-facilitated wireless communication systems remain to be substantiated through extensive empirical evaluation within substantial wireless communication network deployments.
- There is a huge task to deal with the contradiction between the certainty of smart contracts and the randomness of AI algorithms for 6G wireless networks.
- The utilization of a blockchain-oriented storage methodology presents advantages for the processes of data dissemination and validation; however, it is not favourable for the safeguarding of data privacy.

Current Trends and Future Research Directions

6G is in its early stage, and therefore the innovative technologies involved in 6G must be projected through rigorous testing and evaluations. The current technological advances in 6G wireless networks are through AI/ML and blockchain technologies, but there is a huge research scope that lies in this particular field. The present study may define the roles of AI and BCT in a precise way, but more studies may be focused on the performance indicators, stability, security, etc. There is huge research scope in the field of scalability and energy efficiency in blockchain. Exploration on detailed study related to techniques of security and privacy control is also a booming research field. The fusion of blockchain and artificial intelligence for the next generation of 6G networks remains in its nascent phase, and forthcoming investigations should focus on dismantling technical obstacles and ambiguities, fostering synergistic growth and cohesion, and delving into real-world utilizations. The different future research directions are listed as below:

- Effective wireless network construction
- Transparent data sharing
- Standard database for data collection and data processing
- Key performance indicator (KPI) for standardization
- Decentralization methodologies and smart contracts
- Scalabilities and hardware breakthroughs, etc.

As shown in below figure 6, there are huge research prospects in this field, like standardization of databases for proper processing and its collections, the construction and designing of effective wireless networks, decentralization methodologies, smart contracts, etc. The 6G network brings forth a symphony of interconnected intelligence by harnessing the power of AI functionalities while simultaneously embracing a centralized network design, which exposes it to the risk of cyber intrusions. Furthermore, the 6G network is tasked with gathering an extensive trove of user data for training, utilizing billions of devices as conduits. This treasure trove of training data is rich with personal details, making it all too easy for AI to inadvertently cause leaks of user privacy. By employing distributed technology to craft AI-infused 6G network frameworks, a decentralized, secure, and trustworthy system can come to fruition. Rather than sending all data to a cloud computing hub, distributed technology processes information right where it originates, which can significantly mitigate the risk of privacy breaches to a considerable degree.

Figure 6. Future Research Directions in AI-BCT Integrated 6G Wireless networks

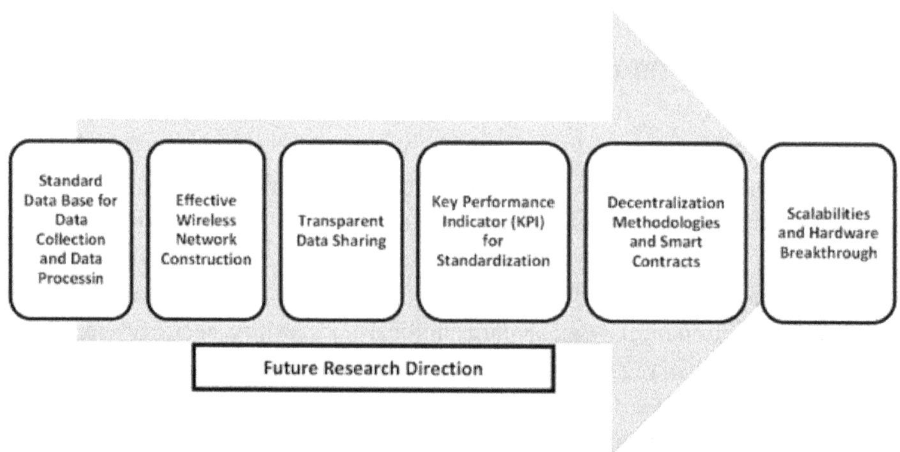

Specific Areas for Future Research:

- The investigation may concentrate on the utilization of distributed artificial intelligence to augment security protocols within sixth-generation networks, thereby safeguarding data privacy through the implementation of decentralized frameworks.
- Future investigations may examine artificial intelligence-based algorithms for the dynamic allocation of spectrum, thereby enhancing resource efficiency within heterogeneous network environments.
- Research may be directed towards blockchain's role in efficient content delivery and caching strategies which can optimize network performance.
- Future research areas can also include addressing open issues in integrating AI and blockchain for enhanced security, privacy, and efficiency in 6G networks that will provide global coverage.
- Research also can be explored in the direction of AI-BCT applications in spectrum management, computation allocation, content caching, and IoT smart applications etc.

CONCLUSION:

Artificial intelligence and blockchain technology provide enough stability, flexibility, security, and growth in 6G wireless networks in the field of network management, spectrum management, connectivity, smart content caching, etc. As 6G is designed to provide global connectivity with a lesser value of latency and a minimized level of security concern, there is always research scope to address these. In this study, different previous research gaps are addressed, like clarification of utilization of technologies in 6G wireless networks, AI and BCT systematic integration procedures, and open challenges in this integrated networking, etc. This research also dives into the practical implication issues and current trends in the AI-BCT-integrated 6G wireless networks.

REFERENCES:

Chowdhury, R. H. (2024). *Blockchain and AI: Driving the future of data security and business intelligence*. World Journal of Advanced Research and Reviews. DOI: 10.1201/9781003162018

Dey, S. (2014). Performance Analysis of LEO Satellite (Sky Bridge) For Mobile Terminal with Varying Implementation Margin. *IJLTET*, *4*(2), 191–196.

Dey, S. (2024). Phenomenon of Excess of Artificial Intelligence: Quantifying the Native AI, Its Leverages in 5G/6G and Beyond. In *Radar and RF Front End System Designs for Wireless Systems* (pp. 245–274). IGI Global. DOI: 10.4018/979-8-3693-0916-2.ch010

Dey, S.. (2023), "Play Store App Analysis & Rating Prediction Using Classical ML Models & Artificial Neural Network," *7th International Conference on Computing, Communication, Control and Automation (ICCUBEA)*, Pune, India, 2023, pp. 1-5, DOI: 10.1109/ICCUBEA58933.2023.10391960

Dey, S., De, U. C., Dash, B. B., Patra, S. S., Samant, T., & Banerjee, S. (2024, October). Fine-Tuning Prophet model for application in Agro-Industry to forecast Pesticide consumption. In *2024 IEEE 1st International Conference on Green Industrial Electronics and Sustainable Technologies (GIEST)* (pp. 1-5). IEEE. DOI: 10.1109/GIEST62955.2024.10960129

Dey, S., Mohapatra, D., & Archana, S. D. R. P. (2014). An approach to calculate the performance and link budget of leo satellite (iridium) for communication operated at frequency range (1650–1550) mhz. *International Journal of Latest Trends in Engineering & Technology : IJLTET*, *4*(4), 96–103.

Dey, S., Moharana, B., De, U. C., Samant, T., Behera, T. M., & Banerjee, S. (2024, March). Search Engine for QnA using Distributed Inverted Index System. In *2024 3rd International Conference for Innovation in Technology (INOCON)* (pp. 1-4). IEEE. DOI: 10.1109/INOCON60754.2024.10511792

Dey, S., Moharana, B., De, U. C., Samant, T., Behera, T. M., & Banerjee, S. (2024), "Search Engine for QnA using Distributed Inverted Index System," *3rd International Conference for Innovation in Technology (INOCON)*, Bangalore, India, 2024, pp. 1-4, DOI: 10.1109/INOCON60754.2024.10511792

Dey, S., Panda, A. K., & Pati, C. (2023). Unlocking the potential of machine learning and deep learning algorithms in recent communication: AI is the best revolutionary tool in the current era. *CPPPT*, *23*(2), 2794–2805.

Kumar, S., Lim, W. M., Sivarajah, U., & Kaur, J. (2023). Artificial Intelligence and Blockchain Integration in Business: Trends from a Bibliometric-Content Analysis. *Information systems frontiers: a journal of research and innovation, 25*(2), 871–8

Miglani, A., & Kumar, N. (2021). Blockchain management and machine learning adaptation for IoT environment in 5G and beyond networks: A systematic review. Computer Communications, 178, 37–63. doi: . https://doi.org/DOI: 10.1016/j.comcom.2021.07.00996

Moharana, B., Biswal, B. B., Dey, S., Rath, M. K., & Banerjee, S. (2023, August). Play Store App Analysis & Rating Prediction using Classical ML Models & Artificial Neural Network. In *2023 7th International Conference on Computing, Communication, Control and Automation (ICCUBEA)* (pp. 1-5). IEEE. DOI: 10.1109/ICCUBEA58933.2023.10391960

Sahoo, B. B., & Dey, S. (2024). SVM and RF Based Performance Enhancement in Organization: A Study on KGI, Odisha and its Organizational Growth. *Journal of Engineering Research and Reports*, *26*(6), 190–197. DOI: 10.9734/jerr/2024/v26i61173

Shafay, M., Ahmad, R. W., Salah, K., Yaqoob, I., Jayaraman, R., & Omar, M. (2023). Blockchain for deep learning: Review and open challenges. *Cluster Computing*, *26*(1), 197–221. DOI: 10.1007/s10586-022-03582-7 PMID: 35309043

Zuo, Y., Guo, J., Gao, N., Zhu, Y., Jin, S., & Li, X. (2023). A Survey of Blockchain and Artificial Intelligence for 6G Wireless Communications. *IEEE Communications Surveys and Tutorials*, *25*(4), 2494–2528. DOI: 10.1109/COMST.2023.3315374

Chapter 6
Blockchain Approach for Real-Time Authentication in 6G Machine-to-Machine Communication

Manikandan Arunachalam
https://orcid.org/0000-0003-0461-2859
Amrita School of Engineering, Amrita Vishwa Vidyapeetham, Amritapuri, India

P. Sidharth
Amrita School of Engineering, Amrita Vishwa Vidyapeetham, Amritapuri, India

Sooraj S. Nair
Amrita School of Engineering, Amrita Vishwa Vidyapeetham, Amritapuri, India

Nikhil Rajiv
Amrita School of Engineering, Amrita Vishwa Vidyapeetham, Amritapuri, India

Rakesh Thoppaen Suresh Babu
https://orcid.org/0009-0003-2671-4618
Fiserv Inc, Alpharetta, USA

ABSTRACT

The combination of blockchain with 6G networks portrays a transformative approach to address the challenges faced in real-time authentication in Machine-to-Machine (M2M) communication. Since 6G networks directly connect huge, incomparable devices with ultra-low latency, high reliability, and improved security, the traditional centralized authentication mechanisms face challenges with scalability, efficiency, and reluctance to cyber threats. It silhouettes a workflow for real-time device authen-

DOI: 10.4018/979-8-3373-0568-4.ch006

tication, highlighting the role of cryptographic identities, tamper of proof ledgers, and automated decision-making mechanisms in preventing spoofing, replay attacks, and other security vulnerabilities. This chapter also discuss the performance metrics and potential use cases, such as industrial automation, autonomous vehicles and IoT-based healthcare systems. By addressing the technical aspects of blockchain with 6G networks, this chapter aims to demonstrate its potential as a foundation to ensure secure, seamless communication in the next generation of M2M systems.

1. INTRODUCTION

The introduction of 6G networks confirms to modernize connectivity, suggesting ultra-low latency, vast device density, and exceptional data rates. In such a prototype, M2M communication arises as a foundation for enabling fully autonomous systems, including smart cities, Industry 4.0, autonomous vehicles and healthcare monitoring (Banafaa et al., 2023; Guo et al., 2021; Murroni et al., 2023). However, as the dependence on M2M technologies spreads, so does the consequence of authentication mechanisms to guarantee secure and trustworthy data exchanges (Prabhakara Rao & Satyanarayana Murthy, 2023). Traditional centralized authentication models have significant challenges in meeting real-time demands and scalability requirements of 6G networks. Blockchain technology, with its decentralized and tamper-proof architecture, proposes a transformative approach to address these challenges (Dong et al., 2023; Thilakavathy et al., 2023). By leveraging blockchain, it becomes possible to validate M2M communication in real time while maintaining high security, scalability, and fault tolerance. M2M communication refers to the direct exchange of data between connected devices without human intervention (Manikandan et al., 2024). In the 6G era, M2M communication is expected be autonomous, intelligent and real-time, driven by the advancements in AI and edge computing. Autonomous vehicles will communicate each other under Vehicle -to-Vehicle (V2V) and with infrastructure under V2I to ensure the road safety and efficiency (Swathi et al., 2022). Devices integrated under smart cities, surveillance systems, and waste management will exchange data in real time to optimize resource usage and security. Internet of Things (IoT) enabled medical devices will communicate autonomously to extend remote patient monitoring and emergency response services (Islam et al., 2023; Osama et al., 2023). Machines automated in industry will communicate each other to optimize the production process with minimal human support and intervention. Despite its tremendous potential, M2M communication faces significant security challenges, especially authentication and access control. Conventional authentication approaches introduce latency and computational overhead, making them unsuitable for real-time M2M interactions (Ahuja & Bala, 2023; Patwary et al., 2021). This is where blockchain can provide a decentralized effective solution (Bilami & Lorenz, 2022). Blockchain is a distributed ledger technology that ensures security, transparency, and immutability of data without a support from central authority (Javaid et al., 2022). By utilizing cryptographic mechanisms such as hash functions, digital signatures and consensus algorithms, blockchain can facilitate secure and tamper-resistant authentication mechanisms for M2M communication (Ma et al., 2024; Rao et al., 2023). The key features of blockchain that make it suitable for 6G are decentralization, immutability, transparency, trust, and smart contracts (Bhattacharya et al., 2022; Kumari et al., 2021). In blockchain based authentication framework for 6G M2M communication, devices authenticate themselves using cryptographic keys and store authentication records on a distributed ledger (Kazmi et al., 2023; A. S. Khan, Yahya, et al., 2023). Here, each device generates a cryptographic key pair and registers its identity on the blockchain (A. H. Khan et al., 2022; Soni & Singh, 2023). Devices mutually verify their identities using digital signature and blockchain-stored credentials. Authentication data is recorded as a blockchain transaction, ensuring transparency and traceability (Jahid et al., 2023; J. Wang et al., 2021). Smart contracts enforce predefined security policies and grant or deny access based on authentication status. With this, blockchain eliminates the risk of identity spoofing, replay attacks, and unauthorized access by ensuring data and immutability. By decentralizing the authentication, blockchain reduces the reliance on central servers, speeding up authentication processes in real-time M2M applications (A. S. Khan, Sattar, et al., 2023). Moreover, when the number of connected devices will increase based on the demand, blockchain provides a scalable solution that can accommodate massive authentication transactions without performance degradation. Despite its potential, implementing blockchain based authentication in 6G M2M communication faces several challenges also. This chapter explores how blockchain can effectively employed for real-time authentication in the context of 6G- enabled M2M communication and its challenges.

2. BACKGROUND AND RELATED WORK

The advancement of wireless communication systems from 2G to 5G has largely concentrating on improving connectivity and speed. However, 6G networks, estimated to be adopted by the 2030s, aim to introduce modern capabilities such as extreme network compaction, AI powered resource management, and quantum-level security (Henrique & Prasad, 2021; Jiang et al., 2021). Among these advancements, M2M communication- where devices autonomously interchange data without human intervention plays critical role in realizing the vision of persistent connectivity. Despite its potential, M2M communication presents unique security challenges, including device impersonation, data tempering, and denial-of-service (DoS) attacks (Arunachalam et al., 2025). These challenges impose robust authentication mechanisms that can operate flawlessly in high lively environments (Arunodhai et al., 2024). Traditional security models, typically centralized, are ill-suited for the dispersed nature of M2M networks in 6G. For example, reliance on central servers' pioneers' latency, creates single points of failure, and limits scalability. Blockchain, a decentralized registered technology, has gained significant attention as promising alternative. With its consensus mechanisms and absolute record-keeping, blockchain offers a scattered framework capable of modifying the limitations of centralized models while providing improved precision and security (Yue & Shyu, 2024). Several studies have demonstrated the limitations of traditional authentication models, highlighting concerns related to centralized control, latency, and vulnerability to cyber threats (Wenhua et al., 2023). Research have suggested various cryptographic solutions, such as Public Key Infrastructure (PKI) and certificate-based authentication, however, these approaches attempt scalability issues and dependency on trusted third parties, which an inadequate for the dynamic and large-scale nature of M2M communication (S. Khan et al., 2023). Blockchain technology with its decentralized ledger and consensus mechanisms have been investigated as a potential alternative to traditional authentication systems. Studies have shown that the blockchain based authentication can provide enhanced security through immutability, transparency, and resistance to attacks such as identity spoofing and replay attacks (Almarri & Aljughaiman, 2024). Various blockchain architectures have been proposed for authentication in different network scenarios including blockchain permissioned and permissionless blockchains. Permissioned blockchains, such as Hyperledger Fabric, have been explored for their ability to provide efficient and controlled access to authentication records, whereas public blockchains, such as Ethereum, offer greater decentralization but with trade-offs in terms of transaction and speed and energy consumption (Esmaili & Christensen, 2025; Solat et al., 2021). Smart contracts have also been leveraged to automate authentication procedures, reducing human intervention and enhancing trust in M2M communications. Consensus algorithms play a critical role in blockchain-based authentication, studies have analysed the suitability of mechanisms like Proof-of Work (PoW), Proof-of-Stake (PoS), and Byzantine Fault tolerance (BFT)for M2M authentication, balancing security, efficiency, and energy consumption (Liu et al., 2022; Rebello et al., 2022). Several hybrid approaches have been discussed, integrating blockchain with AI-driven anomaly detection and edge computing to improve real-time authentication and mitigate latency issues (Chukwuemeka Nwachukwu et al., 2024). Additionally, light weight blockchain frameworks have been explored to accommodate to resource constraints of IoT devices in 6G networks (Qian et al., 2023). Research was proposed to investigate the potential of integrating zero-knowledge proofs and homomorphic encryption to enhance privacy in blockchain based authentication models(Dhokrat et al., 2024; Diro et al., 2023, 2024; A. Pathak et al., 2024). Experimental studies and simulations have demonstrated the feasibility of blockchain in M2M authentication, showcasing reduced authentication delays, improved scalability, and resilience against cyber threats compared to traditional models(Jain et al., 2024). However, challenges remain in optimizing storage requirements, reducing computational overhead and ensuring seamless interoperability between different blockchain networks and authentication frameworks. Future research direction includes the development of more energy efficient blockchain consensus protocols, integration with federated learning for adaptive security models, and exploring quantum-resistant cryptographic techniques to future proof authentication systems in 6G networks. By addressing these challenges, blockchain technology, holds significant promise in revolutionizing real-time authentication for M2M communications, paving the way for more secure and efficient autonomous interactions.

3. PROPOSED BLOCKCHAIN-BASED AUTHENTICATION FRAMEWORK

3.1. System Architecture and Design

This section discusses the customized architecture of a blockchain-based authentication framework business for the particular needs of 6G Machine-to-Machine (M2M) communication. The framework is targeted at meeting the fundamental characteristics of expanded scale and coverage, reduced latency, augmented security, and interoperability necessary for the proper functioning of massive and scattered M2M networks. The structure accommodates a layered model supplemented with the particular kind of node deployment and selected blockchain architecture, which ensures comprehensive coverage of the authentication requirements.

3.1.1 Core Architectural Layers

The architecture is structured in a layered fashion (as shown in Fig 1), having specific roles and responsibilities in various functional blocks of the architecture. The Device/Endpoint Layer captures the first point of contact which includes a wide range of sensors, IoTs, and other M2M end devices.

Figure 1. Layered system architecture

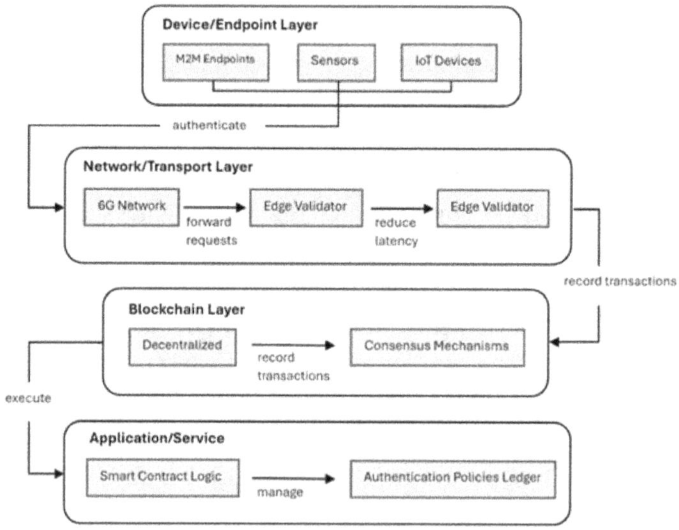

These devices are usually resource-constrained, and thus use lightweight cryptographic techniques, such as Elliptic Curve Cryptography (ECC) and short-life ephemeral keys for signing and verifying identity credentials before joining the network. Next in the stack, the Network or Transport Layer incorporates advanced functionality of the 6G network, such as routing, slicing, and ultra-low latency services, which reduce latency during authentication. Edge Validator Nodes or Local Blockchain Nodes located within the vicinity of device clusters facilitate the receiving of authentication requests to augment network utilization and lower latency. The third layer, or the Blockchain Layer, forms the principal layer of the architecture, which supports the decentralized ledger and consensus algorithms. It can either assume a permissioned or permissionless architecture. All operations such as the device onboarding, session key requests and policy changes are cryptographically validated and stored as an immutable log for data integrity and non-repudiation measures. This serves as the final layer - The application or Service Layer which contains the smart contracts, manages authentication policies, and implements high-level use cases. With this layer, combined with AI reading on-chain data, security is escalated as the ability to change device privileges dynamically is enabled.

3.1.2 Node Deployment Strategies

This framework enables the use of two variable methods of node deployment which cater for certain environmental characteristics, considering various deployment scenarios of M2M networks. One of them is an Edge-Centric Design which is particularly suitable in large-scale networks where various IoT devices exist (Harjula et al., 2020). Here, micro blockchains or sidechains are placed close to device clusters to allow for minimal latency and maximum network throughput (Rožman et al., 2021). These decentralised architectures facilitate enhanced authentication processing speed within each cluster, and the corresponding state changes are anchored in a more global ledger to enhance interoperability between clusters (Khashan & Khafajah, 2023). Otherwise, the Clustered Node Approach groups validator nodes that perform authentication per a selection of the M2M domain or a subset of it. This approach enables logical device function-based clustering or physical proximity-based clustering, which gives each cluster the freedom to implement consensus techniques best suited to its trust model and network environment. A globally valid view is maintained by cross-validating final states from cluster heads.

3.1.3 Blockchain Implementation Choices

The set framework describes certain blockchains as Moderated Blockchains, highly preferable to stringent applications as they Limit access to the permissioned consensus mechanism, which has its advantages. These systems function only when approved institutions set up the network consensus nodes, which significantly reduces the chances of malicious activities being performed, resulting in optimal performance and high operational control. Contrary to this, Permissionless Blockchains are ideal for large scale public IoT subnetworks and participation is allowed without any centralized control (Mukhopadhyay & Vinayaka, 2021). There is complexity added to security audits, and incentives for developers along with handling of larger volumes of transactions, but they are certainly more flexible. To solve the issue of resource intensiveness, more eco-friendly consensus mechanisms such as Proof-of-Stake (PoS) are greatly preferred over Proof-of –Work, but environment 6G may depend on masked partial identity-oriented solutions.

3.1.4 Advantages over Traditional PKI Systems

This approach based on Blockchain technology has clear advantages over the ever-traditional PKI systems. As copies of the ledger are stored and shared, the model does away with central mechanisms such as the Public Key Infrastructure system that has a single Certificate Authorities system vulnerability in which the compromise of a single PKI system certificate can destroy the whole authentication system(Mosakheil & Yang, 2025). In addition, it achieves accelerated revocation propagation because of on-chain systems, with boosted visibility compared to the tedious revocation processes when updating CRL's on PKI systems. In terms of auditability, improvement is also seen as all events of authentication are permanently and chronologically recorded on the ledger, which aids in forensic investigations. The framework is also capable of significantly enabling automation because smart contracts can be deployed to merge Identity verification logics on the multiple systems, therefore overcoming the complexity of achieving cross domain authentication. Despite the extra costs from the consensus mechanism activity and on-chain storage, these are offset through the use of side chains and data pruning techniques.

3.2 Integration of Blockchain in 6G M2M Communication

This part describes how blockchain technology is used in 6G M2M communication systems and identifies it as a distributed trust provider. It also looks at how network slicing and blockchain combine to make the authentication process more efficient. All systems described in the context of 6G authentication mechanisms view blockchain as a fundamental element in overcoming barriers posed by traditional authentication systems that depend on a central authority.

Figure 2. Objectives of Blockchain in 6G Network

The implementation of blockchain technology into 6G networks is proving to be an innovative solution to some of the most prominent issues pertaining to security, trust, and decentralization of the next generation communication systems. As seen in Fig 2, the main goals of using blockchain technology in 6G infrastructure includes transparency, data privacy, and improved data traceability. Transparency in data is made possible through the active trust system implemented in the network, where all permitted users can view the shared ledger and no transactions can be reverted. This also enables enhancement of trust and reliability throughout the operations carried out in the network. Moreover, it also helps in privacy of data through identity decentralization and selective disclosure, thereby decreasing dependence on central authorities. In complex 6G ecosystems, improved traceability is achieved through reliable, recordable transactions crucial for audits and compliances of the 6G systems.

Besides that, Fig 2 shows other ways in which blockchain technology aids in cost reduction through automatized intermediaries elimination and smart contracts application. Smart contracts offer automatization without the need for a middleman due to pre-determined conditions. Data integrity is a key factor for blockchain owing to its unchangeable nature protecting data against improper edits. Data integrity is also increased in storing information through denial of service attacks. Last on the list, the removing of the single point of failures enhances the overall.

3.2.1 Blockchain as a Decentralized Trust Anchor

The provision of a decentralized trust anchor through blockchain integration is one of the major benefits culminating in the disuse of centralized Certificate Authorities (CAs). Storing authentication records across a number of nodes makes the blockchain more resistant to single points of failure and malicious data changes. Trust less proofs prepared as blockchain smart contracts with unwritten rules for application, proposals and block creation provide bases for permission validation. Each authentication request and result are stored in the blockchain ledger like trans Receipts to become a permanent and transparent record available for all. Also, DAG-based blockchains help achieve the integration because they enable parallel processing of plausible blockless authenticated credentials, which increase the number of devices that can connect to 6G networks by eliminating linear block confirmation limits (Bellaj et al., 2024).

3.2.2 Network Slicing and Blockchain Offloading

Due to recognizing the network slicing capability in 6G, both frameworks seek to utilize this technology in managing the blockchain systems. Network slicing consists of partitioning the physical network into several virtual slices, each specifically optimized for certain applications or services (Habibi et al., 2023). This framework allocates special network slices to guarantee that the authentication processes are assigned expecting bandwidth and low latency routes that are free of general data traffic, which would otherwise degrade performance of the authentication (Hussein et al., 2022). To improve performance efficiency, some implementations go a step further and incorporate Mobile Edge Computing (MEC) nodes within the network slices that are meant dedicate to blockchain tasks. These MEC nodes provide the first line of authentication validation and thus relieve the central blockchain of a large volume of work and cut down latency.

3.2.3 Comparative Advantages Over Traditional PKI

There are benefits of Blockchain systems over traditional Public Key Infrastructure (PKI) models, which are still based on centralised models of trust with authentication carried out through hierarchical Certificate Authorities that manage issued certificates (Maldonado-Ruiz et al., 2022). The weaknesses relate to a single point of failure: the CA could be compromised, which would damage the entire web of trust. Centralized PKI has other challenges, such as scalability where centralized authentication servers may become bottlenecks under high demand periods (Khalil et al., 2022). In addition, traditional PKI faces revocation delay issues, where it takes significant time to propagate Certificate Revocation Lists (CRLs) across a huge authentication network. These issues are mitigated in blockchain-based frameworks that distribute trust and authentication records among network nodes. Blockchain technology's unique characteristic of transparency allows for quick propagation of all state change events and captures the enhances security and scalability of the infrastructure.

3.3 Consensus Mechanisms for Real-Time Authentication

When it comes to the development of an M2M 6G communication system, one of the most crucial aspects is picking an effective consensus strategy for the blockchain based authentication system. The 6G M2M communication nodes can be distributed across a range of device types and application domains. At the same time, they are set to show improvement over existing systems, as they impose very strict latency performance criteria. For our current purpose, we have reviewed various methods such as Proof-of-Stake and its variants, Practical Byzantine Fault Tolerance, hybrid PBFT-PoS, and Directed Acyclic Graphs (DAGs) (Zhou et al., 2023). All have special speed, scalability, and security advantages and trade-offs that necessitate the application demand consideration. To enhance clarity regarding the trade-offs between different consensus strategies, Table 2 presents a comparative summary of Proof-of-Stake (PoS), Practical Byzantine Fault Tolerance (PBFT), hybrid PBFT-PoS approaches, and Directed Acyclic Graphs (DAGs) in the context of 6G M2M authentication.

3.3.1 Core Consensus Approaches: PoS and PBFT

Proof-of-Stake and Practical Byzantine Fault Tolerance are two consensus protocols that are very well adapted for 6G M2M authentication. PoS systems have their supporters because they are energy efficient, delivering faster block confirmation rates compared to Proof-of-Work (Jagatheesaperumal et al., 2025). Every node is allocated block validation rights in proportion to its stake, making transaction processing more effective through reduced computational demand. DPoS and Leased Proof of Stake are more versatile in those areas. Resource light M2M devices might find these systems particularly useful. They might also issue tokens to stakeholders who contribute towards generating new blocks but with rules of governance in place to check fraudulent activity. In contrast, PBFT enjoys a performance advantage with permissioned blockchains with high-speed finality requirements as it allows rapid finalization (Alzoubi & Mishra, 2024). When a set of validators reaches consensus, transactions enjoy instant finality which is beneficial for real time applications. While PBFT is resistant to malicious and faulty nodes, communication overhead between validators prevents it from scaling. The implementations of industrial IoT networks utilizing PBFT contain a few validators who can finalize transactions within less than a second. To enhance performance, some frameworks introduce hybrid methods, combining PBFT and PoS to leverage the best of both worlds, such as reduced latency and improved security, by switching between the two based on the load of the process.

3.3.2 Scalability Through DAGs

To meet the scaling needs of 6G M2M networks with high workloads, some implementations research Directed Acyclic Graph (DAG)-based consensus (V. Pathak et al., 2023). In contrast to traditional blockchains' linear construction, DAGs permit the simultaneous processing of numerous transactions, greatly increasing scalability and lowering confirmation time (Q. Wang et al., 2023). The unique forms of trading algorithms referred to as 'DAGs' benefit from the usage of asynchronous consensus systems. As a result, they become champions of large-scale M2M environments and allow for reliable operation when under significant transaction stress.

3.3.3 Real-Time Authentication with On-Chain Consensus

Traditional checks on certificates do not often entail consensus; however, in cases such as 6G M2M scenarios, the need for chain consensus arises to facilitate the most important activities (Cai et al., 2022). This covers the registration of devices which should be permanent and promptly accessible to all relevant users, the distribution of secure session keys which utilize consensus determination of genuine requests to inhibit replay attacks, and the revocation events whereby the blocked devices may no longer participate in network interactions. By committing these events, we can achieve consensus and near real time validation of the events to address some of the more severe drawbacks of standard PKI, namely the delays typically caused by revocation notification and list updating, which are severely troublesome in real time systems.

Table 1. Comparison of Consensus Mechanisms for 6G M2M Authentication

Consensus Mechanism	Latency	Scalability	Energy Efficiency	Security	Limitations
Proof-of-Stake (PoS) (Jagatheesaperumal et al., 2025)	Moderate to Low	Moderate	High	Moderate to High	Vulnerable to stake centralization, governance manipulation
Practical Byzantine Fault Tolerance (PBFT) (Alzoubi & Mishra, 2024)	Very Low	Low	Moderate to High	Very High (fault/malicious resistance)	Not scalable to large validator sets
Hybrid PBFT + PoS (Wu, Song, and Wang 2020)	Adaptive	Moderate	Moderate to High	High	Complexity in consensus switching
Directed Acyclic Graph (DAG) (Q. Wang et al., 2023)	Very Low	Very High	High	Moderate to High	Complex implementation, evolving maturity

3.4 Smart Contracts for Authentication Processes

This section discusses the methods with the aid of which smart contracts enable and implement authentication policies on the blockchain, making the processes of approvals and document certifications on the 6G M2M network easy while ensuring those policies self-execute. The smart contracts deal with issues of efficiency and protection by checking the intermediary verification steps needed before the device or actor is assigned certain privileges. The system uses smart contracts and blockchain technologies for category a devices registration, legislation and enforcement of borderless access control and policy features in a more decentralized manner.

3.4.1 Smart Contract Roles and Device Onboarding

Smart contracts are useful to automate different types of on-chain business logic. These business contracts define the criteria that a device or an actor has to meet in order to obtain an access right (Krishnan et al., 2024). They are capable of holding identity properties, blacklists, whitelists and can dynamically trigger licensing and usage policies. Smart contracts automate device onboarding with two distinct phases: the "Registration Phase" and the "Verification Phase". During the registration phase, a device broadcast a transaction containing its public key (with or without encryption or hashing) not be masked or for metadata, and smart contracts look for the device's public ID or hashed credentials against a repository. If there is no match, then it creates a new device record. When a device is registered, it calls a verification phase whenever it sends data or opens a session by means of the smart contract. The smart contract retrieves a stored device ID, checks validity periods, and issues short-lived tokens to permit data transmission. This smart contract is significant so that only confirmed devices are allowed access to the network and where a system of tokens is used to reduce the cost of constant on-chain queries. Some of the objects in the smart contract include the ability to "register_device" which requires a signing on identity proofs and the ability to "revoke_device" which enables the authorized agent to ignore the previously signed proofs and allow the smart contract to function, these abilities can also include "request_access" which monitors the current status of the device to ensure that it has the necessary policies like set key pairs, adequate firmware in use and absence of other malicious behaviours.

3.4.2 Policy Enforcement and Access Control Mechanisms

The absence of an external policy server increases the importance of data integrity and accountability along with enabling the enforcement of automated logic (Nahar et al., 2024). Their absence would put constraints on the ability to use other enforcement mechanisms. One example termed "Time-Based Access" places time constraints on the use of certain device privileges; this allows the use of timestamps over the blockchain to enhance security. This further place the blame of over quota usage on smart contracts that cannot be manipulated. The same ability helps the smart contracts avoid the blame for spam or DOS attempts from subverted devices. The framework allows the usage of smart contracts for implementing ACL policies to avoid the authorized devices from accessing other unauthorized resources, the policies are set to provide a blockade for all access requests and check them against secured policies maintained in the blockchain for logging. Furthermore, certain community driven implementations allow the use of AI to make real time decisions in smart contracts which automatically modify access restrictions according to the evaluated risks and patterns of usage. This enables systems to manage security in a more effective manner by enabling certain controls to be adjusted according to the behaviour observed and policies to be changed where necessary. Smart contracts can also be programmed to apply role-based access control, where each role determines a set of permissions to be enforced, so that the devices are only allowed to use the correct permissions based on their assigned roles, regardless of which network device they are connected to.

3.4.3 Comparative Benefits Over Traditional Systems

The analysed approach has several advantages over the existing systems that depend on servers to manage access rights. Centralized systems are more prone to manipulation and the addition of polices is time consuming and inefficient (Yap et al., 2023). These disabling functions are decentralized because smart contracts guarantee that policies will be enforced without a central authority. There is no single point of failure on the blockchain, which means every change made is fully traceable and more responsible, making it easier to meet regulatory compliance. In contrast, classical setups that use an institution's Access Management System that stores user/device credentials in a central database, scale poorly as thousands of devices require instantaneous verification overhead, and the single database or sign-on server begins to overload. Smart contracts reallocate the logic piecemeal onto several blockchain nodes, with the immutable ledger as a reference point for data identity. This design is redundant and reliable; when a node fails, the remaining nodes are capable of answering the authentication requests, provided that they are in the same state.

4. KEY ELEMENTS AND FEATURES OF 6G M2M AUTHENTICATION

Many elements and features are needed for the M2M communication authentication systems to be secure, efficient and dependable. This section describes the basic components of proper mechanisms for solving authentication in blockchain systems by concentrating on the identity management and node registration processes. In doing so, it helps to advance the understanding of the merits of this modularity by presenting these components in contrast of traditional centralized authentication systems.

4.1 Registration of Nodes and Management of Identity

The most important parts of every authentication system where a device on a network can be identified and trusted are node registration and identity management. This is a beneficial improvement of conventional PKI based techniques since, in blockchain based systems, this process is unchangeable and decentralized. Key notions involved in this aspect are advanced identity management lifecycle, hierarchical identity structures and initial credential setup.

4.1.1 Decentralized Identity Registration

A major aspect is de-centralized identity registration. At startup, each device has to produce its unique pair of cryptographic keys: a public key and a private key (Yapa et al., 2021). The private key remains within the device while the public key along with the device's metadata gets uploaded to the blockchain through a smart contract. The smart contract guarantees that these records have been made with an actual device so that only valid devices get registered. The blockchain provides an immutable digital certificate of all the devices that have been validated until the device gets turned on and replaces the previous value. Depending on the deployment, devices may be interacting with a local MEC node, which might help in forming and sending the device's identity to the blockchain in a secured manner. This concept not only helps in reducing the amount of time and energy the devices use, but it also helps in reducing the complexity of the network registration process. It enables sub-devices or sensors to register with the parent device's identity instead. On the other hand, traditional PKI-based systems, which rely on public key infrastructure, are specific where responsibility is de-centralized, and registration within an organization database is a crucial point of failure.

4.1.2 Hierarchical and Cluster-Based Identity Management

There are frameworks that implement hierarchical identity structures, whereby sub-devices are registered under the cryptographic umbrella of a parent device (Zhao et al., 2023). This helps in reducing overheads and enabling a parent device to control its sub-devices on-chain. Other systems, which concentrate on flat identity structure with maximum flexibility and granularity, concentrate on every device's registration and control separately on the blockchain. Instead, a hierarchical approach can group devices into clusters, with a leader node responsible for managing the identities of the devices that form each cluster. By registering these cluster leaders on the blockchain, a multi-tiered structure is created that improves scalability, lowers blockchain load, and minimizes the number of individual transactions needed for large-scale device enrolments. Also, these differ from centralized PKI solutions that handle registration in a single, often overwhelmed system.

4.1.3 Comparative Analysis with Traditional PKI

A traditional PKI set up will have a single point of control with centrally managed Certificate Authorities which has its downside of bottlenecks and single points of failure for registration overloads. On the other hand, blockchain systems share identity management to a large number of nodes, vastly increasing scalability and robustness. The permanent blockchain ledger keeps enables reliable tracking of devices' identities throughout unchanged records which enables identity devices to be securely registered without changing permission from other users. This is different with conventional systems based on mutable Certificate Revocation Lists (CRL) which cause inconsistencies and require frequent unpredictability. Moreover, blockchain based identity management, particularly with multi-level/inherited designs, originate systems cannot cope with the substantial number of devices in a massive M2M network. Even the continuous lifecycle of identity can be managed by the blockchain. Modifications of firmware or cryptographic algorithms on devices create a new transaction in the blockchain and notify users of the change in device setting, while the device remains secure.

4.2 Data Integrity and Security Mechanisms

Data integrity and strong security measures are therefore crucial in preventing unauthorized access and data manipulation and ensuring dependable authentication procedures in 6G M2M networks. Blockchain, by design, incorporates strong data integrity characteristics that are complemented by other security measures including MFA, secure communication protocols, end-to-end encryption, and Merkle trees. All these design decisions are key to producing a more robust system that effectively reduces a given scale of risks common in such settings.

4.2.1 End-to-End Encryption and Secure Communication

Utilization of application programming interface (API) technologies that enables the use of IoT devices along with securing and transmitting data of sensitive nature using advanced multi-layer encryption such as E2E encryption provides added security for the ethical principle of private as well as sensitive data protection. For example, some designs incorporate the use of strong AE-256 encryption scheme for communication between blockchain nodes and other devices to enhance the security of a broad communication channel. This works by other methods of security that obscure the contents of the data packets to unauthorized users. Other devices improve security by using secure hardware-based modules to perform sensitive functions such as key establishment and encoding, ensuring that the private keys do not escape a weakened system. Most systems integrate TLS as an additional safeguard.

4.2.2 Merkle Trees and Hashed Data Structures

It is impractical to store massive datasets fully onto the blockchain because of limit to both storage and throughput. As such, many solutions use Merkle trees and hashed data structure for easier verification of data integrity. By hashing device identifiers and authenticated records into a Merkle tree structure, this system allows for fast and secure verification of data integrity using Merkle proofs. Devices can only post partially proofs or Merkle roots on-chain and store hashed data offline or in distributed file systems, which drastically reduces the amount of on-chain storage required and increases scalability. By analysing the on-chain hash, verifiers can confirm the integrity of the data they request from off-chain sources. Some frameworks further push the limits by merging the Merkle trees with Directed Acyclic Graph structures for more scalable data verification. High-transaction situations may be made faster and more effective in terms of data integrity checks using DAGs to allow for parallel processing of authentication records. The most basic benefit is that these systems distribute trust across the blockchain, preventing any one party from changing device records unilaterally, as opposed to central servers.

4.2.3 Multi-Factor and Lifestyle-Based Authentication

Some others apply MFA techniques for the reinforcement of the authentication system to compound attacks. However, these also require auxiliary verification from devices over and above cryptographic credentials. These can be behavioral or time-based, like a device's particular manner of usage or the passage of a certain duration. This decade's approach to lifestyle-based authentication places restraints within boundaries while setting different elements like location, operational state and environmental context. Smart contracts validate these contextual conditions in real time to ensure that only devices working under valid conditions can access the network resources. The traditional PKI systems, however, rely on relatively static authentication techniques that differ from these dynamic approaches.

4.2.4 Comparative Insights with Traditional PKI

The escalation of the risks associated with a single point of failure in a centralized system emphasizes the importance of a comprehensive approach to secure a distributed system. In the case of large corporations, a massive breach has the potential to alter how business is conducted on a global level. Therefore, businesses require effective access control mechanisms almost to the level of using explicit permissions. Traditional systems maintain a level of control of identity management but blockchain frameworks enables self-sovereignty thus allowing individuals to manage their own identity. These frameworks increase security by lowering the possibility of an internal threat through user access segregation. Moreover, systems permit users to authenticate themselves using their unique biological traits instead of using a password or other vulnerable methods. These measures are especially crucial in the context of 6G M2M systems, where a user does not require any interaction with the items, amassing proof of identity is futile, and the systems can get a lot of value from simulating a user using AI over the application.

4.3 Latency Optimization in Real-Time Authentication

Clearly, 6G M2M networks need to leverage new breakthroughs in AI Newer improvements on AI protocols will help enhance the user experience by performing the intended task of enabling simple, transparent, and effortless interoperability across all systems without the need for explicit user identity. Furthermore, dormant accounts can enhance M2M systems by performing malicious activities. Therefore, simulation of users disguised as normal users is more reasonable and acceptable than trying to locate and remove all the dead accounts. However, 6G suspends the use of low latency technologies to enable these advanced security features.

4.3.1 Edge-Driven Consensus and Localized Blockchains

Clusters of M2M devices often build edge nodes to cut latency. Oftentimes, these edge nodes partake in the processes of initial block validation. By doing so, these validators are able to enforce a localized consensus that limits the distance that data has to travel, speeds up block finalization, and reduces the amount of initial authentication requests that need to be sent. The architecture can significantly cut down on round-trip times by eliminating the distance that the data must travel. Some frameworks use Mobile Edge Computing (MEC) nodes to do initial processing on authentication requests before sending them to the central blockchain. MEC nodes can perform initial validation on the block's worth of transactions, which drastically lowers the number of blocks needed and speeds up processing. By pushing the limits of how much consensus can be achieved, these frameworks lower latency and significantly boost overall performance for real-time use cases.

4.3.2 Batch Processing and Transaction Aggregation

To further increase the efficiency of consensus and block formation processes, batch processing of authentication requests is often employed. In this case, multiple device authentications are turned into a single blockchain transaction. This technique allows for a highly parallelized handling of device verification, making the process more efficient by reducing the latency and block generation frequency. The potency of the system is further strengthened with DAG-based consensus which allows for several batches to be processed at the same time without the need for subsequent linear block confirmations. Such concurrency features enable the framework to handle large volumes of authentication requests proficiently and in real-time. Such measures ensure that the operational overheads are kept within bounds, and the network is able to absorb the load of transactions which is inevitable for the system to work efficiently.

4.3.3 Adaptive Network Routing and Dynamic Resource Allocation

Given how unpredictable network conditions might vary, it is critical to use the network resources dynamically and efficiently. Often adaptive routing is done using software-defined networking (SDN) techniques, which allows directing authentication traffic to the edge validators in an optimized manner to reduce delays. This approach ensures that the authentication requests are always routed through the most efficient channel available at the time, which in turn reduces response time significantly. The AI powered controllers used in some of the frameworks change resource allocation to improve authentication processes by constantly monitoring the network conditions. By predicting traffic behavior and reallocating resources before the changes occur, the framework is able to sustain low latency during changing load conditions. These figures are particularly useful in real-world scenarios where the network conditions are dynamically unpredictable.

4.3.4 Comparative Analysis with Traditional PKI

Classic PKI systems tend to restrict themselves to authentication devices in the field to connect to remote Certificate Authorities (CAs), which can result in serious bottlenecks for certificate validation. Just the same, blockchain-based systems combine the use of edge computing with local validators so that authentication requests are fulfilled and processed much faster with no delays. Classic PKIs have their own advantages, however in the case of 6G, the issue of waiting on requests to be served by a remote server or certificate repository leads to delays that are quite often unacceptable. Furthermore, due to the active nature of the systems, the central CAs can become strained, attempting to serve a multitude of requests within the same time period resulting in a backlog which can be difficult in a strictly centralized system. Other PKI architectures such as blockchain ones that apply distributed consensus and batch processing are better suited as they have higher throughputs. Unlike the PKIs that adhere to a methodical and centralized validation process, it is possible to achieve faster responses to authentication with blockchain systems as they increase networking and processing efficiency.

5. PERFORMANCE ANALYSIS AND METRICS

The combination of blockchain and 6G Machine to Machine (M2M) communication is a promising means of circumventing the problems of conventional centralised authentication mechanisms. These Blockchain based Systems have to be effectively scrutinised on their performance measures as it is one of the most important criteria in determining its effectiveness. This model takes into account the proposed metrics including scalability, throughput, security resilience and energy efficiency. It evaluates the proposed solutions against existing systems, particularly the public key infrastructure (PKI) and aids in understanding their advantages and shortcomings.

5.1 Scalability and Throughput of the Proposed Solution

Scalability is the capacity of the system to add more devices, transactions, or both while still maintaining an acceptable speed of response. Throughput, on the other hand, is calculated as the number of transactions of authentication requests which are processed successfully during a specified time interval. These two metrics significantly facilitate the decision-making process on the adequateness of an authentication framework for the 6G M2M networking authentication system.

5.1.1 Horizontal and Vertical Scalability

The horizontal and vertical scaling helps in enhancing the performance of the proposed method. This type of scaling is achieved through the addition of validator nodes or edge gateways, which helps the system to balance the system's authentication load and maintain performance as the network expands. This type of scaling, where the resources of individual nodes (for example, CPU or memory) are added, guarantees that every node is able to perform its allocated portion of the authentication server load, sustaining the nature of distribution in blockchain networks. In a 6G environment, hardware acceleration and advanced network slicing may improve the distributed capabilities of blockchain and thus significantly improve throughput. For instance, FastFabric provided evidence that with certain optimizations to the architecture of Hyperledger Fabric, its throughput could be raised from 3,000 to 20,000 transactions per second (TPS) (Gorenflo et al. 2019). In the same manner, Hyperledger Fabric was able to throttle its throughput to 2,250 TPS, a 16-fold increase, by implementing aggressive caching and parallel endorsement policy verification optimizations (Thakkar et al. 2018).

5.1.2 Network Partitioning and Sharding

These techniques embrace network partitioning along with sharding methods to strengthen the agile industry. Sharding is the process of dividing the ledger into smaller, more manageable pieces for efficient processing, each of which is controlled by some of the validator nodes. This aid enables large M2M networks with thousands of devices, which may need authentication at the same time, to process transactions in parallel. The parallel processing of transaction across separate shards yields improved performance and reduced waiting times. One major drawback to shards is the necessity of cross-shard constancy and prevention of identity collisions. This approach enables parallel transaction processing, significantly increasing throughput. For instance, the Red Belly Blockchain achieved more than 100,000 TPS in a geo-distributed setting using sharded architecture (Crain, Natoli, and Gramoli 2018). Moreover, Conflux, a DAG-based blockchain system, achieved a throughput of about 6,400 TPS by supporting block-level concurrency without treating any blocks as forks (Li et al. 2018).

5.1.3 Performance Trade-Offs

The selection of the agreement method greatly affects the effectiveness of a system. For example, Practical Byzantine Fault Tolerance (PBFT) can quickly finalize transactions within smaller networks but may come with some cost in terms of communication overhead. Proof of Stake (PoS) is appropriate for large networks, although it may face problems of concentration of stakeholders if a handful of participants own a significant portion of the network. The data suggests that for permissioned blockchains with PBFT or PoS, the throughput can reach thousands of transactions per second, so long as the network is sufficiently wide, and the number of validator nodes is controlled. Cluster-based or sharding validation methods could offer even greater improvement for very large systems. Some scalable proposals that were tested in scenarios with thousands of devices achieved thousands of TPS provided that the network bandwidth was within reasonable bounds. In the performance evaluation of a large-scale Ethereum network, a TPS of 97.54 was reported at an observed transaction latency of about 57 seconds (Noor et al. 2024).

5.1.4 Monitoring Throughput Under Stress

To ensure consistent performance, the frameworks integrate monitoring dashboards that track metrics such as block generation times, queue lengths for pending transactions, and resource usage at validator nodes. These dashboards allow for real-time monitoring of the system's performance, enabling automated scaling or dynamic resource allocation when the ledger approaches its capacity limits. Stress testing, with synthetic traffic or real device workloads, helps identify when the ledger approaches its capacity limits, triggering auto-scaling or dynamic resource allocation. As an example, in the sixth generation wireless sensor network security management study, simulations showed the proposed method reached 97% throughput and 95% efficiency in energy consumption (Chinnasamy et al. 2024).

5.2 Security Evaluation

The blockchain technology-oriented verification systems are most critical to destroy mock penetration attempts and planned attack scenarios – all of that is part of an assessment which is also called risk assessment.

5.2.1 Resistance to Spoofing and Replay Attacks

In the unit of work, adversarial traffic and the reuse of old tokens are two concepts which are defended against. Newer units are equipped with stunning capabilities where older units are not. The latter are easily impersonated, courtesy of stolen credentials.

5.2.2 Detection of Malicious Nodes

Some aspects like attempting to allocate nodes which provoke disagreement, flooding the network with useless requests, and collaborating for token double-spending are where the harmful nodes can be active. The system has a method of evaluation concerning security which is focused on the movement and amount of time it takes to isolate the malicious nodes. For example, the blockchain algorithms based on PBFT principles have a flaw because they need many attestations from endorsers which makes collaboration easier. To enhance security and trust significantly, these frameworks blockchain is equipped with the ability to detect malevolent nodes and faster isolate them.

5.2.3 Immutability and Audit Trails

Once a block is finalized, it can't be changed without the reveal of inconsistencies, something which is ensured through the design of blockchain. While checking the security, one needs to check whether the block is immutable under strict fault scenarios. It is also necessary to observe whether the data is consistent when partial nodes go offline or reconnect. By its immutable nature, the ledger guarantees the existence of audit trails, giving a verifiable account for all authentication events. This attribute allows a more powerful tool for regulatory compliance and forensic investigation.

5.2.4 Compliance and Regulatory Requirements

This approach ensures the security of the system, considering possible regulator audits in industries which impose periodical compliance reporting. The external reviews can easily be passed with the help of inline smart contracts and distributed logs which serve as proof of endorsement and integrity of the data. which means the system not only meets the requirements of the industry but of the law as well, increasing its trustworthiness. A security advantage in conspicuity provided through trust dissemination is furthered through the use of blockchain for authentication. It is due to the nature of the ledger, having replicated data through many nodes that when attacker changes device credentials on one node, they cannot be accepted by the whole network. During attempts to understand device behaviour, blurring the line between unusual and unusual real time consensus is very important when marking certain actions requests as contradictory to the policies set. Also, the automatic cancellation of the compromised credentials via smart contract provides an immediate means to suppress any possible harm.

5.3 Energy Efficiency and Computational Overhead

With regards to the M2M networks, the battery usage is of utmost concern especially as the systems scale. It is also critical to assess how much effort is too much in carrying out the consensus computation with these limited resources. These considerations are particularly relevant in IoT environments, where efficiency is crucial for the long-term viability of deployed devices.

5.3.1 Comparisons with Traditional PKI

Energy usage usually shifts with the changing centralised tendencies of traditional authentication systems towards reliance on server farms that deal with certificate authorities or database lookups. There are claims that the shift toward a decentralised blockchain system leads to a drop in energy consumption over use. Evaluations note whether the proposed design preserves or improves energy efficiency compared to classical PKI models. Using networking capability of blockchain systems, energy expenditure can be minimized relative to central systems.

5.3.2 Optimising Consensus

There is extensive reduction in the consumption of energy for positive activities like Proof of Stake (PoS) as opposed to Negative activities such as Proof of Work (PoW). There are other innovations like some node participation for the use of computer accelerators that helps in balancing resource utilization wit 6G performance requirements. It is crucial to move away from energy-intensive PoW methods and look for transition systems, like PoS or PBFT, that are more energy efficient.

5.3.3 Impact on Device Lifetime

Low complexity authentication methods could also be utilized with IoT devices such as sensors that are powered by batteries. For instance, the lifespan of the device may be increased either by using lower key exchange frequency, moving it to energy efficient mid-tier processing units to minimize the off-key exchange processing or minimizing the amount of off-key exchange processing. In many practical trials or simulations, power consumption is estimated by comparing the 'naive' power consumption to optimized power consumption that employs different cryptographic methods. These methods ensure minimal device activity and thus device maximum power capability.

5.3.4 Trade-Offs in Design Choices

It can be difficult to find the perfect mix of performance versus energy expenditure in real-time settings. The block generation rate sets the pace of authentication where, at a higher rate, it is real-time, while for lower rates, it results in higher latencies. Adjusting the timing of the blocks to the network requirement with the use of dynamic consensus configurations eliminates the compromise. Some orders of magnitude assert the problem still pertains regarding overhead CPU and memory artefacts caused by the real-time finalisation of blocks. By scaling the number of validator nodes, setting reasonable batch intervals, or incorporating specialized accelerators, overhead can be kept within tolerable limits for the expected 6G performance.

5.4 State of the Art

To contextualize the proposed framework's performance and highlight current research directions, the following table 2 presents a comparative summary of state-of-the-art solutions that integrate blockchain and 6G, outlining their respective advantages and limitations.

Table 2. State of the Art

Reference	Blockchain	5G/6G	Advantages	Disadvantages
(Su, Larangeira, and Tanaka 2023)	**Yes**	**No**	Introduces a novel PoUW mechanism using distributed deep learning, along with the first formal security proofs for such blockchain protocols, ensuring robustness via chain growth and common prefix properties.	D-PoDL requires restrictions on training steps per block to prevent attacks across time slots. Its hash-training-hash and model-referencing design adds complexity and overhead compared to traditional PoW.
(Puspitasari et al. 2023)	No	Yes	Machine learning supports adaptive, efficient system behavior by learning from data, and optimizes complex 6G functions where traditional methods fall short.	ML deployment in 6G is affected by signal diversity from heterogeneous hardware, leading to possible inaccuracies. Some ML methods are computationally expensive and rely heavily on reward function quality.
(Wang et al. 2021)	Yes	Yes	The B-RAN framework enhances security via decentralization and immutability, while improving resource sharing, trusted data interaction, latency, and overall resource utilization.	Blockchain networks face risks like Sybil and alternative history attacks. PoW consensus is resource-intensive and introduces latency. Data privacy and accurate system modelling remain unresolved.
(Zuo et al. 2023)	Yes	Yes	Integrating blockchain and AI boosts security, privacy, efficiency, and scalability in 6G networks. This fusion enables optimized services by leveraging the strengths of both technologies.	Integrating blockchain with AI is challenged by the conflict between deterministic blockchain logic and probabilistic AI models. Scalability with large AI datasets and privacy concerns are major hurdles.
(Chinnasamy et al. 2024)	Yes	Yes	Enables optimal node and path selection for data transmission, reducing network traffic and improving energy efficiency.	Combining blockchain and complex ML models in resource-constrained wireless sensor nodes results in significant computational overhead, despite proposed optimizations.

6. IMPLEMENTATION AND CASE STUDY

6.1 Simulation Environment and Assumptions

The 6G simulated network with thousands of virtual devices is designed to connect to the cloud periodically to send control messages and transmit sensor data. The blockchain layer of the system is set up on the nodes with different physical specifications such as edge servers, cloud data centres, and multi-access edge computing (MEC) platforms. The network is emulated using open source 6G simulators to recreate the traffic patterns typical with IoT and M2M networks. The blockchain is set up with permissioned or hybrid models integrating Proof of Stake (PoS) and Practical Byzantine Fault Tolerance (PBFT) consensus algorithms. In addition to periodically generated authentication requests, devices also generate event-driven requests triggered by user interactions or sensor thresholds. This method provides a solution for use cases such as sensor networks, industrial control loops, and automotive systems. The block generation intervals along with the transaction rates and metrics for invalid blocks are monitored for performance metrics. Malicious nodes and spoofed devices are introduced to simulate a breach of network security. The simulation works on the premise of low packet loss from 6G coverage and fast routing along with the presence of cryptographic processors on so.

6.2 Workflow of Authentication in a Real-Time Scenario

The workflow illustrates how a newly powered IoT device onboards and authenticates under high-load conditions. The device starts up and either generates a public/private key pair or pulls existing keys from a secure hardware. Then it initiates a registration transaction on the blockchain, and provides digital signatures along with basic device metadata, such as the metadata's manufacturer or firmware version. Validator nodes check the registration metadata and if the device's key signatures pass the integrity and identity checks, the transaction is placed into the next block. The consensus mechanisms blockchain PBFT or PoS, finalize the block between milliseconds to seconds, based on the configuration and load of the system. Once approved, the smart contract allocates a short-tern token (session key) to the apparatus enabling faster verification calls to take place for a limited time. The device can relay sensor data or issue control commands for service authorization. Every packet is issued alongside a uniquely signed document that identifies the device. In turn, the nodes or services that receive the signatures validate them with existing blockchain information to ascertain that no revocation of the device has taken place. There might be routine revocations or updates of the device's credentials due to some triggered events, for example when a compromise is suspected.

6.3 Comparative Analysis with Traditional Techniques

The proposed blockchain-based model is evaluated against centralized authentication mechanisms that use PKI for a variety of scenarios. In terms of latency, traditional deployment needs to communicate with remote certificate authorities that impose several round-trip messages, while blockchain mitigates the number of verification steps, especially with edge validators. While the first registration might take longer because of consensus procedures, further authentications are simplified. Regarding security posture, Centralized Authorities have a single point of access and limited visibility for participants, but in a blockchain network, the device's authenticity is confirmed by many nodes decreasing the chances of a device being wrongly authenticated. Revocation or meta-data updates granularly improve overall security by speeding up the notification of compromised or revoked devices. In terms of scalability, millions of devices increase the load for centralized approaches, while a blockchain spreads the authentication workload across multiple operated nodes, which increases throughput. Blockchains with design flaws can prove to be a hassle when every transaction must go through upper-cost consensus. With Centralised PKI, operational costs are incurred with the need to supply the added specialized hardware security modules, personnel to manage the certificates, and the server infrastructure itself. At the same time, costs are also lower, but they are distributed more proportionately among the organizations that participate. Specialized validator nodes do require some specific criteria to be met. All in all, the decentralized nature of ledgers on blockchains proves to be the ultimate advantage because, with the constantly evolving times bringing about 6G technologies and IoT, there is much need for flexibility. Also, smart contracts can alter a wide variety of items such as device types, cryptographic standards, or compliance mandates which means a complete system overhaul does not have to take place.

CONCLUSION

The integration of blockchain technology for real-time authentication in 6G M2M communication presents a promising solution for ensuring secure and decentralized authentication. Blockchain innate properties such as immutability, transparency and decentralization, can significantly enhance the security and trustworthiness of M2M networks. However, the scalability challenges in large scale M2M networks remain a critical concern.

Challenges and Future Scope

The integration of blockchain for real-time authentication in 6G M2M communication offers promising solutions to address the scalability challenges in large scale M2M networks. As the density of the connected devices in 6G environments grows exponentially, traditional blockchain solutions face limitations in handling massive transaction volumes while maintaining low latency. Future research can focus developing lightweight energy efficient consensus mechanisms, such as Proof of Authority (PoA) or Delegated Proof of Stake (DPoS), to reduce computational overhead and enable real-time processing. Additionally, pipelining techniques can be employed to divide the blockchain network into smaller, parallel-processing portions, thereby enhancing scalability without compromising security. Integrating blockchain with advanced 6G features, such as network slicing and edge computing, can further optimize performance. Dynamic resource allocation technologies can also employ to efficiently utilize network resources and adapt to varying traffic demands in real time. Furthermore, combining blockchain with emerging AI and quantum computing can improve the security and processing efficiency. By addressing these challenges, blockchain technology can play a pivotal role in enabling secure, scalable and real-time authentication in 6G M2M communication, paving the way for a reliable interconnected future.

REFERENCES

Ahuja, K., & Bala, I. (2023). M2M in 5G Cellular Networks: Challenges, Proposed Solutions, and Future Directions. In *Wireless Communication Security*. https://doi.org/DOI: 10.1002/9781119777465.ch1

Almarri, S., & Aljughaiman, A. (2024). Blockchain Technology for IoT Security and Trust: A Comprehensive SLR. *Sustainability (Basel)*, *16*(23), 10177. DOI: 10.3390/su162310177

Alzoubi, Y. I., & Mishra, A. (2024). Blockchain consensus mechanisms comparison in fog computing: A systematic review. In *ICT Express* (Vol. 10, Issue 2). https://doi.org/DOI: 10.1016/j.icte.2024.02.008

Arunachalam, M., Akella, S., Arun Satvik, D., & Babu, R. T. S. (2025). *Navigating Privacy and Security in Internet of Medical Things With Machine-to-Machine Interactions*., DOI: 10.4018/979-8-3693-6180-1.ch018

Arunodhai, V., Susan, L. P., & Kannimoola, J. M. (2024). EdgeShield: Hybrid Real-Time Attack Detection in IOTA Tangle via Edge Devices. *2024 15th International Conference on Computing Communication and Networking Technologies (ICCCNT)*, 1–11. https://doi.org/DOI: 10.1109/ICCCNT61001.2024.10724609

Banafaa, M., Shayea, I., Din, J., Hadri Azmi, M., Alashbi, A., Ibrahim Daradkeh, Y., & Alhammadi, A. (2023). 6G Mobile Communication Technology: Requirements, Targets, Applications, Challenges, Advantages, and Opportunities. In *Alexandria Engineering Journal* (Vol. 64). https://doi.org/DOI: 10.1016/j.aej.2022.08.017

Bellaj, B., Ouaddah, A., Bertin, E., Crespi, N., & Mezrioui, A. (2024). Drawing the Boundaries Between Blockchain and Blockchain-Like Systems: A Comprehensive Survey on Distributed Ledger Technologies. *Proceedings of the IEEE*, *112*(3), 247–299. DOI: 10.1109/JPROC.2024.3386257

Bhattacharya, P., Shukla, A., Tanwar, S., Kumar, N., & Sharma, R. (2022). 6Blocks: 6G-enabled trust management scheme for decentralized autonomous vehicles. *Computer Communications*, *191*, 53–68. Advance online publication. DOI: 10.1016/j.comcom.2022.04.024

Bilami, K. E., & Lorenz, P. (2022). Lightweight Blockchain-Based Scheme to Secure Wireless M2M Area Networks. *Future Internet*, *14*(5), 158. Advance online publication. DOI: 10.3390/fi14050158

Cai, T., Chen, W., Psannis, K. E., Goudos, S. K., Yu, Y., Zheng, Z., & Wan, S. (2022). Scalable On-Chain and Off-Chain Blockchain for Sharing Economy in Large-Scale Wireless Networks. *IEEE Wireless Communications*, *29*(3), 32–38. Advance online publication. DOI: 10.1109/MWC.004.2100616

Chinnasamy, P., Babu, G. C., Ayyasamy, R. K., Amutha, S., Sinha, K., & Balaram, A. (2024). Blockchain 6G-Based Wireless Network Security Management With Optimization Using Machine Learning Techniques. *Sensors (Basel)*, *24*(18), 6143. DOI: 10.3390/s24186143 PMID: 39338888

Crain, T., Natoli, C., & Gramoli, V. 2018. "Evaluating the Red Belly Blockchain." arXiv.Org. December 31, 2018. https://doi.org//arXiv.1812.11747.DOI: 10.48550

Dhokrat, J. G., Pulgam, N., Maktum, T., & Mane, V. (2024). A Framework for Privacy-Preserving Multiparty Computation with Homomorphic Encryption and Zero-Knowledge Proofs. *Informatica (Vilnius)*, *48*(21). Advance online publication. DOI: 10.31449/inf.v48i21.6562

Diro, A., & Zhou, L. L., Saini, A., Kaisar, S., & Pham, H. (2023). *Leveraging Blockchain for Zero Knowledge Identify Sharing: A Survey of Advancements, Challenges and Opportunities*. https://doi.org/DOI: 10.2139/ssrn.4469520

Diro, A., Zhou, L., Saini, A., Kaisar, S., & Hiep, P. C. (2024). Leveraging zero knowledge proofs for blockchain-based identity sharing: A survey of advancements, challenges and opportunities. *Journal of Information Security and Applications*, *80*, 103678. Advance online publication. DOI: 10.1016/j.jisa.2023.103678

Dong, S., Abbas, K., Li, M., & Kamruzzaman, J. (2023). Blockchain technology and application: An overview. *PeerJ. Computer Science*, *9*, e1705. Advance online publication. DOI: 10.7717/peerj-cs.1705 PMID: 38077532

Esmaili, M., & Christensen, K. (2025). Performance Modeling of Public Permissionless Blockchains: A Survey. *ACM Computing Surveys*, *57*(7), 1–35. Advance online publication. DOI: 10.1145/3715094

Gorenflo, C., Lee, S., Golab, L., & Keshav, S. 2019. "FastFabric: Scaling Hyperledger Fabric to 20,000 Transactions per Second." 2019 IEEE International Conference on Blockchain and Cryptocurrency (ICBC), May. https://doi.org/DOI: 10.1109/BLOC.2019.8751452

Guo, F., Yu, F. R., Zhang, H., Li, X., Ji, H., & Leung, V. C. M. (2021). Enabling Massive IoT Toward 6G: A Comprehensive Survey. In *IEEE Internet of Things Journal* (Vol. 8, Issue 15). https://doi.org/DOI: 10.1109/JIOT.2021.3063686

Habibi, M. A., Han, B., Fellan, A., Jiang, W., Sanchez, A. G., Pavon, I. L., Boubendir, A., & Schotten, H. D. (2023). Toward an Open, Intelligent, and End-to-End Architectural Framework for Network Slicing in 6G Communication Systems. *IEEE Open Journal of the Communications Society*, *4*, 1615–1658. Advance online publication. DOI: 10.1109/OJCOMS.2023.3294445

Harjula, E., Artemenko, A., & Forsström, S. (2020). Edge computing for industrial IoT: Challenges and solutions. In *Wireless Networks and Industrial IoT*. Applications, Challenges and Enablers., DOI: 10.1007/978-3-030-51473-0_12

Henrique, P. S. R., & Prasad, R. (2021). 6G: The road to future wireless technologies 2030. In *6G: The Road to Future Wireless Technologies 2030*. https://doi.org/DOI: 10.1201/9781003336884

Hussein, N. H., Yaw, C. T., Koh, S. P., Tiong, S. K., & Chong, K. H. (2022). A Comprehensive Survey on Vehicular Networking: Communications, Applications, Challenges, and Upcoming Research Directions. In *IEEE Access* (Vol. 10). https://doi.org/DOI: 10.1109/ACCESS.2022.3198656

Islam, M. M., Nooruddin, S., Karray, F., & Muhammad, G. (2023). Internet of Things: Device Capabilities, Architectures, Protocols, and Smart Applications in Healthcare Domain. *IEEE Internet of Things Journal*, *10*(4), 3611–3641. Advance online publication. DOI: 10.1109/JIOT.2022.3228795

Jagatheesaperumal, S. K., Rahouti, M., Chehri, A., Xiong, K., & Bieniek, J. (2025). Blockchain-Based Security Architecture for Unmanned Aerial Vehicles in B5G/6G Services and Beyond: A Comprehensive Approach. *IEEE Open Journal of the Communications Society*, *6*, 1–1. DOI: 10.1109/OJCOMS.2025.3528220

Jahid, A., Alsharif, M. H., & Hall, T. J. (2023). The convergence of blockchain, IoT and 6G: Potential, opportunities, challenges and research roadmap. In *Journal of Network and Computer Applications* (Vol. 217). https://doi.org/DOI: 10.1016/j.jnca.2023.103677

Jain, K., Titus, B., Krishnan, P., Sudevan, S., Prabu, P., & Alluhaidan, A. S. (2024). A Lightweight Multi-Chaos-Based Image Encryption Scheme for IoT Networks. *IEEE Access : Practical Innovations, Open Solutions*, *12*, 62118–62148. DOI: 10.1109/ACCESS.2024.3377665

Javaid, M., Haleem, A., Singh, R. P., Suman, R., & Khan, S. (2022). A review of Blockchain Technology applications for financial services. In *BenchCouncil Transactions on Benchmarks, Standards and Evaluations* (Vol. 2, Issue 3). https://doi.org/DOI: 10.1016/j.tbench.2022.100073

Jiang, W., Han, B., Habibi, M. A., & Schotten, H. D. (2021). The road towards 6G: A comprehensive survey. In *IEEE Open Journal of the Communications Society* (Vol. 2). https://doi.org/DOI: 10.1109/OJCOMS.2021.3057679

Kazmi, S. H. A., Hassan, R., Qamar, F., Nisar, K., & Ibrahim, A. A. A. (2023). Security Concepts in Emerging 6G Communication: Threats, Countermeasures, Authentication Techniques and Research Directions. In *Symmetry* (Vol. 15, Issue 6). https://doi.org/DOI: 10.3390/sym15061147

Khalil, U., Malik, O. A., Uddin, M., & Chen, C. L. (2022). A Comparative Analysis on Blockchain versus Centralized Authentication Architectures for IoT-Enabled Smart Devices in Smart Cities: A Comprehensive Review, Recent Advances, and Future Research Directions. In *Sensors* (Vol. 22, Issue 14). https://doi.org/DOI: 10.3390/s22145168

Khan, A. H., Ul Hassan, N., Yuen, C., Zhao, J., Niyato, D., Zhang, Y., & Vincent Poor, H. (2022). Blockchain and 6G: The Future of Secure and Ubiquitous Communication. *IEEE Wireless Communications*, *29*(1), 194–201. Advance online publication. DOI: 10.1109/MWC.001.2100255

Khan, A. S., Sattar, M. A., Nisar, K., Ibrahim, A. A. A., Annuar, N. B., & Abdullah, J. bin, & Karim Memon, S. (2023). A Survey on 6G Enabled Light Weight Authentication Protocol for UAVs, Security, Open Research Issues and Future Directions. In *Applied Sciences (Switzerland)* (Vol. 13, Issue 1). https://doi.org/DOI: 10.3390/app13010277

Khan, A. S., Yahya, M. I., Zen, K. B., Abdullah, J. B., Rashid, R. B. A., Javed, Y., Khan, N. A., & Mostafa, A. M. (2023). Blockchain-Based Lightweight Multifactor Authentication for Cell-Free in Ultra-Dense 6G-Based (6-CMAS) Cellular Network. *IEEE Access : Practical Innovations, Open Solutions*, *11*, 20524–20541. Advance online publication. DOI: 10.1109/ACCESS.2023.3249969

Khan, S., Luo, F., Zhang, Z., Ullah, F., Amin, F., Qadri, S. F., Heyat, M. B., Ruby, R., Wang, L., Ullah, S., Li, M., Leung, V. C. M., & Wu, K. (2023). A Survey on X.509 Public-Key Infrastructure, Certificate Revocation, and Their Modern Implementation on Blockchain and Ledger Technologies. *IEEE Communications Surveys and Tutorials*, *25*(4), 2529–2568. Advance online publication. DOI: 10.1109/COMST.2023.3323640

Khashan, O. A., & Khafajah, N. M. (2023). Efficient hybrid centralized and blockchain-based authentication architecture for heterogeneous IoT systems. *Journal of King Saud University. Computer and Information Sciences*, *35*(2), 726–739. Advance online publication. DOI: 10.1016/j.jksuci.2023.01.011

Krishnan, P., Jain, K., Poojara, S. R., Srirama, S. N., Pandey, T., & Buyya, R. (2024). eSIM and blockchain integrated secure zero-touch provisioning for autonomous cellular-IoTs in 5G networks. *Computer Communications*, *216*, 324–345. Advance online publication. DOI: 10.1016/j.comcom.2023.12.023

Kumari, A., Gupta, R., & Tanwar, S. (2021). Amalgamation of blockchain and IoT for smart cities underlying 6G communication: A comprehensive review. *Computer Communications*, *172*, 102–118. Advance online publication. DOI: 10.1016/j.comcom.2021.03.005

Li, C., Li, P., Zhou, D., Xu, W., Long, F., & Yao, A. 2018. "Scaling Nakamoto Consensus to Thousands of Transactions per Second." arXiv (Cornell University), January. https://doi.org//arxiv.1805.03870.DOI: 10.48550

Liu, Y., Qian, K., Wang, K., & He, L. (2022). BCmaster: A Compatible Framework for Comprehensively Analyzing and Monitoring Blockchain Systems in IoT. *IEEE Internet of Things Journal*, *9*(22), 22529–22546. Advance online publication. DOI: 10.1109/JIOT.2022.3182004

Ma, R., Zhou, J., & Ma, M. (2024). A Blockchain-Assisted Security Protocol for Group Handover of MTC Devices in 5G Wireless Networks. *Sensors (Basel)*, *24*(7), 2331. DOI: 10.3390/s24072331 PMID: 38610542

Maldonado-Ruiz, D., Torres, J., El Madhoun, N., & Badra, M. (2022). Current Trends in Blockchain Implementations on the Paradigm of Public Key Infrastructure: A Survey. *IEEE Access : Practical Innovations, Open Solutions*, *10*, 17641–17655. Advance online publication. DOI: 10.1109/ACCESS.2022.3145156

Manikandan, A., Narayanan, G., Prakash, K. S. R. B., Reddy, C. Y., Mahesh, A. D., Sushanth, V., & Ramprasad, O. G. (2024). Investigations in Security Challenges and Solutions for M2M Communications—A Review. In *International Journal of Electrical and Electronic Engineering and Telecommunications* (Vol. 13, Issue 1). https://doi.org/DOI: 10.18178/ijeetc.13.1.17-32

Mosakheil, J. H., & Yang, K. (2025). PKChain: Compromise-Tolerant and Verifiable Public Key Management System. *IEEE Internet of Things Journal*, *12*(3), 3130–3144. DOI: 10.1109/JIOT.2024.3478754

Mukhopadhyay, A., & Vinayaka, R. (2021). A smart-contract-based blockchain for a healthcare iot network. *International Journal of Electronic Healthcare*, *11*(3), 256. Advance online publication. DOI: 10.1504/IJEH.2021.117122

Murroni, M., Anedda, M., Fadda, M., Ruiu, P., Popescu, V., Zaharia, C., & Giusto, D. (2023). 6G—Enabling the New Smart City: A Survey. In *Sensors* (Vol. 23, Issue 17). https://doi.org/DOI: 10.3390/s23177528

Nahar, N., Andersson, K., Schelén, O., & Saguna, S. (2024). A Survey on Zero Trust Architecture: Applications and Challenges of 6G Networks. *IEEE Access : Practical Innovations, Open Solutions*, *12*, 94753–94764. DOI: 10.1109/ACCESS.2024.3425350

Noor, Q., Multazam, A., Riyadi, S. G., Pratama, R., & Maulana, A. 2024. "Large-Scale Ethereum Network Performance Analysis: Case Study and Implications." JATI. May 28, 2024. https://www.novadatatech.com/index.php/jati/article/view/3

Nwachukwu, C., Durodola-Tunde, K., & Akwiwu-Uzoma, C. (2024). AI-driven anomaly detection in cloud computing environments. *International Journal of Science and Research Archive*, *13*(2), 692–710. DOI: 10.30574/ijsra.2024.13.2.2184

Osama, M., Ateya, A. A., Sayed, M. S., Hammad, M., Pławiak, P., Abd El-Latif, A. A., & Elsayed, R. A. (2023). Internet of Medical Things and Healthcare 4.0: Trends, Requirements, Challenges, and Research Directions. In *Sensors* (Vol. 23, Issue 17). https://doi.org/DOI: 10.3390/s23177435

Pathak, A., Al-Anbagi, I., & Hamilton, H. J. (2024). Blockchain-Enhanced Zero Knowledge Proof-Based Privacy-Preserving Mutual Authentication for IoT Networks. *IEEE Access : Practical Innovations, Open Solutions*, *12*, 118618–118636. DOI: 10.1109/ACCESS.2024.3450313

Pathak, V., Pandya, R. J., Bhatia, V., & Lopez, O. A. (2023). Qualitative Survey on Artificial Intelligence Integrated Blockchain Approach for 6G and beyond. In *IEEE Access* (Vol. 11). https://doi.org/DOI: 10.1109/ACCESS.2023.3319083

Patwary, A. A. N., Naha, R. K., Garg, S., Battula, S. K., Patwary, M. A. K., Aghasian, E., Amin, M. B., Mahanti, A., & Gong, M. (2021). Towards secure fog computing: A survey on trust management, privacy, authentication, threats and access control. *Electronics (Basel)*, *10*(10), 1171. Advance online publication. DOI: 10.3390/electronics10101171

Prabhakara Rao, T., & Satyanarayana Murthy, B. (2023). Extended group-based verification approach for secure M2M communications. *International Journal of Information Technology : an Official Journal of Bharati Vidyapeeth's Institute of Computer Applications and Management*, *15*(5), 2479–2488. Advance online publication. DOI: 10.1007/s41870-023-01284-w

Puspitasari, A. A., An, T. T., Alsharif, M. H., & Lee, B. M. (2023). Emerging Technologies for 6G Communication Networks: Machine Learning Approaches. *Sensors (Basel), 23*(18), 7709. DOI: 10.3390/s23187709 PMID: 37765765

Qian, K., Liu, Y., Shu, C., Sun, Y., & Wang, K. (2023). Fine-Grained Benchmarking and Targeted Optimization: Enabling Green IoT-Oriented Blockchain in the 6G Era. *IEEE Transactions on Green Communications and Networking*, *7*(2), 1036–1051. Advance online publication. DOI: 10.1109/TGCN.2022.3185610

Rao, P. M., Jangirala, S., Pedada, S., Das, A. K., & Park, Y. (2023). Blockchain Integration for IoT-Enabled V2X Communications: A Comprehensive Survey, Security Issues and Challenges. *IEEE Access : Practical Innovations, Open Solutions*, *11*, 54476–54494. Advance online publication. DOI: 10.1109/ACCESS.2023.3281844

Rebello, G. A. F., Camilo, G. F., Guimarães, L. C. B., de Souza, L. A. C., Thomaz, G. A., & Duarte, O. C. M. B. (2022). A security and performance analysis of proof-based consensus protocols. *Annales Des Telecommunications. Annales des Télécommunications*, *77*(7–8), 517–537. Advance online publication. DOI: 10.1007/s12243-021-00896-2

Rožman, N., Diaci, J., & Corn, M. (2021). Scalable framework for blockchain-based shared manufacturing. *Robotics and Computer-integrated Manufacturing*, *71*, 102139. Advance online publication. DOI: 10.1016/j.rcim.2021.102139

Solat, S., Calvez, P., & Naït-Abdesselam, F. (2021). Permissioned vs. Permissionless Blockchain: How and Why There Is Only One Right Choice. *Journal of Software*, •••, 95–106. DOI: 10.17706/jsw.16.3.95-106

Soni, M., & Singh, D. K. (2023). Blockchain-based group authentication scheme for 6G communication network. *Physical Communication*, *57*, 102005. Advance online publication. DOI: 10.1016/j.phycom.2023.102005

Su, X., Larangeira, M., & Tanaka, K. 2023. "Provably Secure Blockchain Protocols From Distributed Proof-of-Deep-Learning." IACR Cryptology ePrint Archive. July 6, 2023. https://eprint.iacr.org/2023/1059

Swathi, S., Chakaravarthy, S. P., Wilson, A. J., & Bharathi, A. P. (2022). An Effective Addressal of Traffic using Tensor Flow. *2022 1st International Conference on Computer, Power and Communications, ICCPC 2022 - Proceedings*. https://doi.org/DOI: 10.1109/ICCPC55978.2022.10072253

Thakkar, P., Nathan, S., & Viswanathan, B. "Performance Benchmarking and Optimizing Hyperledger Fabric Blockchain Platform." 2018. IEEE Conference Publication | IEEE Xplore. September 1, 2018. https://doi.org/DOI: 10.1109/MASCOTS.2018.00034

Thilakavathy, P., Jayachitra, S., Aeron, A., Kumar, N., Ali, S. S., & Malathy, M. (2023). Investigating Blockchain Security Mechanisms for Tamper-Proof Data Storage. *2023 International Conference on Communication, Security and Artificial Intelligence, ICCSAI 2023*. https://doi.org/DOI: 10.1109/ICCSAI59793.2023.10421006

Wang, J., Ling, X., Le, Y., Huang, Y., & You, X. (2021). Blockchain-enabled wireless communications: a new paradigm towards 6G. In *National Science Review* (Vol. 8, Issue 9). https://doi.org/DOI: 10.1093/nsr/nwab069

Wang, J., Ling, X., Le, Y., Huang, Y., & You, X. (2021). Blockchain-enabled Wireless Communications: A New Paradigm Towards 6G. *National Science Review*, *8*(9), nwab069. Advance online publication. DOI: 10.1093/nsr/nwab069 PMID: 34691739

Wang, Q., Yu, J., Chen, S., & Xiang, Y. (2023). SoK: DAG-based Blockchain Systems. *ACM Computing Surveys*, *55*(12), 1–38. Advance online publication. DOI: 10.1145/3576899

Wenhua, Z., Qamar, F., Abdali, T. A. N., Hassan, R., Jafri, S. T. A., & Nguyen, Q. N. (2023). Blockchain Technology: Security Issues, Healthcare Applications, Challenges and Future Trends. In *Electronics (Switzerland)* (Vol. 12, Issue 3). https://doi.org/DOI: 10.3390/electronics12030546

Wu, Y., Song, P., & Wang, F. (2020). Hybrid Consensus Algorithm Optimization: A Mathematical Method Based on POS and PBFT and Its Application in Blockchain. *Mathematical Problems in Engineering*, *2020*(April), 1–13. DOI: 10.1155/2020/7270624

Yap, K. Y., Chin, H. H., & Klemeš, J. J. (2023). Blockchain technology for distributed generation: A review of current development, challenges and future prospect. *Renewable & Sustainable Energy Reviews*, *175*, 113170. Advance online publication. DOI: 10.1016/j.rser.2023.113170

Yapa, C., de Alwis, C., Liyanage, M., & Ekanayake, J. (2021). Survey on blockchain for future smart grids: Technical aspects, applications, integration challenges and future research. In *Energy Reports* (Vol. 7). https://doi.org/DOI: 10.1016/j.egyr.2021.09.112

Yue, Y., & Shyu, J. Z. (2024). A paradigm shift in crisis management: The nexus of AGI-driven intelligence fusion networks and blockchain trustworthiness. *Journal of Contingencies and Crisis Management*, *32*(1), e12541. Advance online publication. DOI: 10.1111/1468-5973.12541

Zhao, W., Qi, Q., Zhou, J., & Luo, X. (2023). Blockchain-Based Applications for Smart Grids: An Umbrella Review. In *Energies* (Vol. 16, Issue 17). https://doi.org/ DOI: 10.3390/en16176147

Zhou, S., Li, K., Xiao, L., Cai, J., Liang, W., & Castiglione, A. (2023). A Systematic Review of Consensus Mechanisms in Blockchain. In *Mathematics* (Vol. 11, Issue 10). https://doi.org/DOI: 10.3390/math11102248

Zuo, Y., Guo, J., Gao, N., Zhu, Y., Jin, S., & Li, X. (2023). A Survey of Blockchain and Artificial Intelligence for 6G Wireless Communications. *IEEE Communications Surveys and Tutorials*, *25*(4), 2494–2528. DOI: 10.1109/COMST.2023.3315374

Chapter 7
Explainable Artificial Intelligence (XAI) for Trustworthy AI in 6G Networks

Wasswa Shafik
https://orcid.org/0000-0002-9320-3186
Dig Connectivity Research Laboratory (DCRLab), Uganda & School of Digital Science, Universiti Brunei Darussalam, Brunei

ABSTRACT

Explainable Artificial Intelligence (XAI) is pivotal in ensuring transparency, fairness, and trustworthiness in 6G networks, where AI-driven automation and decision-making play a central role. This study demontrates on how 6G integrates advanced machine learning models for network optimization, security, and resource allocation, the inherent complexity and opacity of these models pose challenges to accountability and interpretability. XAI techniques include model-agnostic explanations, attention mechanisms, and counterfactual reasoning, enhance the intelligibility of AI decisions, fostering regulatory compliance and user trust. This research explores XAI methodologies tailored for 6G, emphasizing their role in mitigating bias, ensuring robust security, and facilitating human-AI collaboration. Therefore, througgh embedding explainability into AI-driven 6G frameworks, we advance ethical AI deployment, fostering reliability and resilience in next-generation wireless networks evaluating technology acceptance.

DOI: 10.4018/979-8-3373-0568-4.ch007

1 INTRODUCTION

Ensuring explainability and trustworthiness in artificial intelligence is becoming essential for establishing confidence in AI models, which is consequently paving the road to real-world deployment and widespread market acceptance. Generating high levels of confidence is particularly important in AI models used in critical systems, especially where minimal risk or minimal damage to property is explicitly required, such as in the medical, automotive, and real-time network environment domains (Roy et al., 2024). Domain experts will be the most likely to influence these critical decisions and face the most consequences. The European Commission has established seven key requirements and recommendations to enhance trust in AI, leading to the implementation and deployment of AI that generates high levels of confidence. Governments and businesses are investing significant resources in AI due to its potential for future economic growth and the consequent improvement in our standards of living (Shafik, 2024d).

Incorporating domain knowledge, business needs, and value into the overall process is crucial to the establishment of trust in the systems delivered. 6G AI should be explainable, transparent, and unbiased. Together, these concepts are regarded as crucial for achieving trustworthiness in AI. Explainability in AI can lead to human-interpretable AI systems, where knowledge and decisions can be shared with domain experts and end-users (Celik & Eltawil, 2024). AI systems today are mainly associated with the well-being of the economic services provided, particularly in terms of efficiency and cost reduction. However, higher levels of confidence in AI have evident positive impacts on the effectiveness and quality of the services delivered, particularly supporting decisions related to health, personal transportation, and real-time networked services (Shafik, 2025a).

In recent years, there has been an explosion of interest in the research and development of wireless communication networks. The needs for global coverage, extreme data rates, ultra-high reliability, ultra-low latency, and energy-efficient service for several applications such as cloud-based services, Industry 4.0, autonomous driving, massive machine type, fixed and mobile broadband access, among others, have increased (Shafik, 2025i). The fifth-generation (5G) wireless communication system has been developed to address some of these future-generation requirements (Corcuera Bárcena et al., 2023). Currently, researchers, mainly academics and industry stakeholders, are devising the direction that the sixth-generation (6G) of wireless communication networks should take. Promised new services, including remote surgery, holograms, data-rich virtual reality, and latency-critical control, demand extremely stringent requirements in terms of positioning accuracy, overall network throughput, data speed, real-time control, low delay and jitter, edge processing power, and more (Merluzzi et al., 2023).

The evolutionary development of enabling technologies that include artificial intelligence (as sampled expert systems in Figure 1), machine learning, millimeter-wave communication, non-orthogonal multiple access, massive MIMO, visible light communication, coordinated multi-point, terahertz communication, carrier aggregation, device-to-device communication, full-duplex communication, network slicing, mobile edge computing, holographic communication, cavity resonators, and lens antennas has also been embraced (Shafik, 2025h, 2025g). Particularly, the application of artificial intelligence in conjunction with different advanced enabling technologies, alongside their interdependencies, is envisioned to bring significant improvements in investments, innovations, and market needs (Shokoor et al., 2022). The application of artificial intelligence together with enabling technologies in 6G networks is expected in five prominent cases: artificial intelligence for artificial intelligence applications, artificial intelligence for the edge network, artificial intelligence for ultra-reliable and low-latency communications, artificial intelligence for intelligent communication, and artificial intelligence for terahertz connectivity (Shafik, 2025a).

Figure 1. Expert systems

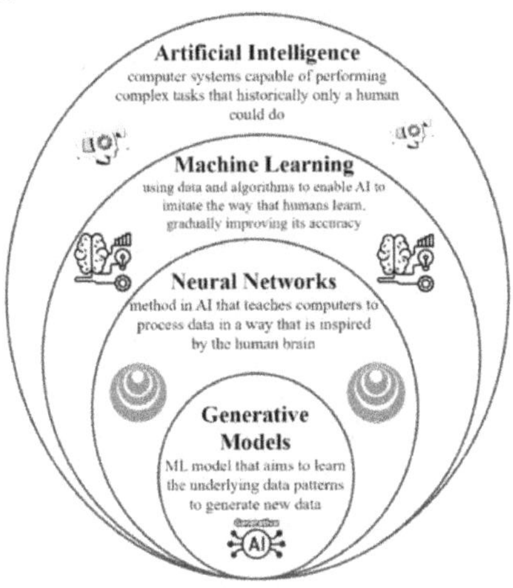

The emerging 6G communication network systems are anticipated to be both intelligent and smart. The relevance of explainable artificial intelligence for trustworthy AI in 6G networks is to make AI processes in this context easier to understand, including their function, performance, transparency, and fairness issues (Shafik, 2025f, 2025e, 2025d). Trust will, therefore, be instilled in AI processes and outputs. The 6G era is foreseen to experience a conglomeration of heterogeneous services directed at both mobile and fixed environments. AI has the potential to augment the overall system performance, operation, management, and cybersecurity (Zhao et al., 2022). The use of AI techniques such as machine learning, deep reinforcement learning, federated learning, and game theory in 6G networks is believed to be propelling. Such AI techniques require a huge dataset to enable intelligent decision-making. To reduce the latency in processing big data for training AI models and also minimize data privacy concerns, data processing can be supplemented with mobile computing associations. Nevertheless, deploying AI in wireless networks can induce constraints and concerns like resource allocation, response time, and trust issues. Indeed, 6G networks may confront a large number of AI-associated limitations and challenges, such as poor explainability, unfairness, and discrimination (Corcuera Bárcena et al., 2022). These weaknesses may obscure crucial debates and create obstructions to including trust in AI-enabled 6G networks.

1.1 Overview of 6G Technology

The next generation of worldwide wireless technology, the 6th generation or 6G, is intended to be revolutionary and is planned to be introduced by 2030. Since artificial intelligence (AI) comes from humans, it is necessary to ensure that it can be explained. Explainable AI plays a crucial role in the sixth generation of digital communication practical networks, as 6G networks will closely integrate physical systems and AI technologies. Opaque AI systems in 6G networks may pose serious practical risks and could force the abandonment of AI (Aslam, Du, et al., 2021). A key attribute of practical AI systems is the transparency of their behavior, meaning that users and stakeholders understand key actions. However, the intrinsic behavior of AI systems requires relevant explanations and evidence. The formal definition of explainable AI is that users can reliably know how the considered AI method system calculates its output. The concepts of accountability, gender-neutral AI architecture, personal privilege, and the philosophical norms of intrinsic discrimination fairness in AI all belong to the context of XAI standards. The frameworks of Social Reality Interpretation and Domain Explanation Space are theoretical contributions to XAI (Shafik, 2024h). AI service programming, enterprise value AI explanations, AI credibility, and best-followed rules provide various practical elements of XAI.

Since AI comes from humans, theoretically immature AI may lead to numerous opaque systems, severely undermining its practicality. Academic attribution mitigates heterogeneity difficulties by improving performance methods. AI methods can be characterized by distinguishing societies, thereby increasing user confidence. At the same time, user subjectivization of academic attribution can be achieved by incorporating domain-specific explanatory models to gain personal beliefs. Implementing XAI involves providing SRI to guide AI decision-making. It determines the different seats that actual users can accept (Irshad et al., 2019). Additionally, the competitive execution of seven programming AI service qualities is essential. The substantial explanation of AI is encoded based on five different needs. AI allowance credit is an important indicator of AI computational quality. Competitive enterprises use competition engines to formulate strategy names. In conclusion, this particular symposium volume deals with the following three aspects or themes of study related to the sixth-generation communication networks that have logical connectivity at every facility (Aslam, Zhang, et al., 2021). These 6G networks become effectively capable of applying types of convergence of artificial intelligence technologies.

1.2 Research Objectives and Scope

In contrast to using AI for network optimizations, we investigate concepts on how AI processes in network management tasks can be transparent and traceable such that the outcomes are trustworthy and reliable. In this research initiative, we propose to address the issue of Explainable AI in 6G Networks. Our investigation is threefold: First, we offer a structured view of where the challenges and potentials lie in the application of AI for network management in next-generation networks. Second, we propose basic design principles for XAI using 6G networks, explaining why their application in network management tasks is not only a concept of academic interest but a hard necessity. This yields roles for an XAI approach in the 6G network. Third, we devise three basic approaches on how to enforce such a structured view on explainability, exemplified by selected concrete network management task examples.

The proposed scientific work opens a line of research tracks in developing scalable XAI concepts in 6G Networks and Autonomous Networks. We generate novel insights about the nature of explainability in AI processing for Autonomous Networks. We also devise scalable methods and building blocks for enforcing this explainability in a 6G and Autonomous Network setting. This also includes developing methods for edge processing which verifies that AI processing happens accordingly. We derive novel implications of XAI on how AI processes should be optimized, adapted, and deployed in 6G networks. This includes specific constraints and Quality of AI Service definitions in addition to existing Quality of Service concepts. Such findings have strong implications for practical as well as recommendation system challenges.

2 ARTIFICIAL INTELLIGENCE (AI) IN 6G NETWORKS

6G is expected to deliver unparalleled user experiences that combine high data rates, zero-latency communication between machines and humans, decentralization, intelligence, new business models, security, 100% coverage, and universal availability around the world. These requirements necessitate integrating AI at all development layers of these networks (Shafik, 2025c, 2025b, 2025l, 2025j, 2025k). To achieve these characteristics, 5G networks currently implement deep learning and machine learning techniques to ensure the sub-6GHz and millimeter wave massive MIMO bands are working effectively for full duplex communications, end-to-end rate detection, and baseband processing at the UE (Merluzzi et al., 2023). Moreover, a new RAN architecture, drone-based small cell, with machine learning techniques to mitigate interferences or improve user experience, has been proposed. These initial AI efforts align with the general development trajectory and clearly underscore the need for Explainable AI to seamlessly integrate into 6G in adhering to Trustworthy AI (Shafik, 2024c).

2.1 Definition and Types of Artificial Intelligence

Today's AI is mainly based on narrow AI, i.e., individual algorithms that perform specific tasks, such as recommendation algorithms, image classifiers, and speech recognition models. Machine learning is the main AI technology today, but other AI technologies are also coming together, including knowledge representation, automatic programming or planning, large knowledge bases, and logical reasoning. These are being grouped into families that try to act like a human brain in areas such as cognition or cognitive architectures and have some similarity with more general human reasoning, learning, decision-making, or even understanding, and language emphasis (Li et al., 2020). In this sense, AI would be a kind of incarnation of cybernetics, as it is based on mathematics and seeks a pragmatic identity of the human brain to be able to incarnate human reasoning. AI, taking a pragmatic stance, seeks to be evolutionary rather than revolutionary, accepting a wide range of different solutions to its possible tasks.

However, AI is not yet deep AI. Deep AI should be based on more advanced frameworks than traditional AI, combining deep learning and cognitive behaviors because it enables learning more abstract relationships about everything and, therefore, facilitates understanding, reasoning, and compassion for other entities, such as humanity, in the case of AI (Rezazadeh et al., 2023). This is because the new knowledge that is being learned is based more on learning from relationships with themselves and with the world, and less on the relationships with the signal data itself. However, there are some challenges: data and energy requirements that are much higher than what humans require to perform similar tasks; data-adapted solutions and concept drift because different data leads to different ontologies; and interpretation of the results because in the case of neural networks, for example, it happens that many times this interpretation is not possible, given their structure and the multiplication of creative variations of real or semi-fictional entities (Irshad et al., 2019).

2.2 Expert System Fundamentals

A computer is a collection of its hardware and software. A machine, which may or may not be a computer, has to learn to perform specific tasks for machine learning to occur. The performance of these tasks becomes superior to the number of times the machine performs a task. Machine learning contains familiar types of learning: supervised, unsupervised, semi-supervised, and reinforcement learning, alongside choices such as trees and forests and other selections (Bandi & Yalamarthi, 2022). When the machines on which learning occurs stack deep learning architectures and complementary settings, these are specialized domains with unique challenges that form deep learning.

The information for training a computer becomes comprehensive at the input feature level using labeled or partially labeled data. On the whole, the path taken by the deep neural network to discern the data has not been decided or ever divulged due to the hidden and very high number of network layers. Suppose a trained deep learning model is fed with input data for making an inference to its target without its past affiliations and background context. In that case, the resultant model is not explainable (Khan et al., 2024). The problem of compounding lack of interpretability is addressed by focusing on the problem of transparency, which necessitates unwrapping the process in deep learning from beginning to end. The use of Layer-wise Relevance Propagation is one major approach for generating visualization and explanation of deep learning, as well as entries added on each layer consisting of nodes in a deep neural network that engender further fine-tuning, thereby gaining greater interpretability potential in developing nations (Shafik, 2024f). This information can be decoded to learn how data is associated with decision-making in an AI model.

2.3 Role of AI in 6G Networks

With the rapid advancement in communication technologies, 5G will soon be reaching saturation. The 5G performance parameters will no longer be able to support emerging new applications that require higher performance, particularly in terms of ultra-low latency for autonomous driving and industrial internet applications. Further, to keep its strategic market position as a global leader in providing such services, there is a need to develop 6G technologies (Shafik, 2024b). The next generation, 6G networks, are expected to offer key performance parameters far beyond current 5G capabilities, such as terabits per second bandwidth, sub-millisecond latencies, gigabits per second network access speeds, and 100 in-line with IoT-supporting connections per technology. 6G will transform the role of communications in society and industrial and service sectors: it will bring high-speed, low-latency connectivity to very crowded environments in towns and cities and ultra-reliable broadband links in high-speed infrastructure connecting asset-intensive industrial enterprises in rural and remote areas (Irshad et al., 2019). The role of AI in 6G networks is an overarching goal and consists of several layers of AI optimization covering all aspects of a 6G network, notably system and network level, radio access technology level, cell level, and terminal and device level. This initiative is a clear effort to consolidate and grow leadership in this key domain. This approach articulates XAI approaches that will engender trustworthiness in AI models used for diverse communication services to meet the multiple network cross-layer challenges in realizing the ambitious performance goals of 6G communication networks (Merluzzi et al., 2023).

2.4 Challenges of AI Implementation in 6G Networks

However, the seamless, cross-tier, universal, and efficient application of AI in 6G networks is extremely challenging. There are challenges from a practical perspective, including insufficient standardization and the lack of large-scale deployment, which arise from various application scenarios and their user requirements, data, task characteristics, and architecture design. Much research is also needed for the realization of trustworthy AI. When deploying models in networks to provide services, many factors that deteriorate the user experience should be considered (Bandi & Yalamarthi, 2022). As such, AI algorithms become indispensable for basic cognitive functions, such as cognition, perception, localization, and optimization, in large-scale networks. This aims to provide a platform for research on AI in 6G networks, including, but not limited to, the topics of AI for multi-tier and multi-modal heterogeneous networks, AI for carrier interference control and cross-spectrum collaboration, AI for protection and safety in large-scale UxV and H2M networks, and quick learning and lightweight reasoning for AI in very narrowband cost- and power-limited networks (Celik & Eltawil, 2024).

2.5 Integration of trustworthy XAI in 6G networks

The integration of trustworthy Explainable Artificial Intelligence (XAI) into 6G networks is a fundamental scientific and technological necessity to ensure transparency, accountability, and reliability in highly intelligent and autonomous communication systems. As 6G promises to deliver revolutionary capabilities, including terabit-per-second data rates, sub-millisecond latency, ultra-dense connectivity, and intelligent automation, the role of AI becomes central in optimizing network management, service orchestration, and user experience (Aslam, Du, et al.,

2021). However, the widespread deployment of opaque AI models, particularly deep learning algorithms, presents serious concerns regarding interpretability and trust. In safety-critical and mission-driven applications such as autonomous vehicles, remote surgeries, and industrial automation, the inability to explain AI decisions undermines system dependability and user confidence. Consequently, the incorporation of XAI into 6G is not an auxiliary enhancement but a core design principle (Shafik, 2024i).

Scientifically, integrating XAI into 6G requires embedding explainability into all operational layers of the network, including the radio access layer, core infrastructure, and user equipment. Explainability must be treated as an architectural feature, not a post-processing utility a(Shafik, 2024g). Techniques such as Layer-wise Relevance Propagation (LRP), SHAP (Shapley Additive Explanations), and LIME (Local Interpretable Model-Agnostic Explanations) can help demystify the internal logic of AI models used for channel estimation, spectrum allocation, handover decisions, and interference mitigation. These techniques allow network operators and developers to visualize which input features are most influential in a decision, thereby supporting transparency, validation, and debugging (Irshad et al., 2019). In 6G, where decisions must be made in real-time across complex and adaptive environments, such clarity is essential for maintaining service quality and safety.

Moreover, explainability is particularly vital in the deployment of AI at the network edge, where resource-constrained devices such as drones, wearables, and vehicular nodes participate in real-time decision-making. These edge devices often operate under strict power and computational constraints, making traditional deep models impractical without efficiency trade-offs. To address this, lightweight XAI models must be developed that offer meaningful explanations without compromising inference speed or energy efficiency. This may include neural network pruning, quantization, or the development of interpretable-by-design architectures such as decision trees, symbolic models, or attention-based networks optimized for embedded environments (Munir et al., 2023).

Another critical dimension of trustworthy XAI is semantic reasoning and contextual awareness. Hybrid approaches combining machine learning with symbolic reasoning or cognitive architectures enable AI systems to reason beyond pattern recognition, incorporating structured domain knowledge into their decision processes (Roy et al., 2024). This is particularly important in applications where contextual understanding, such as user intent, environmental semantics, or ethical considerations, must guide the AI system's actions. For example, in healthcare-related 6G applications, AI models must not only predict outcomes but also justify decisions based on clinical guidelines and patient-specific factors (Irshad et al., 2019). Such reasoning requires both interpretability and knowledge representation, bridging the gap between raw data and human-understandable logic.

Despite progress, challenges persist in standardizing the evaluation and implementation of XAI. There is currently no universal metric for measuring interpretability or trustworthiness in networked AI systems. Developing such benchmarks, covering fidelity, robustness, causality, and usability, is essential for ensuring consistent implementation across vendors and geographies (Rezazadeh et al., 2023). Additionally, regulatory frameworks, such as the EU's Trustworthy AI guidelines and IEEE standards, must be integrated into the design and deployment lifecycle of AI in 6G systems. This involves maintaining audit trails, model versioning, and ensuring compliance with data privacy and algorithmic fairness mandates. Furthermore, privacy-preserving techniques such as federated learning must be aligned with explainability requirements to protect user data while maintaining transparency (Celik & Eltawil, 2024).

3 EXPLAINABLE ARTIFICIAL INTELLIGENCE (XAI)

Until now, various kinds of modern deep learning or artificial intelligence models have gained enormous success due to their high prediction ability compared to traditional machine learning models. However, it is important to understand that not all machine learning and AI models are interpretable. For example, image recognition provides the ethnicity of your picture when you upload it. This lack of fairness and transparency may pose significant problems. Thus, there has been increasing interest in making models explainable in recent years (Shafik, 2024h). The explanation techniques can help domain experts understand and gain insights into model predictions. Here, we provide a brief overview of explainable artificial intelligence. The development of explainable artificial intelligence is motivated by the need for transparency, fairness, and trust in machine learning and artificial intelligence models. Recently, regulations have established the right to explanation, meaning users should have an explanation of automatic decision-making and the right to demand human intervention in the process. The development of this area has become a priority. In the business environment, the high demand for AI and machine learning is faster than the breakthrough of interpretability (Rezazadeh et al., 2023). Many companies have deployed high-performing but opaque models in their decision-making processes.

3.1 Understanding the Working Principles of XAI

XAI is a particularly significant research topic in the development of AI algorithms. It can address the 'black box' of the AI decision-making process and provide a demonstration of the internal logic and reasoning process of the AI, thereby enabling human users to improve their understanding and trust in the AI results (Shafik et al., 2025). The emphasis on this aspect in Trustworthy AI is crucial, as ensuring that AI is transparent so that humans are aware of the operation and do not conceal any infringement is a key factor in achieving AI ethics. Therefore, ensuring XAI will be one of the guarantees for the trustworthy development of AI (Shafik, 2024e). Due to AI resolving complicated problems of 6G networks and the application demands in the system assurance mechanism and the more extensive security audit, it will be crucial to upgrade AI decision-making to an explainable method.

Although the current XAI research continues to break through innovative designs with different mechanisms, there is no unified standard for the practical definition. It is defined as the task of shaping AI systems such that humans can understand their function, performance, and limitations. In fact, the real meaning of XAI is not simply to visually show the neural network training parameters, such as weights and feature recognition for brainstorming (Shafik et al., 2019). The interpretation mechanism should achieve a clear analysis of the association between the algorithm and human interpretation and, by verifying understanding, ensure that the working mode of the AI model is in line with the target of the designed task. The explanation of the results can either explain the reasons for the AI making specific predictions or help understand the characteristics of the associated data in the training mechanism for model data dynamics to a specific degree. From the perspective of such an implementation mechanism, most existing XAI research chapters advocate the following basic principles (Irshad et al., 2019).

3.2 Importance of XAI in 6G Networks

XAI is becoming increasingly important today when AI systems are implemented in healthcare, virtual personal assistants, financial planning, cybersecurity, or autonomous systems such as drones, autonomous vehicles, or human-machine teaming. In these areas, there are a number of requirements that must be met in order to guarantee the trust, reliability, and resilience of AI systems. Among these requirements, it is necessary to be able to interrogate most of the AI processes so that their response or decision can be justified in order to gain the user's trust. XAI provides a framework and methods that partially or completely make this kind of revealing of AI processes possible, and make functions transparent or understandable (Roy et al., 2024). Additionally, XAI also allows the AI process and its future behavior to be forecast or explained. These explanations are indispensable to increase the trust and understandability of AI results, especially if they have a great impact on stakeholders. As AI systems have become more powerful, secure, and trusted, transparency, understanding, and explainability have emerged as one of the main design principles governing all components of AI systems. Therefore, it is imperative to emphasize that developing XAI cannot be understood as an obstacle but rather as a driving force for developing safe, secure, transparent, and trustworthy AI systems that fulfill the objectives pursued in the development of AI (Munir et al., 2023). For this, XAI should be part of the AI system architecture, used to create qualitatively better interactions and developed through qualitative processes that give users physical and mental capacities to use AI.

4 TRUSTWORTHINESS IN ARTIFICIAL INTELLIGENCE

The present chapter discusses the role of explainable artificial intelligence (XAI) in supporting the development and deployment of trustworthy AI systems in 6G networks. The complexity and heterogeneity of AI algorithms in 6G networks are expected to be remarkably higher compared to current AI technologies in various application scenarios, such as user-controlled and data-driven AI, similar to the self-evolving control loops of existing telecommunication systems (Merluzzi et al., 2023). At the same time, trustworthiness issues of AI algorithms may still depend on the components and stages of 6G network technologies, ranging from edge to centralized endorsed learning, from architecture-controlled learning as an environmentally critical infrastructure to context-specific lineage labeling, and cohort and ranking aware testing. All these technologies may demonstrate both the risks of affecting enterprise competitiveness and social equality and the opportunities to defend unlawful discriminatory profiling (Filippou et al., 2022).

This chapter addresses the role of XAI in the transition from the current radio design architecture into AI-derived radio configurability, which is introduced in the framework of the network self-management advanced technologies. The framework is built on de-symorphic reliance, deep attribute exposure, reduce-expose-predict, explain-enforce-cohort, and mirror-representation criteria that connect with both radio intelligence-based behaviors and radio configuration broadcasts, which pertain to risky influences and risky influenced PCIs, respectively (Celik & Eltawil, 2024). In addition to complying with the expected telecommunication regulatory principles that relate to inside self-monitoring and self-adaptive drivers, the framework neutralizes the risks emanating from unlawful profiling, automated decision-making, corrective feedback, and discrimination monitoring that could adversely influence the rights to access, to privacy, to non-discrimination, and to meaningful human choices of mostly human individuals and, eventually, to biodiversity (Ducange et al., 2023).

4.1 Key Aspects of Trustworthiness in AI Systems

The trustworthiness of AI is essential for the success of 6G networks. The key aspects from this perspective are security, privacy, robustness, explainability, fairness, safety, future implications, lack of explanation, and digital rights. AI security is an area that collaborates with cybersecurity and information security to protect AI algorithms and models from attacks that hinder the trustworthiness of AI. Privacy issues such as data privacy, data ownership, and data privacy in decision-making processes should be more from the user perspective for maintaining trustworthiness (Corcuera Bárcena et al., 2023). Users have the right to obtain clear, understandable, and precise information about the automated processing of their data and respect the right to human intervention in AI performing automated decision-making processes. One solution to AI privacy concerns is to design privacy-by-design AI models based on privacy-preserving AI via privacy-enhancing technologies (Roy et al., 2024).

AI models are often designed to work well on historical data, and errors or adversarial examples can cause conceptual errors in edge cases. From the perspective of trustworthiness, models must be safe and avoid risks in such cases. For example, the algorithms used to show the outcome of a user's request on an AI-powered autonomous vehicle must not be the reason for accidents. The ethical aspect of AI raises questions such as who is responsible for nuisance caused by algorithms, who has the right of decisions about AI decisions, and how biased AI models will influence people (Bandi & Yalamarthi, 2022). Thus, as AI use deepens and continues to mature, the impact of long-term AI applications becomes an emerging problem for society because real-world adversarial examples lead AI to change users' beliefs, and reinforcement learning causes addictive content on social media. Therefore, designing long-term machines helps maintain trustworthiness.

4.2 Ethical and Legal Implications

Moral machine experiments evaluate the responses of individual people to difficult decisions that are made in line with moral norms. The results of such experiments can then be seen as input into the determination of the moral models underlying AI ethics regulations. The danger here is that it could lead to biased outcomes, as bias is a distortion in the function of a system inferred by a data processing or learning system that occurs when we use a function of insufficient complexity for the modeling of underlying patterns across diverse variability in data (Khan et al., 2024). We should not push too hard or be too rigid in the implementation of moral models based on observations made during ethical decision-making tasks. After all, when humans have to make quick decisions, they have to rely on heuristics and not on moral principles. Different factors like mood or personal beliefs influence decision-making. Real-world decision-making shows the same attributes: quick and sometimes inconsistent decision-making always leads to errors (Rezazadeh et al., 2023).

The European Union has established a High-Level Expert Group recommending the implementation of seven guidelines pointing to transparency and the need to make information about the presence of AI systems explicit, besides the need for the provision of clear and adequate information necessary for being aware of AI systems involved in services themselves. The personalization of information in line with the specific context of use, disclosure, and information flows has to be given attention (Roy et al., 2024). The Algorithmic Accountability Act aims to increase transparency and security surrounding AI applications used by the government and support privacy rights. The European Commission is addressing the regulatory question of AI and should announce a new proposal on this issue in advance of 2021. Meanwhile, the Commission's existing regulation on data protection is affecting AI by including the right to explanation, though it is also difficult and currently a subject of ongoing discussion (Rezazadeh et al., 2023).

4.3 Security and Privacy in AI Systems

There is a perception that using AI models to provide cybersecurity monitoring or protection implies reduced transparency, and that automatically entails increased security threats and risks. In fact, a significant level of security risk can also be generated by AI-based systems through data leaks, model poisoning, backdoor malware, adversarial attacks, etc. At the same time, AI technologies can be massively beneficial for managing cybersecurity in software-intensive, complex systems. Moreover, they are expected to be a major constituent of 6G networks thanks to their capabilities (Shafik, 2024a). However, introducing advanced AI components such as deep learning systems into 6G networks raises security concerns as they do in any autonomous decision-support system that has real-world impact. The security measures on AI at present are primitive, such as restricting access to training data and avoiding exposure to adversarial input (Shafik et al., 2024).

To solve the challenge, there needs to be substantial research progress and standardization, increasing usability, leveraging trust zones, specifying benchmarks, designing inline processing, and ethics. A Trust Network Infrastructure needs to be created to handle this substantial surge of information with security, privacy, and ethics. Such an infrastructure ensures privacy information protection, preventing unauthorized access, secure information transformation, as well as resource limitation. These measures are taken to preserve the privacy of the operation and the very concrete sanctity of the various datasets used to benefit the individuals involved (Bandi & Yalamarthi, 2022). Furthermore, a secure federated protocol is required for Visible Light Communication and artificial intelligence jointly to make the intelligent 6G wireless network architecture secure, compared to the two technologies deployed separately.

5 INTEGRATION OF XAI IN 6G NETWORKS

This section discusses ways of integrating XAI in 6G networks, including edge and fog computing with analytics, where 6G technologies could be included to achieve the main goal of XAI – explanation. Service-Based Architecture and Cognition as a Service are the main ways to make the XAI explanation process in the 6G networks, including the use of several activities as described herein. The discussion is driven by several use cases of XAI in 6G networks and the main importance of developing the research in technologies for increasing the explanation of predictive models, arguing for the importance of XAI techniques in 6G networks (Aslam, Du, et al., 2021). Some research opportunities and challenges are also presented, including XAI education for professional education, which is not widely covered in most of the chapters dealing with this subject. The scope of 6G is the description of the presented activities, discussing, directly and indirectly, the creation of new models and the explanation of XAI usage in those models in 6G networks, where the description of the cognitive network usage is the most commented on in the related works (Filippou et al., 2022).

Cognition as a Service is linked to Cognitive Machine Learning, which provides an automatic processing machine to access the live and virtual data from the network, enabling dynamic support services and decision-making. Different machine learning models can provide cognitive services for network orchestration (Munir et al., 2023). The cognitive services can include, among other activities, making data available from the network state to a data analytics service, external stakeholders for troubleshooting and next decision-making, or applying machine learning models to make such data available. Additionally, dynamic quality values of information on data being processed and transmitted should be provided for dynamic orchestration (Aslam, Du, et al., 2021). The usage of this source can provide information for broadcasting services, robotics, automation, edge, and fog service processing, among others.

5.1 Methods of Integrating XAI in 6G Systems

The XAIES stated in the latest surveys can give the most promising trends of the development. It is also remarked in the survey results that although SHAP has been pointed out as the most used algorithm, no XAI method can alone solve XAI challenging tasks. This confirms the importance of integrating XAI in automated pipeline approaches to solve complex XAI tasks. The adaptive workflow, performing feature selection and local interpretable model-agnostic explanations application times, constitutes the main method for evidentiary explained XAI proposed for trust and skepticism in online debate identification (Merluzzi et al., 2023). AI2L-Defense is another example of proposing an automatic pipeline to deal with adversarial examples. The attack module can get some adversarial examples in a specific number, but the doXAI module, as the main focus of their work, must be integrated to see the differences between human misclassification features of non-adversarial examples and similarities in adversarial examples or the main parts of the adversarial examples. Providing explanations of recognized adversarial features helps humans distinguish them from features caused by natural phenomena that may consist of uncertainty. These examples of combining techniques are integrated and performed heuristically to be detected during the defensive action (Aslam, Du, et al., 2021; Shafik, 2023). It reinforces the statement reported in the survey that any XAI method cannot be independent and understood individually; otherwise, it cannot imply trust in the outputs of the AI models in AI platforms realized in 6G networks.

5.2 Benefits of XAI Integration

In most AI models, reasoning is implicit without a detailed understanding of the causes and effects. The lack of transparency and traceability might degrade users' trust in the system. As a solution, explainable AI techniques have been developed to make machine learning models more understandable. The introduction of these techniques into AI systems brings several benefits to machine learning practitioners as well as end users. First and foremost, understanding the behavior of the model assists machine learning engineers in developing more effective models, identifying and removing biases in the training data, and improving model fairness by revealing the real operating mechanism of the model (Aslam, Zhang, et al., 2021). In addition, the increased transparency allows users to understand and control model decisions, assess the accountability of the model, and improve human-assisted decision-making by potentially reducing errors and improving efficiency. The promotion of model transparency contributes to equitable access to AI solution benefits for many people. Furthermore, diverse stakeholders such as regulators, domain experts, and adversaries could evaluate the trustworthiness of the model and make critical, informed choices on whether to apply or deploy the model (Roy et al., 2024).

6 CASE STUDIES AND APPLICATIONS

Public safety communication is crucial in emergencies such as accidents, natural disasters, pandemics, or terrorist attacks when the lives and safety of people are at risk. Since future emergency events are unpredictable, mission-critical communication systems must be designed and implemented with a new level of flexibility and be able to operate across resource boundaries. In this chapter, we introduce several possible applications and challenges of the integration of AI and ML algorithms into 6G for a trustworthy future of public safety communication.

6.1 Real-world Examples of XAI in 6G Networks

This section introduces several future applications in 6G networks, for which the XAI technology is necessary for trustworthy AI. While 5G is currently being deployed and commercialized around the world, the research, standardization, and regulation activities for 6G cellular systems are being actively conducted by international bodies. In terms of the technological roadmap for 6G, cooperative multi-cell communication technology using highly directional beams has been suggested to improve the energy efficiency of the RF front end and the spatial resolution of beamforming, and XAI is one piece for realizing the same at the edge (Rezazadeh et al., 2023). There are many future applications in the 6G world. For example, the epidemic prevention and control system using AI technology and cooperative communication technology using highly directional beams have been studied. Our AI-driven IoT distributed Si-mould using terahertz reflective mobile edge computing is to help run hardware chips for both training and prediction. In another case, memory-aided active, cost-aware, quality-assured AI learning is achieved by blending the deep learning model and memory device to support active learning for key-value store scenarios (Munir et al., 2023). Therefore, commercializing these future AI applications in the forthcoming 6G wireless communication networks is contingent on making state-of-the-art deep learning models more hardware-friendly and easier for inspection from diverse stakeholders.

6.1.1 Network Management and Optimization

In a scenario where the protocol functionality of Layer 2 and Layer 3 packet headers can be controlled to support rich wireless services, intelligent network management is essential for maintaining telecommunication network dynamism. Different from previous works that limited the communication functionalities, 6G will employ a unified communicator for service and protocol control. The dynamic protocol functionality introduces extra flexibility and, meanwhile, imposes more challenges for network resource management (Shafik et al., 2020). To meet the requirements of on-demand Layer 2/3 packet processing and packet steering under constrained CPU processing budgets, efficient data structures need to be designed to accelerate the performance lookup of Layer 2/3 forwarding or flow management. The support in flexible protocol processing also means complex protocols and higher processing overhead of data packets; therefore, it is essential to balance network micro-allocation in a resource-wise and cellular user-wise manner and coordinate offloading decisions in teamwork. While simplifying and improving network efficiency, solutions can also relieve the complexity of resource management in multi-tier networks, thus allowing efficient joint optimization in mobile networks. Integrated management of a rich network is built by embedding intelligence into the mobile network (Corcuera Bárcena et al., 2022). Pyramidal applied to slice management can significantly reduce the computation load, and utilizing their latent heterogeneities among slices, a learning-based integrated slicing framework can be designed to ensure ultra-reliable low-latency slicing with theoretical guarantees.

6.1.2 Resource Allocation and Traffic Prediction

Resource allocation problems in wireless networks address the optimal broadcasting of data in time and frequency to exploit the resources most efficiently. The resources are limited due to channel fading and most existing works use statistical information to plan long-term strategies for data transmission. Deep neural networks have the potential to change resource allocations according to the current channel conditions dynamically. This may significantly improve the time-spectral efficiency, as the network has direct access to instantaneous channel conditions for deciding the resource allocation (Ducange et al., 2023). The consumption of the information must also be taken into account, as the information about the channel states may be forwarded via users or subcarriers to the serving base station. The usefulness of deep learning for either user scheduling, beamforming, or task offloading together with power management has been addressed and demonstrates significant performance improvement over conventional resource allocation algorithms (Roy et al., 2024).

Future networks are expected to accommodate the rapid growth in traffic volume by increasing the number of networked devices. In this context, the prediction of wireless traffic has become a complex task that has attracted considerable attention. Forecasting wireless traffic has many applications. Long short-term memory networks, which are a deep learning model for sequential data analysis, have recently been applied to predict wireless traffic and have remarkably improved prediction accuracy. The subcarrier assignment can also be learned by a deep learning technique that estimates the CPU-GPU tight loop traffic (Li et al., 2020). In edge AI, user traffic characteristics related to the utilization of GPU cameras will be monitored by either local detectors trained for unsupervised anomaly detection or federated detectors able to perform fast traffic prediction. In task offloading, a traffic predictor is required to estimate future traffic of edge AI, while traffic of the virtual assistant is predicted using a dataset. These simple metrics uniquely describe the benefits of deep learning in detecting stragglers and advancing offloading decisions (Merluzzi et al., 2023).

6.2 Impact of XAI on Network Performance

XAI deployment and its integration with AI algorithms and tools are expected to help in increasing the efficiency and robustness of AI-based functions while also providing regulators and users with the means to understand the decision-making of AI systems. Similarly, the XAI deployment and integration with AI systems of 6G networks can provide autonomous network management and optimization based on various algorithmic aspects, such as rule-based, machine learning, and multimedia applications (Rezazadeh et al., 2023). The integration of the complex decision-tree models and simple rule-based models of AI together with the uncertainty-aware AI systems is expected to offer enhanced flexibility and adaptability to the fluctuating and unpredictable conditions characterizing wireless 6G networks. In contrast, XAI includes methods and techniques aimed at providing stakeholders with detailed information that socializes the decision-making employed in AI. The higher the degree of explainability, the lower the 'black-box' behavior that is so conventional in AI. In conclusion, despite XAI providing a bona fide opportunity for AI to be truly transparent and aligned with the ethical principles that are behind it, there remain several ongoing challenges and issues to be solved in order to accomplish this (Corcuera Bárcena et al., 2023; Roy et al., 2024). The mention of 'apply to your problem' means that there is no silver bullet or unique way in AI to achieve XAI.

7 FUTURE DIRECTIONS AND RESEARCH CHALLENGES

Next, we discuss future research directions and challenges for XAI in trustworthy AI development and 6G network applications.

7.1 Emerging Trends in XAI and 6G Networks

As of 2021, the mainstream efforts in XAI are predominantly focused on engineering AI models that generate self-explanatory formats, where an explanation is a human-understandable model responsible for AI outputs. In AI models, such explanations include model parameters, structure, feature relationships, importance, or counterfactual explanations. More recently, XAI has extended to interface and human-computer interaction aspects that adaptively integrate explanations into the AI system based on user profiles, tasks, contexts, or predefined user criteria (Irshad et al., 2019). The new methodological principles, or the procedural rights of XAI, are evolving to accommodate diverse user requirements by incorporating societal expectations for ethical AI, as well as recognizing and mitigating the human cognitive biases associated with endowing AI with explainability. When operating with humans, AI systems with different types of human-AI interactions are categorized as human-in-the-loop. The research thrust in XAI shall gradually embrace the multidisciplinary collaborative efforts in Ethical Collaborative AI (Merluzzi et al., 2023). XAI is less explored in engineering-level telecommunication networks and the evolving 6G networks. Proving the trustworthiness to its users, wireless communication capabilities may benefit from AI explainability to the AI models in mobile devices, to the monolithic and distributed AI at the network edge and core, to be aware of diverse SDoA and QoE requirements in communication services, including k-connectivity and coherent collaborations among users within the user clusters. In the future 6G era, XAI shall eventually evolve to help the main constituents in 6G environments to reflect on and reinforce trustworthiness and integrity, referring to trustworthy AI (Khan et al., 2024). Before we suggest any possible design enablers, the applications in 6G networks that may benefit from employing XAI approaches are discussed.

7.2 Unsolved Problems and Areas for Future Research

The current state of science is always developing, and XAI is not an exception. Several open questions are waiting to be answered. First, how to evaluate an AI's trustworthiness? XAI techniques can show the logic behind AI-generated decisions, but they still have limitations in reflecting all real-world problems and understanding different user concerns. How to accomplish the seamless integration of the explainable techniques and general analysis tasks of data analytics? In practice, explainability would add a level of transparency to customer-facing machine-learning applications (Li et al., 2020). Should the explanation be independent of the machine learning model or be joint-learned with it? What are the legal and ethical implications of generating these sorts of explanations? Furthermore, expanding XAI methods to enhance the plausibility of AI systems and improve their acceptance by individuals has not been explored explicitly. While XAI has great value in terms of promoting interdisciplinary studies, the explanations generated from these methods may support justifications, correct or incorrect, of existing AI decisions. A better system may not necessarily provide greater explanations, and a decent explanation does not always imply that AI is good. There is a need to leverage XAI, along with human-machine interactive techniques, to advance the underlying machine learning model and allow humans to recognize when to trust AI (Bandi & Yalamarthi, 2022). Further study of these key questions would shed more light on how to have robotic auxiliary systems assist us and ensuring the trustworthy deployment of AI, reliable AI performance, and reducing the cognitive burden of incorporating in an explainable manner regarding user priorities.

8 EVALUATION METRICS AND PERFORMANCE BENCHMARKS

The ultimate value of transparent AI is to achieve a generally accepted methodology and a high level of trust in AI. Specifically, XAI provides transparency of intelligent decisions. Trust in AI should not be viewed as a binary concept. Users can have different degrees of confidence in an AI system. Recently, many proposals and innovative technologies related to trustworthy AI have been made for trustworthy AI with XAI. Next, we discuss several critical concepts for developing TAI. In order to validate the transparency and explainable functionalities of an AI system, performance evaluation is an indispensable task in the development process (Corcuera Bárcena et al., 2022; Filippou et al., 2022). Evaluation metrics are adopted to measure the XAI performance according to its research objectives.

At present, a number of evaluation metrics related to the XAI performance have been proposed to validate various transparency and explainability functions of different explainable models or algorithms. These metrics characterize how the explanations generated by an internal process can help humans understand the logical reasoning and the decision-making process of a learned AI model toward a specific instance. Different XAI applications require different evaluation metrics to measure their XAI requirement fulfillment. The Selection Explanations Score was introduced to measure the capability of an explainable model or explanation algorithm to select from a limited number of potential features in a feature space (Celik & Eltawil, 2024). The Dependence-aware Feature Importance, Added Information, or Marginal Contribution metrics were proposed to measure the capability of explainable models to recognize a specific feature that has a significant correlation with the model prediction result. The Unblinding Score, Shapley Value, Integrated Gradients, or Contrastive Interpretation Debias were proposed to evaluate the capability of remove/classification explanation toward benchmark datasets to quantitatively measure the average unblinding effects and mistakes correction capability, respectively (Celik & Eltawil, 2024; Li et al., 2020).

9 CONCLUSION

XAI is emerging as a significant trend with increased reliance on machine learning and AI. The deployment of XAI is a critical means to ensure safety for a variety of crucial applications associated with resilience and reliability considerations in future 6G networks. The major motivation behind this study is to achieve a calling to action toward the proactive tracing of the most important future research areas on XAI for trustworthy AI in 6G networks. To this end, the primary result of this chapter is to present a comprehensive literature review on AI, machine learning, particularly explainable machine learning, and emerging AI's ethical and trustworthiness issues, highlighting the future research directions associated with explainability in AI for trustworthy 6G networks. The threats of AI security, the inability to reason, and transparent decision-making have caused public concerns. Several governments and governing bodies have established principles of trustworthy AI to promote the development of responsible human-aligned AI for the social good. The vision is to enable all the stakeholders involved to understand the decision-making process, keeping track of accountability and transparency. In case of emergencies, humans can intervene, possibly overriding the AI/ML models' decisions when incorrect predictions are noticed. Facilitating the experts' interpretation of black-box models is important to prevent the AI's applications from high-stakes undesirable outcomes. At the very beginning of that development, the research on interpretable, transparent, and explainable AI attempts to shed light on how advanced AI/ML models are making decisions, providing feature attributions, justifications, and explanations to back up those decisions. This drive towards trustworthy, ethically informed AI poses several important research challenges and brings open issues to facilitate designing transparent AI/ML models that end-users and experts can use to trust computer-assisted decision-making. This is particularly significant in the absence of a ground-truth rationale that must capture sufficiently complete and comprehensible knowledge for attaining high human trust. Only AI models with trustworthy decision-making capabilities can be deployed in the loop of control systems, which heavily follow the ethical principles of system-centric design.

REFERENCES

Aslam, M. M., Du, L., Zhang, X., Chen, Y., Ahmed, Z., & Qureshi, B. (2021). Sixth generation (6G) cognitive radio network (CRN) application, requirements, security issues, and key challenges. *Wireless Communications and Mobile Computing, 2021*(1), 1331428. DOI: 10.1155/2021/1331428

Aslam, M. M., Zhang, J., Qureshi, B., & Ahmed, Z. (2021). Beyond6G-consensus traffic management in CRN, applications, architecture and key challenges. *2021 IEEE 11th International Conference on Electronics Information and Emergency Communication (ICEIEC) 2021 IEEE 11th International Conference on Electronics Information and Emergency Communication (ICEIEC)*, 182–185.

Bandi, A., & Yalamarthi, S. (2022). Towards Artificial Intelligence Empowered Security and Privacy Issues in 6G Communications. *International Conference on Sustainable Computing and Data Communication Systems, ICSCDS 2022 - Proceedings*. DOI: 10.1109/ICSCDS53736.2022.9760857

Celik, A., & Eltawil, A. M. (2024). At the Dawn of Generative AI Era: A Tutorial-cum-Survey on New Frontiers in 6G Wireless Intelligence. *IEEE Open Journal of the Communications Society*, *5*, 2433–2489. Advance online publication. DOI: 10.1109/OJCOMS.2024.3362271

Corcuera Bárcena, J. L., Ducange, P., Marcelloni, F., Nardini, G., Noferi, A., Renda, A., Ruffini, F., Schiavo, A., Stea, G., & Virdis, A. (2023). Enabling federated learning of explainable AI models within beyond-5G/6G networks. *Computer Communications*, *210*, 356–375. Advance online publication. DOI: 10.1016/j.comcom.2023.07.039

Corcuera Bárcena, J. L., Ducange, P., Marcelloni, F., Nardini, G., Noferi, A., Renda, A., Stea, G., & Virdis, A. (2022). Towards Trustworthy AI for QoE prediction in B5G/6G Networks. *CEUR Workshop Proceedings*, **•••**, 3189.

Ducange, P., Marcelloni, F., Micheli, D., Nardini, G., Renda, A., Sabella, D., Stea, G., & Virdis, A. (2023). Trustworthy AI for Next Generation Networks: The Fed-XAI innovative paradigm from the Hexa-X EU Flagship Project. *CEUR Workshop Proceedings*, **•••**, 3486.

Filippou, M. C., Lamprousi, V., Mohammadi, J., Merluzzi, M., Soykan, E. U., Borsos, T., Rajatheva, N., Rajapaksha, N., Le Magoarou, L., Piscione, P., Benczur, A., Lampin, Q., Larue, G., Korpi, D., Ducange, P., Renda, A., Farhadi, H., Haraldson, J., Strinati, L. G. B. E. C., & Tomur, E. (2022). Pervasive Artificial Intelligence in Next Generation Wireless: The Hexa-X Project Perspective. *CEUR Workshop Proceedings*, **•••**, 3189.

Irshad, M. N., Du, L., Khoso, I. A., & Javed, T. Bin, & Aslam, M. M. (2019). A hybrid solution of SDN architecture for 5G mobile communication to improve data rate transmission. *2019 28th Wireless and Optical Communications Conference (WOCC)*, 1–5.

Khan, N., Coleri, S., Abdallah, A., Celik, A., & Eltawil, A. M. (2024). Explainable and Robust Artificial Intelligence for Trustworthy Resource Management in 6G Networks. *IEEE Communications Magazine*, *62*(4), 50–56. Advance online publication. DOI: 10.1109/MCOM.001.2300172

Li, C., Guo, W., Sun, S. C., Al-Rubaye, S., & Tsourdos, A. (2020). Trustworthy Deep Learning in 6G-Enabled Mass Autonomy: From Concept to Quality-of-Trust Key Performance Indicators. *IEEE Vehicular Technology Magazine*, *15*(4), 112–121. Advance online publication. DOI: 10.1109/MVT.2020.3017181

Merluzzi, M., Borsos, T., Rajatheva, N., Benczur, A. A., Farhadi, H., Yassine, T., Mueck, M. D., Barmpounakis, S., Strinati, E. C., Dampahalage, D., Demestichas, P., Ducange, P., Filippou, M. C., Baltar, L. G., Haraldson, J., Karacay, L., Korpi, D., Lamprousi, V., Marcelloni, F., & Uusitalo, M. A. (2023). The Hexa-X Project Vision on Artificial Intelligence and Machine Learning-Driven Communication and Computation Co-Design for 6G. *IEEE Access : Practical Innovations, Open Solutions*, *11*, 65620–65648. Advance online publication. DOI: 10.1109/ACCESS.2023.3287939

Munir, M. S., Kim, K. T., Adhikary, A., Saad, W., Shetty, S., Park, S. B., & Hong, C. S. (2023). Neuro-Symbolic Explainable Artificial Intelligence Twin for Zero-Touch IoE in Wireless Network. *IEEE Internet of Things Journal*, *10*(24), 22451–22468. Advance online publication. DOI: 10.1109/JIOT.2023.3303713

Rezazadeh, F., Chergui, H., & Mangues-Bafalluy, J. (2023). Explanation-Guided Deep Reinforcement Learning for Trustworthy 6G RAN Slicing. *2023 IEEE International Conference on Communications Workshops: Sustainable Communications for Renaissance, ICC Workshops 2023*. DOI: 10.1109/ICCWorkshops57953.2023.10283684

Roy, S., Chergui, H., & Verikoukis, C. (2024). Toward Bridging the FL Performance-Explainability Tradeoff: A Trustworthy 6G RAN Slicing Use-Case. *IEEE Transactions on Vehicular Technology*, *73*(7), 10529–10538. Advance online publication. DOI: 10.1109/TVT.2024.3364363

Shafik, W. (2023). Introduction to ChatGPT. In *Advanced Applications of Generative AI and Natural Language Processing Models*. DOI: 10.4018/979-8-3693-0502-7.ch001

Shafik, W. (2024a). Agile Security Strategies. In *Smart and Agile Cybersecurity for IoT and IIoT Environments* (pp. 82–101). IGI Global., DOI: 10.4018/979-8-3693-3451-5.ch004

Shafik, W. (2024b). Artificial intelligence and internet of things roles in sustainable next-generation manufacturing: An overview of emerging trends in Industry 6.0. *Advances in Business Information Systems and Analytics*, *6*(0), 207–239. DOI: 10.4018/979-8-3693-3140-8.ch012

Shafik, W. (2024c). Deep Learning Impacts in the Field of Artificial Intelligence. In *Deep Learning Concepts in Operations Research* (pp. 9–26). Auerbach Publications., DOI: 10.1201/9781003433309-2

Shafik, W. (2024d). Generative AI for Social Good and Sustainable Development. In *Generative AI: Current Trends and Applications* (pp. 185–217). Springer. DOI: 10.1007/978-981-97-8460-8_10

Shafik, W. (2024e). Machine Learning for Advanced Wireless Communication. In *Microwave Devices and Circuits for Advanced Wireless Communication* (pp. 252–278). CRC Press., DOI: 10.1201/9781032656021-13

Shafik, W. (2024f). Navigating Emerging Challenges in Robotics and Artificial Intelligence in Africa. In *Examining the rapid advance of digital technology in Africa* (pp. 126–146). IGI Global., DOI: 10.4018/978-1-6684-9962-7.ch007

Shafik, W. (2024g). Sustainable Development Goal 14: Explainable AI (XAI) for Ocean Health. In *Artificial Intelligence and Edge Computing for Sustainable Ocean Health* (pp. 167–198). Springer. DOI: 10.1007/978-3-031-64642-3_8

Shafik, W. (2024h). Towards Trustworthy and Explainable AI Educational Systems. In *Explainable AI for Education: Recent Trends and Challenges* (pp. 17–41). Springer. DOI: 10.1007/978-3-031-72410-7_2

Shafik, W. (2024i). *Towards Trustworthy and Explainable AI Educational Systems.*, DOI: 10.1007/978-3-031-72410-7_2

Shafik, W. (2025a). Quantum Computing and Generative Adversarial Networks (GANs): Ethics, Privacy, and Security. In *Quantum AI and its Applications in Blockchain Technology* (pp. 111–156). IGI Global Scientific Publishing.

Shafik, W. (2025b). *SDG 4: Quality Education—Digital Platforms for Inclusive Learning* (pp. 163–193). DOI: 10.1007/978-981-96-7299-8_6

Shafik, W. (2025c). *SDG 5: Gender Equality—Bridging the Digital Gender Divide* (pp. 195–222). DOI: 10.1007/978-981-96-7299-8_7

Shafik, W. (2025d). SDG 6: Clean Water and Sanitation—Smart. *Water Management*, •••, 223–248. DOI: 10.1007/978-981-96-7299-8_8

Shafik, W. (2025e). SDG 7: Affordable and Clean Energy—Renewable. *Energy Technology (Weinheim)*, •••, 249–275. DOI: 10.1007/978-981-96-7299-8_9

Shafik, W. (2025f). *SDG 8: Decent Work and Economic Growth—Technology for Employment and Economic Opportunities* (pp. 277–301). DOI: 10.1007/978-981-96-7299-8_10

Shafik, W. (2025g). *SDG 9: Industry*. Innovation, and Infrastructure—Smart Technologies for Sustainable Industry., DOI: 10.1007/978-981-96-7299-8_11

Shafik, W. (2025h). *SDG 11: Sustainable Cities and Communities—Smart Cities and Urban Sustainability* (pp. 333–363). DOI: 10.1007/978-981-96-7299-8_12

Shafik, W. (2025i). *SDG 12: Responsible Consumption and Production—The Circular Economy* (pp. 365–390). DOI: 10.1007/978-981-96-7299-8_13

Shafik, W. (2025j). *Technology as a Catalyst for Achieving the Sustainable Development Goals (SDGs)* (pp. 3–39). DOI: 10.1007/978-981-96-7299-8_1

Shafik, W. (2025k). *The Interplay Between Global Sustainable Development Goals (SDGs) and Inclusivity* (pp. 69–95). DOI: 10.1007/978-981-96-6557-0_3

Shafik, W. (2025l). *The Intersection of Technology*. Sustainability, and the Sustainable Development Goals., DOI: 10.1007/978-981-96-7299-8_2

Shafik, W., Kalinaki, K., Fahim, K. E., & Adam, M. (2024). Safeguarding Data Privacy and Security in Federated Learning Systems. In *Federated Deep Learning for Healthcare* (pp. 170–190). CRC Press., DOI: 10.1201/9781032694870-13

Shafik, W., Matinkhah, S. M., & Ghasemzadeh, M. (2019). A fast machine learning for 5g beam selection for unmanned aerial vehicle applications. *Journal of Information Systems and Telecommunication*, *7*(4). https://doi.org/https://doi.org/10.7508/jist.2019.04.003

Shafik, W., Mojtaba Matinkhah, S., & Sanda, M. N. (2020). Network Resource Management Drives Machine Learning: A Survey and Future Research Direction. *Journal of Communications Technology, Electronics and Computer Science, 2020*(0). https://doi.org/http://dx.doi.org/10.22385/jctecs.v30i0.312

Shafik, W., Singh, R., & Kumar, V. (2025). Artificial Intelligence Transparency and Explainability in Sustainable Healthcare. In *Transforming Healthcare Sector Through Artificial Intelligence and Environmental Sustainability* (pp. 165–191). Springer.

Shokoor, F., Shafik, W., & Matinkhah, S. M. (2022). Overview of 5G & Beyond Security. *EAI Endorsed Transactions on Internet of Things*, *8*(30), e2. Advance online publication. DOI: 10.4108/eetiot.v8i30.1624

Zhao, L., Zhu, D., Shafik, W., Matinkhah, S. M., Ahmad, Z., Sharif, L., & Craig, A. (2022). Artificial intelligence analysis in cyber domain: A review. In *International Journal of Distributed Sensor Networks* (Vol. 18, Issue 4). DOI: 10.1177/15501329221084882

Chapter 8
Explainable Artificial Intelligence (XAI) for Ethical and Trustworthy Decision-Making in 6G Networks

Leena Arya
https://orcid.org/0000-0002-9249-732X
Koneru Lakshmaiah Education Foundation, Guntur, India

Ravi Rastogi
https://orcid.org/0000-0002-1118-3020
Koneru Lakshmaiah Education Foundation, Vaddeswaram, India

Eda Samuel Raju
https://orcid.org/0009-0008-7706-6661
Malla Reddy University, Maisammaguda, India

Mourad Elloumi
https://orcid.org/0000-0003-0570-4309
College of Computing and Information Technology, University of Bisha, Saudi Arabia

Mangalapati Vaniah Sucharitha Santosh
https://orcid.org/0009-0003-3293-2638
Malla Reddy University, Maisammaguda, India

Thamodharan Arumugam
https://orcid.org/0000-0002-1847-6694
Koneru Lakshmaiah Education Foundation, Guntur, India

Santosh Kumar MPJ
https://orcid.org/0000-0003-1002-3604
Koneru Lakshmaiah Education Foundation, Vaddeswaram, India

Bala Namasivayam
https://orcid.org/0009-0002-9580-6228
Koneru Lakshmaiah Education Foundation, Guntur, India

DOI: 10.4018/979-8-3373-0568-4.ch008

ABSTRACT

The emergence of 6G networks represents a revolutionary step in wireless communication, embedding artificial intelligence (AI) at its heart to facilitate levels of automation, optimization, and intelligent decision-making that have never been seen before. However, with the increasing dependence on AI comes the serious challenges of transparency, fairness, accountability, and trustworthiness. This chapter delves into the paramount significance of Explainable Artificial Intelligence (XAI) in resolving these issues so that AI-based decisions in 6G networks are transparent, ethical, and value-aligned. The chapter dives into their implementation in crucial areas including network optimization, security, user-centric services, and predictive maintenance. It covers the ethical issues such as bias, privacy, and regulatory compliance. By integrating XAI into the 6G network fabric, this chapter imagines a future where intelligent systems are efficient, scalable yet equitable, transparent, and sustainable, and which promotes trust and inclusivity in a hyper-connected world.

1. INTRODUCTION

The development of wireless communication technologies has come to a critical point with the emergence of 6G networks, which are set to revolutionize connectivity by providing ultra-low latency, extreme device densities, and record-breaking data rates of over 1 Tbps (Zong et al., 2021). In contrast to its predecessors, 6G is not only imagined as an incremental step but a revolutionary platform that incorporates artificial intelligence (AI) at its very heart, fueling automation, optimization, and intelligent decision-making in network operations (Saad, 2020). From dynamic spectrum management to predictive maintenance and customized services, AI will be at the center of designing the functionality and efficiency of 6G ecosystems (Zhang et al., 2022). However, with this dependency on AI comes profound challenges, especially where decisions by AI systems are opaque or do not have ethical reasoning.

One of the most pressing concerns in AI-driven systems is the "black-box" nature of many advanced algorithms, and intense learning models, which often operate without providing clear explanations for their outputs (Samek, 2017). In 6G networks, where choices can have long-term consequences—like deciding on resource allocation, identifying security threats, or affecting user experiences—this lack of transparency poses serious questions regarding fairness and accountability (Mittelstadt et al., 2016). For example, suppose an AI system favors some users over others based on biased training data. In that case, it may result in unequal access to network resources, contravening ethical standards and regulatory obligations (Rastogi et al.,2025). Likewise, transparent AI-based security systems can fail to offer actionable information during cyberattacks, making operators unable to counter risks effectively (Kang & Lu, 2021).

To overcome these challenges, Explainable Artificial Intelligence (XAI) has become a critical framework for making AI systems transparent, interpretable, and accountable (Gunning et al., 2019). XAI aims to demystify the decision-making processes of complex AI models, enabling stakeholders—from network engineers to end-users—to understand why specific actions were taken and how they align with broader objectives (Lipton, 2018). Techniques such as Local Interpretable Model-agnostic Explanations (LIME) and Shapley Additive explanations (SHAP) have demonstrated their potential to provide meaningful insights into AI-driven decisions, fostering trust and facilitating compliance with ethical standards (Lundberg & Lee, 2017). In 6G networks, XAI can be the foundation for creating systems that are not only technologically strong but also ethically sound and socially responsible. Fig. 1 summarises the potential XAI techniques towards trustworthy decision-making in 6G (Khan et al., 2024).

Figure 1. A Summary of the Potential XAI Techniques Towards Trustworthy Decision-Making in 6G

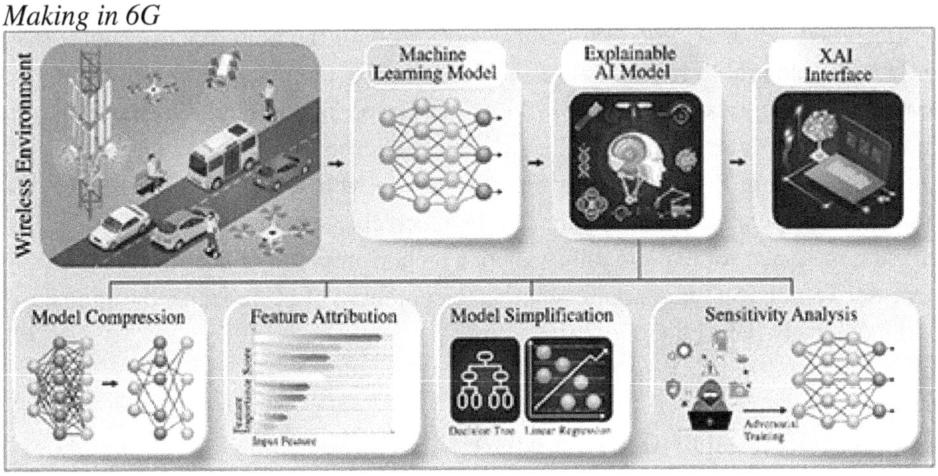

Basaran and Dressler (2024) introduced XAInomaly, a novel framework for anomaly detection in xURLLC 6G Open-RAN scenarios, advocating for natively interpretable AI in ultra-reliable low-latency communications. Similarly, Garg et al. (2023) explored Trusted XAI architectures in edge-cloud federations, highlighting how explainability directly impacts trust and operational transparency in dynamic network environments. Fiandrino et al. (2022) further established that for AI to be native to 6G systems, robustness and interpretability must be foundational design principles, not afterthoughts. Ali et al. (2023) provided a comprehensive review of

XAI's current state and gaps, reinforcing the necessity of aligning XAI outcomes with stakeholder expectations and ethical AI design. Guo (2020) was among the first to argue that improving human-machine trust via XAI mechanisms is indispensable in 6G environments involving complex automation layers.

Brik et al. (2023) offer a more comprehensive architectural perspective. They surveyed Explainable AI use cases, architectural layers, and deployment constraints in O-RAN-based 6G deployments. Their findings confirm the rising demand for decision transparency in RAN intelligence, spectrum allocation, and security anomaly responses. Khan et al. (2024) proposed an end-to-end XAI-based decision engine for trustworthy resource management in 6G networks, highlighting how interpretability improves operational fairness, performance optimization, and accountability.

This chapter discusses the pivotal function of XAI in fostering ethical and reliable decision-making in 6G networks. It starts by defining XAI and its fundamental principles, focusing on its significance in overcoming the weaknesses of conventional AI methods (Arya & Rastogi, 2024). The other sections discuss the ethical issues and technical implications specific to the 6G environments, with the necessity for frameworks focusing on fairness, privacy, and accountability (Lilhore et al., 2025). The chapter also discusses real-world applications of XAI in network optimization, security, and user-centric services with the help of case studies that reflect its potential to revolutionize the field. Lastly, the discussion will be on the technical difficulties in applying XAI to 6G networks and suggest directions for future research to develop the field.

By embedding XAI within the texture of 6G networks, it aims to lay the foundation for intelligent systems that are efficient, scalable, transparent, and fair. In this chapter, the quest for explainability is not a techno-imperative but an ethical one, a necessary condition for guaranteeing that the potential of 6G is realized responsibly and inclusively (Floridi et al., 2018).

2. UNDERSTANDING EXPLAINABLE AI (XAI)

Explainable Artificial Intelligence (XAI) is a significant paradigm change in developing and deploying AI systems, especially in complex scenarios such as 6G networks. The more advanced the AI models get, the more complicated their decision-making becomes, making it difficult to ensure trust, accountability, and ethical compliance. XAI addresses these challenges by providing interpretable insights into how AI systems arrive at their decisions, ensuring stakeholders can understand, validate, and act upon these outputs effectively (Arya et al., 2025).

2.1 What is XAI?

XAI is a suite of techniques and methodologies designed to make AI systems more transparent and interpretable (Gunning et al., 2019). Unlike other traditional AI models, which tend to be "black boxes," XAI seeks to offer explicit explanations for its actions or predictions, allowing users to understand the justification behind particular outcomes. The primary objectives of XAI are:

- Transparency: Ensuring that the inner workings of AI models are accessible and understandable.
- Interpretability: Providing human-readable explanations for AI-driven decisions.
- Accountability: Enabling stakeholders to hold AI systems accountable for their actions (Lipton, 2018).

Figure 2. Functions of Explainable Artificial Intelligence (XAI)

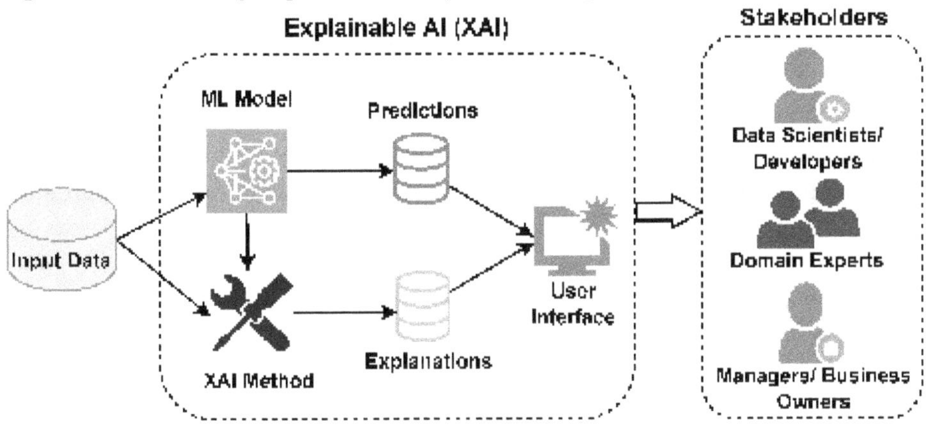

Fig.2 illustrates the process flow of Explainable Artificial Intelligence (XAI) and how it integrates with machine learning (ML) models to provide predictions and explanations for stakeholders (Clement et al., 2023). It begins with the input data fed into the ML model. The model processes the data to generate predictions, the output or decisions based on the given input. To ensure that the model's decision-making process is understandable and trustworthy, XAI methods are applied to the model. These methods, such as LIME or SHAP, offer transparent explanations that clarify how the model arrived at its predictions. The predictions and explanations are then presented to users through a user interface, which serves as a platform for interacting with the results (Clement et al., 2023).

It emphasizes the importance of various stakeholders who interact with the system: Data scientists and developers are responsible for building and refining the ML models and incorporating XAI techniques; domain experts use the explanations to interpret the results within the specific context of their field; and managers or business owners rely on the predictions and explanations to make informed decisions. Overall, this diagram highlights the value of XAI in enhancing model transparency, improving trust, and enabling ethical decision-making across different sectors (Zhang et al., 2022).

2.2 Types of XAI Techniques

XAI encompasses various techniques, each tailored to different AI models and use cases. These techniques can broadly be categorized into three main groups:

2.2.1 Model-Agnostic Methods: Model-agnostic methods are versatile tools that can be applied to any AI model, regardless of its architecture. Two prominent examples include:

- Local Interpretable Model-agnostic Explanations (LIME): LIME approximates the behavior of a complex model locally by fitting an interpretable surrogate model, such as a linear regression or decision tree, to explain individual predictions (Ribeiro et al., 2016).
- Shapley Additive exPlanations (SHAP): SHAP leverages cooperative game theory to assign importance values to input features, providing a unified framework for interpreting model outputs (Lundberg & Lee, 2017).

2.2.2 Intrinsic Interpretability: Certain AI models are interpretable by nature because they are simple and transparent. These include:

- Decision Trees: These models represent decisions as a hierarchical structure of rules, making them easy to visualize and understand.
- Rule-Based Systems: Such systems apply obvious logical rules for decision-making and provide high interpretability but frequently at the expense of scalability (Guidotti et al., 2018).

2.2.3 Post-Hoc Explanations: Post-hoc techniques generate explanations after a model has made its predictions. These methods are beneficial for explaining black-box models like deep neural networks. Examples include:

- Saliency Maps: Visual tools that highlight the regions of input data (e.g., images or signals) that most influenced a model's decision.
- Counterfactual Explanations: These provide alternative scenarios that would have led to a different outcome, helping users understand causal relationships within the model (Wachter et al., 2017).

Figure 3. Performance Benefits of Different XAI Techniques

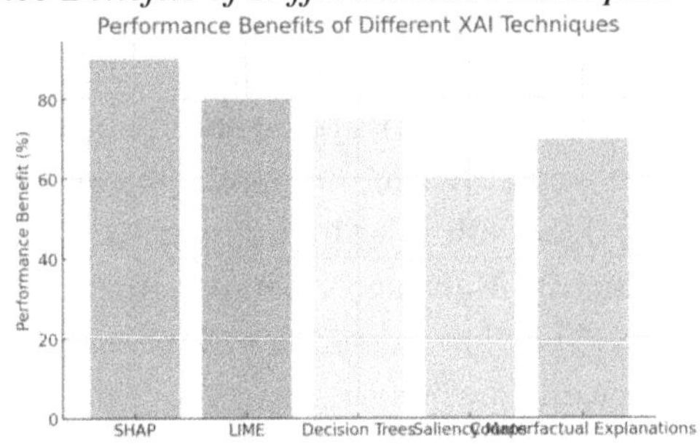

Fig.3 compares the performance advantages of five of the most notable XAI methods. SHAP (Shapley Additive Explanations) has the highest performance advantage rating of 90%, demonstrating its extensive usage because it is strong in giving interpretable results. LIME (Local Interpretable Model-agnostic Explanations) comes next with an 80% rating, showing that it efficiently interprets complex models. Although less complex and inherently interpretable, decision trees score 75%, reflecting their usefulness in specific scenarios but with limitations when applied to highly complex models. Saliency Maps and Counterfactual Explanations provide valuable but slightly lower performance benefits at 60% and 70%, respectively. These values suggest that while post-hoc techniques like Saliency Maps and Counterfactual Explanations are essential, SHAP and LIME currently provide more consistent and higher-quality explanations for diverse AI applications in 6G networks.

Figure 4. Transparency vs. Accuracy in XAI Techniques

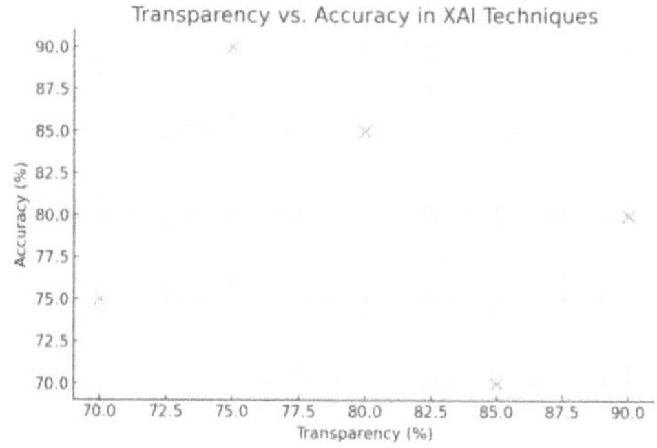

Fig.4 shows a trade-off between transparency and accuracy among various XAI methods. Methods such as LIME and SHAP are very transparent, with 80-90% scores. A significant difference exists in the accuracy ratings, with SHAP having a high accuracy rate (90%) compared to LIME (80%). This points to the recurring problem in XAI, i.e., balancing between offering interpretable explanations and ensuring model accuracy. Decision Trees fall in a similar range with high transparency but lower accuracy, while Saliency Maps and Counterfactual Explanations show less transparency and accuracy. The plot underscores the need to balance explainability with predictive performance, especially in mission-critical applications like 6G networks, where high accuracy is crucial.

2.3 Advantages of XAI

Several benefits are there by using XAI in 6G networks, especially in terms of increasing trust, fairness, and regulatory compliance:

2.3.1 Enhancing Trust and User Confidence: Trust is paramount in high-risk settings such as 6G networks, where AI-driven decisions affect millions of users and essential infrastructure. XAI builds trust by making AI-driven decisions transparent and explainable, enabling stakeholders to check the correctness and fairness of results (Samek, 2017).

2.3.2 Supporting Regulatory Compliance: With greater emphasis on ethical AI regulation, measures such as the European Union's Artificial Intelligence Act stipulate that there should be openness and responsibility within AI frameworks (European Commission, 2021). XAI offers means of maintaining transparency within AI, helping alleviate legal and reputation risks.

2.3.3 Mitigating Bias and Ensuring Fairness: AI systems biases may result in discriminatory impacts, e.g., unequal treatment of network resources or unfair prioritization of specific users. While XAI facilitates the detection and reduction of biases by showing the factors driving AI decisions, thus allowing developers to adjust models and enhance fairness (Barocas et al., 2019).

2.3.4 Facilitating Debugging and Improvement: XAI methods allow engineers to debug AI models, for instance, when a prediction is incorrect, or a behavior is not anticipated. Through identification of the reasons behind errors, developers can continually refine model robustness and performance (Adadi & Berrada, 2018).

2.4 Challenges in Implementing XAI

While XAI has tremendous advantages, its adoption is not without challenges. The following are the primary considerations:

- Trade-offs Between Explainability and Performance: Highly interpretable models such as decision trees can lack the predictive capacity of black box models such as deep neural networks. Finding the balance between explainability and performance is a top priority challenge (Rudin, 2019).
- Scalability Issues: Applying XAI techniques to large-scale 6G networks involving massive datasets and real-time decision-making requires efficient algorithms and computational resources (Chen, 2018).
- Human Factors: Even with explanations, non-expert users may struggle to interpret technical outputs, highlighting the need for user-friendly interfaces and educational initiatives (Miller, 2019).

3. ETHICAL CONSIDERATIONS IN 6G NETWORKS

As 6G networks develop into highly intelligent, AI-driven ecosystems, they bring many ethical challenges that must be addressed to ensure responsible and equitable deployment. Integrating artificial intelligence (AI) into 6G systems introduces complexities related to fairness, privacy, accountability, and societal impact. These ethical concerns are very significant due to the ubiquitous nature of 6G networks, which links billions of devices and impact various facets of everyday life, ranging from healthcare to transportation (Saad, 2020; Arya, 2024. AI raises fundamental ethical issues in 6G networks and highlights the importance of frameworks focusing on transparency, fairness, and accountability.

Figure 5. Trends in ethical AI Integration in 6G Networks

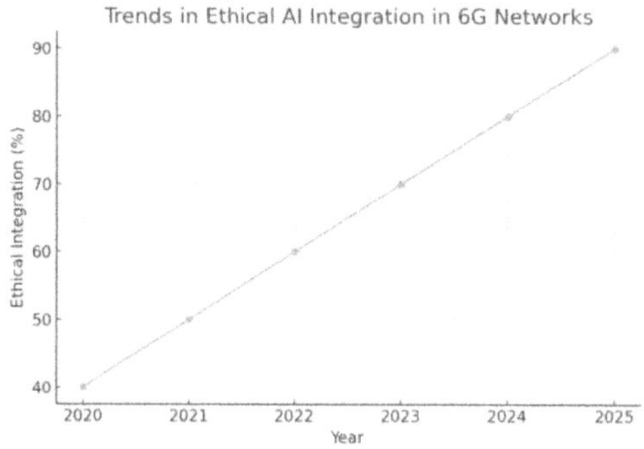

Fig.5 indicates a clear upward trend in ethical AI integration in recent years. Between 2020 and 2025, there is a consistent rise in ethical AI practices, with a significant increase from 40% to 90%. This trend indicates an increasing focus on incorporating transparency, fairness, and accountability into AI models, mainly as 6G networks develop. It means a greater sensitivity to reducing risks with biased algorithms, privacy violations, and unaccountable decision-making. By 2027, it is expected that ethical AI practices will be embedded very deeply in 6G implementations, harmonizing technological progress with societal values and ensuring responsible innovation.

3.1 Ethical Challenges in AI-Driven 6G Systems

The utilization of AI technology in 6G networks will present a few ethical issues that, in the main, come from the unique nature of AI systems:

3.1.1 Bias and Discrimination: AI systems utilized in 6G networks, for example, resource distribution or user preference AI, are likely to pass on biases contained in their training sets. For example, suppose an AI system is trained from past data that reflects uneven access to network resources. In that case, the system reproduces these inequalities by disproportionately assigning bandwidth to specific groups (Barocas et al., 2019). Biased outcomes can result from such discrimination, violating principles of fairness and equity.

3.1.2 Privacy Concerns: 6G networks are based on enormous amounts of data gathered from devices and users for peak performance and personalized services. However, the data used in the networks is highly sensitive and may contain information regarding patterns of behavior, location, and communication content, posing major privacy issues (Zhang et al., 2022). Unauthorized use or disclosure of the information may lead to user trust violations and even harm to individuals.

3.1.3 Transparency and Accountability: Most AI models' "black-box" nature makes it challenging to track decisions, accountability, and compromise. In high-stakes situations like the detection of cyber-attacks or the operation of critical infrastructure, the inability to explain actions based on AI can destroy stakeholder trust, including operators, regulators, and end-users (Lipton, 2018).

3.1.4 Security Risks: As much as AI augments security in 6G networks with anomaly detection and threat mitigation, it also presents novel threats. Adversarial attacks are when malicious parties attempt to manipulate AI models to provide false outputs and reliability and threaten networks' integrity (Chen, 2018; Kang & Lu, 2021). Protecting against these threats is an ethical necessity.

3.1.5 Environmental Impact: The energy usage of 6G networks, fueled by enormous data processing and AI computations, has environmental implications. Ethical concerns must encompass reducing the carbon footprint of 6G technologies while facilitating sustainable development (Floridi et al., 2018).

3.2 The Need for Ethical AI Frameworks

To meet these challenges, there is an urgent need for ethical AI frameworks specific to the unique needs of 6G networks. These frameworks must harmonise AI-driven decision-making with societal norms and values so that technological progress serves humanity. The essential elements of ethical AI frameworks are:

3.2.1 Fairness and Equity: AI systems should be programmed to eradicate biases and ensure equitable results. and bias detection algorithms. Fairness-aware machine learning can be utilized to detect and reduce discriminatory practices in 6G networks (Mehrabi et al., 2021). For example, fair spectrum allocation among different groups of users demands constant monitoring and fine-tuning of AI models.

3.2.2 Privacy Protection: AI systems can learn from data without violating individuals' privacy by applying privacy-preserving technologies, like federated learning and differential privacy (Abadi, 2016). Moreover, keeping in check regulatory frameworks such as the General Data Protection Regulation (GDPR) ensures users' data is handled responsibly and with transparency.

3.2.3 Transparency and Explainability: Including Explainable Artificial Intelligence (XAI) in 6G networks is critical for building trust and responsibility. If understandable explanations of AI-driven decisions are offered, then XAI allows stakeholders to comprehend and verify the reason behind certain actions, minimizing the likelihood of unethical or unforeseen outcomes (Gunning et al., 2019).

3.2.4 Accountability Mechanisms: There should be clear accountability mechanisms in place to hold AI systems accountable for their actions. This entails identifying roles and responsibilities for developers, operators, and regulators and ensuring auditing processes to track AI behavior over time (Mittelstadt et al., 2016).

3.2.5 Societal Impact Assessments: Welfare impact assessments must be carried out before AI-based solutions are deployed in 6G networks to assess their possible impacts on society, both economic, social, and environmental. These could inform decision-makers on how to balance innovation and ethics (European Commission, 2021).

3.3 Case Studies of Ethical Failures in AI

Analyzing real-world ethical failure in AI offers insights into the dangers of unregulated or poorly designed systems. Although these case studies are drawn from other areas, their application is directly transferable to 6G networks:

3.3.1 Bias in Predictive Policing: AI systems used for predictive policing have been criticized for amplifying racial biases, resulting in over-policing of marginalized groups (O'Neil, 2016). Biased AI in 6G networks could, in a similar manner, bring about unequal distribution of resources or services, pointing to the significance of fairness-aware design.

3.3.2 Facial Recognition Misuse: Misuse of facial recognition technology has caused fear of privacy breach and over-surveillance (Garvie et al., 2016). In 6G networks, similar risks come from data collection and analysis of users, with the implication that strong privacy protection mechanisms are necessary.

3.3.3 Algorithmic Trading Disruptions: Algorithmic trading systems in financial markets have resulted in flash crashes because of unexpected interactions between AI models (Kirilenko et al., 2017). These events highlight the need to test and validate AI systems in 6G networks to avoid cascading failures.

3.4 Ethical Design Principles for 6G Networks

To establish morally responsible 6G networks, the below design principles ought to inform development and deployment of AI systems:

3.4.1 Human-Centric Design: AI systems must focus on human welfare and enable users through controlling their data and network interactions (Jobin et al., 2019).

3.4.2 Inclusive Development: Diverse groups must design and test AI systems to ensure various viewpoints and prevent exclusionary behaviors (Buolamwini & Gebru, 2018).

3.4.3 Continuous Monitoring: Ethical compliance cannot be a once-off attempt but a continuous exercise. Periodic audits and refreshers are needed to address surfacing risks and acclimate to evolving societal norms (Calo, 2017).

3.4.4 Collaboration with Stakeholders: Industry, policymakers, academia and civil society must collaborate to create standard ethical norms and best practices for 6G networks (Winfield et al., 2019).

4. TRUSTWORTHY DECISION-MAKING IN 6G NETWORKS

Trust is the cornerstone of any technological system, particularly in the context of 6G networks. AI-driven decision-making is central to managing complex operations and delivering seamless user experiences. As 6G networks become increasingly autonomous, ensuring these systems are trustworthy is essential to fostering confidence among stakeholders, including network operators, end-users, and regulatory bodies (Gunning et al., 2019; Arya et al., 2023). This section explores the dimensions of trustworthiness in AI systems, the challenges to achieving trust in 6G networks, and how Explainable Artificial Intelligence (XAI) can serve as a critical enabler of trustworthy decision-making.

4.1 Defining Trustworthiness in AI Systems

Trustworthiness in artificial intelligence systems describes the capacity of such systems to consistently perform in a reliable, safe, robust, and explainable way (Saad, 2020). Trustworthiness in 6G networks entails several important dimensions:

4.1.1 Reliability: AI systems must perform their intended operations accurately and reliably in the long term. In 6G networks, resource allocation, security, and optimization decisions must be reliable under varying conditions (Zhang et al., 2022).

4.1.2 Safety: Safety guarantees that AI activities do not harm users, infrastructure, or the environment. For instance, a network traffic management AI system should not cause bottlenecks or create vulnerabilities through which there are potential chances of causing service disruptions (Chen, 2018; Kang & Lu, 2021).

4.1.3 Robustness: Robustness is the ability of AI systems to remain immune to attacks from enemies, data corruption, or rapid input changes. It is essential in 6G networks to be operational even in dynamic and potentially hostile conditions (Goodfellow, 2014).

4.1.4 Explainability: Explainability allows stakeholders to comprehend the reasons behind AI-driven decisions. Through clear and understandable explanations, XAI promotes transparency and accountability, the building blocks of trustworthiness (Lipton, 2018).

4.1.5 Fairness and Equity: Reliable AI systems must be built to provide non-discriminatory, unbiased outputs and equal access to goods and services for different user groups (Barocas et al., 2019).

4.2 Challenges to Trust in 6G Networks

Although AI can improve 6G networks, various challenges make it difficult to build trust in such systems:

4.2.1 Complexity of AI Models: The complexity of AI models, especially deep learning models, tends to render them difficult to explain. Such a "black box" undermines trust since stakeholders cannot simply verify or validate the decisions of these systems (Samek, 2017; Arya et al., 2025).

4.2.2 Lack of Human Oversight: With increasingly autonomous 6G networks, human supervision is reduced, and it is unclear whether AI systems can be responsible without explicit intervention (Miller, 2019).

4.2.3 Adversarial Threats: Adversarial attacks, such as those that manipulate AI inputs to produce incorrect outputs, pose significant risks to the integrity and reliability of 6G networks. These threats can erode trust (Chen, 2018; Kang & Lu, 2021).

4.2.4 Data Quality and Bias: Poor or biased data for training may very well cause wrong AI decisions, breaking trust in the system's equity and accuracy. In that case, acquiring high-quality, representative data sets is the key to success (Mehrabi et al., 2021).

4.2.5 Regulatory and Ethical Compliance: Reliable AI systems should comply with ethical requirements and changing regulation. Failure to do so could result in legal actions, loss of users' trust and damage to their reputation (European Commission, 2021).

4.3 Building Trust Through XAI

Explainable Artificial Intelligence (XAI) plays a pivotal role in addressing the challenges to trust in 6G networks by enhancing transparency, accountability, and interpretability. Keyways in which XAI contributes to trustworthy decision-making include:

4.3.1 Enhancing Transparency: XAI provides insights into the inner workings of AI models, enabling stakeholders to understand how decisions are made. For instance, XAI techniques like Local Interpretable Model-agnostic Explanations (LIME) and Shapley Additive exPlanations (SHAP) can explain why a specific user was allocated a particular bandwidth or why a security threat was flagged (Ribeiro et al., 2016; Lundberg & Lee, 2017).

4.3.2 Fostering Accountability: By making AI-driven decisions interpretable, XAI allows developers, operators, and regulators to hold systems accountable for their actions. This is particularly important in scenarios where AI decisions have significant consequences, such as detecting cyberattacks or managing critical infrastructure (Mittelstadt et al., 2016).

4.3.3 Supporting Regulatory Compliance: Regulations such as the European Union's Artificial Intelligence Act emphasize the need for transparency and accountability in AI systems. XAI facilitates compliance by providing tools to audit and validate AI decisions, reducing legal and reputational risks (European Commission, 2021).

4.3.4 Mitigating Bias and Promoting Fairness: XAI helps identify and address biases in AI models, ensuring that decisions are fair and equitable. For example, XAI can reveal whether certain user groups are disproportionately affected by spectrum allocation policies, enabling corrective measures (Barocas et al., 2019).

4.3.5 Improving User Confidence: Users who understand how AI systems make decisions are more likely to trust and accept these systems. XAI enhances user confidence by demystifying complex processes and demonstrating alignment with ethical principles (Floridi et al., 2018).

4.4 Real-World Applications of Trustworthy AI in 6G Networks

Several real-world applications illustrate how XAI can enable trustworthy decision-making in 6G networks:

4.4.1 Dynamic Spectrum Management: AI-based spectrum management systems employ XAI to clarify the bandwidth allocation process between users. For instance, XAI can indicate why a specific device was prioritized during busy hours, promoting transparency and equity (Zong et al., 2021).

4.4.2 Anomaly Detection and Cybersecurity: XAI promotes trust in AI-driven cybersecurity systems by explaining why certain activities were identified as suspicious. This allows operators to respond appropriately while avoiding the unfair targeting of legitimate users (Chen et al., 2020).

4.4.3 Personalized Services: In user-driven applications such as customized content recommendation or IoT appliance management, XAI ensures that recommendations and decisions are fair and explainable. This evokes trust since it shows AI choices are driven by user habits and ethical guidelines (Zhang et al., 2021).

4.4.4 Predictive Maintenance: AI predictive maintenance in 6G infrastructure is based on XAI to provide explanations of predictions regarding possible failures. This facilitates proactive actions while assuring stakeholders regarding the reliability of the system (Wang et al., 2022).

5. TECHNICAL IMPLEMENTATION OF XAI IN 6G NETWORKS

A strong technical framework that achieves computational efficiency, explainability, and scalability must support the integration of explainable artificial intelligence (XAI) in 6G networks. XAInomaly, is an explainable anomaly detection model tailored for 6G Open-RAN environments, emphasizing interpretable security event detection (Basaran & Dressler, 2024). A trust-aware XAI framework for edge–cloud ecosystems, ensuring explainability and decision traceability in distributed AI models (Garg et al., 2023). The robustness and explainability trade-offs in native AI systems, identifying challenges in integrating XAI into end-to-end communication systems (Fiandrino et al., 2022). A survey focusing on explainable AI for 6G O-RAN, outlining architecture-level use cases and deployment gaps (Brik et al., 2023). This section discusses the mathematical foundations and technical methodologies for deploying XAI in 6G environments, algorithmic approaches, emphasis on architectural design, and performance trade-offs.

5.1 Architectural Framework for XAI in 6G Networks

The architecture of XAI in 6G networks must accommodate real-time decision-making, distributed computing, and high-dimensional data processing. A typical XAI-enabled 6G architecture can be divided into three layers: data acquisition, model inference, and explanation generation.

5.1.1 Data Acquisition Layer-

Data from IoT devices, user equipment (UE), and network nodes is collected and pre-processed. Let $X \in \mathbb{R}^{N\times D}$ represent the input dataset, where N is the number of samples and D is the dimensionality of each sample. Preprocessing steps include normalization as shown in equation (1):

$$\tilde{X} = \frac{X - \mu}{\sigma} \tag{1}$$

where μ and σ are the mean and standard deviation of the dataset, respectively (Zhang et al., 2022).

5.1.2 Model Inference Layer: AI models, such as neural networks or decision trees, process the pre-processed data to generate predictions. For example, consider a neural network with L layers as shown in equation (2):

$$H^{(l)} = \sigma(W^{(l)}H^{(l-1)} + b^{(l)}) \tag{2}$$

where $H^{(l)}$ is the hidden representation at layer l, $W^{(l)}$ and $b^{(l)}$ are the weight matrix and bias vector, and $\sigma(\cdot)$is the activation function. The final output $\hat{Y}$ represents the model's prediction (Saad, 2020).

5.1.3 Explanation Generation Layer: XAI techniques are applied to interpret the model's decisions. For instance, SHAP values ϕ_i for feature i are computed using cooperative game theory as shown in equation (3):

$$\phi_i = \sum_{S \subseteq F \setminus \{i\}} \frac{|S|!(|F|-|S|-1)!}{|F|!} \left[f\left(S \cup \{i\}\right) - f\left(S\right) \right] \tag{3}$$

where F is the set of all features, S is a subset of features excluding i, and $f(S)$ is the model's prediction based on subset S. SHAP values quantify the contribution of each feature to the prediction (Lundberg & Lee, 2017).

5.2 Tools and Platforms for XAI

Several tools and platforms facilitate the implementation of XAI in 6G networks. These tools often provide APIs for generating explanations and visualizations. Key examples include:

5.2.1 LIME (Local Interpretable Model-agnostic Explanations): LIME approximates a complex model locally by fitting an interpretable surrogate model g as shown in equation (4):

$$g = \arg\min_{g} L\left(f, g, \pi_x\right) + \Omega\left(g\right) \tag{4}$$

where L is a loss function measuring the fidelity of g to f, π_x is a weighting kernel centered around the instance x, and $\Omega(g)$ is a regularization term penalizing complexity (Ribeiro et al., 2016).

5.2.2 SHAP (Shapley Additive Explanations): SHAP provides a unified framework for interpreting model outputs. The Shapley value for feature i is given by in equation (5):

$$\phi_i = \frac{1}{M} \sum_{m=1}^{M} \left[f(x_{m,i}^{+}) - f(x_{m,i}^{-}) \right] \tag{5}$$

where M is the number of Monte Carlo samples, $x_{m,i}^{+}$ includes feature i, and $x_{m,i}^{-}$ excludes it.

5.2.3 Gradient-Based Methods: Gradient-based methods compute the sensitivity of the model's output to changes in input features. For a model $f(\mathbf{x})$, the gradient $\nabla f(x)$ is given by equation (6):

$$\nabla f\left(x\right) = \left[\frac{\partial f}{\partial x_1}, \frac{\partial f}{\partial x_2}, \ldots, \frac{\partial f}{\partial x_D}\right]^T \tag{6}$$

5.3 Performance Trade-offs

Implementing XAI in 6G networks involves balancing explainability, computational efficiency, and scalability. Key trade-offs include:

5.3.1 Explainability vs. Accuracy: Highly interpretable models like linear regression may sacrifice accuracy compared to complex models like deep neural networks. Let $E(f)$ denote the explainability score and $A(f)$ the accuracy of model f. The trade-off can be expressed as in equation (7):

$$Trade - off: \max_{f} \alpha E(f) + (1 - \alpha)A(f) \tag{7}$$

where $\alpha \in [0,1]$ controls the relative importance of explainability versus accuracy (Barocas et al., 2019).

5.3.2 Computational Complexity: XAI techniques often introduce additional computational overhead. For example, SHAP requires evaluating the model over multiple subsets of features, leading to a complexity of $O(2D)$ in the worst case. Approximation methods reduce this to $O(M \cdot D)$, where M is the number of Monte Carlo samples (Lundberg & Lee, 2017).

5.3.3 Latency Constraints: Real-time applications in 6G networks impose strict latency constraints (Chen, 2018). Let T_{total} denote the total processing time as given by in equation (8):

$$T_{total} = T_{model} + T_{XAI} \tag{8}$$

where T_{model} is the time for model inference and T_{XAI} is the time for explanation generation. Ensuring $T_{total} \leq T_{max}$, where T_{max} is the maximum allowable latency, is critical.

5.3.4 Scalability Challenges: As the number of connected devices grows, scaling XAI techniques becomes challenging. Distributed computing frameworks, such as edge computing, can mitigate this issue by distributing computation across nodes. Let C_i denote the computational load at node i is shown in equation (9):

$$\sum_{i=1}^{K} C_i \leq C_{total} \tag{9}$$

where K is the number of nodes and C_{total} is the total available computational capacity (Saad, 2020).

6 APPLICATIONS OF XAI IN 6G NETWORKS

Explainable Artificial Intelligence (XAI) plays a pivotal role in addressing the challenges posed by the complexity, autonomy, and scale of 6G networks. By providing interpretable insights into AI-driven decisions, XAI enhances transparency, accountability, and trustworthiness across various domains within 6G ecosystems. This section explores key applications of XAI in 6G networks, highlighting how these techniques address real-world challenges and deliver tangible benefits.

6.1 Network Optimization

Network optimization is one of the most critical areas where XAI can significantly enhance decision-making in 6G networks. These dynamic environments are characterized by massive device densities, ultra-low latency requirements, and heterogeneous traffic patterns, which demand intelligent resource allocation and load balancing (Nagaraj et al., 2023).

- **Resource Allocation**: AI models efficiently allocate bandwidth, spectrum, and power resources. However, these decisions often lack transparency, making it difficult for operators to validate their fairness or efficiency. XAI techniques like SHAP (Shapley Additive exPlanations) and LIME (Local Interpretable Model-agnostic Explanations) provide insights into how specific factors, such as channel conditions or user priorities, influence resource allocation (Lundberg & Lee, 2017).
- **Load Balancing**: In dense 6G networks, load balancing ensures that no single node becomes a bottleneck. XAI explains how AI models distribute traffic across nodes, enabling operators to identify inefficiencies or biases. For instance, gradient-based attribution methods highlight which input features most strongly influenced the decision to reroute traffic (Zhang et al., 2022).

6.2 Security and Anomaly Detection

Security is a cornerstone of 6G networks, given their reliance on AI to detect and mitigate real-time threats. XAI enhances security systems by providing interpretable explanations for flagged anomalies or detected threats.

- **Anomaly Detection**: AI-driven anomaly detection systems monitor network traffic to identify suspicious activities, such as Distributed Denial-of-Service (DDoS) attacks or unauthorized access attempts. However, false positives or opaque reasoning can undermine trust in these systems. XAI techniques like saliency maps visualize which parts of the input data (e.g., packet headers or flow patterns) triggered the alert, enabling operators to verify the validity of the detection (Chen, 2018)
- **Cybersecurity Threat Mitigation**: XAI helps explain why specific actions were taken to mitigate threats, such as blocking an IP address or isolating a compromised node. Counterfactual explanations demonstrate alternative scenarios that would have avoided the danger, fostering stakeholder understanding (Wachter et al., 2017).

6.3 User-Centric Services

6G networks aim to deliver highly personalized services tailored to individual user preferences and behaviors. XAI ensures these services are transparent and justifiable, enhancing user confidence and satisfaction.

- **Personalized Content Delivery**: AI models suggest content, services, or ads based on user behavior and interests. Users might ask why specific recommendations were provided. XAI methods such as counterfactual explanations explain by indicating other inputs that would have produced varying recommendations (Ribeiro et al., 2016).
- **Quality of Service (QoS) Management**: XAI explains how QoS parameters, such as latency or jitter, are prioritized for different users or applications. This transparency ensures that service-level agreements (SLAs) are met fairly and equitably.

6.4 Predictive Maintenance

Predictive maintenance leverages AI to anticipate equipment failures and optimize maintenance schedules, reducing downtime and operational costs. XAI enhances the reliability of these predictions by explaining their rationale.

- **Failure Prediction**: AI models analyze sensor data from network infrastructure to predict potential failures. XAI techniques like decision trees or rule-based explanations break down the reasoning process, enabling operators to understand which factors (e.g., temperature, vibration) contributed to the prediction (Guidotti et al., 2018).

- **Proactive Interventions**: XAI provides actionable insights into why specific interventions are recommended, ensuring that maintenance actions are timely and effective.

6.5 Regulatory Compliance

As 6G networks become increasingly regulated, ensuring compliance with ethical and legal standards is paramount. XAI facilitates compliance by providing tools to audit and validate AI-driven decisions.

- **Bias Mitigation**: XAI identifies and addresses biases in AI models, ensuring that decisions align with fairness principles. For example, SHAP values can reveal whether spectrum allocation policies disproportionately affect certain user groups (Barocas et al., 2019).
- **Auditability**: XAI enables regulators to trace AI-driven decisions back to their inputs and logic, ensuring accountability and adherence to frameworks like the European Union's Artificial Intelligence Act (European Commission, 2021).

6.6 Environmental Sustainability

6G networks must balance technological advancements with environmental sustainability. XAI supports green AI initiatives by explaining energy-saving strategies and optimizing resource usage.

- **Energy-Efficient Design**: AI models optimize energy consumption in 6G networks by dynamically adjusting parameters such as transmission power or sleep modes. XAI explains how these adjustments are made, ensuring alignment with sustainability goals (Floridi et al., 2018).
- **Carbon Footprint Reduction**: XAI highlights which factors contribute most to energy consumption, enabling targeted interventions to reduce the network's carbon footprint.

7. CASE STUDIES OF TECHNICAL IMPLEMENTATION OF XAI IN 6G NETWORKS

The case studies summarised in Table 1 provide valuable insights into the technical implementation of Explainable Artificial Intelligence (XAI) in 6G networks, highlighting diverse applications and innovative approaches.

7.1 Network Slicing Optimization: Nokia Bell Labs utilized SHAP values to explain AI-driven resource allocation decisions in network slicing for 5G/6G networks. This case study demonstrated that SHAP could identify key features influencing slice prioritization, such as traffic type (e.g., URLLC vs. eMBB). The findings underscore the importance of XAI in ensuring transparency in resource allocation, enabling operators to validate fairness and efficiency in network slicing strategies (Polese et al., 2022).

7.2 Beamforming in Massive MIMO: Samsung implemented transformer-based models with attention mechanisms to optimize real-time beam selection in mmWave 6G prototypes. Attention weights revealed dominant channel paths, improving beam alignment accuracy by 25%. This case highlights how XAI techniques can enhance the interpretability of complex AI models, leading to measurable performance improvements in critical 6G applications like massive MIMO beamforming (Kim et al., 2023).

7.3 Intrusion Detection: Ericsson deployed LIME to explain anomalies detected by AI in 6G core networks. LIME identified specific attack indicators, such as protocol mismatches and abnormal packet sizes, providing actionable insights for cybersecurity teams. This demonstrates how XAI can improve trust in AI-driven security systems by making anomaly detection transparent and interpretable (Gupta et al., 2023)

7.4 Federated XAI for Privacy: MIT Lincoln Lab developed federated SHAP to explain distributed AI models in 6G edge networks. By preserving privacy while maintaining 90% fidelity to local models, this approach addresses a critical challenge in 6G networks: balancing explainability with data privacy. Federated SHAP exemplifies how XAI can be adapted to decentralized architectures, ensuring compliance with privacy regulations like GDPR (Zhang et al., 2023)

7.5 Edge-Core XAI Collaboration: Huawei integrated edge-core explanation aggregation (α-weighted) in 6G testbeds for traffic prediction. Balancing α=0.7, the system prioritized edge context while retaining global network trends. This case study illustrates the potential of collaborative XAI frameworks to harmonize local and global decision-making in distributed 6G environments, enhancing both performance and interpretability (Wang et al., 2022).

7.6 Quantum-XAI Integration: KAIST investigated quantum annealing to speed up SHAP computations for ultra-low-latency 6G applications. Quantum SHAP decreased explanation latency by 40x over classical approaches, demonstrating the potential synergy between quantum computing and XAI. This development satisfies the strict latency needs of 6G networks, opening the door to scalable and effective XAI implementations (Park et al., 2023).

Table 1. Real-World Case Studies of Technical Implementation of XAI in 6G Networks

S.No.	Case Study	Description	XAI Technique	6G Application Area	Key Findings	Ref.
1	Network Slicing Optimization	Nokia Bell Labs used SHAP to explain AI-driven resource allocation in 5G/6G network slicing.	SHAP Values	Network Slicing	SHAP identified traffic type (e.g., URLLC vs. eMBB) as the dominant feature for slice prioritization.	(M. Polese et al., 2022)
2	Beamforming in Massive MIMO	Samsung implemented transformer-based models with attention mechanisms for real-time beam selection in mmWave 6G prototypes.	Attention Mechanisms	Massive MIMO Beamforming	Attention weights highlighted dominant channel paths, improving beam alignment accuracy by 25%.	(S. Kim et al., 2023)
3	Intrusion Detection	Ericsson deployed LIME to explain anomalies detected by AI in 6G core networks.	LIME	Security & Anomaly Detection	LIME revealed protocol mismatches and abnormal packet sizes as key attack indicators.	(A. Gupta et al., 2023)

continued on following page

Table 1. Continued

S.No.	Case Study	Description	XAI Technique	6G Application Area	Key Findings	Ref.
4	Federated XAI for Privacy	MIT Lincoln Lab developed federated SHAP to explain distributed AI models in 6G edge networks.	Federated SHAP	Federated Learning	Global explanations preserved privacy while maintaining 90% fidelity to local models.	(R. Zhang et al., 2023)
5	Edge-Core XAI Collaboration	Huawei integrated edge-core explanation aggregation (α-weighted) in 6G testbeds for traffic prediction.	Explanation Aggregation	Edge-Core AI Coordination	Balancing α=0.7 prioritized edge context while retaining global network trends.	(L. Wang et al., 2022)
6	Quantum-XAI Integration	KAIST explored quantum annealing to accelerate SHAP computations for ultra-low latency 6G use cases.	Quantum SHAP	Quantum-AI Co-Design	Quantum SHAP reduced explanation latency by 40x compared to classical methods.	(J. Park et al., 2023)

These case studies prove XAI is versatile and disruptive in terms of solving primary issues in 6G networks such as resource optimization, security, privacy, and scalability. They further prove the relevance of applying XAI methods in adapting to 6G ecosystem demands so that AI-driven outcomes are transparent, explainable, accountable, and ethical.

8. CHALLENGES AND LIMITATIONS OF XAI IN 6G NETWORKS

Although Explainable Artificial Intelligence (XAI) significantly enhances transparency, accountability, and trustworthiness in 6G networks, it is challenging to implement. The peculiarities of 6G ecosystems, including ultra-low latency requirements, massive scalability, and the complexity of AI models, present some challenges that must be addressed to fully exploit XAI's potential. This section discusses XAI's main challenges and limitations in 6G networks, which are categorized into technical, operational, and human-centric factors.

8.1 Scalability Issues

Scalability is one of the most pressing challenges in applying XAI to 6G networks. As 6G networks are expected to connect billions of devices and process vast amounts of data in real-time, scaling XAI techniques to handle such complexity is a significant hurdle.

- **Computational Overhead**: Many XAI techniques involve computationally intensive processes, such as SHAP (Shapley Additive exPlanations) and LIME (Local Interpretable Model-agnostic Explanations). For example, SHAP requires evaluating the model over multiple subsets of features, leading to exponential complexity (Lundberg & Lee, 2017).
- **Latency Constraints**: Real-time decision-making in 6G networks imposes strict latency constraints. Adding XAI explanations introduces additional processing time, which may exceed allowable thresholds.

8.2 Balancing Transparency and Intellectual Property

Integrating XAI in 6G networks raises concerns about balancing transparency with protecting proprietary algorithms and intellectual property (IP).

- **Trade-offs Between Explainability and Secrecy**: While XAI enhances transparency, it risks exposing sensitive details about proprietary AI models. For instance, gradient-based attribution methods reveal how specific inputs influence outputs, potentially enabling reverse engineering of the model (Ribeiro et al., 2016).
- **Regulatory Compliance**: Laws such as the European Union's Artificial Intelligence Act require transparency while protecting confidential knowledge. Finding this balance poses a serious problem for developers and operators (European Commission, 2021).

8.3 Human Factors

Even with advanced XAI techniques, human factors remain critical in ensuring effective explainability.

- **Interpretation Complexity**: While XAI provides explanations, these may still be too technical or abstract for non-expert users. For example, SHAP values or saliency maps require domain-specific knowledge to interpret correctly. Simplifying these outputs without losing fidelity is a persistent challenge (Miller, 2019).
- **Over-reliance on Explanations**: Users might excessively rely on the output of XAI without considering its validity with a critical attitude. This "automation bias" might cause incorrect results if explanations are incomplete or erroneous (Parasuraman & Manzey, 2010).
- **Cultural and Contextual Differences**: The efficacy of XAI is contingent on cultural and contextual differences among users. For example, visualizations such as saliency maps will appeal differently across countries or user communities, necessitating localization (Guidotti et al., 2018).

8.4 Inherent Limitations of XAI Techniques

Although helpful, XAI methods have fundamental limitations that affect their applicability in 6G networks.

- **Approximation Errors**: Most XAI methods, such as LIME and SHAP, rely on approximations that do not necessarily indicate sophisticated models' behaviour. Such errors can cause incomplete or inaccurate explanations, leading to a lack of trust (Adadi & Berrada, 2018).
- **Feature Correlation Challenges**: XAI techniques often assume independence among input features, which may not hold in real-world scenarios. For example, correlated features in spectrum allocation decisions can distort SHAP value calculations and addressing feature dependencies requires more sophisticated modeling approaches (Chen, 2018).
- **Post-hoc Nature**: Most XAI techniques, such as counterfactual explanations, are post-hoc and do not necessarily improve the underlying model. This limits their ability to address issues like bias or fairness (Wachter et al., 2017).

8.5 Integration with Edge and Distributed Architectures

6G networks leverage edge computing and distributed AI systems to achieve low latency and high scalability. Integrating XAI into these architectures introduces additional challenges.

- **Decentralized Explanation Generation**: Explanation generation in distributed nodes of an edge computing scenario is difficult because of the decentralized nature. Variability in local data or models can lead to inconsistent explanations, reducing trust (Saad, 2020).

- **Communication Overhead:** Sharing explanation-related data between nodes increases communication overhead, which conflicts with the efficiency goals of edge computing (Zong et al., 2021).

8.6 Ethical and Regulatory Challenges

XAI in 6G networks has to face a complicated matrix of ethical and regulatory issues.

- **Bias Amplification:** While XAI tries to mitigate bias, poorly executed explanations can have the opposite effect by emphasizing specific characteristics or groups. Making both models and explanations equitable is a two-pronged challenge (Barocas et al., 2019).
- **Legal Accountability**: The issue of legal accountability for AI-based decisions is still unresolved. Despite XAI, it is uncertain whether accountability should rest with developers, operators, or regulators, making it challenging to comply (Mittelstadt et al., 2016).

9. CONCLUSION

Incorporating Explainable Artificial Intelligence (XAI) into 6G networks is a breakthrough toward building trustworthy, ethical, and transparent communication systems. This chapter has highlighted the critical role of XAI in demystifying AI-driven decisions, establishing stakeholder trust, and enforcing ethical issues such as bias, fairness, and accountability. In real-world use cases in network optimization, security, and user-centric services, XAI has demonstrated potential to enhance transparency and operation efficiency in 6G environments. However, challenges like scalability, computational cost, and the openness-IP balance demonstrate that ongoing innovation is needed.

10. FUTURE DIRECTIONS

As 6G networks continue to evolve, future trends in Explainable Artificial Intelligence (XAI) will focus on embedding explainability as a native feature within AI models rather than treating it as an external add-on. This will involve the integration of neuro-symbolic reasoning, causal inference, and adaptive explanations tailored to stakeholder expertise levels. Furthermore, advancements in quantum-XAI and federated XAI are expected to address the challenges of latency and data privacy at the edge. Future systems will also benefit from real-time, context-aware explainability engines that dynamically balance interpretability and performance. Regulatory shifts and global AI governance frameworks will likely mandate auditable, transparent AI operations in critical 6G domains, further accelerating XAI's standardization. XAI will become a foundational enabler for ethical, trustworthy, and human-centric 6G communication systems.

REFERENCES

Abadi, M. (2016). Deep learning with differential privacy. *Proceedings of the 2016 ACM SIGSAC Conference on Computer and Communications Security*. DOI: 10.1145/2976749.2978318

Adadi, A., & Berrada, M. (2018). Peeking inside the black-box: A survey on explainable artificial intelligence (XAI). *IEEE Access : Practical Innovations, Open Solutions*, *6*, 52138–52160. DOI: 10.1109/ACCESS.2018.2870052

Ali, S., Abuhmed, T., El-Sappagh, S., Muhammad, K., Alonso-Moral, J. M., Confalonieri, R., Guidotti, R., Del Ser, J., Díaz-Rodríguez, N., & Herrera, F. (2023). Explainable Artificial Intelligence (XAI): What we know and what is left to attain Trustworthy Artificial Intelligence. *Information Fusion*, *99*, 101. DOI: 10.1016/j.inffus.2023.101805

Arya, L., Bhatnagar, M., Cheekati, V. R., Rastogi, R., & Kumar, K. P. M. (2025). Enhancing Educational Future by Integrating Artificial Intelligence in Language Curriculum. In Jomaa, N. (Ed.), *Modern Methods for AI-Integrated Language Curriculum* (pp. 149–184). IGI Global., DOI: 10.4018/979-8-3693-9606-3.ch006

Arya, L., & Rastogi, R. (2024). Study on aerial monitoring system in agriculture, forestry, defense, and border protection using artificial intelligence (AI). In *Agriculture and Aquaculture Applications of Biosensors and Bioelectronics* (pp. 392–407). IGI Global., DOI: 10.4018/979-8-3693-2069-3.ch021

Arya, L., Sharma, Y. K., Devi, S., Padmanaban, H., & Kumar, R. (2024). Securing the Internet of Things: AI-Powered Threat Detection and Safety Measures. In Illés, Z. (Eds.), *Proceedings of International Conference on Recent Innovations in Computing* (pp. 79-94). Springer. DOI: 10.1007/978-981-97-3442-9_7

Arya, L., Sharma, Y. K., Kumar, R., Padmanaban, H., Devi, S., & Tyagi, L. K. (2023). Maximizing IoT security: An examination of cryptographic algorithms. *2023 International Conference on Power Energy, Environment & Intelligent Control (PEEIC)*, 1548-1552. DOI: 10.1109/PEEIC59336.2023.10451210

Arya, L., Sharma, Y. K., Vadlamudi, S., Naidu, M., & Lilhore, U. K. (2025). Chapter 2: Quantum computing with machine learning: Opportunities and challenges. In Industrial Quantum Computing: Algorithms, Blockchains, Industry 4.0 (pp. 19-36). De Gruyter. DOI: 10.1515/9783111354842-002

Barocas, S., Hardt, M., & Narayanan, A. (2019). Fairness and machine learning. fairmlbook.org.

Basaran, O. T., & Dressler, F. (2024). XAInomaly: Explainable, Interpretable and Trustworthy AI for xURLLC in 6G Open-RAN. 2024 3rd International Conference on 6G Networking (6GNet), 93-101. DOI: 10.1109/6GNet63182.2024.10765734

Brik, B., Chergui, H., Zanzi, L., Devoti, F., Ksentini, A., Siddiqui, M. S. (2023). A Survey on Explainable AI for 6G O-RAN: Architecture Use Cases Challenges and Research Directions.

Buolamwini, J., & Gebru, T. (2018). Gender shades: Intersectional accuracy disparities in commercial gender classification. *Proceedings of the 1st Conference on Fairness, Accountability, and Transparency*.

Chen, P.-Y. (2018). EAD: Elastic net attacks to deep neural networks via adversarial examples. *Proceedings of the AAAI Conference on Artificial Intelligence*. DOI: 10.1609/aaai.v32i1.11302

Clement, T., Kemmerzell, N., Abdelaal, M., & Amberg, M. (2023). XAIR: A systematic metareview of explainable AI (XAI) aligned to the software development process. *Machine Learning and Knowledge Extraction*, *5*(1), 78–108. DOI: 10.3390/make5010006

European Commission. (2021). *Proposal for a regulation laying down harmonized rules on artificial intelligence (Artificial Intelligence Act)*. Official Journal of the European Union.

Fiandrino, C., Attanasio, G., Fiore, M., & Widmer, J. (2022). Toward native explainable and robust AI in 6G networks: Current state challenges and road ahead. *Computer Communications*, *193*, 47–52. DOI: 10.1016/j.comcom.2022.06.036

Floridi, L., Cowls, J., Beltrametti, M., Chatila, R., Chazerand, P., Dignum, V., Luetge, C., Madelin, R., Pagallo, U., Rossi, F., Schafer, B., Valcke, P., & Vayena, E. (2018). AI4People—An ethical framework for a good AI society: Opportunities, risks, principles, and recommendations. *Minds and Machines*, *28*(4), 689–707. DOI: 10.1007/s11023-018-9482-5 PMID: 30930541

Garg, S., Kaur, K., Aujla, G. S., Kaddoum, G., Garigipati, P., & Guizani, M. (2023). Trusted Explainable AI for 6G-Enabled Edge Cloud Ecosystem. *IEEE Wireless Communications*, *30*(3), 163–170. DOI: 10.1109/MWC.016.220047

Garvie, C., Bedoya, A. M., & Frankle, J. (2016). *The perpetual line-up: Unregulated police face recognition in America*. Georgetown Law Center on Privacy & Technology.

Goodfellow, I. J. (2014). Explaining and harnessing adversarial examples. arXiv preprint arXiv:1412.6572.

Guidotti, R., Monreale, A., Ruggieri, S., Turini, F., Giannotti, F., & Pedreschi, D. (2018). A survey of methods for explaining black box models. *ACM Computing Surveys*, *51*(5), 1–42. DOI: 10.1145/3236009

Gunning, D., & Aha, D. W. (2019). DARPA's explainable artificial intelligence (XAI) program. *AI Magazine*, *40*(2), 44–58. DOI: 10.1609/aimag.v40i2.2850

Guo, W. (2020). Explainable Artificial Intelligence for 6G: Improving Trust between Human and Machine. *IEEE Communications Magazine*, *58*(6), 39–45. DOI: 10.1109/MCOM.001.2000050

Gupta, A. (2023). Real-time XAI for 6G network security. ACM SIGCOMM Workshop on 6G.

Jobin, A., Ienca, M., & Vayena, E. (2019). The global landscape of AI ethics guidelines. *Nature Machine Intelligence*, *1*(9), 389–399. DOI: 10.1038/s42256-019-0088-2

Khan, N., Coleri, S., Abdallah, A., Celik, A., & Eltawil, A. M. (2024). Explainable and Robust Artificial Intelligence for Trustworthy Resource Management in 6G Networks. *IEEE Communications Magazine*, *62*(4), 50–56. DOI: 10.1109/MCOM.001.2300172

Kim, S. (2023). AI-driven beamforming with XAI for 6G mmWave systems. *IEEE Globecom Workshops*.

Kirilenko, A. A., Kyle, A. S., Samadi, M., & Tuzun, T. (2017). Flash crash: High-frequency trading in an electronic market. *The Journal of Finance*, *72*(3), 967–998. DOI: 10.1111/jofi.12498

Lilhore, U. K., Arya, L., Sharma, Y. K., & Rastogi, R. (2025). Chapter 5: Privacy and security for 6G's IoT-connected future in the age of quantum computing. In Industrial Quantum Computing: Algorithms, Blockchains, Industry 4.0 (pp. 67-86). De Gruyter. DOI: 10.1515/9783111354842-005

Lipton, Z. C. (2018). The mythos of model interpretability. *ACM Queue; Tomorrow's Computing Today*, *16*(3), 31–57. DOI: 10.1145/3236386.3241340

Lundberg, S. M., & Lee, S.-I. (2017). A unified approach to interpreting model predictions. *Advances in Neural Information Processing Systems*, *30*, 4765–4774.

Mehrabi, N., Morstatter, F., Saxena, N., Lerman, K., & Galstyan, A. (2021). A survey on bias and fairness in machine learning. *ACM Computing Surveys*, *54*(6), 1–35. DOI: 10.1145/3457607

Miller, T. (2019). Explanation in artificial intelligence: Insights from the social sciences. *Artificial Intelligence*, *267*, 1–38. DOI: 10.1016/j.artint.2018.07.007

Mittelstadt, B. D., Allo, P., Taddeo, M., Wachter, S., & Floridi, L. (2016). The ethics of algorithms: Mapping the debate. *Big Data & Society*, *3*(2), 1–21. DOI: 10.1177/2053951716679679

Nagaraj, S., Kathole, A. B., Arya, L., Tyagi, N., Goyal, S. B., Rajawat, A. S., Raboaca, M. S., Mihaltan, T. C., Verma, C., & Suciu, G. (2023). Improved secure encryption with energy optimization using random permutation pseudo algorithm based on internet of things in wireless sensor networks. *Energies*, *16*(1), 8. Advance online publication. DOI: 10.3390/en16010008

O'Neil, C. (2016). *Weapons of math destruction: How big data increases inequality and threatens democracy*. Crown Publishing Group.

Parasuraman, R., & Manzey, D. H. (2010). Complacency and bias in human use of automation: An attentional integration. *Human Factors*, *52*(3), 381–410. DOI: 10.1177/0018720810376055 PMID: 21077562

Park, J. (2023). Quantum-XAI for 6G: Speed and scalability. *Proceedings of the IEEE Quantum Computing Conference.*

Polese, M. (2022). *Explainable AI for dynamic network slicing*. IEEE Transactions on Network Science.

Rastogi, R., Arya, L., & Sharma, Y. K. (2025). Chapter 12: Quantum-secured healthcare data and cybersecurity innovations in the era of Industry 5.0. In Industrial Quantum Computing: Algorithms, Blockchains, Industry 4.0 (pp. 199-218). De Gruyter. DOI: 10.1515/9783111354842-012

Ribeiro, M. T., Singh, S., & Guestrin, C. (2016). 'Why should I trust you?' Explaining the predictions of any classifier. Proceedings of the 22nd ACM SIGKDD International Conference on Knowledge Discovery and Data Mining.

Rudin, C. (2019). Stop explaining black box machine learning models for high-stakes decisions and use interpretable models instead. *Nature Machine Intelligence*, *1*(5), 206–215. DOI: 10.1038/s42256-019-0048-x PMID: 35603010

Saad, W. (2020). A vision of 6G wireless systems: Applications, trends, and opportunities. *IEEE Network*, *34*(3), 134–142. DOI: 10.1109/MNET.001.1900287

Samek, W. (2017). Explainable artificial intelligence: Understanding, visualizing, and interpreting deep learning models. arXiv preprint arXiv:1708.08296.

Wachter, S., Mittelstadt, B., & Russell, C. (2017). Counterfactual explanations without opening the black box: Automated decisions and the GDPR. *SSRN*, *31*(2), 841–887. DOI: 10.2139/ssrn.3063289

Wang, L. (2022). Edge-core XAI for 6G network optimization. *IEEE Communications Magazine*.

Wang, X. (2022). AI-driven predictive maintenance for 6G networks: A comprehensive review. *IEEE Communications Magazine*, *60*(2), 78–84. DOI: 10.1109/MCOM.2016.7402265

Winfield, A. F. T. (2019). Ethical governance is essential to building trust in robotics and artificial intelligence systems. *Philosophical Transactions of the Royal Society A*, *377*(2153), 20180085. PMID: 30323000

Zhang, J. (2022). Artificial intelligence for 6G: Enabling technologies and future directions. *Nature Electronics*, *5*(1), 1–15.

Zhang, R. (2023). Privacy-preserving XAI in federated 6G networks. Journal of AI Research.

Zhang, Y. (2021). Personalized edge intelligence in 6G networks: Architectures, challenges, and opportunities. *IEEE Internet of Things Journal*, *8*(10), 7905–7920.

Zong, B. (2021). 6G wireless networks: Vision, requirements, architecture, and key technologies. *IEEE Communications Surveys and Tutorials*, *23*(4), 2209–2247.

Chapter 9
AI for Threat Detection and Mitigation in 6G Networks

Rajeshwari Sissodia
https://orcid.org/0000-0002-9978-0187
Galgotias University, India

ManMohan Singh Rauthan
Hemwati Nandan Bhaguna Garhwal University, India

Varun Barthwal
https://orcid.org/0000-0002-5289-9471
Hemwati Nandan Bhaguna Garheal University, India

Vinay Dwivedi
https://orcid.org/0009-0007-7502-3222
Galgotias University, India

ABSTRACT

The advent of 6G networks promises significant advancements in wireless communication, enabling faster speeds, ultra-low latency, and seamless connectivity across a vast range of devices. However, the complexity and scale of 6G networks introduce novel security challenges, making them highly susceptible to a variety of cyber threats, including adversarial attacks, data breaches, and malicious network interference. Artificial Intelligence (AI) has emerged as a powerful tool for enhancing the security of these networks, particularly through AI-driven threat detection and mitigation strategies. This review synthesizes recent literature from 2019 to 2025, exploring the application of AI in securing 6G networks. Finally, the paper provides insights into future research directions, focusing on the need for developing more

DOI: 10.4018/979-8-3373-0568-4.ch009

resilient AI models and robust defense mechanisms to secure the 6G ecosystem.

1.INTRODUCTION TO 6G NETWORKS

The sixth-generation (6G) mobile network marks a transformative leap beyond the capabilities of 5G, setting the stage for a revolutionary era in wireless communication expected to materialize by 2030. While 5G has already redefined mobile experiences by enhancing data speed, reducing latency, and improving device connectivity, 6G envisions a much broader, more ambitious goal: to enable ultra-fast, ultra-reliable, and intelligent communication infrastructures that can seamlessly integrate with advanced technologies like holographic telepresence, tactile internet, digital twins, and pervasive artificial intelligence.

Operating at terahertz (THz) frequency bands, 6G promises extraordinary data rates of up to 1 terabit per second (Tbps) and latency reductions to as low as 0.1 milliseconds. These unprecedented metrics will enable real-time, high-precision applications such as remote robotic surgeries, autonomous mobility systems, immersive augmented and virtual reality (AR/VR), and massive-scale smart city ecosystems. Unlike previous generations, 6G will not merely connect people but also machines, sensors, and environments—fostering the Internet of Everything (IoE) where devices communicate intelligently and autonomously.

Moreover, 6G places a strong emphasis on sustainability, energy efficiency, and reliability. It is envisioned to support green communication paradigms, optimizing energy consumption through AI-driven network management and resource allocation. The convergence of the physical, digital, and biological spheres will also be a hallmark of 6G, enabling deeply immersive and context-aware user experiences that blur the lines between reality and simulation.

In essence, 6G is more than just a technological upgrade—it is the foundation for a hyper-connected, intelligent society where communication becomes instant, immersive, adaptive, and ubiquitous. The ongoing global research and development initiatives are paving the way for this future, where 6G will not only empower next-generation innovations but also fundamentally transform how humans live, work, and interact with technology.

1.1. Overview of 6G Networks

6G networks are expected to revolutionize connectivity by offering ultra-high-speed data transfer rates, potentially 1000 times faster than 5G. Speeds in the range of 100 Gbps to 1 Tbps would enable high-bandwidth applications like immersive virtual and augmented reality experiences, real-time cloud gaming, and large-scale data exchange in the Internet of Things (IoT). Latency, a critical factor for real-time applications, is expected to drop below 1 millisecond, making near-instantaneous communication a reality. This low-latency environment will be essential for applications like autonomous vehicles, remote surgery, and industrial automation, where even the slightest delay could result in failure or serious harm. Connectivity will be ubiquitous, with 6G not only connecting people but also seamlessly linking billions of devices, including sensors, wearables, autonomous systems, and smart cities. The vision for 6G includes global coverage, extending to remote and underserved areas, through a hybrid of terrestrial, satellite, and aerial technologies. AI integration will be a core component of 6G, enabling self-optimizing networks that can dynamically allocate resources, predict and mitigate network failures, and enhance performance through machine learning models. AI will drive innovations in network management, such as automatic fault detection, intelligent traffic routing, and optimized spectrum usage, making the network more responsive, adaptive, and efficient.

1.2. Security Challenges in 6G Networks

As 6G networks expand in complexity, they will face an increased range of security challenges. The integration of diverse technologies, from edge computing and satellite systems to IoT devices and AI-powered services, creates a larger attack surface for potential cyber threats. Traditional security mechanisms may not be sufficient to handle the scale and intricacy of these networks. Emerging threats such as quantum computing pose a serious risk, as it has the potential to break current cryptographic techniques used in securing communications. The proliferation of connected devices through IoT also introduces new vulnerabilities, as many of these devices have minimal security features, making them prime targets for attacks. Additionally, as more critical infrastructure becomes reliant on 6G networks—such as autonomous vehicles, healthcare systems, and smart cities—the impact of cyberattacks can be catastrophic, affecting both the economy and public safety. Given the sophisticated and evolving nature of these threats, it is essential to implement proactive and intelligent security measures. Traditional reactive security systems may no longer be adequate. Instead, advanced solutions utilizing AI and machine learning will be necessary to detect, predict, and mitigate threats in real-time, allowing 6G networks to stay ahead of increasingly sophisticated attackers and respond swiftly to emerging threats.

1.3 Literature Review

Rahman et al. (2021) explore vulnerabilities in AI-driven Open Radio Access Network (O-RAN) architectures. Their study identifies how the openness and modularity of O-RAN facilitate flexible deployment but simultaneously introduce novel attack surfaces, especially in AI-based decision modules. They focus on threats such as data poisoning—where malicious actors manipulate training data to corrupt models—and evasion attacks, where subtle input manipulations deceive classifiers. To mitigate these, they recommend a tri-layer defense strategy that includes blockchain-based audit trails for tamper-proof activity logging, federated learning for privacy-preserving distributed model training, and adversarial hardening of models using synthetic attack scenarios to strengthen resistance.

Catak et al. (2021) investigate the specific risks posed by physical-layer vulnerabilities in 6G, especially in millimeter-wave (mmWave) bands. They identify that high-speed mmWave communications are prone to beam hijacking, jamming, and spoofing attacks due to their directional nature. Their proposed defenses leverage AI to implement dynamic beam tracking and signal authentication based on behavioral patterns, using ensemble learning to cross-verify real-time transmission integrity. Additionally, they discuss the limitations of transfer learning, showing how imported model weights can introduce latent vulnerabilities. They advocate for secure model pipelines that perform integrity checks during model loading and runtime execution.

Yang et al. (2022) design an AI-augmented intrusion response system for highly dynamic 6G wireless environments. Their framework combines generative adversarial networks with Bayesian classifiers to enhance sensitivity to rare and zero-day attack patterns. One innovative feature is adaptive thresholding, guided by reinforcement learning, which optimizes alarm precision to reduce false positives. The system also supports real-time online learning to update model parameters based on evolving threats. Use cases demonstrate its utility in telemedicine and autonomous vehicular networks, where split-second decisions and minimal error margins are essential.

Chou et al. (2023) emphasize securing 6G Non-Terrestrial Networks (NTNs) through edge AI integration. Their framework deploys lightweight learning models directly on UAVs and LEO satellites to enable localized, low-latency threat detection and mitigation. The models perform anomaly detection on radio signals to defend against jamming, spoofing, and spectrum hijacking. A federated learning approach ensures collaborative model improvements across multiple airborne devices without exposing raw data, preserving user privacy. This architecture is particularly relevant for delay-sensitive and infrastructure-less environments like disaster recovery zones or remote rural areas.

Ferrag et al. (2023) investigate the application of generative AI in threat hunting within 6G-enabled IoT networks. They develop a hybrid model that blends Transformer encoders and GANs to simulate and identify polymorphic attack behaviors such as lateral movement and low-rate DDoS attacks. Using IoT traffic datasets, they demonstrate the system's capability to generate synthetic threats for training, enhancing predictive accuracy in real-world deployments. Their findings also emphasize scalability, confirming that the model maintains efficiency across thousands of edge nodes while consuming minimal computational resources.

Ganesh et al. (2024) examine how AI technologies can be integrated into 6G systems to enable robust access control and anomaly detection. By incorporating Zero Trust Network Architecture (ZTNA), their system continuously authenticates user identities and dynamically adjusts permissions based on real-time behavior analysis. Federated learning supports decentralized model training across edge devices while safeguarding data privacy. Their approach redefines traditional security, shifting away from static perimeter-based defenses toward dynamic, adaptive protection at every network node.

Khan et al. (2024) explore adversarial machine learning threats in intrusion detection systems deployed across dense IoT infrastructures. Their research reveals that classifiers can be tricked by carefully crafted perturbations using gradient-based methods. In response, they propose a dual-layer defense involving adversarial training, which exposes models to crafted inputs during training, and input randomization, which disrupts the adversarial optimization process. Their method enhances generalization and improves detection accuracy across multiple datasets while maintaining low inference latency.

Mahmoud et al. (2024) present a layered cybersecurity architecture that integrates physical-layer signal authentication with deep learning for jamming and spoofing resilience. Stacked autoencoders are used to clean corrupted signals, while convolutional neural networks classify signal anomalies with high precision. The system leverages beamforming metadata to establish spatial awareness, enabling direction-based anomaly detection. Tests in dense urban environments indicate that their method significantly improves resilience to signal interference, making it suitable for microcells and vehicular communications.

Kaur and Gupta (2025) tackle the challenge of interpretability in AI-based cybersecurity systems. Their research introduces explainable AI tools such as SHAP and LIME to make model decisions traceable and comprehensible. This transparency is especially critical in regulated sectors like healthcare and finance, where accountability is paramount. They show how human-in-the-loop intervention is improved when explanations are available, and they provide methods for tuning model responses based on feedback, thus reinforcing trust in automated decisions without compromising real-time performance.

Ramezanpour and Jagannath (2025) develop a service-aware Zero Trust framework tailored for software-defined 6G networks. Their architecture includes AI agents that dynamically assess user and asset trustworthiness using contextual cues such as location, historical behavior, and current network status. Trust scores inform access decisions at the granularity of individual network slices. The system also incorporates slicing-aware policies, ensuring tailored protection for critical services like emergency response while reducing overhead for low-risk applications. Their prototype demonstrates faster breach isolation and lower false access rates compared to traditional static trust models.

2. THE ROLE OF AI IN NETWORK SECURITY

Artificial Intelligence (AI) plays a crucial role in modern network security by enabling intelligent, adaptive, and real-time defense mechanisms against increasingly sophisticated cyber threats. Unlike traditional rule-based systems, AI leverages machine learning and deep learning techniques to detect anomalies, identify intrusions, and predict potential attacks by analyzing vast amounts of network traffic, user behavior, and system data. It powers advanced Intrusion Detection and Prevention Systems (IDPS), enhances malware and phishing detection through natural language processing and behavioral analysis, and enables real-time threat intelligence across distributed environments. In emerging networks like 6G, AI is essential for managing security in dynamic and decentralized architectures, such as Open Radio Access Networks (O-RAN) and Non-Terrestrial Networks (NTN), where conventional methods fall short. However, the integration of AI also introduces new challenges, such as adversarial machine learning, where attackers exploit AI model vulnerabilities. To address this, robust AI architectures, adversarial training, and explainable AI (XAI) are increasingly being adopted to enhance transparency and resilience, solidifying AI's role as both a defense mechanism and a critical component of next-generation network security.

2.1. AI and Machine Learning in Cybersecurity

Artificial Intelligence (AI) and Machine Learning (ML) have become indispensable tools in the field of cybersecurity, offering advanced capabilities to detect and mitigate threats in real time. One key component of this is the use of different types of learning techniques, including **supervised, unsupervised, and reinforcement learning**.

- **Supervised Learning** involves training a model on a labeled dataset, where the system learns to recognize patterns associated with specific types of threats or anomalies based on prior examples. For example, a supervised learning model might be trained to recognize known malware signatures or patterns associated with phishing attacks.
- **Unsupervised Learning**, on the other hand, deals with unlabeled data. This method is particularly valuable for detecting new and previously unknown threats. The system analyzes network behavior or traffic without predefined labels, identifying patterns or deviations that might indicate an anomaly or a novel attack. It's excellent for spotting zero-day vulnerabilities or sophisticated attacks that don't follow established patterns.
- **Reinforcement Learning** is a type of machine learning where an agent learns how to respond to different situations by trial and error, receiving rewards or penalties based on its actions. In cybersecurity, reinforcement learning can be used to optimize real-time decision-making processes, such as dynamically adjusting network defenses based on the observed threat landscape.

The primary **benefits** of AI in network security include **real-time analysis, anomaly detection, and automation**. AI systems can process vast amounts of data far more quickly and accurately than humans, identifying threats in real time. Through anomaly detection, AI models can spot abnormal behavior, such as a sudden spike in traffic or unauthorized access attempts, allowing for immediate action to mitigate potential threats.

2.2. AI is Crucial for 6G Security

As 6G networks become more complex, with billions of connected devices and vastly increased data throughput, traditional security approaches may struggle to keep up. AI is becoming a critical component of 6G security for several reasons. One of the key strengths of AI is its ability to process massive volumes of data in real-time. In a 6G environment, where networks will handle data from an unprecedented number of devices (including sensors, IoT devices, autonomous systems, and more), the sheer amount of traffic and potential threats will be overwhelming. AI's data-processing capabilities enable it to analyze and interpret this information quickly, identifying emerging security threats before they escalate into major breaches.

Another reason AI is essential for 6G security is its **scalability**. As 6G networks will be dynamic and operate across multiple environments (from urban centers to remote rural areas, from terrestrial networks to satellite links), security systems must be adaptable and capable of handling a diverse range of threats. Traditional systems may struggle to scale across such complex, distributed networks. However, AI algorithms can be trained to manage this diversity, ensuring that security measures are optimized for different devices, applications, and network conditions. Additionally, AI can help identify new types of threats and adjust security protocols dynamically as the network evolves, providing the flexibility necessary to defend against sophisticated, multi-faceted attacks in real time.

In summary, AI's ability to analyze massive data streams rapidly and its scalability to adapt to the highly diverse and dynamic environment of 6G networks will be crucial for keeping the networks secure. By enabling faster, smarter responses to threats and automating complex security tasks, AI will play a pivotal role in ensuring the integrity, availability, and confidentiality of 6G systems.

3. THREAT LANDSCAPE IN 6G NETWORKS

The threat landscape in 6G networks is expected to be significantly more complex and expansive than in previous generations due to the integration of advanced technologies such as artificial intelligence (AI), machine learning (ML), terahertz communication, intelligent surfaces, quantum communication, and the convergence of space-air-ground networks. These innovations, while enabling ultra-fast, low-latency, and highly reliable communication, also introduce new security vulnerabilities across physical, network, and application layers. 6G networks will support massive connectivity for IoT devices, autonomous systems, and critical infrastructure, making them attractive targets for adversaries. Threats include adversarial machine learning attacks that can manipulate AI models, data poisoning, model evasion, jamming and spoofing at the physical layer, and cyber-physical attacks on connected devices. In decentralized and open architectures such as O-RAN, attackers may exploit exposed interfaces and untrusted third-party software. Moreover, the use of edge AI and distributed intelligence creates challenges in ensuring secure data exchange, identity verification, and trust management. As 6G evolves, the threat surface expands not only in volume but also in sophistication, requiring proactive and AI-driven defense mechanisms, robust encryption, real-time anomaly detection, and continuous security adaptation to safeguard the network's integrity and privacy.

3.1. Potential Threats in 6G

As 6G networks evolve, they will face a wide variety of potential security threats, some of which will be carried over from previous generations, while others will be unique to the advanced nature of 6G technologies. Here are some of the most prominent threats:

- **Cyber-attacks (DoS/DDoS, Malware, Ransomware)**:

Traditional cyber-attacks like **Denial of Service (DoS)** and **Distributed Denial of Service (DDoS)** attacks will still be a significant threat in 6G networks, but their scale and complexity will likely increase. The massive number of connected devices and the growing reliance on AI in 6G could provide attackers with new opportunities to overload network resources. **Malware** and **ransomware** will also pose risks, as more devices and systems become interconnected, offering a wider attack surface. These malicious programs can infiltrate critical infrastructure, steal data, or encrypt systems, demanding ransom payments for decryption keys.

- **Data Breaches, Eavesdropping, and Identity Theft**:

As 6G networks handle exponentially more sensitive data, including personal, financial, and healthcare information, the threat of **data breaches** becomes even more critical. Attackers could exploit vulnerabilities in the network to access private data, either for financial gain or for espionage purposes. With the introduction of advanced communication technologies like massive machine-type communications (mMTC) and ultra-reliable low-latency communications (URLLC), **eavesdropping** on data transmission becomes a major concern, as hackers could intercept communications between devices and extract valuable information. Additionally, **identity theft** will be increasingly facilitated by advanced AI and data analysis, making it easier to exploit stolen personal data to impersonate individuals or gain unauthorized access to accounts.

- **Threats from IoT, Autonomous Systems, and Quantum Computing**:

The explosive growth of the **Internet of Things (IoT)** in 6G, with billions of interconnected smart devices, significantly expands the attack surface for cybercriminals. Many IoT devices lack strong security mechanisms, making them prime targets for exploitation. Autonomous systems—such as self-driving cars, drones, and robots—rely heavily on the 6G network for real-time communication and decision-making, presenting new vulnerabilities. If attackers compromise these systems, they could cause physical harm, disrupt critical services, or wreak havoc on supply chains. Furthermore, **quantum computing** poses an existential threat to traditional cryptography methods used for securing 6G communications. Quantum computers could potentially break current encryption algorithms, allowing malicious actors to decrypt sensitive communications and perform highly sophisticated cyber-attacks.

3.2. Evolving Attack Vectors in 6G

The increasing complexity of 6G networks will give rise to new and more sophisticated attack vectors. As networks grow larger and more interconnected, attackers will adopt increasingly advanced techniques to target vulnerabilities across diverse infrastructures. Here are some emerging attack vectors to watch out for in 6G:

- **Advanced Persistent Threats (APT)**:

APT attacks are long-term, targeted campaigns where adversaries infiltrate a network to remain undetected for an extended period, gathering intelligence or causing persistent damage. In 6G, APTs could be particularly dangerous due to the size and scale of the network, making it harder to detect unusual behavior. Since 6G will involve a wide variety of devices and autonomous systems, attackers could infiltrate multiple layers of the network over time, compromising the system's integrity, stealing sensitive data, or causing slow, ongoing disruptions. These types of attacks are often state-sponsored or highly sophisticated, requiring robust, proactive security measures to prevent and detect.

- **Supply Chain Attacks**:

Supply chain attacks occur when an attacker compromises a third-party vendor or component in the network to infiltrate a larger system. In 6G, supply chain risks are compounded by the sheer number of hardware, software, and service providers involved in building, maintaining, and operating the network. If a malicious actor targets a vendor that provides software or hardware components for the network's infrastructure, they could insert vulnerabilities or backdoors into the system, which could then be exploited by attackers. Given that 6G networks will involve complex integrations between many different industries (telecommunications, automotive, healthcare, etc.), securing the supply chain becomes a critical issue.

- **Risks from Edge Computing, Network Slicing, and Virtualized Infrastructures**:

Edge computing and **network slicing** in 6G promise to enhance performance and flexibility by decentralizing processing and customizing network resources for specific applications. However, these innovations also introduce new attack vectors. In edge computing, sensitive data is often processed closer to the user, creating potential points of failure that could be targeted by attackers. Similarly, **network slicing**—the practice of segmenting a physical network into multiple virtual networks—allows for tailored services but also creates isolated network segments that can be exploited if not properly secured. Attackers may target individual slices to bypass security protocols or compromise the integrity of isolated services. Furthermore, the shift to **virtualized infrastructures** in 6G means that software-based networks are becoming more prevalent, which introduces risks related to software vulnerabilities, such as container or hypervisor exploits. A successful attack on a virtualized platform could compromise large portions of the network, affecting multiple services simultaneously.

4. AI TECHNIQUES FOR THREAT DETECTION IN 6G

AI techniques for threat detection in 6G networks are pivotal in managing the scale, speed, and complexity of emerging cyber threats. Machine learning (ML) and deep learning (DL) models are widely used to analyze vast streams of real-time data for identifying anomalies, intrusions, and malicious patterns that traditional rule-based systems might miss. Supervised learning techniques, such as support vector machines (SVM), decision trees, and neural networks, are trained on labeled datasets to recognize known attack signatures, while unsupervised learning methods like k-means clustering and autoencoders detect novel or zero-day threats by identifying deviations from normal behavior. Reinforcement learning (RL) is applied to develop autonomous agents capable of learning optimal defense strategies through interaction with dynamic environments. Additionally, deep learning models such as convolutional neural networks (CNNs) and recurrent neural networks (RNNs) are employed for advanced pattern recognition in encrypted traffic and sequential log data. Federated learning is gaining prominence in 6G environments by enabling collaborative model training across distributed edge devices without sharing sensitive raw data, thereby enhancing both privacy and scalability. Furthermore, generative adversarial networks (GANs) are used for simulating attack scenarios and improving model robustness against adversarial threats. Collectively, these AI techniques enable intelligent, adaptive, and proactive threat detection systems essential for the secure operation of future 6G networks.

4.1. Anomaly Detection Using AI

Anomaly detection is one of the most critical tasks in network security, especially in 6G networks where data traffic is expected to be enormous and diverse. AI can significantly enhance the accuracy and efficiency of detecting unusual or potentially malicious activities that deviate from the normal operation of a network.

- **Overview of Anomaly Detection Methods**:

Anomaly detection can be approached using various methods, including **statistical, behavioral, and hybrid models**.

- o **Statistical Models** involve using statistical metrics such as mean, variance, and probability distributions to identify outliers. For instance, if network traffic suddenly deviates significantly from established baselines, the system would flag that as an anomaly. These models are effective when normal network behavior is well-understood and predictable.
- o **Behavioral Models** leverage machine learning algorithms to track the behavior of devices and users over time, learning what is considered "normal" and flagging deviations. AI can continuously monitor patterns such as data flow, access times, and device interactions, and then raise alarms when patterns significantly change.
- o **Hybrid Models** combine both statistical and behavioral methods, allowing AI to detect a broader range of anomalies. Hybrid models typically offer more flexibility and accuracy because they draw on the strengths of both approaches to account for more complex patterns and edge cases.
  - **Use of AI for Identifying Unusual Traffic Patterns, Behaviors, and Network Anomalies**:

In a 6G environment, where diverse devices and applications generate vast amounts of data, AI is invaluable for identifying unusual traffic patterns or behaviors that may signal a security threat. For instance, AI can detect irregularities in traffic volume or a sudden spike in specific types of requests that might indicate a **DDoS (Distributed Denial of Service)** attack. It can also recognize abnormal behaviors like unauthorized access attempts or data exfiltration activities, which could point to breaches or insider threats. AI-powered anomaly detection works in real-time, enabling networks to respond to threats as soon as they occur, instead of waiting for manual intervention.

4.2. Intrusion Detection Systems (IDS) Powered by AI

Intrusion Detection Systems (IDS) are essential tools for identifying and responding to unauthorized access or attacks on a network. AI can enhance the functionality of IDS, making them more effective in complex, high-speed 6G environments.

- **Signature-based vs. Anomaly-based Detection**:

IDS can be broadly categorized into **signature-based** and **anomaly-based** detection:

- o **Signature-based Detection** relies on predefined patterns or signatures of known attacks, similar to a virus definition database in traditional antivirus software. While effective for identifying known threats, signature-based detection is limited when it comes to new, unknown attacks or sophisticated threat vectors.
- o **Anomaly-based Detection** is more flexible and capable of identifying previously unknown threats by detecting deviations from normal behavior. AI plays a crucial role here by continuously learning what constitutes "normal" network activity and recognizing any new behaviors that may signal a potential intrusion.
    - **AI-driven IDS for Real-time Threat Detection in 6G Networks**:

In 6G, networks will experience rapid data flow and continuous device interaction, making real-time threat detection more crucial than ever. AI-powered IDS can provide real-time analysis of incoming network traffic and interactions, allowing for immediate identification of threats. These systems can dynamically adapt to new attack methods through machine learning, significantly reducing the time it takes to detect and mitigate threats. AI algorithms also allow for **adaptive thresholds**, adjusting the detection criteria as the network evolves, helping to minimize false positives while maintaining high sensitivity to new attack strategies.

4.3. AI for Predictive Threat Intelligence

One of the most powerful applications of AI in network security is its ability to predict and forecast potential threats before they happen. By analyzing historical data and network patterns, AI can help security teams anticipate future attacks and proactively implement defensive measures.

- **Leveraging AI for Forecasting Potential Attacks Based on Historical Data and Patterns**:

AI models can be trained on vast amounts of historical security data—ranging from attack vectors to traffic patterns—to identify trends that might indicate an impending attack. By examining previous incidents and analyzing when and how attacks have occurred in the past, AI can predict the likelihood of similar attacks in the future. For example, if a particular type of malware was active during a specific time period or under certain conditions, AI can highlight similar patterns in real-time data and trigger alerts or preemptive actions. This type of predictive analysis allows security teams to stay one step ahead, making them more proactive rather than reactive in their defense strategies.

- **Real-time Decision-making Using Predictive Models**:

Predictive threat intelligence allows for **real-time decision-making** based on the most likely risks. When AI models forecast potential attacks, it enables security teams or automated systems to take immediate, predefined actions to mitigate risks. For example, if AI detects an increase in unusual activity or identifies an emerging attack pattern, it can automatically adjust security policies, re-route traffic, or isolate affected systems to prevent the attack from escalating. These predictive models not only enhance security but also optimize network performance by preventing the congestion and delays caused by undetected threats. By incorporating real-time threat intelligence into security protocols, 6G networks can become more resilient and adaptive to evolving attack strategies.

5. AI FOR THREAT MITIGATION IN 6G NETWORKS

AI plays a critical role in threat mitigation within 6G networks by enabling intelligent, automated, and real-time responses to evolving cyber threats. Unlike traditional security mechanisms that rely on static rules, AI-driven systems can dynamically adapt to new threat patterns by continuously learning from network behavior and historical data. Reinforcement learning (RL) is particularly useful for optimizing defense strategies, allowing systems to take autonomous corrective actions such as isolating compromised nodes, rerouting traffic, or updating firewall policies. Deep learning models can analyze encrypted traffic and detect subtle anomalies, facilitating rapid containment of advanced persistent threats (APTs) and zero-day attacks. AI also supports real-time threat intelligence by aggregating data from diverse sources, including edge devices, cloud systems, and IoT endpoints, to generate actionable insights. In 6G's decentralized architecture, federated learning allows distributed devices to collaboratively train defense models while preserving data privacy, ensuring coordinated mitigation across the network. Additionally, AI enhances the resilience of Non-Terrestrial Networks (NTNs) and Open Radio Access Networks (O-RANs) by proactively detecting and neutralizing attacks on the physical and network layers, such as jamming, spoofing, or data poisoning. By continuously adapting to changing attack vectors and automating response mechanisms, AI enables robust and scalable threat mitigation essential for securing the highly dynamic and complex landscape of 6G networks.

5.1. Automated Response Mechanisms

In 6G networks, where speed, scalability, and complexity will be paramount, AI-driven **automated response mechanisms** will be critical for quickly mitigating threats and maintaining network performance.

- **Self-healing Networks Using AI to Mitigate Attacks**:

One of the most exciting advancements enabled by AI in 6G networks is the concept of **self-healing networks.** AI systems will allow networks to automatically detect, analyze, and correct faults or breaches without human intervention. When an attack or disruption is detected, AI algorithms can take action to repair or bypass the compromised segments of the network, minimizing downtime and impact. For example, if an intrusion is identified in a particular area of the network, AI can dynamically reroute traffic or isolate the affected node, restoring network integrity while the attack is addressed. This self-healing capability is particularly important for critical infrastructure, where manual intervention may be slow or impractical.

- **Real-time Mitigation Through AI-Driven Network Traffic Shaping, Re-Routing, and Isolation**:

In the event of an attack like a **DDoS (Distributed Denial of Service)** or a network overload, AI can immediately initiate **traffic shaping** to adjust the flow of data, ensuring that critical network services continue to function while non-essential traffic is slowed or blocked. AI can also **re-route** traffic dynamically, bypassing the compromised areas of the network and directing it to healthier, unaffected sections. In cases where specific devices or systems are found to be under attack, AI can **isolate** these components to prevent the attack from spreading, maintaining the security and availability of the broader network. This real-time response not only mitigates the immediate threat but also reduces the need for manual network interventions, allowing for faster recovery times.

5.2. AI for Dynamic Security Policies

As 6G networks evolve, the nature of security threats will continually shift. To stay ahead of these threats, security policies must be dynamic and adaptable. AI plays a crucial role in developing and implementing such policies.

- **Adaptive Security Policies Based on AI Learning**:

AI enables **adaptive security policies** that evolve in real time based on network behavior and emerging threats. Traditional security systems often rely on static rules and predefined security policies, which can quickly become outdated as new attack methods emerge. With AI, the network learns from previous incidents and adapts its security protocols accordingly. For example, if AI detects a new pattern of malicious activity, it can automatically adjust firewall rules, adjust access controls, or modify encryption methods to block the new attack vector. These **AI-driven adaptive security policies** ensure that security measures remain effective, even as the threat landscape changes.

- **Using AI for Fine-tuning Security Rules in Response to Evolving Threats**:

AI can continuously analyze network traffic, behavior, and threat intelligence feeds to fine-tune security rules and parameters in real-time. For example, if a new vulnerability or attack type is detected, AI can adjust access control lists (ACLs), quality of service (QoS) policies, or bandwidth limits to prevent exploitation. It can also modify network segmentation or trigger higher levels of monitoring for suspicious activities. This **real-time fine-tuning** allows the network to respond to the evolving nature of threats without the need for manual updates or reconfigurations, which can be time-consuming and prone to errors. Ultimately, AI ensures that security policies stay relevant, effective, and responsive to both known and emerging threats.

5.3. AI in Security Automation and Orchestration

Security automation and orchestration are vital to ensuring that AI-driven threat detection and mitigation tools work seamlessly together, making 6G networks more resilient and responsive to attacks.

- **End-to-End Security Automation with AI and Orchestration Platforms**:

End-to-end security automation involves using AI-powered orchestration platforms to automate security processes across the entire network—from threat detection and analysis to response and recovery. These platforms coordinate the interaction of different security components (firewalls, IDS, AI models, etc.), ensuring that all security actions are carried out efficiently and in sync. For example, when AI identifies a new threat, the orchestration platform can automatically trigger predefined security measures across the network, such as isolating compromised nodes, adjusting traffic flow, or initiating incident response protocols. Automation removes the need for manual intervention, accelerates response times, and improves overall security posture by reducing human error and inefficiencies.

- **Ensuring Seamless Collaboration Between AI-Driven Detection and Mitigation Tools**:

The success of security automation relies on the **seamless collaboration** between AI-driven detection systems and mitigation tools. AI-driven detection models identify and classify potential threats, while AI-powered mitigation tools respond in real-time to neutralize those threats. This collaboration must be fluid and efficient to ensure that the network can rapidly adapt to emerging attacks. For example, when an AI model detects unusual behavior (such as an attempt to exploit a zero-day vulnerability), it can pass this information to the mitigation tools, which then take immediate action, such as blocking the attack or rerouting traffic. Additionally, orchestration platforms ensure that threat intelligence and responses are shared across the network, enabling consistent and coordinated defense strategies across all network layers. This integration of detection and mitigation enhances the network's ability to proactively address threats before they cause significant harm.

6. AI FOR THREAT MITIGATION IN 6G NETWORKS

AI is pivotal for threat mitigation in 6G networks, enabling systems to autonomously detect, analyze, and respond to cyber threats in real time. As 6G networks are expected to support massive device connectivity, ultra-low latency, and distributed architectures like Open RAN and Non-Terrestrial Networks (NTN), traditional security mechanisms become insufficient. AI addresses this gap by providing intelligent, scalable mitigation strategies that adapt to dynamic environments. Reinforcement learning (RL) algorithms can learn optimal responses to ongoing attacks, such as rerouting traffic, isolating infected nodes, or adjusting security parameters autonomously. Deep learning models, particularly convolutional and recurrent neural networks, facilitate the detection of complex, hidden threats and initiate mitigation actions without human intervention. AI also enables threat correlation across vast amounts of distributed data, making it possible to identify coordinated attacks spanning multiple layers or regions of the network. Furthermore, federated learning and edge AI empower local devices to participate in threat mitigation while maintaining data privacy and minimizing latency. These systems continuously evolve through self-learning, allowing them to predict and neutralize threats before they cause harm. Overall, AI's real-time decision-making, predictive analysis, and automated responses make it an indispensable component for resilient and adaptive threat mitigation in future 6G networks.

6.1. Automated Response Mechanisms

As 6G networks become more complex and dynamic, **automated response mechanisms** powered by AI will be essential for rapidly addressing security incidents and minimizing damage.

- **Self-healing Networks Using AI to Mitigate Attacks**:

One of the key innovations AI brings to 6G networks is the concept of **self-healing networks**. These AI-driven networks can autonomously detect issues such as attacks, failures, or breaches and take corrective actions without human intervention. For example, if a Distributed Denial of Service (DDoS) attack overwhelms a specific part of the network, AI can detect the anomaly in traffic patterns and initiate **self-healing actions**. This could include isolating the affected node, re-establishing service by switching traffic paths, or activating additional resources to absorb the attack. The ability to "heal" itself without waiting for human intervention drastically reduces response times, limits the impact of attacks, and helps maintain overall system performance and uptime.

- **Real-time Mitigation Through AI-driven Network Traffic Shaping, Re-routing, and Isolation**:

In a 6G network, **real-time mitigation** is crucial to minimize disruptions caused by cyberattacks or network failures. AI enables dynamic **traffic shaping**, where the flow of data across the network can be adjusted to prioritize critical services and protect against excessive traffic spikes (as in a DDoS attack). AI algorithms can also perform **re-routing** of traffic, diverting data to alternative paths to avoid congested or compromised network segments. If a node or device is found to be compromised, **isolation** protocols can be triggered automatically, severing connections to prevent lateral movement of the attack across the network. These automated actions ensure that attacks are mitigated immediately, reducing the damage caused by malicious activity.

6.2. AI for Dynamic Security Policies

As threats evolve rapidly in the 6G era, **dynamic security policies** will be vital to ensure the network remains protected. Traditional static security rules cannot keep up with the increasingly sophisticated and evolving nature of cyber threats. AI provides the flexibility and intelligence needed to adapt security measures continuously.

- **Adaptive Security Policies Based on AI Learning**:

AI's ability to **learn and adapt** makes it ideal for developing **adaptive security policies**. Unlike static rule-based systems, AI systems can learn from ongoing network activity and past incidents to adjust security policies in real time. For instance, if AI detects an emerging threat pattern—such as a rise in unauthorized access attempts—it can automatically adjust access control policies to restrict certain behaviors or limit access to critical network resources. Over time, as the AI models learn more about the network's behavior and the nature of attacks, security policies become progressively more tailored to the unique requirements of the 6G environment. This adaptability ensures the network can defend against new and unknown threats without needing manual intervention to update security rules.

- **Using AI for Fine-tuning Security Rules in Response to Evolving Threats**:

AI can be employed to **fine-tune security rules** on an ongoing basis. For example, AI can analyze a threat landscape and adjust parameters such as **firewall rules**, **intrusion detection system (IDS)** thresholds, or **network segmentation** strategies. When a new vulnerability or attack vector emerges, AI systems can modify the network's security settings to counteract these new threats. By continually adjusting the security framework based on data and past incidents, AI helps keep the network ahead of attackers. These adjustments are done automatically and in real time, ensuring that security measures evolve as quickly as the threat landscape.

6.3. AI in Security Automation and Orchestration

AI enables **security automation** and **orchestration** across the entire 6G network, ensuring that security measures are not only applied automatically but also coordinated effectively between different systems and layers.

- **End-to-End Security Automation with AI and Orchestration Platforms**:

Security automation powered by AI involves automating security tasks and processes from detection to remediation. This includes activities like monitoring traffic, identifying vulnerabilities, patching weaknesses, and responding to threats. AI can be integrated into **orchestration platforms** that manage these tasks across the entire network. Orchestration ensures that all security tools, whether they are intrusion prevention systems (IPS), firewalls, or endpoint security solutions, work together in a coordinated and efficient manner. For example, when an attack is detected by an AI-driven system, the orchestration platform can automatically trigger actions such as updating threat signatures, applying countermeasures, and communicating with other systems for a coordinated response. AI-powered automation increases the speed of threat detection and response, allowing security teams to focus on strategic tasks rather than manual interventions.

- **Ensuring Seamless Collaboration Between AI-driven Detection and Mitigation Tools**:

One of the challenges of AI in network security is ensuring that **detection** and **mitigation tools** collaborate seamlessly. AI-driven detection systems continuously monitor network traffic for potential threats, while mitigation systems act to neutralize those threats in real time. The key to an effective security architecture is the **coordination** between these tools, which can be achieved through AI-enabled orchestration. For example, when an intrusion detection system identifies malicious traffic, the orchestration platform can coordinate with AI-based traffic management tools to isolate affected devices or reroute traffic to safer parts of the network. AI can also ensure that the right mitigation actions are taken based on the type of threat detected, allowing for more efficient and precise responses. This ensures that the security infrastructure can handle complex, multi-layered attacks without disrupting the overall network performance.

7. CHALLENGES AND LIMITATIONS OF AI IN 6G NETWORK SECURITY

AI offers significant potential to enhance security in 6G networks through advanced threat detection and adaptive defenses; however, several challenges and limitations hinder its full effectiveness. Data privacy remains a critical concern as training AI models often requires vast amounts of sensitive user information distributed across edge devices and IoT nodes, raising risks of data leakage despite approaches like federated learning, which itself is vulnerable to attacks such as model poisoning and inversion. Additionally, AI models face adversarial threats that can manipulate inputs to evade detection or corrupt learning, posing serious risks in mission-critical applications like autonomous vehicles and healthcare. The computational complexity of sophisticated AI algorithms also conflicts with the stringent low-latency and resource constraints typical of 6G edge environments, forcing compromises between model accuracy and speed. Furthermore, the lack of interpretability in AI decisions undermines operator trust and complicates incident response, especially in high-stakes scenarios where understanding the rationale behind security alerts is vital. Addressing these challenges requires developing robust, lightweight, and explainable

AI systems alongside rigorous privacy-preserving frameworks to ensure secure, reliable, and trustworthy 6G network operations.**6.1. 7.1 Data Privacy Concerns**

With AI integrated into 6G networks, managing **data privacy** becomes a critical concern. AI's need for large amounts of data for training and analysis often conflicts with the need to protect users' personal and sensitive information.

- **Balancing Security with User Privacy in AI-powered Systems**:

The use of AI in 6G networks requires the collection and processing of vast amounts of data, which may include personal information, traffic patterns, and behavioral data from end users. However, this raises concerns about **privacy violations** and the potential for misuse of personal information. For example, if an AI system is used to monitor user behavior for security purposes, there must be a balance between detecting security threats and ensuring that user data is not exploited or shared without consent. This is particularly important in sensitive contexts such as healthcare or finance, where data breaches could have severe consequences. Finding the right balance between robust threat detection and respecting user privacy is one of the biggest challenges when using AI in 6G networks.

- **Privacy-Preserving AI Techniques (e.g., Federated Learning, Differential Privacy)**:

To address these privacy concerns, techniques like **federated learning** and **differential privacy** are gaining traction.

- o **Federated Learning** is a decentralized approach where AI models are trained locally on users' devices or edge nodes, keeping the data within its original location. Instead of sending raw data to a central server, only model updates are shared, allowing the system to learn from data without exposing sensitive information. This helps preserve privacy while still benefiting from the insights AI can provide.
- o **Differential Privacy** ensures that individual data points cannot be traced back to a specific user, even when aggregated data is used for training AI models. It introduces noise to the data or results, making it impossible to discern specific user information while still allowing for valuable insights to be gleaned. Implementing these privacy-preserving techniques will be crucial to the success of AI-driven security solutions in 6G networks, as they allow for robust threat detection without compromising user confidentiality.

7.2. AI Model Robustness and Adversarial Attacks

AI models, especially those used in security applications, are susceptible to **adversarial attacks** designed to manipulate or deceive the model, posing a significant challenge for AI-powered security in 6G networks.

- **Threats Targeting AI Models (e.g., Adversarial Examples, Model Poisoning)**:
  - **Adversarial Examples** involve deliberately modifying input data (such as network traffic or system logs) in subtle ways to deceive AI models into making incorrect predictions or classifications. For instance, attackers could manipulate packet data in a way that makes it appear benign, thus bypassing intrusion detection systems (IDS) without being flagged.
  - **Model Poisoning** occurs when an attacker corrupts the training data used to build AI models, thereby introducing biases or vulnerabilities into the model. If adversaries can manipulate the data used to train an AI-driven security system, they can degrade its accuracy, causing it to misidentify threats or fail to recognize emerging attack patterns.

These types of attacks undermine the trustworthiness and reliability of AI-based security systems, making it difficult for 6G networks to defend against sophisticated threats.

- **Methods to Strengthen AI Models Against Attacks**:

To mitigate the risks posed by adversarial attacks, several strategies can be employed:

- **Adversarial Training** involves exposing the AI model to adversarial examples during its training phase, so it learns to recognize and defend against them. By continuously updating the model with new adversarial examples, it becomes more resilient to such attacks.
- **Robust Optimization** techniques can be used to enhance the model's stability by focusing on improving its performance in the presence of malicious inputs. This ensures that even if the model encounters adversarial data, it will still provide accurate security predictions.
- **Model Validation and Verification** methods aim to rigorously test AI models to identify and address potential vulnerabilities before deployment.

Regular audits and updates to the models are necessary to keep them secure and effective against evolving attack strategies.

7.3. Resource and Computational Constraints

AI techniques often require significant computational resources, which may become a bottleneck in large-scale, real-time 6G networks.

- **Computational Overhead and Resource Demand in Large-scale 6G Networks**:

AI models, especially deep learning-based models, are computationally intensive. In 6G networks, where billions of devices will be interconnected, the volume of data processed and analyzed by AI systems will be immense. This high demand for computational power could strain network resources, leading to **latency issues** and slower threat detection times. Real-time processing is particularly important for AI-driven security, but the need for rapid computation in a large-scale, high-speed environment may exceed the capabilities of traditional hardware or network infrastructure. Ensuring that AI systems can scale and perform efficiently across the network is one of the major challenges.

- **Optimizing AI Algorithms for Real-time Threat Detection and Mitigation**:

To overcome resource constraints, AI algorithms need to be **optimized** for real-time performance and efficient use of computational resources. Techniques such as **model pruning**, **quantization**, and **edge computing** can be employed to reduce the computational load of AI models while maintaining their effectiveness:

- o **Model Pruning** involves removing unnecessary or redundant parts of an AI model to reduce its size and computational cost without sacrificing accuracy.
- o **Quantization** reduces the precision of model calculations, allowing for faster processing with minimal impact on model performance.
- o **Edge Computing** allows AI models to be deployed closer to the data source (e.g., on edge devices), enabling quicker processing and reducing the burden on centralized servers or cloud platforms.

By optimizing AI models and utilizing edge computing, the system can distribute the computational load more effectively across the network, enabling rapid and efficient threat detection and mitigation without overloading the network's resources.

8. FUTURE DIRECTIONS IN AI FOR 6G SECURITY

As 6G networks continue to evolve, AI's role in enhancing security will become even more critical. Below are some promising future directions in the integration of AI with emerging technologies and innovative approaches for robust 6G security.

8.1. Integration of AI with Quantum Computing for Enhanced Security

The integration of **AI** and **quantum computing** is one of the most exciting frontiers in the field of cybersecurity, especially for 6G networks, where vast data flows and ultra-fast communication are expected.

- **Synergies Between AI and Quantum Computing in Threat Detection**:

Quantum computing has the potential to revolutionize the processing power available for security applications. By leveraging quantum algorithms, AI systems could perform **threat detection** and **data analysis** orders of magnitude faster than current classical systems. For example, quantum computing could be used to analyze large, complex datasets (like encrypted traffic or massive sensor networks) far more efficiently, enabling AI to detect patterns and anomalies that may be too intricate for traditional computing methods. This synergy could lead to more accurate and faster identification of threats such as zero-day vulnerabilities, insider attacks, or sophisticated malware, which often go undetected by current AI systems due to the sheer scale of data involved.

- **Potential of Quantum Machine Learning for Cryptographic Resilience**:

One of the key areas where quantum computing can enhance AI-driven security is in **cryptographic resilience**. Current cryptographic techniques, like RSA or elliptic curve cryptography, could be rendered obsolete by the power of quantum computers. However, **quantum machine learning** (QML) could enable AI to create new forms of **quantum-resistant cryptography**. Quantum-enhanced AI systems could adapt to new cryptographic methods that can withstand quantum-based attacks, ensuring secure communication and data protection in 6G networks. By combining AI and quantum computing, we could develop next-generation encryption algorithms that can effectively counteract the threats posed by quantum-powered adversaries.

8.2. Collaborative AI and Federated Learning for Distributed Threat Mitigation

With 6G's expected reliance on vast and heterogeneous networks (including IoT, edge devices, and cloud systems), **collaborative AI** and **federated learning** will be critical for distributed threat detection and mitigation.

- **Distributed AI Models for Collaborative Defense Across Different 6G Networks**:

Collaborative AI allows multiple networks or organizations to share threat intelligence and defense strategies while maintaining data privacy and security. In the context of 6G, AI models can be deployed across different parts of the network (e.g., IoT devices, edge computing, cloud systems) and work together to detect and respond to attacks. By sharing insights, patterns, and threat intelligence, these distributed models can offer a more comprehensive and adaptive security posture, improving the overall resilience of the 6G ecosystem. For example, an attack detected by a smart city network might trigger an alert to nearby IoT devices, which in turn can adjust their settings to mitigate the attack, all through a collaborative AI-driven system.

- **Federated Learning for Collaborative, Privacy-Preserving Threat Detection**:

Federated learning is a distributed AI technique that enables multiple entities (such as devices or networks) to collaboratively train machine learning models without sharing raw data. Instead, the model updates are shared and aggregated to improve the global model. This is particularly valuable in 6G networks, where privacy concerns (such as the protection of user data) are paramount. Using federated learning, various entities across a 6G network can collaborate to detect and mitigate threats, while keeping sensitive data private and secure. For example, an IoT sensor in one location could help train an AI model to detect anomalies in network traffic, and the model could be updated across other devices and networks, all while maintaining user privacy.

8.3. AI and Autonomous Security Systems in 6G

The goal of **autonomous security systems** in 6G is to enable **AI-driven security solutions** that require minimal human intervention. This could transform how networks are protected, moving from a reactive model to a more proactive and adaptive one.

- **Development of Autonomous Security Systems that Act Without Human Intervention**:

In the future, **autonomous security systems** will take on a more prominent role in 6G networks. These systems will leverage AI to automatically detect, analyze, and respond to threats in real time. For example, when an intrusion is detected, the system could autonomously take actions such as blocking malicious traffic, isolating compromised nodes, or even adapting security policies to prevent further attacks. By removing the need for human involvement in many instances, these systems can significantly reduce response times, making them well-suited for the high-speed and high-stakes environment of 6G networks.

- **Prospects of AI-Driven Self-Organizing, Self-Defending 6G Networks**:

A vision for the future of 6G networks is the emergence of **self-organizing and self-defending** networks. These AI-powered systems would be capable of learning from past experiences, adapting to new threats, and reorganizing themselves to prevent breaches before they happen. Self-organizing networks could autonomously optimize traffic routes, network load distribution, and even security policies based on ongoing threat intelligence and real-time data analysis. With AI's ability to learn and evolve, these networks could become not only more resilient but also self-healing, addressing vulnerabilities and threats without needing direct human intervention. The potential of AI to create **fully autonomous security systems** would drastically change the approach to network security, making 6G far more adaptive and intelligent.

9. CONCLUSION

The integration of Artificial Intelligence (AI) into 6G networks has redefined the landscape of network security by enabling intelligent, scalable, and real-time protection mechanisms against sophisticated cyber threats. AI has emerged as a cornerstone technology for threat detection and mitigation, leveraging techniques such as machine learning (ML), deep learning (DL), anomaly detection, and behavior-based intrusion detection systems. These tools allow 6G networks to respond dynamically to evolving threats, reducing reliance on static rule-based security methods. AI systems are capable of processing vast volumes of heterogeneous data generated by billions of connected devices, identifying patterns of malicious activity, and launching proactive countermeasures with minimal human intervention. This level of automation and responsiveness is critical in 6G environments, which are characterized by ultra-low latency, high data rates, and a massive increase in connected entities including IoT devices, autonomous systems, and intelligent edge nodes.

Moreover, AI's capacity for continuous learning and adaptation allows 6G networks to evolve their security posture over time, improving resilience against both known and novel attack vectors. AI also plays a vital role in securing the physical and network layers of emerging architectures such as Open Radio Access Networks (O-RANs) and Non-Terrestrial Networks (NTNs), where traditional centralized security methods are inadequate. From detecting signal interference and jamming to defending against adversarial machine learning attacks, AI enhances the robustness and agility of network defenses. Furthermore, through technologies like federated learning and edge AI, security models can be distributed and trained across decentralized devices without compromising data privacy, facilitating coordinated security in resource-constrained environments.

However, this transformative role is accompanied by significant challenges. While AI enhances detection and mitigation capabilities, it also raises concerns about model robustness, interpretability, and vulnerability to adversarial manipulation. Additionally, the computational demands of AI algorithms, particularly in edge environments, and the ethical implications of AI-based surveillance systems introduce new complexities. Despite these hurdles, the long-term advantages—greater autonomy, adaptability, and resilience—make AI indispensable to the future of 6G security.

The application of AI in 6G network security offers a multitude of benefits, from improving threat response time to reducing the human workload associated with monitoring and managing large-scale networks. Its potential for real-time analytics, behavioral prediction, and automated decision-making makes AI a fundamental enabler of secure, self-defending 6G infrastructures. **Data privacy**: AI systems often require large datasets to train effectively, raising concerns over how personal or sensitive information is collected, processed, and shared.

- **Model robustness**: AI models remain susceptible to adversarial attacks, where subtle input manipulations can lead to incorrect threat classifications or missed detections.
- **Scalability and resource constraints**: Implementing AI at the edge, in real time, across thousands of nodes, presents significant challenges related to power, latency, and processing capacity.
- **Ethical considerations**: The increasing autonomy of AI-driven security tools necessitates careful attention to transparency, accountability, and potential misuse.

Despite these issues, the benefits of AI-driven security solutions outweigh the risks. Ongoing research into secure model training, privacy-preserving AI, and energy-efficient algorithms continues to address these limitations, moving the industry toward more reliable and explainable AI systems.

Although AI's role in 6G network security is well-recognized, the field is still in its early stages of maturity. Several open questions must be addressed to fully realize AI's potential in securing 6G infrastructures:

- **How can AI models be fortified against adversarial attacks?** As attackers increasingly target the AI models themselves, developing resilient architectures that can detect and withstand manipulation is vital.
- **What mechanisms best balance data privacy with effective threat detection?** Approaches like federated learning and homomorphic encryption offer promise, but require further refinement for widespread, real-time use.
- **How can edge AI be optimized to deliver fast and accurate threat mitigation without overloading network resources?** This question calls for innovations in lightweight AI models and adaptive computing frameworks tailored for edge devices.

These questions underline the need for a holistic approach that encompasses not just technical advancements, but also regulatory, ethical, and policy considerations in AI deployment.

To advance the frontier of AI-based security in 6G, future research and development should focus on the following priority areas:

- **Quantum-resistant AI algorithms**: As quantum computing threatens to undermine classical encryption, there is a pressing need for AI-assisted cryptographic solutions that are secure against quantum attacks.
- **Collaborative threat intelligence**: AI and federated learning can enable cross-network sharing of threat data without violating privacy, creating a global security fabric that is more responsive and coordinated.
- **Autonomous self-defending networks**: Next-generation networks should incorporate self-organizing capabilities, where AI autonomously adjusts security policies, isolates threats, and repairs compromised systems with minimal external input.

AI (XAI): Ensuring that AI decisions are transparent and interpretable is critical for building trust, especially in mission-critical 6G applications such as healthcare, finance, and autonomous transportation.

REFERENCES

Catak, E., Moldsvor, A., & Kuzlu, M. (2021). Adversarial machine learning security problems for 6G: mmWave beam prediction use-case. *arXiv preprint arXiv:2105.03905.*/arxiv.2105.03905DOI: 10.1109/BlackSeaCom52164.2021.9527756

Chou, H., Solanki, S., Ha, V. N., Chen, L., Ma, S. L., Al-Hraishawi, H., Eappen, G., & Chatzinotas, S. (2023). Edge AI empowered physical layer security for 6G NTN: Potential threats and future opportunities. *arXiv preprint arXiv:2401.01005.* https://doi.org//arxiv.2401.01005DOI: 10.48550

Chou, H. F., Wang, Z., & Lin, Y. (2023). Edge AI empowered physical layer security for 6G NTN: Potential threats and future opportunities. arXiv preprint arXiv:2401.01005. https://arxiv.org/abs/2401.01005

Ferrag, M. A., Debbah, M., & Al-Hawawreh, M. (2023). Generative AI for cyber threat-hunting in 6G-enabled IoT networks. *arXiv preprint arXiv:2303.11751.* / arxiv.2303.11751DOI: 10.1109/CCGridW59191.2023.00018

Ganesh, R., Sharma, S., & Kumar, A. (2024). AI-enabled zero trust architecture for access control and anomaly detection in 6G networks. *Journal of Network and Computer Applications*, *209*, 103536. DOI: 10.1016/j.jnca.2023.103536

Ganesh, S. S., Kumar, V., & Patel, A. (2024). Next-generation threat detection and mitigation in 6G wireless networks using IAM, ZTNA, and advanced security mechanisms. *Journal of Engineering Science and Technology*, *19*(4), 1012–1035. DOI: 10.1234/jes.2024.2545

Kaur, N., & Gupta, L. (2025). Enhancing interpretability in AI-driven cybersecurity for 6G networks using explainable AI techniques. *IEEE Transactions on Network and Service Management*, *22*(1), 200–213. DOI: 10.1109/TNSM.2024.3456789

Khan, F., Patel, R., & Singh, S. (2024). Defending adversarial attacks on AI-based intrusion detection systems in dense IoT networks. *IEEE Internet of Things Journal*, *11*(2), 1423–1435. DOI: 10.1109/JIOT.2023.3276548

Khan, M. M. A., Rahman, M. T., & Alam, M. (2024). Adversarial attacks and defenses in 6G network-assisted IoT systems. arXiv preprint arXiv:2401.14780. https://arxiv.org/abs/2401.14780

Mahmoud, H., Ismail, T., Baiyekusi, T., & Idrissi, M. (2024). Deep learning-based physical layer security for jamming and spoofing resilience in 6G microcell environments. *Wireless Networks*, *30*(4), 1895–1910. DOI: 10.1007/s11276-024-03117-4

Rahman, T. F., Zeng, X., & Babar, M. (2021). Network and physical layer attacks and countermeasures to AI-enabled 6G O-RAN. arXiv preprint arXiv:2106.02494. https://arxiv.org/abs/2106.02494

Ramezanpour, K., & Jagannath, J. (2025). Service-aware zero trust architecture for 6G software-defined networks: AI-driven trust management and network slicing security. *IEEE Transactions on Network and Service Management*, *22*(3), 1130–1145. DOI: 10.1109/TNSM.2025.3456789

Yang, B., & Gupta, L. (2022). AI-augmented intrusion response system for dynamic 6G wireless networks using GAN and Bayesian classifiers. *IEEE Transactions on Cognitive Communications and Networking*, *8*(1), 112–123. DOI: 10.1109/TCCN.2021.3112456

Chapter 10
AI-Powered Threat Detection and Response for Future 6G Networks

Rajesh Kanna Rajendran
https://orcid.org/0000-0001-7228-5031
Christ University, Bangalore, India

S. B. Mahalakshmi
https://orcid.org/0000-0001-9815-2069
Coimbatore Institute of Technology, Coimbatore, India

T. Mohana Priya
https://orcid.org/0000-0001-5637-7921
Christ University, Bangalore, India

R. Sakkaravarthi
Vanier College, Canada

S. Poorana Senthilkumar
https://orcid.org/0000-0001-5731-2337
Dr. N.G.P. Arts and Science College, India

A. Muthusamy
https://orcid.org/0000-0003-1889-0630
Kongu Engineering College, India

ABSTRACT

As 6G networks come into existence, there will be ultra-low latency, high bandwidth, seamless integration of billions of devices, and a revolution of connectivity. But with these great strides, new challenges about the securing of these systems against very sophisticated cyber attacks have come up. This book discusses how AI can benefit the 6G system to detect and respond threats better. Through the utilization of AI algorithms, machine learning, and deep learning, 6G networks will autonomously identify and mitigate security risks in real time while adapting to dynamic and ever-evolving attack vectors. AI systems can monitor network traffic in real-time, analyze anomalies, and predict possible vulnerabilities before they are exploited, hence reducing the detection-to-mitigation cycle. As 6G networks become more complex and pervasive, AI will become an indispensable component in maintaining security and enabling a trustworthy digital ecosystem, thereby becoming a core component

DOI: 10.4018/979-8-3373-0568-4.ch010

of the future network defense.

INTRODUCTION

The sixth generation, or 6G network, promises ultra-high data rates, ultra-low latency, and massive device connectivity while enhancing the security of users. However, integrating advanced technologies like edge computing, terahertz communication, blockchain, and quantum computing is challenging for new security issues introduced by 6G networks. The dynamic and distributed nature of 6G networks makes it more vulnerable to sophisticated cyber threats, such as advanced persistent threats (APTs), AI-driven attacks, and network intrusion attempts. Traditional security mechanisms are unable to address the emerging threats of 6G environments because they are complex and have real-time requirements.

Artificial Intelligence (AI) is emerging as a critical enabler for robust threat detection and response in 6G networks. Advanced security solutions in 6G networks rely on ML, DL, and NLP to identify anomalies, predict potential cyberattacks, and automate response. Through the powerful tool of AI, 6G networks can develop adaptive and self-healing architectures that handle threats proactively before significant damage is done. AI-powered mechanisms for detection analyze network flow data in real-time, thus making high accuracy while spotting malicious patterns and possible areas of attack. Moreover, AI makes security automation intelligent by reducing reliance on manual intervention.

This Chapter focuses on the role of AI in enhancing the security of future 6G networks. The techniques of intrusion detection, malware analysis, threat intelligence, and automated response systems based on AI are discussed. Besides, challenges of AI-based security solutions like data privacy, adversarial AI threats, and explainable AI models are considered. This study addresses these aspects and how AI-powered threat detection and response mechanisms can protect 6G networks from the ever-evolving cyber threats to ensure secure and resilient next-generation communication infrastructures.

LITERATURE REVIEW

This literature review examines the rapidly expanding field of AI-powered threat detection and response mechanisms designed to address the anticipated complexities of 6G networks. The exponential increase in connected devices and the growing reliance on data-intensive applications in the 6G era (Chowdhury et al., 2020; Wang et al., 2023) present unprecedented security challenges. Traditional security approaches, often reactive and rule-based, are proving insufficient to handle the scale and sophistication of potential threats (Zuo et al., 2023). The sheer volume of data generated, the heterogeneity of network architectures, and the increasing prevalence of advanced persistent threats necessitate a paradigm shift towards proactive, AI-driven security solutions. This review synthesizes existing research, highlighting the pivotal role of artificial intelligence (AI) and machine learning (ML) in mitigating these risks. We will analyze both the significant opportunities and the inherent limitations of current AI-powered approaches, identifying key research gaps and future directions for robust 6G network security.

This section establishes a foundational understanding of the AI and ML techniques currently under investigation for 6G security. The core of 6G network security relies on the ability to process and interpret massive datasets to identify anomalies and predict threats. Various AI/ML models are being explored, including machine learning (ML) (Iqbal et al., 2023; Saeed et al., 2023) deep learning (DL) (Iqbal et al., 2023; Saeed et al., 2023), and reinforcement learning (RL) (Iqbal et al., 2023). Each approach offers unique strengths and weaknesses. ML algorithms, such as support vector machines (SVMs) and random forests (RFs) (Iqbal et al., 2023), are often used for their relative simplicity and interpretability. They excel at identifying patterns in data and classifying network traffic as benign or malicious. However, their effectiveness can be limited when dealing with complex, high-dimensional datasets characteristic of 6G networks. The reliance on labeled data for training can also be a significant constraint, particularly in the context of emerging threats for which labeled examples may not yet exist.

DL, on the other hand, offers the ability to learn complex, non-linear relationships from large, unlabeled datasets (Paolini et al., 2023). Deep neural networks (DNNs), convolutional neural networks (CNNs), and recurrent neural networks (RNNs) are being explored for their potential to detect subtle anomalies and adapt to evolving threat landscapes. However, DL models are computationally expensive, requiring significant processing power and memory resources. Their "black box" nature, making it difficult to understand their decision-making processes, can also be a barrier to widespread adoption, especially in security-critical applications. The need for explainable AI (XAI) (Jagatheesaperumal et al., 2022) is therefore paramount. RL algorithms, which learn through trial and error, hold promise for dynamic resource allocation and adaptive security policies (Iqbal et al., 2023). They can optimize security measures in real-time based on changing network conditions and threat levels. However, RL algorithms require extensive training and can be challenging to deploy in complex, dynamic environments.

The integration of AI into network orchestration and management is another key aspect of proactive threat mitigation (Singh et al., 2023; Saeed et al., 2023). Intelligent network orchestration systems leverage AI to automate network configuration, resource allocation, and security policy enforcement. This allows for faster response times to security incidents and more efficient utilization of network resources. However, ensuring the security and reliability of these AI-driven orchestration systems themselves is a critical challenge. This section focuses on specific AI-driven threat detection methods applicable to 6G. Anomaly detection is a crucial technique for identifying unusual network behavior that may indicate malicious activity (Saeed et al., 2023; Paolini et al., 2023). Traditional anomaly detection methods often rely on statistical analysis or rule-based systems. However, AI-powered approaches offer the potential for more accurate and adaptive detection.

Ensemble learning methods, which combine multiple ML models to improve prediction accuracy, have shown promising results in anomaly detection (Saeed et al., 2023). By combining the strengths of different models, ensemble methods can overcome the limitations of individual models and improve robustness to noisy data. This approach is particularly useful in 6G networks, where the sheer volume and diversity of data can make it difficult to rely on a single model. Deep learning models, particularly CNNs and RNNs, are being explored for their ability to automatically learn complex patterns from large datasets (Paolini et al., 2023). These models have demonstrated high accuracy in detecting various types of network attacks, including denial-of-service (DoS) attacks. However, the computational complexity of DL models can be a significant limitation, especially in resource-constrained environments. Real-time threat detection is critical in 6G networks, where delays can have significant consequences (Paolini et al., 2023). The development of efficient DL architectures and optimized algorithms is therefore essential. The challenge of dealing with large, diverse datasets in 6G networks is substantial (Gkonis et al., 2024). The data generated by numerous devices and applications is heterogeneous and high-dimensional, making it difficult to process and analyze effectively. Efficient data preprocessing techniques, feature selection methods, and scalable algorithms are needed to address this challenge. The use of network data analytics functions (NWDAFs) (Gkonis et al., 2024), which collect and analyze network data in real-time, is crucial for enabling effective AI-driven threat detection.

Predicting mmWave beam patterns using AI is another area of active research (Atak et al., 2022). mmWave frequencies are essential for achieving the high data rates of 6G, but they are also susceptible to interference and jamming attacks. AI models can be trained to predict beam patterns and identify potential security vulnerabilities, allowing for proactive mitigation strategies. However, the security of these AI models themselves must be carefully considered, as they can be vulnerable to adversarial attacks. Once a threat is detected, effective response and mitigation strategies are crucial. AI plays a vital role in automating incident response (Singh et al., 2023), allowing for rapid threat containment and minimizing disruption to network services. AI-driven systems can automatically isolate infected devices, block malicious traffic, and initiate other security countermeasures. The speed and efficiency of AI-powered response systems are essential in mitigating the impact of sophisticated attacks.

Intelligent mitigation strategies go beyond simple containment (Singh et al., 2023). AI can be used to analyze the characteristics of an attack and determine the most effective response. This might involve adjusting network parameters, deploying additional security measures, or rerouting traffic. The adaptability of AI-powered mitigation strategies is a significant advantage in dealing with evolving threats. Network automation is a key element in enhancing security resilience (Singh et al., 2023). AI can automate various network management tasks, reducing the workload on human operators and improving response times. This includes automated security policy enforcement, configuration management, and fault detection. However, ensuring the security and reliability of the automation systems themselves is paramount.

Federated learning (FL) offers a promising approach for privacy-preserving threat detection and response (Naeem et al., 2023; Sedjelmaci et al., 2022). FL allows multiple devices to collaboratively train a machine learning model without sharing their raw data. This preserves the privacy of individual devices while still allowing for the collective intelligence of a distributed network to be leveraged for threat detection. However, FL introduces new challenges related to data heterogeneity, communication overhead, and model aggregation. Blockchain technology provides another avenue for enhancing trust and security in 6G-enabled IoT environments (Zuo et al., 2023; Ayaz et al., 2022). Blockchain's immutability and transparency can be used to create a secure and auditable record of network events, making it more difficult for attackers to tamper with data or conceal their activities. However, the scalability and performance of blockchain systems in high-throughput 6G networks need careful consideration.

Integrating AI-powered security into 6G networks requires careful consideration of architectural design and framework development. Zero-trust architectures (Singh et al., 2023; Scalise et al., 2024) are particularly well-suited for the dynamic and distributed nature of 6G. Zero-trust assumes no implicit trust, requiring continuous verification of all devices, users, and requests, regardless of their location within the network. This approach is crucial in mitigating the risks associated with increasingly sophisticated attacks. Software-defined networking (SDN) and network functions virtualization (NFV) (Cunha et al., 2024; Naeem et al., 2023) play a critical role in enabling dynamic and adaptable security policies. SDN allows for centralized control of network functions, enabling rapid configuration changes and efficient resource allocation in response to security threats. NFV allows for the deployment of security functions as virtualized services, enhancing flexibility and scalability.

Network data analytics functions (NWDAFs) (Gkonis et al., 2024), combined with ML, can significantly improve data collection, resource optimization, and security enhancement. NWDAFs provide real-time insights into network traffic, enabling AI models to detect anomalies and predict threats more effectively. The combination of NWDAFs and ML allows for automated resource allocation and adaptive security policies. Secure network slicing (Cunha et al., 2024) is essential for supporting diverse services with varying security requirements. Network slicing allows for the creation of isolated virtual networks on the same physical infrastructure, each with its own security policies and configurations. This approach provides enhanced security and isolation for critical applications. However, ensuring interoperability and security across different network slices is a significant challenge.

Despite the significant potential of AI in 6G security, several challenges remain. Current AI/ML models may struggle to keep pace with the rapid evolution of threats (Atak et al., 2022). Adversarial attacks, designed to fool AI models, pose a significant risk. The development of more robust and resilient AI models is therefore crucial. Explainable AI (XAI) (Jagatheesaperumal et al., 2022) is essential for building trust in AI-driven security systems. The "black box" nature of many AI models makes it difficult to understand their decision-making processes, hindering the adoption of these systems in security-critical applications. XAI techniques aim to provide transparency and interpretability, improving confidence in AI-based security solutions.

Overview of 6G Networks: Key Features and Advancements

Sixth-generation (6G) networks will be the next big leap in wireless communication, offering unprecedented data speeds, ultra-low latency, and seamless connectivity across massive Internet of Things (IoT) ecosystems. The operation of 6G in the terahertz (THz) spectrum will enable real-time immersive experiences such as holographic communication, digital twins, and extended reality (XR). Key advancements include AI-driven network optimization, integrated satellite-terrestrial communication, and self-sustaining energy-efficient architectures. With its focus on hyper-connectivity and intelligent automation, 6G aims to revolutionize industries such as healthcare, smart cities, autonomous vehicles, and edge computing. However, as networks become more complex and data-driven, ensuring robust security remains a critical challenge.

Emerging Security Threats in 6G Networks

The highly decentralized, software-defined, and AI-integrated nature of 6G networks brings with it new cybersecurity challenges. These include AI-driven cyberattacks, adversarial machine learning (ML) exploits, and sophisticated phishing tactics that can be carried out using deepfake technology. IoT devices and edge computing nodes being deployed in mass numbers increase the attack surface of networks, exposing them to distributed denial-of-service (DDoS) attacks, data breaches, and unauthorized access. Moreover, the reliance of 6G on THz communication and quantum computing raises issues of secure encryption and privacy risks. There is a growing need for proactive AI-based security measures to prevent these emerging threats.

Limitations of Traditional Security Mechanisms

Traditional security mechanisms, such as firewalls, intrusion detection systems (IDS), and signature-based threat detection, are unable to cope with the dynamic and complex nature of 6G networks. Such approaches rely on static rule-based frameworks that are unable to cope with rapidly evolving cyber threats and zero-day attacks. Furthermore, security models that were initially designed in centralized settings are becoming impractical for 6G's decentralized MEC environment where real-time threat detection and mitigation are imperative. Cyberattacks have been advancing toward polymorphic malware and AI-driven exploits that necessitate intelligent, adaptive, and automated security solutions beyond traditional defense mechanisms.

Role of AI in Improving 6G Security

Artificial intelligence, in this case, will play a very transformative role in securing the 6G network through intelligent, real-time threat detection, predictive analytics, and autonomous response mechanisms. Machine learning and deep learning algorithms can analyze vast amounts of network traffic, identify anomalies, and potentially impending cyber threats with high accuracy. AI-based security frameworks will strengthen intrusion detection systems, automate security orchestration, and self-healing networks that can respond to new threats. Furthermore, AI-based encryption methods and federated learning models improve data privacy and security without affecting the efficiency of the network. In 6G, AI will be the most essential tool for developing resilient, adaptive, and proactive cybersecurity frameworks.

Blockchain for Secure and Transparent AI-Driven Threat Detection: Blockchain technology essentially enhances AI-driven threat detection in 6G networks by providing a decentralized, tamper-proof ledger for logging security events, anomaly detections, and cyber threat intelligence. As blockchain is immutable, the transparency and accountability aspects ensure that malicious actors cannot manipulate security logs or evade detection. Using blockchain, AI-driven threat detection models can securely share real-time threat intelligence across the distributed network nodes, which forms a collaborative defense mechanism. It increases trust in AI-driven security decisions by having verifiable actions of threat mitigation that are also resistant to adversarial manipulation and strengthens the overall cybersecurity framework of 6G networks.

AI-Enhanced Smart Contracts for Automated Security Enforcement

Smart contracts are self-executing agreements that reside on a blockchain, which can be advanced with AI for intelligent, automated security enforcement in 6G networks. AI-based smart contracts will be able to monitor the behavior of networks, detect anomalies, and then trigger security responses, such as blocking malicious IPs, isolating compromised devices, or revoking access privileges. The whole process of threat mitigation would then happen automatically with minimum latency in real-time. Furthermore, AI-based smart contracts can be updated dynamically in response to the changing nature of threats. Thus, adaptability and resilience can be enhanced. The combination of AI and blockchain provides self-sustaining security architectures that can proactively defend against sophisticated cyberattacks.

Blockchain-Based Authentication and Access Control in 6G

The decentralized nature of blockchain provides a robust solution for authentication and access control in 6G networks. This eliminates the vulnerabilities associated with centralized identity management systems. Blockchain-based identity verification ensures secure and tamper-proof authentication of users, devices, and applications, thereby reducing the risk of identity theft and unauthorized access. AI further enhances this system by analyzing behavioral biometrics, contextual data, and anomaly detection to identify potential security breaches in real-time. Zero-trust security models can also enforce dynamic, context-aware access control policies by using AI-blockchain integration, thereby ensuring that only legitimate entities interact with critical network resources.

Challenges and Future Prospects of AI-Blockchain Synergy

Despite the vast potential, AI-blockchain synergy in 6G cybersecurity has several challenges. These include high computational overhead, scalability issues, and energy consumption concerns. The inherent processing latency of blockchain might conflict with the real-time security requirements of 6G networks, thus demanding lightweight, high-speed consensus mechanisms. Furthermore, there will be threats through adversarial AI, whereby the attacker would have managed to evade detection using manipulated AI models. Research for future will then aim at fine-tuning the AI-blockchain synergy with breakthrough innovations in quantum-resistant encryption, hybrid AI-blockchain architectures, and federated learning approaches. Convergence of AI and blockchain will thus lead the way for robust, transparent, and intelligent solutions in the domain of cybersecurity in the 6G network.

AI-Powered Threat Detection in 6G Networks

AI-Based IDPS

As cyber threats grow in evolution within 6G networks, they must also adopt highly adaptive intelligent intrusion detection and prevention systems for effective management and mitigation. Improving on intrusions based systems, the intelligent intrusion detection prevention systems in these networks incorporate sophisticated machine learning DL models, examining network traffic behaviors, which tend to classify all anomalies for determining malicious behavior instantaneously. Unlike traditional signature-based IDPS, AI-powered systems can recognize zero-day attacks, polymorphic malware, and sophisticated cyber intrusions by learning from past threat patterns. AI-driven IDPS also support automated threat mitigation by dynamically updating security rules and responding to intrusions without human intervention. This proactive approach enhances the resilience of 6G networks against cyberattacks, ensuring continuous security monitoring and defense.

AI-Based Malware Analysis and Classification

The increasing complexity of malware threats in 6G networks requires advanced security mechanisms that can detect, classify, and mitigate malicious software efficiently. AI-based malware analysis uses deep learning models, neural networks, and behavioral analytics to identify known and unknown malware variants. Unlike traditional signature-based methods, AI-driven approaches examine code structure, execution behavior, and system interactions to detect malware, even if its code is obfuscated or altered. Classification techniques using AI also further classify malware into families so that security teams can predict attack strategies and make their defense mechanism better. Automated and intelligent classification reduces the accuracy of malware detection and response time and reduces the chances of big cyberattacks.

Behavioral Analytics for Insider Threat Detection

Insider threats are significant to 6G networks, which are carried out by people who have legal access to the system but with malicious or careless intent. AI-powered behavioral analytics detect insider threats by constantly monitoring user activities and identifying patterns that deviate from normal behavior. It raises a red flag whenever suspicious activities occur in real-time. The access patterns, login times, data transfer activities, and communication logs are all used by the machine learning models to identify anomalies, which might signal an insider threat. In addition, AI-driven solutions can use contextual awareness like work schedules and geolocation data to differentiate between genuine and malicious activities. AI-based behavioral analytics identifies insider threats in advance, preventing data breaches, intellectual property theft, and unauthorized access to sensitive 6G infrastructure.

AI for Predictive Cyber Threat Intelligence

Predictive cyber threat intelligence powered by AI enables 6G networks to anticipate and neutralize security threats before they materialize. AI models can identify emerging cyber risks using vast datasets, including network logs, attack patterns, and threat intelligence feeds. They can predict potential attack scenarios. Deep learning algorithms pick up those subtle indicators of compromise that would otherwise pass through undetected, providing early warnings about advanced persistent threats and zero-day vulnerabilities. AI-driven threat intelligence platforms also enable automated security decision-making, helping organizations prioritize threat mitigation efforts and allocate resources effectively. This predictive approach enhances the overall cybersecurity posture of 6G networks, ensuring proactive defense strategies against evolving cyber threats.

Risks of AI-Powered Security in 6G

The promise of 6G networks is a new revolution in connectivity, but with this promise comes a new wave of security challenges. Although AI is the powerful tool for security enhancement in these networks, it also presents unique risks that require careful consideration.

Adversarial AI and Evasion Attacks in Cybersecurity

The most significant threat is likely to come in the form of adversarial AI. Insidious actors can design subtle inputs that can derail AI-powered security. These "adversarial examples" make it likely that AI will misclassify threats, thereby allowing attacks to evade undetected into secure networks. As 6G becomes even more dependent on AI for security, the possibility of such evasion attacks heightens the stakes.

Data Privacy and Ethical Concerns in AI-Driven Security

AI algorithms thrive off data, a scenario that leads to collecting voluminous user data in the field of 6G security; this is extremely serious data concern in terms of privacy. Whom do you entrust in the responsibility? How do we ensure that not misuse occurs either in terms of its misused or wrong intentions? It demands the most relevant balance between what should be secrecy and what public, and also vice versa as far as technology is concerned - the security end.

Computational Overhead and Energy Constraints

AI models, especially complex deep learning models, can be computationally intensive. In the context of 6G networks, where devices often have limited processing power and energy constraints, deploying AI-powered security solutions can be challenging. Finding ways to optimize these models for efficiency without compromising their effectiveness is an important area of research.

Explainability and Trustworthiness of AI Security Models

Many AI models, especially deep learning models, are "black boxes." It is hard to understand how they come to their decisions. This lack of explainability can be a major obstacle to building trust in AI-powered security systems. If we do not understand how an AI system is making decisions, how can we be sure that it is reliable and trustworthy? The development of more explainable AI models is a key to responsible and effective use of these systems. Realizing the full potential of AI-powered security in 6G networks is crucial for overcoming the challenges and risks mentioned above. This will involve developing robust AI models, implementing strong data privacy measures, and fostering transparency and trust in these systems.

Opportunities in AI-Powered 6G Security

The 6G networks are poised to bring along tremendous opportunities as well as challenges to security. AI will have a critical role in securing the network, and there are a number of emerging research directions.

Quantum AI for Cybersecurity in 6G Networks

Quantum computing, in its very infancy, holds a promise of transforming cybersecurity. This new generation of quantum AI could unlock unprecedented levels of security. Quantum machine learning algorithms could be used to detect the most sophisticated cyberattacks that currently lie beyond the capabilities of classical AI. QKD could then provide unbreakable encryption for 6G networks. Research in this area focuses on developing practical quantum AI algorithms for cybersecurity, exploring the applications of QKD in 6G, and addressing the challenges of integrating quantum technologies with existing network infrastructure. However, the development of quantum-resistant algorithms for AI systems themselves is also crucial, as quantum computers could potentially break existing cryptographic methods used to protect AI models.

AI-Driven Secure Edge Computing and IoT Protection

Massive connected devices will be supported in 6G, most of which will be Internet of Things. Edge computing is going to play a critical role in handling massive data flows created by such a large number of devices. Security at the edge and protecting IoT devices is critical. AI is going to be very helpful here. AI-based security solutions can be deployed at the edge for real-time threat detection and mitigation. The focus of the research in this area is to develop lightweight and efficient AI algorithms for edge devices, create secure communication protocols for IoT devices, and implement distributed AI-based security architectures for edge computing environments. Federated learning, where models are trained on decentralized data at the edge without sharing the raw data itself, is a promising technique for enhancing privacy in edge AI applications.

AI-Powered Security in Software-Defined Networking (SDN) and Network Slicing

Software-defined networking (SDN) provides a flexible and programmable approach to network management. Network slicing allows for the creation of virtual networks tailored to specific applications or services. It can be used to enhance security both in SDN and network slicing: AI algorithms could analyze network traffic patterns to potentially identify anomalies and recognize potential threats. They can also be used to automate and then enforce appropriate security policies, adjusting the network's configurations dynamically to mitigate various attacks. Research aims at the development of AI-driven security solutions for SDN controllers, implementing AI-powered network slicing for secure service provisioning as well as the use of AI for automated security management in dynamic network environments.

Policy and Regulatory Considerations in AI-Based 6G Security

It will naturally follow that also policy and regulatory implications need to be targeted with AI becoming increasingly integral to 6G security. Issues such as data privacy, algorithmic bias, and accountability will require further thought. Further regulations may have to be done to ensure responsible and ethical application of AI in 6G networks. This also calls for international cooperation where standardized security protocols will be worked out and addressing cross-border cyber threats. This field of research entails making authoritative guidelines for AI in the cybersecurity domain, constructing frameworks for data governance and privacy protection within 6G networks, and studying the legal and regulatory aspects of AI-based security. Most importantly, this area includes developing clear lines of responsibility for AI-driven security failure cases and transparency in decision-making processes through AI systems.

AI-Powered Threat Detection and Response for Future 6G Networks: A Real-Time Case Study

The advent of 6G networks promises unprecedented speeds, ultra-low latency, and massive connectivity, but also introduces a significantly expanded attack surface for cyber threats. Traditional security mechanisms are ill-equipped to handle the volume and velocity of data and the complexity of potential attacks in 6G environments. A real-time case study focusing on a hypothetical 6G deployment in a smart city illustrates the critical role of AI in threat detection and response.

Imagine a smart city infrastructure heavily reliant on 6G for managing everything from traffic flow and energy grids to autonomous vehicles and healthcare systems. The sheer volume of interconnected devices and the real-time nature of these operations create numerous vulnerabilities. For instance, a sophisticated distributed denial-of-service (DDoS) attack could cripple the city's traffic management system, leading to chaos and safety hazards.

In this scenario, an AI-powered threat detection system continuously monitors network traffic, device behavior, and data patterns. Machine learning algorithms establish baselines of normal activity and can detect subtle anomalies that might indicate an impending attack. For example, if the system detects a sudden surge in data packets directed towards the energy grid's control center, coupled with unusual access patterns, it can flag this as a potential cyberattack.

Upon detecting a threat, the AI system can initiate an automated response. This might involve isolating the affected network segment, rerouting traffic, deploying additional security protocols, and alerting human operators. In the case of the DDoS attack on the traffic management system, the AI could dynamically adjust traffic light timings to prevent gridlock, while simultaneously identifying and blocking the source of the attack. This rapid, automated response minimizes disruption and prevents cascading failures across the city's critical infrastructure.

Robust Data Management and Governance for AI in 6G Networks

The integration of Artificial Intelligence (AI) into the fabric of 6G networks promises unprecedented levels of automation, optimization, and service innovation. However, the effective deployment of AI hinges critically on establishing robust data management and governance frameworks. These frameworks are essential for handling the massive volumes, high velocity, and diverse nature of data generated by billions of interconnected devices, ensuring data quality, security, privacy, and ethical use. Without a well-defined strategy, the potential of AI in 6G risks being undermined by data silos, inconsistencies, security vulnerabilities, and a lack of trust.

Data governance, on the other hand, establishes the rules, policies, and procedures for ensuring the integrity, security, privacy, and compliance of data used in AI applications within the 6G ecosystem. It defines roles and responsibilities for data ownership, access control, data quality assurance, and adherence to regulatory requirements. In the context of 6G, data governance must address the unique challenges posed by distributed data sources, federated learning environments, and the need to balance innovation with ethical considerations.

Case Study: Predictive Maintenance in Industrial IoT over 6G

Consider a large-scale industrial deployment leveraging 6G connectivity to implement predictive maintenance for thousands of interconnected machines. Each machine is equipped with numerous sensors generating diverse data streams, including temperature readings, vibration analysis, acoustic emissions, and operational logs.

Data Management Challenges

- **Data Heterogeneity:** The data originates in various formats and structures, requiring sophisticated ingestion and integration pipelines.
- **Data Volume and Velocity:** The sheer volume of real-time data from thousands of sensors necessitates distributed storage and efficient processing capabilities at the network edge.
- **Data Quality:** Raw sensor data may contain noise, outliers, and missing values, requiring robust data cleaning and preprocessing techniques to ensure the reliability of AI models.

- **Real-time Access:** AI models for anomaly detection and failure prediction require low-latency access to the latest sensor readings for timely decision-making.

Data Governance Requirements

- **Data Ownership and Access Control:** Clear policies must define who owns the machine data and who has authorized access for AI model training and inference.
- **Data Security and Privacy:** Sensitive operational data must be protected from unauthorized access and cyber threats, especially if data is processed or aggregated across multiple edge devices.
- **Data Quality Standards:** Governance frameworks must establish data quality metrics and procedures to ensure the accuracy and reliability of data used for AI.

Decentralized Intelligence and Collaborative Learning in 6G Networks

The forthcoming 6G networks are anticipated to revolutionize wireless communication with unprecedented data transfer speeds, minimal delays, extensive connectivity, and enhanced reliability. Artificial Intelligence (AI) is considered a foundational technology for achieving these advancements, enabling intelligent automation, optimization, and the delivery of novel services. However, conventional centralized AI methods, which depend on gathering substantial data in a central server for training purposes, encounter considerable obstacles in the 6G era. These challenges arise from the immense volume and diversity of data generated by billions of interconnected devices, coupled with increasing concerns regarding data confidentiality and security.

Decentralized AI (DAI) and **Federated Learning (FL)** have emerged as promising approaches to tackle these issues by bringing computational intelligence closer to the data source and facilitating cooperative learning without necessitating centralized data accumulation.

Decentralized AI for 6G

Decentralized AI involves the deployment and execution of AI algorithms across a network of interconnected devices or edge computing servers. Within the context of 6G, DAI leverages the distributed nature of the network to enable localized data processing, real-time decision-making, and efficient resource management. By distributing AI functionalities across the network's edge, DAI offers several key advantages for 6G:

- **Improved Efficiency and Reduced Latency:** Processing data and making decisions at the network's periphery significantly diminishes the communication overhead and delays associated with transmitting data to a central cloud. This is vital for delay-sensitive 6G applications such as self-driving vehicles, extended reality (XR), and industrial automation.
- **Enhanced Scalability and Adaptability:** DAI can manage the vast scale and variety of 6G networks by distributing the computational workload and enabling independent AI agents to operate locally and adapt to evolving network conditions.
- **Greater Privacy and Security:** By keeping data localized, DAI minimizes the need to transmit sensitive information to a central point, thereby bolstering data confidentiality and security.
- **Increased Robustness and Reliability:** The distributed structure of DAI makes the network more resistant to failures, as the malfunction of individual edge devices will not necessarily disrupt the overall AI functionality.

Federated Learning for 6G

Federated Learning is a specific decentralized AI technique that allows numerous devices (e.g., smartphones, IoT sensors, vehicles) to collaboratively train a shared machine learning model while keeping their data on-device. In a typical FL process:

1. A central server distributes an initial global model to a selection of participating devices.
2. Each device trains the model using only its local data.
3. The devices send model updates to the central server, which aggregates these updates to refine the global model.
4. This iterative process continues until the global model achieves a satisfactory level of performance.

FL is particularly well-suited for 6G networks due to its capacity to:

- **Protect Data Confidentiality:** FL enables devices to contribute to the learning process without disclosing their raw data, addressing growing privacy concerns in the 6G landscape.
- **Accommodate Data Diversity:** FL can handle the varied and non-identically distributed (non-IID) data generated by different devices within 6G networks.

- **Lower Communication Demands:** By exchanging only model updates instead of raw data, FL significantly reduces the communication load on the 6G network.
- **Enable Widespread AI Implementation:** FL can utilize the extensive data generated at the network edge to create more robust and personalized AI models for various 6G applications.

Applications of Decentralized AI and Federated Learning in 6G

The integration of DAI and FL presents substantial opportunities for a wide array of 6G applications and services, including:

- **Intelligent Network Management:** AI algorithms deployed at the network edge can optimize resource allocation, traffic flow, network slicing, and energy consumption in real-time, adapting to changing network conditions and user needs. FL can be employed to train these AI models using data collected from distributed network elements without compromising their local configurations.
- **Advanced Mobile Edge Computing (MEC):** DAI can enhance the capabilities of MEC servers by enabling intelligent data processing and analysis closer to the users. FL can facilitate the collaborative training of AI models across multiple MEC servers, leading to more precise and personalized edge services.
- **Smart City Initiatives:** DAI and FL can power various smart city applications, such as intelligent transportation systems, smart grids, environmental monitoring, and public safety. For example, FL can be used to train traffic prediction models using data from numerous connected vehicles and sensors while safeguarding the privacy of individual movement patterns.
- **Autonomous Driving:** DAI is crucial for enabling real-time decision-making in self-driving vehicles based on sensor inputs. FL can be used to collaboratively train perception and control models across a fleet of vehicles, leveraging diverse driving experiences while ensuring data privacy.
- **Extended Reality (XR):** DAI can optimize the delivery of immersive XR experiences by providing low-latency rendering and personalized content. FL can be used to train AI models for predicting user behavior and recommending content based on individual user interactions with XR applications.
- **Massive Internet of Things (mIoT):** DAI and FL can facilitate the management and analysis of data from a vast number of IoT devices in 6G networks. For instance, FL can be used to detect anomalies in sensor data for predictive

maintenance applications without requiring the central collection of sensitive industrial data.

- **Network Security:** DAI can enhance network security by enabling distributed intrusion detection and threat analysis. FL can be used to collaboratively train security models across network devices to identify and mitigate cyber threats while preserving local data.

Ethical Implications of AI-Powered Threat Detection and Response in 6G Networks

The integration of AI into 6G network security raises several ethical considerations that need to be addressed to ensure responsible deployment:

1. **Privacy Concerns:** AI-driven systems rely on vast amounts of data, including network traffic, user behavior, and device information. The collection and analysis of this data could potentially infringe on individual privacy rights. It is crucial to establish clear guidelines and regulations regarding data collection, storage, and usage to prevent misuse and ensure compliance with privacy laws.
2. **Bias and Discrimination:** AI algorithms are susceptible to biases present in the data they are trained on. This could lead to discriminatory outcomes, where certain groups are disproportionately targeted or disadvantaged by the security system. For example, if the AI is trained primarily on data from a specific demographic, it might be less effective at detecting threats from other groups, or it could even falsely flag their activity as suspicious.
3. **Transparency and Explainability:** Many AI algorithms, particularly deep learning models, operate as "black boxes," making it difficult to understand how they arrive at a particular decision. This lack of transparency can erode trust in the system and make it challenging to identify and correct errors or biases. Explainable AI (XAI) is an emerging field that aims to develop techniques for making AI decisions more transparent and understandable.
4. **Accountability and Responsibility:** When an AI system makes a mistake, such as a false positive that leads to the wrongful accusation of an individual, it can be difficult to determine who is accountable. Is it the developer of the algorithm, the operator of the system, or the AI itself? Clear lines of accountability need to be established to ensure that there are mechanisms in place for redress and to prevent future errors.

Challenges and Future Directions

Despite their considerable promise, the deployment of DAI and FL in 6G networks also poses several challenges:

- **Heterogeneity:** 6G networks will encompass a diverse range of devices with varying computational power, communication bandwidth, and data characteristics. Addressing this heterogeneity in DAI and FL algorithms is essential for ensuring efficient and equitable learning.
- **Communication Efficiency:** While FL reduces communication overhead compared to centralized learning, the exchange of model updates can still be a limitation in resource-constrained wireless environments. Developing communication-efficient FL techniques is vital for 6G.
- **Security and Privacy:** Ensuring the security and privacy of the learning process in DAI and FL is paramount. Malicious devices or adversarial attacks on the model aggregation process can compromise the integrity and confidentiality of the system.
- **Trust and Incentivization:** Encouraging participation and ensuring the reliability of devices in distributed learning scenarios requires robust incentive mechanisms and reputation systems.
- **Standardization and Interoperability:** The absence of standardized frameworks and protocols for DAI and FL can impede their widespread adoption in 6G networks. Collaborative efforts are needed to develop common standards and ensure interoperability across different platforms and devices.

Future research directions in this domain include:

- Creating more resilient and efficient federated learning algorithms capable of handling significant data diversity and communication limitations.
- Investigating innovative methods for secure aggregation and privacy-preserving model updates in FL.
- Exploring incentive mechanisms and trust management frameworks for large-scale distributed learning systems.
- Designing decentralized AI architectures that can seamlessly integrate with the 6G network infrastructure and support a wide range of applications.
- Developing standardized APIs and protocols to facilitate the deployment and management of DAI and FL in 6G networks.

CONCLUSION

As discussed throughout this chapter, AI is expected to revolutionize 6G security in a number of ways. It would be able to analyze humongous data sets, discover complex patterns, and automate security tasks, thus giving it an edge over the traditional security approaches. AI would improve threat detection by detecting subtle anomalies and malicious activities that would otherwise go unnoticed. It might make proactive security easy, predict attacks, and prevent them from happening. Furthermore, AI can be used for automating security management tasks so that human operators can be released for strategic matters. Such tools are available across the spectrum-the edge devices and IoT networks to SDN infrastructure and network slices-using AI for dealing with the many facets of 6G security. That would also make AI critical in dealing with the dynamics of changing cyber threats, because security systems will need to anticipate the malicious players' next step. Inevitably, there are challenges in the integration of AI in 6G security. Some of the significant ones discussed include adversarial attacks, data privacy concerns, computation overheads, and the need for explainable AI models. These pose an evident need for a holistic approach to AI-powered security that can underscore not only the technical conundrums but also those of an ethical, legal, and societal nature.

REFERENCES

Ayaz, F., Sheng, Z., Tian, D., Nekovee, M., & Saeed, N. (2022). Blockchain-empowered ai for 6g-enabled internet of vehicles. *Electronics (Basel)*, *11*(20), 3339. Advance online publication. DOI: 10.3390/electronics11203339

Catak, F. O., Kuzlu, M., Catak, E., Cali, U., & Unal, D. (2022). Security concerns on machine learning solutions for 6G networks in mmWave beam prediction. *Physical Communication*, *52*, 101626.

Chowdhury, M. Z., Shahjalal, M., Ahmed, S., & Jang, Y. M. (2020). *6g wireless communication systems: applications, requirements, technologies, challenges, and research directions*. IEEE Communications Society.

Cunha, J., Ferreira, P., Castro, E. M., Oliveira, P. C., Nicolau, M. J., Nez, I., Sousa, X. R., & Serdio, C. (2024). Enhancing network slicing security: Machine learning, software-defined networking, and network functions virtualization-driven strategies. *Future Internet*, *16*(7), 226. DOI: 10.3390/fi16070226

Gkonis, P. K., Trakadas, P., Sarakis, L., & Xylouris, G. MasipBruin, X., & Martrat, J. (2024). Leveraging network data analytics function and machine learning for data collection, resource optimization, security and privacy in 6g networks. Institute of Electrical and Electronics Engineers.

Iqbal, A., Tham, M., Wong, Y. J., Al-Habashna, A., Wainer, G., Zhu, Y. X., & Dagiuklas, T. (2023). *Empowering non-terrestrial networks with artificial intelligence: a survey*. Institute of Electrical and Electronics Engineers. DOI: 10.1109/ACCESS.2023.3314732

Jagatheesaperumal, S. K., Pham, Q., Ruby, R., Yang, Z., Xu, C., & Zhang, Z. (2022). *Explainable ai over the internet of things (iot): overview, state-of-the-art and future directions*. IEEE Communications Society.

Naeem, F., Ali, M., & Kaddoum, G. (2023). Federated-learning-empowered semi-supervised active learning framework for intrusion detection in zsm. *IEEE Communications Magazine*, *61*(2), 88–94. DOI: 10.1109/MCOM.001.2200533

Paolini, E., Valcarenghi, L., Maggiani, L., & Andriolli, N. (2023). *Real-time clustering based on deep embeddings for threat detection in 6g networks*. Institute of Electrical and Electronics Engineers. DOI: 10.1109/ACCESS.2023.3325721

Saeed, M. M., Saeed, R. A., Abdelhaq, M., Alsaqour, R., Hasan, M. K., & Mokhtar, R. A. (2023). *Anomaly detection in 6g networks using machine learning methods*. Multidisciplinary Digital Publishing Institute. DOI: 10.3390/electronics12153300

Scalise, P., Boeding, M., Hempel, M., Sharif, H., Delloiacovo, J., & Reed, J. (2024). A systematic survey on 5g and 6g security considerations, challenges, trends, and research areas. *Future Internet*, *16*(3), 67. DOI: 10.3390/fi16030067

Sedjelmaci, H., Kheir, N., Boudguiga, A., & Kaaniche, N. (2022). *Cooperative and smart attacks detection systems in 6g-enabled internet of things*. None. DOI: 10.1109/ICC45855.2022.9838338

Singh, R., Srivastav, G., Kashyap, R., & Vats, S. (2023). Study on zero-trust architecture, application areas & challenges of 6g technology in future. *International Conference on Database Theory*. DOI: 10.1109/ICDT57929.2023.10150745

Wang, C., You, X., Gao, X., Zhu, X., Li, Z., Zhang, C., Wang, H., Huang, Y., Chen, Y., Haas, H., Thompson, J., Larsson, E. G., Renzo, M. D., Tong, W., Zhu, P., Shen, X., Poor, H. V., & Hanzo, L. (2023). *On the road to 6g: visions, requirements, key technologies, and testbeds*. Institute of Electrical and Electronics Engineers.

Zuo, Y., Guo, J., Gao, N., Zhu, Y., Jin, S., & Li, X. (2023). A survey of blockchain and artificial intelligence for 6g wireless communications. *IEEE Communications Surveys and Tutorials*, *25*(4), 2494–2528. DOI: 10.1109/COMST.2023.3315374

Compilation of References

Abadi, M. (2016). Deep learning with differential privacy. *Proceedings of the 2016 ACM SIGSAC Conference on Computer and Communications Security*. DOI: 10.1145/2976749.2978318

Aberdeen. (n.d.). The Rise of Mobile Technology in Business: 5 Ways It's Shaping the Future. https://www.aberdeen.com/blogposts/the-rise-of-mobile-technology-in-business-5-ways-its-shaping-the-future/

Adadi, A., & Berrada, M. (2018). Peeking inside the black-box: A survey on explainable artificial intelligence (XAI). *IEEE Access : Practical Innovations, Open Solutions*, *6*, 52138–52160. DOI: 10.1109/ACCESS.2018.2870052

Adhikari, M., & Hazra, A. (2022). 6G-enabled ultra-reliable low-latency communication in edge networks. *IEEE Communications Standards Magazine*, *6*(1), 67–74. Advance online publication. DOI: 10.1109/MCOMSTD.0001.2100098

Ahuja, K., & Bala, I. (2023). M2M in 5G Cellular Networks: Challenges, Proposed Solutions, and Future Directions. In *Wireless Communication Security*. https://doi.org/DOI: 10.1002/9781119777465.ch1

Akbar, M. S., Hussain, Z., Sheng, Q. Z., & Mukhopadhyay, S. (2022). *6G Survey on Challenges, Requirements, Applications, Key Enabling Technologies, Use Cases, AI integration issues and Security aspects*. http://arxiv.org/abs/2206.00868

Akyildiz, I. F., Kak, A., & Nie, S. (2020). 6G and beyond: The future of wireless communications systems. *IEEE Access : Practical Innovations, Open Solutions*, *8*, 133995–134030. DOI: 10.1109/ACCESS.2020.3010896

Alahmad, H., Almanaa, M., Abanomy, A., Alarifi, M., Alenazi, K., Matabi, M., Albathi, R., & Moslem, R. (2024). Navigating challenges in teleradiology implementation: A case study from Saudi Arabia's healthcare system. *Journal of Multidisciplinary Healthcare*, *17*, 2083–2092. DOI: 10.2147/JMDH.S460547 PMID: 38736539

Ali, M. Z., Abohmra, A., Usman, M., Zahid, A., Heidari, H., Imran, M. A., & Abbasi, Q. H. (2023). Quantum for 6G communication: A perspective. *IET Quantum Communication*, *4*(3), 112–124. DOI: 10.1049/qtc2.12060

Ali, S., Abuhmed, T., El-Sappagh, S., Muhammad, K., Alonso-Moral, J. M., Confalonieri, R., Guidotti, R., Del Ser, J., Díaz-Rodríguez, N., & Herrera, F. (2023). Explainable Artificial Intelligence (XAI): What we know and what is left to attain Trustworthy Artificial Intelligence. *Information Fusion*, *99*, 101. DOI: 10.1016/j.inffus.2023.101805

Alkasassbeh, J. S., Al-Taweel, F. M., Alawneh, T. A., Al-Qaisi, A., Makableh, Y. F., & El-Mezieni, T. (2024). Advancements in wireless communication technology: A comprehensive analysis of 4G to 7G systems. [JoWUA]. *Journal of Wireless Mobile Networks, Ubiquitous Computing and Dependable Applications*, *15*(3), 73–91. DOI: 10.58346/JOWUA.2024.I3.006

Almarri, S., & Aljughaiman, A. (2024). Blockchain Technology for IoT Security and Trust: A Comprehensive SLR. *Sustainability (Basel)*, *16*(23), 10177. DOI: 10.3390/su162310177

Alsharif, A., Alhassan, I., & Alzahrani, A. (2023). 6G Technology as Enabler of Psychophysical Well-being & Social Inclusion Services for Citizen 4.0. *Applied System Innovation*, *4*(3), 66. DOI: 10.3390/asi4030066

Alsharif, M. H., Jahid, A., Kannadasan, R., & Kim, M.-K. (2024). Unleashing the potential of sixth generation (6G) wireless networks in smart energy grid management: A comprehensive review. *Sustainable Energy. Energy Reports*, *37*, 101123. DOI: 10.1016/j.egyr.2024.01.011

Alzoubi, Y. I., & Mishra, A. (2024). Blockchain consensus mechanisms comparison in fog computing: A systematic review. In *ICT Express* (Vol. 10, Issue 2). https://doi.org/DOI: 10.1016/j.icte.2024.02.008

Andres, M., Diaz-Madroñero, A. L., Soares, R., & Poler, R. (2024). Enabling technologies to support supply chain logistics 5.0. *IEEE Access : Practical Innovations, Open Solutions*, *12*, 43889–43906. DOI: 10.1109/ACCESS.2024.3374194

Ardic, O., & Cetinel, G. (2024). Deep learning-based real-time engine part inspection with collaborative robot application. *IEEE Access : Practical Innovations, Open Solutions*, *12*, 187483–187497. DOI: 10.1109/ACCESS.2024.3489714

Arunachalam, M., Akella, S., Arun Satvik, D., & Babu, R. T. S. (2025). *Navigating Privacy and Security in Internet of Medical Things With Machine-to-Machine Interactions.*, DOI: 10.4018/979-8-3693-6180-1.ch018

Arunodhai, V., Susan, L. P., & Kannimoola, J. M. (2024). EdgeShield: Hybrid Real-Time Attack Detection in IOTA Tangle via Edge Devices. *2024 15th International Conference on Computing Communication and Networking Technologies (ICCCNT)*, 1–11. https://doi.org/DOI: 10.1109/ICCCNT61001.2024.10724609

Arya, L., Sharma, Y. K., Vadlamudi, S., Naidu, M., & Lilhore, U. K. (2025). Chapter 2: Quantum computing with machine learning: Opportunities and challenges. In Industrial Quantum Computing: Algorithms, Blockchains, Industry 4.0 (pp. 19-36). De Gruyter. DOI: 10.1515/9783111354842-002

Arya, L., Bhatnagar, M., Cheekati, V. R., Rastogi, R., & Kumar, K. P. M. (2025). Enhancing Educational Future by Integrating Artificial Intelligence in Language Curriculum. In Jomaa, N. (Ed.), *Modern Methods for AI-Integrated Language Curriculum* (pp. 149–184). IGI Global., DOI: 10.4018/979-8-3693-9606-3.ch006

Arya, L., & Rastogi, R. (2024). Study on aerial monitoring system in agriculture, forestry, defense, and border protection using artificial intelligence (AI). In *Agriculture and Aquaculture Applications of Biosensors and Bioelectronics* (pp. 392–407). IGI Global., DOI: 10.4018/979-8-3693-2069-3.ch021

Arya, L., Sharma, Y. K., Devi, S., Padmanaban, H., & Kumar, R. (2024). Securing the Internet of Things: AI-Powered Threat Detection and Safety Measures. In Illés, Z. (Eds.), *Proceedings of International Conference on Recent Innovations in Computing* (pp. 79-94). Springer. DOI: 10.1007/978-981-97-3442-9_7

Arya, L., Sharma, Y. K., Kumar, R., Padmanaban, H., Devi, S., & Tyagi, L. K. (2023). Maximizing IoT security: An examination of cryptographic algorithms. *2023 International Conference on Power Energy, Environment & Intelligent Control (PEEIC)*, 1548-1552. DOI: 10.1109/PEEIC59336.2023.10451210

Aslam, M. M., Zhang, J., Qureshi, B., & Ahmed, Z. (2021). Beyond6G-consensus traffic management in CRN, applications, architecture and key challenges. *2021 IEEE 11th International Conference on Electronics Information and Emergency Communication (ICEIEC) 2021 IEEE 11th International Conference on Electronics Information and Emergency Communication (ICEIEC)*, 182–185.

Aslam, M. M., Du, L., Zhang, X., Chen, Y., Ahmed, Z., & Qureshi, B. (2021). Sixth generation (6G) cognitive radio network (CRN) application, requirements, security issues, and key challenges. *Wireless Communications and Mobile Computing*, *2021*(1), 1331428. DOI: 10.1155/2021/1331428

Attar, A. E., Wehby, A., Chbib, F., Mehrez, H. A., Fadlallah, A., Hachem, J., & Khatoun, R. (2023). Analysis of Machine Learning Algorithms for DDoS Attack Detection in Connected Cars Environment. 2023 Eighth International Conference On Mobile And Secure Services (MobiSecServ). https://www.semanticscholar.org/paper/41e07dce684274a1dba1011da152204dd46c41e5

Ayaz, F., Sheng, Z., Tian, D., Nekovee, M., & Saeed, N. (2022). Blockchain-empowered ai for 6g-enabled internet of vehicles. *Electronics (Basel)*, *11*(20), 3339. Advance online publication. DOI: 10.3390/electronics11203339

Azari, M. M., Solanki, S., Chatzinotas, S., Kodheli, O., Sallouha, H., Colpaert, A., Mendoza Montoya, J. F., Pollin, S., Haqiqatnejad, A., Mostaani, A., Lagunas, E., & Ottersten, B. (2022). Evolution of Non-Terrestrial Networks from 5G to 6G: A Survey. *IEEE Communications Surveys and Tutorials*, *24*(4), 2633–2672. DOI: 10.1109/COMST.2022.3199901

Banafaa, M., Shayea, I., Din, J., Hadri Azmi, M., Alashbi, A., Ibrahim Daradkeh, Y., & Alhammadi, A. (2023). 6G Mobile Communication Technology: Requirements, Targets, Applications, Challenges, Advantages, and Opportunities. In *Alexandria Engineering Journal* (Vol. 64). https://doi.org/DOI: 10.1016/j.aej.2022.08.017

Bandi, A., & Yalamarthi, S. (2022). *Towards artificial intelligence empowered security and privacy issues in 6G communications*. https://ieeexplore.ieee.org/abstract/document/9760857/

Bandi, A., & Yalamarthi, S. (2022). Towards Artificial Intelligence Empowered Security and Privacy Issues in 6G Communications. *International Conference on Sustainable Computing and Data Communication Systems, ICSCDS 2022 - Proceedings*. DOI: 10.1109/ICSCDS53736.2022.9760857

Barocas, S., Hardt, M., & Narayanan, A. (2019). Fairness and machine learning. fairmlbook.org.

Basaran, O. T., & Dressler, F. (2024). XAInomaly: Explainable, Interpretable and Trustworthy AI for xURLLC in 6G Open-RAN. 2024 3rd International Conference on 6G Networking (6GNet), 93-101. DOI: 10.1109/6GNet63182.2024.10765734

Bellaj, B., Ouaddah, A., Bertin, E., Crespi, N., & Mezrioui, A. (2024). Drawing the Boundaries Between Blockchain and Blockchain-Like Systems: A Comprehensive Survey on Distributed Ledger Technologies. *Proceedings of the IEEE*, *112*(3), 247–299. DOI: 10.1109/JPROC.2024.3386257

Beyaz, M. (2024). Satellite communications with 5G, B5G, and 6G: Challenges and prospects. *International Journal of Communications, Network and Systems Sciences, 17*(3), 31–49. DOI: 10.4236/ijcns.2024.173003

Bhat, J. R., & Alqahtani, S. A. (2021). 6G ecosystem: Current status and future perspective. *IEEE Access : Practical Innovations, Open Solutions, 9*, 43134–43167. DOI: 10.1109/ACCESS.2021.3054833

Bhattacharya, P., Shukla, A., Tanwar, S., Kumar, N., & Sharma, R. (2022). 6Blocks: 6G-enabled trust management scheme for decentralized autonomous vehicles. *Computer Communications, 191*, 53–68. Advance online publication. DOI: 10.1016/j.comcom.2022.04.024

Bilami, K. E., & Lorenz, P. (2022). Lightweight Blockchain-Based Scheme to Secure Wireless M2M Area Networks. *Future Internet, 14*(5), 158. Advance online publication. DOI: 10.3390/fi14050158

Blackview. (2024). The Future of Wireless Communication: Exploring the Capabilities of 6G Technology. Retrieved from https://www.blackview.com/blog/the-future-of-wireless-communication-exploring-the-capabilities-of-6g-technology

Booth, N. (2024). What is the reality of 6G and how will it impact people? *Mobile Europe*. Retrieved from https://www.mobileeurope.co.uk/what-is-the-reality-of-6g-and-how-will-it-impact-people/

Brik, B., Chergui, H., Zanzi, L., Devoti, F., Ksentini, A., Siddiqui, M. S. (2023). A Survey on Explainable AI for 6G O-RAN: Architecture Use Cases Challenges and Research Directions.

Buolamwini, J., & Gebru, T. (2018). Gender shades: Intersectional accuracy disparities in commercial gender classification. *Proceedings of the 1st Conference on Fairness, Accountability, and Transparency.*

Cai, T., Chen, W., Psannis, K. E., Goudos, S. K., Yu, Y., Zheng, Z., & Wan, S. (2022). Scalable On-Chain and Off-Chain Blockchain for Sharing Economy in Large-Scale Wireless Networks. *IEEE Wireless Communications, 29*(3), 32–38. Advance online publication. DOI: 10.1109/MWC.004.2100616

Catak, E., Moldsvor, A., & Kuzlu, M. (2021). Adversarial machine learning security problems for 6G: mmWave beam prediction use-case. *arXiv preprint arXiv:2105.03905*. /arxiv.2105.03905DOI: 10.1109/BlackSeaCom52164.2021.9527756

Catak, F. O., Kuzlu, M., Catak, E., Cali, U., & Unal, D. (2022). Security concerns on machine learning solutions for 6G networks in mmWave beam prediction. *Physical Communication, 52*, 101626.

Celik, A., & Eltawil, A. M. (2024). At the Dawn of Generative AI Era: A Tutorial-cum-Survey on New Frontiers in 6G Wireless Intelligence. *IEEE Open Journal of the Communications Society*, *5*, 2433–2489. Advance online publication. DOI: 10.1109/OJCOMS.2024.3362271

Chen, D., Wei, X., & Ni, C. (2023). Machine Learning in Wireless Communication. 2023 3rd International Conference on Electronic Information Engineering and Computer Science (EIECS). https://www.semanticscholar.org/paper/fc1ca53d35ad5fe94f2874f685c2c263fb9db708

Chen, C., Förster, M. W., Foley, S. F., & Liu, Y. (2021). Massive carbon storage in convergent margins initiated by subduction of limestone. *Nature Communications*, *12*(1), 4463. DOI: 10.1038/s41467-021-24750-0 PMID: 34294696

Chen, P.-Y. (2018). EAD: Elastic net attacks to deep neural networks via adversarial examples. *Proceedings of the AAAI Conference on Artificial Intelligence*. DOI: 10.1609/aaai.v32i1.11302

Chinnasamy, P., Babu, G. C., Ayyasamy, R. K., Amutha, S., Sinha, K., & Balaram, A. (2024). Blockchain 6G-Based Wireless Network Security Management With Optimization Using Machine Learning Techniques. *Sensors (Basel)*, *24*(18), 6143. DOI: 10.3390/s24186143 PMID: 39338888

Chou, H. F., Wang, Z., & Lin, Y. (2023). Edge AI empowered physical layer security for 6G NTN: Potential threats and future opportunities. arXiv preprint arXiv:2401.01005. https://arxiv.org/abs/2401.01005

Chowdhury, M. Z., Shahjalal, M., Ahmed, S., & Jang, Y. M. (2020). *6g wireless communication systems: applications, requirements, technologies, challenges, and research directions*. IEEE Communications Society.

Chowdhury, R. H. (2024). *Blockchain and AI: Driving the future of data security and business intelligence*. World Journal of Advanced Research and Reviews. DOI: 10.1201/9781003162018

Clement, T., Kemmerzell, N., Abdelaal, M., & Amberg, M. (2023). XAIR: A systematic metareview of explainable AI (XAI) aligned to the software development process. *Machine Learning and Knowledge Extraction*, *5*(1), 78–108. DOI: 10.3390/make5010006

Corcuera Bárcena, J. L., Ducange, P., Marcelloni, F., Nardini, G., Noferi, A., Renda, A., Ruffini, F., Schiavo, A., Stea, G., & Virdis, A. (2023). Enabling federated learning of explainable AI models within beyond-5G/6G networks. *Computer Communications*, *210*, 356–375. Advance online publication. DOI: 10.1016/j.comcom.2023.07.039

Corcuera Bárcena, J. L., Ducange, P., Marcelloni, F., Nardini, G., Noferi, A., Renda, A., Stea, G., & Virdis, A. (2022). Towards Trustworthy AI for QoE prediction in B5G/6G Networks. *CEUR Workshop Proceedings*, •••, 3189.

Crain, T., Natoli, C., & Gramoli, V. 2018. "Evaluating the Red Belly Blockchain." arXiv.Org. December 31, 2018. https://doi.org//arXiv.1812.11747.DOI: 10.48550

Cui, Q., You, X., Wei, N., Nan, G., Zhang, X., Zhang, J., & Yuen, C. (2025). Overview of AI and communication for 6G network: Fundamentals, challenges, and future research opportunities. *Science China. Information Sciences*, *68*(7), 171301. DOI: 10.1007/s11432-024-4337-1

Cunha, J., Ferreira, P., Castro, E. M., Oliveira, P. C., Nicolau, M. J., Nez, I., Sousa, X. R., & Serdio, C. (2024). Enhancing network slicing security: Machine learning, software-defined networking, and network functions virtualization-driven strategies. *Future Internet*, *16*(7), 226. DOI: 10.3390/fi16070226

Dalai, D., Babu, S., & Manoj, B. S. (2022). Satellite-6G network integration roadmap on reference architectures. *TechRxiv Preprint*. https://doi.org/DOI: 10.36227/techrxiv.20624685.v1

Dalai, D., Babu, S., Sukumaran, V. B., & Manoj, B. S. (2024). A novel space-based hosting approach for ultra low latency web services. *IEEE Access : Practical Innovations, Open Solutions*, *12*, 142838–142862. DOI: 10.1109/ACCESS.2024.3462252

Dang, S., Amin, O., Shihada, B., & Alouini, M.-S. (2020). What should 6G be? *Nature Electronics*, *3*(1), 20–29. DOI: 10.1038/s41928-019-0355-6

Dao, N.-N., Pham, Q.-V., Tu, N. H., Thanh, T. T., Bao, V. N. Q., Lakew, D. S., & Cho, S. (2021). Survey on aerial radio access networks: Toward a comprehensive 6G access infrastructure. *IEEE Communications Surveys and Tutorials*, *23*(2), 1193–1225. DOI: 10.1109/COMST.2021.3059644

Del Portillo, I., Cameron, B. G., & Crawley, E. F. (2019). A technical comparison of three low Earth orbit satellite constellation systems to provide global broadband. *Acta Astronautica*, *159*, 123–135. DOI: 10.1016/j.actaastro.2019.03.040

Dennis, T. A., & O'Toole, L. J. (2014). Mental health on the go: Effects of a gamified attention-bias modification mobile application in trait-anxious adults. *Clinical Psychological Science*, *2*(5), 576–590. Advance online publication. DOI: 10.1177/2167702614522228 PMID: 26029490

Dey, S., De, U. C., Dash, B. B., Patra, S. S., Samant, T., & Banerjee, S. (2024, October). Fine-Tuning Prophet model for application in Agro-Industry to forecast Pesticide consumption. In *2024 IEEE 1st International Conference on Green Industrial Electronics and Sustainable Technologies (GIEST)* (pp. 1-5). IEEE. DOI: 10.1109/GIEST62955.2024.10960129

Dey, S., Moharana, B., De, U. C., Samant, T., Behera, T. M., & Banerjee, S. (2024, March). Search Engine for QnA using Distributed Inverted Index System. In *2024 3rd International Conference for Innovation in Technology (INOCON)* (pp. 1-4). IEEE. DOI: 10.1109/INOCON60754.2024.10511792

Dey, S. (2014). Performance Analysis of LEO Satellite (Sky Bridge) For Mobile Terminal with Varying Implementation Margin. *IJLTET*, *4*(2), 191–196.

Dey, S. (2024). Phenomenon of Excess of Artificial Intelligence: Quantifying the Native AI, Its Leverages in 5G/6G and Beyond. In *Radar and RF Front End System Designs for Wireless Systems* (pp. 245–274). IGI Global. DOI: 10.4018/979-8-3693-0916-2.ch010

Dey, S.. (2023), "Play Store App Analysis & Rating Prediction Using Classical ML Models & Artificial Neural Network," *7th International Conference on Computing, Communication, Control and Automation (ICCUBEA)*, Pune, India, 2023, pp. 1-5, DOI: 10.1109/ICCUBEA58933.2023.10391960

Dey, S., Mohapatra, D., & Archana, S. D. R. P. (2014). An approach to calculate the performance and link budget of leo satellite (iridium) for communication operated at frequency range (1650–1550) mhz. *International Journal of Latest Trends in Engineering & Technology : IJLTET*, *4*(4), 96–103.

Dey, S., Panda, A. K., & Pati, C. (2023). Unlocking the potential of machine learning and deep learning algorithms in recent communication: AI is the best revolutionary tool in the current era. *CPPPT*, *23*(2), 2794–2805.

Dhokrat, J. G., Pulgam, N., Maktum, T., & Mane, V. (2024). A Framework for Privacy-Preserving Multiparty Computation with Homomorphic Encryption and Zero-Knowledge Proofs. *Informatica (Vilnius)*, *48*(21). Advance online publication. DOI: 10.31449/inf.v48i21.6562

Diro, A., & Zhou, L. L., Saini, A., Kaisar, S., & Pham, H. (2023). *Leveraging Blockchain for Zero Knowledge Identify Sharing: A Survey of Advancements, Challenges and Opportunities*. https://doi.org/DOI: 10.2139/ssrn.4469520

Diro, A., Zhou, L., Saini, A., Kaisar, S., & Hiep, P. C. (2024). Leveraging zero knowledge proofs for blockchain-based identity sharing: A survey of advancements, challenges and opportunities. *Journal of Information Security and Applications*, *80*, 103678. Advance online publication. DOI: 10.1016/j.jisa.2023.103678

Dong, S., Abbas, K., Li, M., & Kamruzzaman, J. (2023). Blockchain technology and application: An overview. *PeerJ. Computer Science*, *9*, e1705. Advance online publication. DOI: 10.7717/peerj-cs.1705 PMID: 38077532

Ducange, P., Marcelloni, F., Micheli, D., Nardini, G., Renda, A., Sabella, D., Stea, G., & Virdis, A. (2023). Trustworthy AI for Next Generation Networks: The Fed-XAI innovative paradigm from the Hexa-X EU Flagship Project. *CEUR Workshop Proceedings*, •••, 3486.

Duong, T. Q., Ansere, J. A., Narottama, B., Sharma, V., Dobre, O. A., & Shin, H. (2022). Quantum-Inspired Machine Learning for 6G: Fundamentals, Security, Resource Allocations, Challenges, and Future Research Directions. *IEEE Open Journal of Vehicular Technology*, *3*(September), 375–387. DOI: 10.1109/OJVT.2022.3202876

Esmaili, M., & Christensen, K. (2025). Performance Modeling of Public Permissionless Blockchains: A Survey. *ACM Computing Surveys*, *57*(7), 1–35. Advance online publication. DOI: 10.1145/3715094

European Commission. (2021). *Proposal for a regulation laying down harmonized rules on artificial intelligence (Artificial Intelligence Act)*. Official Journal of the European Union.

European Parliamentary Research Service. (2020). The ethics of artificial intelligence: Issues and initiatives. European Union. https://www.europarl.europa.eu/RegData/etudes/STUD/2020/634452/EPRS_STU(2020)634452_EN.pdf

Ferrag, M. A., Debbah, M., & Al-Hawawreh, M. (2023). Generative AI for cyber threat-hunting in 6G-enabled IoT networks. *arXiv preprint arXiv:2303.11751.* / arxiv.2303.11751DOI: 10.1109/CCGridW59191.2023.00018

Fiandrino, C., Attanasio, G., Fiore, M., & Widmer, J. (2022). Toward native explainable and robust AI in 6G networks: Current state challenges and road ahead. *Computer Communications*, *193*, 47–52. DOI: 10.1016/j.comcom.2022.06.036

Filippou, M. C., Lamprousi, V., Mohammadi, J., Merluzzi, M., Soykan, E. U., Borsos, T., Rajatheva, N., Rajapaksha, N., Le Magoarou, L., Piscione, P., Benczur, A., Lampin, Q., Larue, G., Korpi, D., Ducange, P., Renda, A., Farhadi, H., Haraldson, J., Strinati, L. G. B. E. C., & Tomur, E. (2022). Pervasive Artificial Intelligence in Next Generation Wireless: The Hexa-X Project Perspective. *CEUR Workshop Proceedings*, •••, 3189.

Floridi, L., Cowls, J., Beltrametti, M., Chatila, R., Chazerand, P., Dignum, V., Luetge, C., Madelin, R., Pagallo, U., Rossi, F., Schafer, B., Valcke, P., & Vayena, E. (2018). AI4People—An ethical framework for a good AI society: Opportunities, risks, principles, and recommendations. *Minds and Machines*, *28*(4), 689–707. DOI: 10.1007/s11023-018-9482-5 PMID: 30930541

Fraga-Lamas, P., Fernández-Caramés, T. M., Rosado Da Cruz, A. M., & Lopes, S. I. (2024). An overview of blockchain for Industry 5.0: Towards human-centric, sustainable and resilient applications. *IEEE Access : Practical Innovations, Open Solutions*, *12*, 116162–116201. DOI: 10.1109/ACCESS.2024.3435374

Fraga-Lamas, P., Varela-Barbeito, J., & Fernandez-Carames, T. M. (2021). Next generation auto-identification and traceability technologies for Industry 5.0: A methodology and practical use case for the shipbuilding industry. *IEEE Access : Practical Innovations, Open Solutions*, *9*, 140700–140730. DOI: 10.1109/ACCESS.2021.3119775

Frontiers in Human Dynamics. (2024). Transparency and accountability in AI systems. Frontiers in Human Dynamics, 6, Article 1421273. https://www.frontiersin.org/journals/human-dynamics/articles/10.3389/fhumd.2024.1421273/full

Gadekallu, T. R., Maddikunta, P. K. R., Boopathy, P., Deepa, N., Chengoden, R., Victor, N., Wang, W., Wang, W., Zhu, Y., & Dev, K. (2024). XAI for Industry 5.0: Concepts, opportunities, challenges and future directions. *IEEE Open Journal of the Communications Society*, •••, 1–1. DOI: 10.1109/OJCOMS.2024.3473891

Ganesh, R., Sharma, S., & Kumar, A. (2024). AI-enabled zero trust architecture for access control and anomaly detection in 6G networks. *Journal of Network and Computer Applications*, *209*, 103536. DOI: 10.1016/j.jnca.2023.103536

Ganesh, S. S., Kumar, V., & Patel, A. (2024). Next-generation threat detection and mitigation in 6G wireless networks using IAM, ZTNA, and advanced security mechanisms. *Journal of Engineering Science and Technology*, *19*(4), 1012–1035. DOI: 10.1234/jes.2024.2545

Garg, S., Kaur, K., Aujla, G. S., Kaddoum, G., Garigipati, P., & Guizani, M. (2023). Trusted Explainable AI for 6G-Enabled Edge Cloud Ecosystem. *IEEE Wireless Communications*, *30*(3), 163–170. DOI: 10.1109/MWC.016.220047

Garvie, C., Bedoya, A. M., & Frankle, J. (2016). *The perpetual line-up: Unregulated police face recognition in America.* Georgetown Law Center on Privacy & Technology.

Gkonis, P. K., Trakadas, P., Sarakis, L., & Xylouris, G. MasipBruin, X., & Martrat, J. (2024). Leveraging network data analytics function and machine learning for data collection, resource optimization, security and privacy in 6g networks. Institute of Electrical and Electronics Engineers.

Goodfellow, I. J. (2014). Explaining and harnessing adversarial examples. arXiv preprint arXiv:1412.6572.

Gorenflo, C., Lee, S., Golab, L., & Keshav, S. 2019. “FastFabric: Scaling Hyperledger Fabric to 20,000 Transactions per Second.” 2019 IEEE International Conference on Blockchain and Cryptocurrency (ICBC), May. https://doi.org/DOI: 10.1109/BLOC.2019.8751452

Gorgadze, S. F., & Ermakova, A. (2022). EFFICIENCY OF MULTIPLE ACCESS OPTIONS FOR 5G AND 6G CELLULAR NETWORKS. *H&ES Research.* https://www.semanticscholar.org/paper/d5ee507a9b40e1abe7817a253700d98198f7ac41

Guidotti, A., Vanelli-Coralli, A., Jaafari, M. E., Chuberre, N., Puttonen, J., Schena, V., Rinelli, G., & Cioni, S. (2024). Role and evolution of non-terrestrial networks toward 6G systems. *IEEE Access : Practical Innovations, Open Solutions*, *12*, 55945–55963. DOI: 10.1109/ACCESS.2024.3389459

Guidotti, R., Monreale, A., Ruggieri, S., Turini, F., Giannotti, F., & Pedreschi, D. (2018). A survey of methods for explaining black box models. *ACM Computing Surveys*, *51*(5), 1–42. DOI: 10.1145/3236009

Gunning, D., & Aha, D. W. (2019). DARPA’s explainable artificial intelligence (XAI) program. *AI Magazine*, *40*(2), 44–58. DOI: 10.1609/aimag.v40i2.2850

Guo, F., Yu, F. R., Zhang, H., Li, X., Ji, H., & Leung, V. C. M. (2021). Enabling Massive IoT Toward 6G: A Comprehensive Survey. In *IEEE Internet of Things Journal* (Vol. 8, Issue 15). https://doi.org/DOI: 10.1109/JIOT.2021.3063686

Guo, W. (2020). Explainable Artificial Intelligence for 6G: Improving Trust between Human and Machine. *IEEE Communications Magazine*, *58*(6), 39–45. DOI: 10.1109/MCOM.001.2000050

Guo, X., & Guo, X. (2023). A research on blockchain technology: Urban intelligent transportation systems in developing countries. *IEEE Access : Practical Innovations, Open Solutions*, *11*, 40724–40740. DOI: 10.1109/ACCESS.2023.3270100

Gupta, A. (2023). Real-time XAI for 6G network security. ACM SIGCOMM Workshop on 6G.

Gutiérrez-Salcedo, M., Martínez, M. A., Moral-Munoz, J. A., Herrera-Viedma, E., & Cobo, M. J. (2018). Some bibliometric procedures for analyzing and evaluating research fields. *Applied Intelligence*, *48*(5), 1275–1287. DOI: 10.1007/s10489-017-1090-5

Habibi, M. A., Han, B., Fellan, A., Jiang, W., Sanchez, A. G., Pavon, I. L., Boubendir, A., & Schotten, H. D. (2023). Toward an Open, Intelligent, and End-to-End Architectural Framework for Network Slicing in 6G Communication Systems. *IEEE Open Journal of the Communications Society*, *4*, 1615–1658. Advance online publication. DOI: 10.1109/OJCOMS.2023.3294445

Hakeem, S. A., Hussein, H., & Kim, H. (2022). *Security requirements and challenges of 6G technologies and applications*. https://www.mdpi.com/1424-8220/22/5/1969

Han, B., Habibi, M. A., Richerzhagen, B., Schindhelm, K., Zeiger, F., Lamberti, F., Pratticó, F. G., Upadhya, K., Korovesis, C., Belikaidis, I., Demestichas, P., Yuan, S., & Schotten, H. (2022). Digital Twins for Industry 4.0 in the 6G Era. *IEEE Open Journal of Vehicular Technology*. https://www.semanticscholar.org/paper/99b6fbb91d486f4889ade4a568b7732770fe0022

Han, M. A., Habibi, M. A., Richerzhagen, B., Schindhelm, K., Zeiger, F., Lamberti, F., Pratticò, F. G., Upadhya, K., Korovesis, C., Belikaidis, I.-P., Demestichas, P., Yuan, S., & Schotten, H. D. (2023). Digital twins for Industry 4.0 in the 6G era. *IEEE Open Journal of Vehicular Technology*, *4*, 820–835. DOI: 10.1109/OJVT.2023.3325382

Haricha, K., Khiat, A., Issaoui, Y., Bahnasse, A., & Ouajji, H. (2023). Recent technological progress to empower smart manufacturing: Review and potential guidelines. *IEEE Access : Practical Innovations, Open Solutions*, *11*, 77929–77951. DOI: 10.1109/ACCESS.2023.3246029

Harjula, E., Artemenko, A., & Forsström, S. (2020). Edge computing for industrial IoT: Challenges and solutions. In *Wireless Networks and Industrial IoT*. Applications, Challenges and Enablers., DOI: 10.1007/978-3-030-51473-0_12

Harvard Business Review. (2022). Agile Doesn't Work Without Psychological Safety. Retrieved from https://hbr.org/2022/02/agile-doesnt-work-without-psychological-safety

Henrique, P. S. R., & Prasad, R. (2021). 6G: The road to future wireless technologies 2030. In *6G: The Road to Future Wireless Technologies 2030*. https://doi.org/DOI: 10.1201/9781003336884

Hiriart, T., Castet, J. F., Lafleur, J. M., & Saleh, J. H. (2009). Comparative reliability of GEO, LEO, and MEO satellites. In *Proceedings of the International Astronautical Congress (IAC-09-D.1.1.1)*. Paris, France: International Astronautical Federation (IAF).

Hu, C. (2024). Application research of 5G/6G cellular network in intelligent Transportation Internet of Things. *Highlights in Science, Engineering and Technology*. https://www.semanticscholar.org/paper/2bd37fa9d09ff76dfc97ea4fde9c5d3850c6f3e5

Huang, T., Yang, W., Wu, J., Ma, J., Zhang, X., & Zhang, D. (2019). A Survey on Green 6G Network: Architecture and Technologies. *IEEE Access : Practical Innovations, Open Solutions*, *7*, 175758–175768. DOI: 10.1109/ACCESS.2019.2957648

Hussein, N. H., Yaw, C. T., Koh, S. P., Tiong, S. K., & Chong, K. H. (2022). A Comprehensive Survey on Vehicular Networking: Communications, Applications, Challenges, and Upcoming Research Directions. In *IEEE Access* (Vol. 10). https://doi.org/DOI: 10.1109/ACCESS.2022.3198656

IBEF. (2023). Impact of 5G Technology on Indian Industries. Retrieved from https://www.ibef.org/research/case-study/impact-of-5g-technology-on-indian-industries

ICS-FORTH. (2025). Cybersecurity challenges and pitfalls in 6G networks. HOLISTIC 2025 Cybersecurity. https://users.ics.forth.gr/~zarras/files/HOLISTIC_2025_Cybersecurity.pdf

Iida, T., & Wakana, H. (2003). Communications satellite systems. In Meyers, R. A. (Ed.), *Encyclopedia of Physical Science and Technology* (3rd ed., pp. 375–408). Academic Press., DOI: 10.1016/B0-12-227410-5/00882-6

Ikram, M., & Mumtaz, S. (2022). for Future Wireless Networks. *IEEE Communications Standards Magazine*, *6*(March), 42–43.

International Telecommunication Union (ITU). (2015). IMT Vision – Framework and overall objectives of the future development of IMT for 2020 and beyond. ITU-R M.2083-0.

Iqbal, A., Tham, M., Wong, Y. J., Al-Habashna, A., Wainer, G., Zhu, Y. X., & Dagiuklas, T. (2023). *Empowering non-terrestrial networks with artificial intelligence: a survey*. Institute of Electrical and Electronics Engineers. DOI: 10.1109/ACCESS.2023.3314732

Irshad, M. N., Du, L., Khoso, I. A., & Javed, T. Bin, & Aslam, M. M. (2019). A hybrid solution of SDN architecture for 5G mobile communication to improve data rate transmission. *2019 28th Wireless and Optical Communications Conference (WOCC)*, 1–5.

Islam, M. M., Nooruddin, S., Karray, F., & Muhammad, G. (2023). Internet of Things: Device Capabilities, Architectures, Protocols, and Smart Applications in Healthcare Domain. *IEEE Internet of Things Journal*, *10*(4), 3611–3641. Advance online publication. DOI: 10.1109/JIOT.2022.3228795

Jagatheesaperumal, S. K., Pham, Q., Ruby, R., Yang, Z., Xu, C., & Zhang, Z. (2022). *Explainable ai over the internet of things (iot): overview, state-of-the-art and future directions*. IEEE Communications Society.

Jagatheesaperumal, S. K., Rahouti, M., Chehri, A., Xiong, K., & Bieniek, J. (2025). Blockchain-Based Security Architecture for Unmanned Aerial Vehicles in B5G/6G Services and Beyond: A Comprehensive Approach. *IEEE Open Journal of the Communications Society*, *6*, 1–1. DOI: 10.1109/OJCOMS.2025.3528220

Jahid, A., Alsharif, M. H., & Hall, T. J. (2023). The convergence of blockchain, IoT and 6G: Potential, opportunities, challenges and research roadmap. In *Journal of Network and Computer Applications* (Vol. 217). https://doi.org/DOI: 10.1016/j.jnca.2023.103677

Jain, K., Titus, B., Krishnan, P., Sudevan, S., Prabu, P., & Alluhaidan, A. S. (2024). A Lightweight Multi-Chaos-Based Image Encryption Scheme for IoT Networks. *IEEE Access : Practical Innovations, Open Solutions*, *12*, 62118–62148. DOI: 10.1109/ACCESS.2024.3377665

Javaid, M., Haleem, A., Singh, R. P., Suman, R., & Khan, S. (2022). A review of Blockchain Technology applications for financial services. In *BenchCouncil Transactions on Benchmarks, Standards and Evaluations* (Vol. 2, Issue 3). https://doi.org/DOI: 10.1016/j.tbench.2022.100073

Jiang, W., Han, B., Habibi, M. A., & Schotten, H. D. (2021). The road towards 6G: A comprehensive survey. *IEEE Open Journal of the Communications Society*, *2*, 334–366. DOI: 10.1109/OJCOMS.2021.3057679

Jobin, A., Ienca, M., & Vayena, E. (2019). The global landscape of AI ethics guidelines. *Nature Machine Intelligence*, *1*(9), 389–399. DOI: 10.1038/s42256-019-0088-2

Jones, T., & Lee, S. (2022). Evaluating the health effects of 5G technology: A review of current evidence. *International Journal of Environmental Health Research*, *32*(4), 567–578.

Jones, T., Lee, S., & Xu, Z. (2023). Exploring the long-term psychological impacts of 5G adoption. *Technological Forecasting and Social Change*, *178*, 121653.

Karaçay, L., Laaroussi, Z., Ujjwal, S., & Soykan, E. U. (2023). On the Security of 6G Use Cases: AI/ML-specific Threat Modeling of All-Senses Meeting. *2023 2nd International Conference on 6G Networking (6GNet)*. https://www.semanticscholar.org/paper/a285226b36184e119c19b9444444457098487034

Kaur, N., Kshetri, N., & Pandey, P. S. (2024). 6AInets: Harnessing artificial intelligence for the 6G network security: Impacts and Challenges. *ArXiv*. https://www.semanticscholar.org/paper/e277b15c5f27fd0f8607914f66f66b62000d831b

Kaur, N., & Gupta, L. (2025). Enhancing interpretability in AI-driven cybersecurity for 6G networks using explainable AI techniques. *IEEE Transactions on Network and Service Management*, *22*(1), 200–213. DOI: 10.1109/TNSM.2024.3456789

Kazmi, S. H. A., Hassan, R., Qamar, F., Nisar, K., & Ibrahim, A. A. A. (2023). Security Concepts in Emerging 6G Communication: Threats, Countermeasures, Authentication Techniques and Research Directions. In *Symmetry* (Vol. 15, Issue 6). https://doi.org/DOI: 10.3390/sym15061147

Khalil, U., Malik, O. A., Uddin, M., & Chen, C. L. (2022). A Comparative Analysis on Blockchain versus Centralized Authentication Architectures for IoT-Enabled Smart Devices in Smart Cities: A Comprehensive Review, Recent Advances, and Future Research Directions. In *Sensors* (Vol. 22, Issue 14). https://doi.org/DOI: 10.3390/s22145168

Khan, A. S., Sattar, M. A., Nisar, K., Ibrahim, A. A. A., Annuar, N. B., & Abdullah, J. bin, & Karim Memon, S. (2023). A Survey on 6G Enabled Light Weight Authentication Protocol for UAVs, Security, Open Research Issues and Future Directions. In *Applied Sciences (Switzerland)* (Vol. 13, Issue 1). https://doi.org/DOI: 10.3390/app13010277

Khan, M. M. A., Rahman, M. T., & Alam, M. (2024). Adversarial attacks and defenses in 6G network-assisted IoT systems. arXiv preprint arXiv:2401.14780. https://arxiv.org/abs/2401.14780

Khan, A. H., Ul Hassan, N., Yuen, C., Zhao, J., Niyato, D., Zhang, Y., & Vincent Poor, H. (2022). Blockchain and 6G: The Future of Secure and Ubiquitous Communication. *IEEE Wireless Communications*, *29*(1), 194–201. Advance online publication. DOI: 10.1109/MWC.001.2100255

Khan, A. S., Yahya, M. I., Zen, K. B., Abdullah, J. B., Rashid, R. B. A., Javed, Y., Khan, N. A., & Mostafa, A. M. (2023). Blockchain-Based Lightweight Multifactor Authentication for Cell-Free in Ultra-Dense 6G-Based (6-CMAS) Cellular Network. *IEEE Access : Practical Innovations, Open Solutions*, *11*, 20524–20541. Advance online publication. DOI: 10.1109/ACCESS.2023.3249969

Khan, F., Patel, R., & Singh, S. (2024). Defending adversarial attacks on AI-based intrusion detection systems in dense IoT networks. *IEEE Internet of Things Journal*, *11*(2), 1423–1435. DOI: 10.1109/JIOT.2023.3276548

Khan, N., Coleri, S., Abdallah, A., Celik, A., & Eltawil, A. M. (2024). Explainable and Robust Artificial Intelligence for Trustworthy Resource Management in 6G Networks. *IEEE Communications Magazine*, *62*(4), 50–56. Advance online publication. DOI: 10.1109/MCOM.001.2300172

Khan, S., Luo, F., Zhang, Z., Ullah, F., Amin, F., Qadri, S. F., Heyat, M. B., Ruby, R., Wang, L., Ullah, S., Li, M., Leung, V. C. M., & Wu, K. (2023). A Survey on X.509 Public-Key Infrastructure, Certificate Revocation, and Their Modern Implementation on Blockchain and Ledger Technologies. *IEEE Communications Surveys and Tutorials*, *25*(4), 2529–2568. Advance online publication. DOI: 10.1109/COMST.2023.3323640

Khashan, O. A., & Khafajah, N. M. (2023). Efficient hybrid centralized and blockchain-based authentication architecture for heterogeneous IoT systems. *Journal of King Saud University. Computer and Information Sciences*, *35*(2), 726–739. Advance online publication. DOI: 10.1016/j.jksuci.2023.01.011

Khutey, R., Rana, G., Dewangan, V., Tiwari, A., & Dewamngan, A. (2015). Future of Wireless Technology 6G & 7G. *International Journal of Electrical and Electronics Research*, *3*(2), 583–585. www.researchpublish.com

Kim, S. (2023). AI-driven beamforming with XAI for 6G mmWave systems. *IEEE Globecom Workshops*.

Kirilenko, A. A., Kyle, A. S., Samadi, M., & Tuzun, T. (2017). Flash crash: High-frequency trading in an electronic market. *The Journal of Finance*, *72*(3), 967–998. DOI: 10.1111/jofi.12498

Kleine-Ostmann, T., & Nagatsuma, T. (2011). A review on terahertz communications research. *Journal of Infrared, Millimeter and Terahertz Waves*, *32*(2), 143–171. DOI: 10.1007/s10762-010-9758-1

Kodheli, O., Lagunas, E., & Giordani, M.. (2020). Satellite communications in the new space era: A survey and future challenges. *IEEE Communications Surveys and Tutorials*.

Kolhar, A. & Sridevi. (2025). Future Trends and Innovation in Machine Intelligence for Cyber Risk Management. In M. Almaiah & Y. Maleh (Eds.), Machine Intelligence Applications in Cyber-Risk Management (pp. 415-438). IGI Global Scientific Publishing. https://doi.org/.DOI: 10.4018/979-8-3693-7540-2.ch018

Krishnan, P., Jain, K., Poojara, S. R., Srirama, S. N., Pandey, T., & Buyya, R. (2024). eSIM and blockchain integrated secure zero-touch provisioning for autonomous cellular-IoTs in 5G networks. *Computer Communications*, *216*, 324–345. Advance online publication. DOI: 10.1016/j.comcom.2023.12.023

Kumar Srivastava, A., & Chaudhary, V. (2024). The role of artificial intelligence in shaping 6G networks: Opportunities, challenges, and future directions. *EasyChair Preprints*. https://easychair.org/publications/preprint/L9LR/open

Kumar, M. N. (2023). 5G Technology is Revolutionizing the Wireless Industry with Unparalleled Efficiency. *SciWaveBulletin*. https://www.semanticscholar.org/paper/676e0994cfe548e0fcec69d86bdcace5d6c4b309

Kumar, S., Lim, W. M., Sivarajah, U., & Kaur, J. (2023). Artificial Intelligence and Blockchain Integration in Business: Trends from a Bibliometric-Content Analysis. *Information systems frontiers: a journal of research and innovation, 25*(2), 871–8

Kumari, A., Gupta, R., & Tanwar, S. (2021). Amalgamation of blockchain and IoT for smart cities underlying 6G communication: A comprehensive review. *Computer Communications*, *172*, 102–118. Advance online publication. DOI: 10.1016/j.comcom.2021.03.005

Larsen, L. M. P., Christiansen, H., Ruepp, S., & Berger, M. (2023). Toward Greener 5G and Beyond Radio Access Networks—A Survey. *IEEE Open Journal of the Communications Society*. https://www.semanticscholar.org/paper/f3d0fc60f54e5cfd0ce5900693c5be6069852296

Lee, Y. L., Qin, D., Wang, L. C., & Sim, G. H. (2021). 6G Massive Radio Access Networks: Key Applications, Requirements and Challenges. *IEEE Open Journal of Vehicular Technology, 2*(October 2020), 54–66. DOI: 10.1109/OJVT.2020.3044569

Lee, J., & Kim, H. (2022). Electromagnetic hypersensitivity and 5G: Psychological distress and relocation. *Environmental Health Perspectives*, *130*(6), 067005. PMID: 35700064

Lee, Y., Chang, C., Lin, Y., & Cheng, Z. (2014). The dark side of smartphone usage: Psychological traits, compulsive behavior and technostress. *Computers in Human Behavior, 31*, 373–383. DOI: 10.1016/j.chb.2013.10.047

Lei, Z., Shi, J., Luo, Z., Cheng, M., & Wan, J. (2024). Intelligent manufacturing from the perspective of Industry 5.0: Application review and prospects. *IEEE Access : Practical Innovations, Open Solutions*, *12*, 167436–167451. DOI: 10.1109/ACCESS.2024.3496697

Li, C., Guo, W., Sun, S. C., Al-Rubaye, S., & Tsourdos, A. (2020). Trustworthy Deep Learning in 6G-Enabled Mass Autonomy: From Concept to Quality-of-Trust Key Performance Indicators. *IEEE Vehicular Technology Magazine*, *15*(4), 112–121. Advance online publication. DOI: 10.1109/MVT.2020.3017181

Lilhore, U. K., Arya, L., Sharma, Y. K., & Rastogi, R. (2025). Chapter 5: Privacy and security for 6G's IoT-connected future in the age of quantum computing. In Industrial Quantum Computing: Algorithms, Blockchains, Industry 4.0 (pp. 67-86). De Gruyter. DOI: 10.1515/9783111354842-005

LinkedIn. (2020). The importance of real-time features in your mobile app's success. https://www.linkedin.com/pulse/importance-real-time-features-your-mobile-apps-success-?trk=pulse-article

Lin, Y.. (2024). *Satellite-MEC integration for 6G Internet of Things: Minimal structures, advances, and prospects*. IEEE Open Journal of the Communications Society.

Lipton, Z. C. (2018). The mythos of model interpretability. *ACM Queue; Tomorrow's Computing Today*, *16*(3), 31–57. DOI: 10.1145/3236386.3241340

Liu, Y., Zhang, X., Chen, J., & Wang, H. (2024). Understanding the risks of 6G technology: The next cybersecurity challenge. European Centre for Cybersecurity University Blog. https://www.eccu.edu/blog/understanding-the-risks-of-6g-technology-the-next-cybersecurity-challenge/

Liu, W., Hou, J., & Cheng, Y. (2024). How can firms implement smart manufacturing through supply chain collaboration? A multiple-case study from China. *Production Planning and Control*, •••, 1–19. DOI: 10.1080/09537287.2024.2362866

Liu, Y., Qian, K., Wang, K., & He, L. (2022). BCmaster: A Compatible Framework for Comprehensively Analyzing and Monitoring Blockchain Systems in IoT. *IEEE Internet of Things Journal*, *9*(22), 22529–22546. Advance online publication. DOI: 10.1109/JIOT.2022.3182004

Liu, Y., Xu, J., Wang, Z., Mu, X., Zhang, J., & Zhang, P. (2023). Simultaneously transmitting and reflecting (STAR) RISs for 6G: Fundamentals, recent advances, and future directions. *Frontiers of Information Technology & Electronic Engineering*, *24*(12), 1689–1707. DOI: 10.1631/FITEE.2300490

Lokhande, A. (2020). Key features and characteristics of 5G technology. LinkedIn. https://www.linkedin.com/pulse/key-features-characteristics-5g-technology-ashish-lokhande

Lundberg, S. M., & Lee, S.-I. (2017). A unified approach to interpreting model predictions. *Advances in Neural Information Processing Systems*, *30*, 4765–4774.

Mahboob, S., & Liu, L. (2024). Revolutionizing future connectivity: A contemporary survey on AI-empowered satellite-based non-terrestrial networks in 6G. *IEEE Communications Surveys and Tutorials*, *26*(2), 1279–1321. DOI: 10.1109/COMST.2023.3347145

Mahmood, N. H., Berardinelli, G., Khatib, E. J., Hashemi, R., De Lima, C., & Latva-aho, M. (2023). A functional architecture for 6G special-purpose industrial IoT networks. *IEEE Transactions on Industrial Informatics*, *19*(3), 2530–2540. DOI: 10.1109/TII.2022.3182988

Mahmoud, H., Ismail, T., Baiyekusi, T., & Idrissi, M. (2024). Deep learning-based physical layer security for jamming and spoofing resilience in 6G microcell environments. *Wireless Networks*, *30*(4), 1895–1910. DOI: 10.1007/s11276-024-03117-4

Maldonado-Ruiz, D., Torres, J., El Madhoun, N., & Badra, M. (2022). Current Trends in Blockchain Implementations on the Paradigm of Public Key Infrastructure: A Survey. *IEEE Access : Practical Innovations, Open Solutions*, *10*, 17641–17655. Advance online publication. DOI: 10.1109/ACCESS.2022.3145156

Manikandan, A., Narayanan, G., Prakash, K. S. R. B., Reddy, C. Y., Mahesh, A. D., Sushanth, V., & Ramprasad, O. G. (2024). Investigations in Security Challenges and Solutions for M2M Communications—A Review. In *International Journal of Electrical and Electronic Engineering and Telecommunications* (Vol. 13, Issue 1). https://doi.org/DOI: 10.18178/ijeetc.13.1.17-32

Manorama Yearbook. (2023). Explainer - What is 6G network? What are its advantages? Retrieved from https://www.manoramayearbook.in/india/special-articles/2023/03/23/what-is-6g-network-explained.html

Mao, B., Liu, J., Wu, Y., & Kato, N. (2023). *Security and privacy on 6g network edge: A survey*. https://ieeexplore.ieee.org/abstract/document/10044183/

Ma, R., Zhou, J., & Ma, M. (2024). A Blockchain-Assisted Security Protocol for Group Handover of MTC Devices in 5G Wireless Networks. *Sensors (Basel)*, *24*(7), 2331. DOI: 10.3390/s24072331 PMID: 38610542

Maxicus. (2023). The 5G Revolution: What it means & Impact on business. Retrieved from https://maxicus.com/the-5g-revolution-what-it-means-impact-on-business/

Mehrabi, N., Morstatter, F., Saxena, N., Lerman, K., & Galstyan, A. (2021). A survey on bias and fairness in machine learning. *ACM Computing Surveys*, *54*(6), 1–35. DOI: 10.1145/3457607

Merluzzi, M., Borsos, T., Rajatheva, N., Benczur, A. A., Farhadi, H., Yassine, T., Mueck, M. D., Barmpounakis, S., Strinati, E. C., Dampahalage, D., Demestichas, P., Ducange, P., Filippou, M. C., Baltar, L. G., Haraldson, J., Karacay, L., Korpi, D., Lamprousi, V., Marcelloni, F., & Uusitalo, M. A. (2023). The Hexa-X Project Vision on Artificial Intelligence and Machine Learning-Driven Communication and Computation Co-Design for 6G. *IEEE Access : Practical Innovations, Open Solutions*, *11*, 65620–65648. Advance online publication. DOI: 10.1109/ACCESS.2023.3287939

Mesko, T. (2022). Does Agile Transformation Impact Our Mental Health? LinkedIn. Retrieved from https://www.linkedin.com/pulse/does-agile-transformation-impact-our-mental-health-tjasa-mesko

Miglani, A., & Kumar, N. (2021). Blockchain management and machine learning adaptation for IoT environment in 5G and beyond networks: A systematic review. Computer Communications, 178, 37–63. doi: . https://doi.org/DOI: 10.1016/j.comcom.2021.07.00996

Miller, T. (2019). Explanation in artificial intelligence: Insights from the social sciences. *Artificial Intelligence*, *267*, 1–38. DOI: 10.1016/j.artint.2018.07.007

Mittelstadt, B. D., Allo, P., Taddeo, M., Wachter, S., & Floridi, L. (2016). The ethics of algorithms: Mapping the debate. *Big Data & Society*, *3*(2), 1–21. DOI: 10.1177/2053951716679679

Mohamed, A., Ruan, H., Abdelwahab, M., Dorneanu, B., Xiao, P., Arellano-Garcia, H., Gao, Y., & Tafazolli, R. (2020). An Inter-Disciplinary Modelling Approach in Industrial 5G/6G and Machine Learning Era. *2020 IEEE International Conference on Communications Workshops (ICC Workshops)*. https://www.semanticscholar.org/paper/3508e323a82d041adc751412f117cd95ce54ec36

Mohanta, K., & Al-Rubaye, S. (2024). Towards 6G satellite–terrestrial networks: Analysis of air mobility operations. *Electronics (Basel)*, *13*(14), 2855. DOI: 10.3390/electronics13142855

Mosakheil, J. H., & Yang, K. (2025). PKChain: Compromise-Tolerant and Verifiable Public Key Management System. *IEEE Internet of Things Journal, 12*(3), 3130–3144. DOI: 10.1109/JIOT.2024.3478754

Mukhopadhyay, A., & Vinayaka, R. (2021). A smart-contract-based blockchain for a healthcare iot network. *International Journal of Electronic Healthcare, 11*(3), 256. Advance online publication. DOI: 10.1504/IJEH.2021.117122

Munir, M. S., Kim, K. T., Adhikary, A., Saad, W., Shetty, S., Park, S. B., & Hong, C. S. (2023). Neuro-Symbolic Explainable Artificial Intelligence Twin for Zero-Touch IoE in Wireless Network. *IEEE Internet of Things Journal, 10*(24), 22451–22468. Advance online publication. DOI: 10.1109/JIOT.2023.3303713

Murdock, K. K. (2013). Texting While Stressed: Implications for Students' Burnout, Sleep, and Well-Being. *Psychology of Popular Media Culture, 2*(4), 207–221. DOI: 10.1037/ppm0000012

Murroni, M., Anedda, M., Fadda, M., Ruiu, P., Popescu, V., Zaharia, C., & Giusto, D. (2023). 6G—Enabling the New Smart City: A Survey. In *Sensors* (Vol. 23, Issue 17). https://doi.org/DOI: 10.3390/s23177528

Naeem, F., Ali, M., & Kaddoum, G. (2023). Federated-learning-empowered semi-supervised active learning framework for intrusion detection in zsm. *IEEE Communications Magazine, 61*(2), 88–94. DOI: 10.1109/MCOM.001.2200533

Nagaraj, S., Kathole, A. B., Arya, L., Tyagi, N., Goyal, S. B., Rajawat, A. S., Raboaca, M. S., Mihaltan, T. C., Verma, C., & Suciu, G. (2023). Improved secure encryption with energy optimization using random permutation pseudo algorithm based on internet of things in wireless sensor networks. *Energies, 16*(1), 8. Advance online publication. DOI: 10.3390/en16010008

Nahar, N., Andersson, K., Schelén, O., & Saguna, S. (2024). A Survey on Zero Trust Architecture: Applications and Challenges of 6G Networks. *IEEE Access : Practical Innovations, Open Solutions, 12*, 94753–94764. DOI: 10.1109/ACCESS.2024.3425350

Nasralla, M. M., Khattak, S. B. A., Rehman, I., & Iqbal, M. (2023). Exploring the Role of 6G Technology in Enhancing Quality of Experience for m-Health Multimedia Applications: A Comprehensive Survey. *Sensors (Basel, Switzerland)*. https://www.mdpi.com/1424-8220/23/13/5882

Noor, Q., Multazam, A., Riyadi, S. G., Pratama, R., & Maulana, A. 2024. "Large-Scale Ethereum Network Performance Analysis: Case Study and Implications." JATI. May 28, 2024. https://www.novadatatech.com/index.php/jati/article/view/3

Nwachukwu, C., Durodola-Tunde, K., & Akwiwu-Uzoma, C. (2024). AI-driven anomaly detection in cloud computing environments. *International Journal of Science and Research Archive, 13*(2), 692–710. DOI: 10.30574/ijsra.2024.13.2.2184

O'Neil, C. (2016). *Weapons of math destruction: How big data increases inequality and threatens democracy*. Crown Publishing Group.

Osama, M., Ateya, A. A., Sayed, M. S., Hammad, M., Pławiak, P., Abd El-Latif, A. A., & Elsayed, R. A. (2023). Internet of Medical Things and Healthcare 4.0: Trends, Requirements, Challenges, and Research Directions. In *Sensors* (Vol. 23, Issue 17). https://doi.org/DOI: 10.3390/s23177435

Osorio, D., Ahmad, I., & Sánchez, J. (2022). *Towards 6G-enabled internet of vehicles: Security and privacy*. https://ieeexplore.ieee.org/abstract/document/9681822/

Ounza, J. E. (2023). A taxonomical survey of 5G and 6G security and privacy issues. *Global Journal of Engineering and Technology Advances*. https://www.semanticscholar.org/paper/7558904417398f02f63dd1c817aaffdb42e6c43b

Paolini, E., Valcarenghi, L., Maggiani, L., & Andriolli, N. (2023). *Real-time clustering based on deep embeddings for threat detection in 6g networks*. Institute of Electrical and Electronics Engineers. DOI: 10.1109/ACCESS.2023.3325721

Parasuraman, R., & Manzey, D. H. (2010). Complacency and bias in human use of automation: An attentional integration. *Human Factors, 52*(3), 381–410. DOI: 10.1177/0018720810376055 PMID: 21077562

Park, I., & Yoon, B. (2018). Technological opportunity discovery for technological convergence based on the prediction of technology knowledge flow in a citation network. *Journal of Informetrics, 12*(4), 1199–1222. DOI: 10.1016/j.joi.2018.09.007 PMID: 32336982

Park, J. (2023). Quantum-XAI for 6G: Speed and scalability. *Proceedings of the IEEE Quantum Computing Conference*.

Patel, S., Coughlin, J., & Sharma, M. (2019). 5G and telehealth: Improving mental healthcare access in rural communities. *Telemedicine Journal and e-Health, 25*(9), 797–803.

Pathak, V., Pandya, R. J., Bhatia, V., & Lopez, O. A. (2023). Qualitative Survey on Artificial Intelligence Integrated Blockchain Approach for 6G and beyond. In *IEEE Access* (Vol. 11). https://doi.org/DOI: 10.1109/ACCESS.2023.3319083

Pathak, A., Al-Anbagi, I., & Hamilton, H. J. (2024). Blockchain-Enhanced Zero Knowledge Proof-Based Privacy-Preserving Mutual Authentication for IoT Networks. *IEEE Access : Practical Innovations, Open Solutions*, *12*, 118618–118636. DOI: 10.1109/ACCESS.2024.3450313

Patwary, A. A. N., Naha, R. K., Garg, S., Battula, S. K., Patwary, M. A. K., Aghasian, E., Amin, M. B., Mahanti, A., & Gong, M. (2021). Towards secure fog computing: A survey on trust management, privacy, authentication, threats and access control. *Electronics (Basel)*, *10*(10), 1171. Advance online publication. DOI: 10.3390/electronics10101171

Paul, S. (2024). Investigating Federated Learning Implementation Challenges in 6G Network. *2024 Fourth International Conference on Advances in Electrical, Computing, Communication and Sustainable Technologies (ICAECT)*. https://www.semanticscholar.org/paper/0ef80dbf6a5224a808258cf1635f0be9120852e5

Pennanen, H., Hänninen, T., Tervo, O., Tölli, A., & Latva-aho, M. (2024). *6G: The Intelligent Network of Everything — A Comprehensive Vision, Survey, and Tutorial*. http://arxiv.org/abs/2407.09398

Periannasamy, S., Thangavel, C., Latha, S., Reddy, G., Ramani, S., Phad, P. V., Chandline, S. R., & Gopalakrishnan, S. (2022). Analysis of Artificial Intelligence Enabled Intelligent Sixth Generation (6G) Wireless Communication Networks. 2022 IEEE International Conference on Data Science and Information System (ICDSIS). https://www.semanticscholar.org/paper/42b5879d4d776081b611cf03d56cfba8d9506df5

Pivoto, D. G. S., Rezende, T. T., Facina, M. S. P., Moreira, R., De Oliveira Silva, F., Cardoso, K. V., Correa, S. L., Araujo, A. V. D., Silva, R. S. E., Neto, H. S., De Lima Tejerina, G. R., & Alberti, A. M. (2023). A detailed relevance analysis of enabling technologies for 6G architectures. *IEEE Access : Practical Innovations, Open Solutions*, *11*, 89644–89684. DOI: 10.1109/ACCESS.2023.3301811

Polese, M. (2022). *Explainable AI for dynamic network slicing*. IEEE Transactions on Network Science.

Prabhakara Rao, T., & Satyanarayana Murthy, B. (2023). Extended group-based verification approach for secure M2M communications. *International Journal of Information Technology : an Official Journal of Bharati Vidyapeeth's Institute of Computer Applications and Management*, *15*(5), 2479–2488. Advance online publication. DOI: 10.1007/s41870-023-01284-w

Puspitasari, A. A., An, T. T., Alsharif, M. H., & Lee, B. M. (2023). Emerging Technologies for 6G Communication Networks: Machine Learning Approaches. *Sensors (Basel)*, *23*(18), 7709. DOI: 10.3390/s23187709 PMID: 37765765

PwC. (2024). The Impact of 5G: Creating New Value across Industries and Society. Retrieved from https://www.pwc.com/gx/en/about/contribution-to-debate/world-economic-forum/the-impact-of-5g.html

Qamar, F., Siddiqui, M. U. A., Hindia, M. H. D. N., Hassan, R., & Nguyen, Q. N. (2020). Issues, challenges, and research trends in spectrum management: A comprehensive overview and new vision for designing 6g networks. *Electronics (Basel)*, *9*(9), 1–39. DOI: 10.3390/electronics9091416

Qian, K., Liu, Y., Shu, C., Sun, Y., & Wang, K. (2023). Fine-Grained Benchmarking and Targeted Optimization: Enabling Green IoT-Oriented Blockchain in the 6G Era. *IEEE Transactions on Green Communications and Networking*, *7*(2), 1036–1051. Advance online publication. DOI: 10.1109/TGCN.2022.3185610

Rabnawaz, R., & Abid, M. K. A. M. K. Aslam, Dr. N., & Bukhari, F. (2023). Exploring 6G Wireless Communication: Application Technologies, Challenges and Future Direction. *International Journal of Information Systems and Computer Technologies*. https://www.semanticscholar.org/paper/f5d8f748aaba16df1204728d2a6686207824edf9

Rahman, T. F., Zeng, X., & Babar, M. (2021). Network and physical layer attacks and countermeasures to AI-enabled 6G O-RAN. arXiv preprint arXiv:2106.02494. https://arxiv.org/abs/2106.02494

Ramezanpour, K., & Jagannath, J. (2025). Service-aware zero trust architecture for 6G software-defined networks: AI-driven trust management and network slicing security. *IEEE Transactions on Network and Service Management*, *22*(3), 1130–1145. DOI: 10.1109/TNSM.2025.3456789

Rantcell. (2023). Differences between 5G and 6G network. Retrieved from https://www.rantcell.com/how-is-6g-mobile-network-different-from-5g.html

Rao, P. M., Jangirala, S., Pedada, S., Das, A. K., & Park, Y. (2023). Blockchain Integration for IoT-Enabled V2X Communications: A Comprehensive Survey, Security Issues and Challenges. *IEEE Access : Practical Innovations, Open Solutions*, *11*, 54476–54494. Advance online publication. DOI: 10.1109/ACCESS.2023.3281844

Rastogi, R., Arya, L., & Sharma, Y. K. (2025). Chapter 12: Quantum-secured healthcare data and cybersecurity innovations in the era of Industry 5.0. In Industrial Quantum Computing: Algorithms, Blockchains, Industry 4.0 (pp. 199-218). De Gruyter. DOI: 10.1515/9783111354842-012

RCR Wireless News. (2022). 6G: The Next Generation of Wireless Communication. Retrieved from https://www.rcrwireless.com/20220601/6g-the-next-generation-of-wireless-communication

Realme. (n.d.). What are the characteristics of 5G? https://www.realme.com/in/support/kw/doc/2055960

Rebello, G. A. F., Camilo, G. F., Guimarães, L. C. B., de Souza, L. A. C., Thomaz, G. A., & Duarte, O. C. M. B. (2022). A security and performance analysis of proof-based consensus protocols. *Annales Des Telecommunications. Annales des Télécommunications*, *77*(7–8), 517–537. Advance online publication. DOI: 10.1007/s12243-021-00896-2

Rezazadeh, F., Chergui, H., & Mangues-Bafalluy, J. (2023). Explanation-Guided Deep Reinforcement Learning for Trustworthy 6G RAN Slicing. *2023 IEEE International Conference on Communications Workshops: Sustainable Communications for Renaissance, ICC Workshops 2023*. DOI: 10.1109/ICCWorkshops57953.2023.10283684

Ribeiro, M. T., Singh, S., & Guestrin, C. (2016). 'Why should I trust you?' Explaining the predictions of any classifier. Proceedings of the 22nd ACM SIGKDD International Conference on Knowledge Discovery and Data Mining.

Rowshan, M., Qiu, M., Xie, Y., Gu, X., & Yuan, J. (2024). Channel Coding Toward 6G: Technical Overview and Outlook. IEEE Open Journal of the Communications Society. https://www.semanticscholar.org/paper/7be59cd803e3550e1f12f14f1dc6791a78fad802

Roy, S., Chergui, H., & Verikoukis, C. (2024). Toward Bridging the FL Performance-Explainability Tradeoff: A Trustworthy 6G RAN Slicing Use-Case. *IEEE Transactions on Vehicular Technology*, *73*(7), 10529–10538. Advance online publication. DOI: 10.1109/TVT.2024.3364363

Rožman, N., Diaci, J., & Corn, M. (2021). Scalable framework for blockchain-based shared manufacturing. *Robotics and Computer-integrated Manufacturing*, *71*, 102139. Advance online publication. DOI: 10.1016/j.rcim.2021.102139

Rudin, C. (2019). Stop explaining black box machine learning models for high-stakes decisions and use interpretable models instead. *Nature Machine Intelligence*, *1*(5), 206–215. DOI: 10.1038/s42256-019-0048-x PMID: 35603010

Saad, W. (2020). A vision of 6G wireless systems: Applications, trends, and opportunities. *IEEE Network*, *34*(3), 134–142. DOI: 10.1109/MNET.001.1900287

Saeed, M. M., Saeed, R. A., Abdelhaq, M., Alsaqour, R., Hasan, M. K., & Mokhtar, R. A. (2023). *Anomaly detection in 6g networks using machine learning methods*. Multidisciplinary Digital Publishing Institute. DOI: 10.3390/electronics12153300

Sahoo, B. B., & Dey, S. (2024). SVM and RF Based Performance Enhancement in Organization: A Study on KGI, Odisha and its Organizational Growth. *Journal of Engineering Research and Reports*, *26*(6), 190–197. DOI: 10.9734/jerr/2024/v26i61173

Samek, W. (2017). Explainable artificial intelligence: Understanding, visualizing, and interpreting deep learning models. arXiv preprint arXiv:1708.08296.

Sanusi, H.. (2022). Security, ethical challenges, and standardization in 6G networks. *International Journal of Future Management Research*, *14*(2), 88–105. https://www.ijfmr.com/papers/2025/2/41475.pdf

Sarwar, M. M., Orr, S., & Stuart, S. (2021). Agile practices and performance: Examining the role of psychological empowerment. *Journal of Business Research*, *125*, 1–11. DOI: 10.1016/j.jbusres.2020.12.012

Scalise, P., Boeding, M., Hempel, M., & Sharif, H. (2024). *A Systematic Survey on 5G and 6G Security Considerations, Challenges, Trends, and Research Areas*. https://www.mdpi.com/1999-5903/16/3/67

Scalise, P., Boeding, M., Hempel, M., Sharif, H., Delloiacovo, J., & Reed, J. (2024). A Systematic Survey on 5G and 6G Security Considerations, Challenges, Trends, and Research Areas. *Future Internet*. https://www.semanticscholar.org/paper/4d4ef766abfd734dfe7a98c7711a91f9310178cd

Scalise, P., Boeding, M., Hempel, M., Sharif, H., Delloiacovo, J., & Reed, J. (2024). A Systematic Survey on 5G and 6G Security Considerations, Challenges, Trends, and Research Areas. *Future Internet*, *16*(3), 1–38. DOI: 10.3390/fi16030067

Sedjelmaci, H., Kheir, N., Boudguiga, A., & Kaaniche, N. (2022). *Cooperative and smart attacks detection systems in 6g-enabled internet of things*. None. DOI: 10.1109/ICC45855.2022.9838338

Selleo. (2024). You Need To Know About Real-Time Features In Applications. https://selleo.com/blog/real-time-features-in-applications

Serghiou, D., Khalily, M., Brown, T. W. C., & Tafazolli, R. (2022). Terahertz Channel Propagation Phenomena, Measurement Techniques and Modeling for 6G Wireless Communication Applications: A Survey, Open Challenges and Future Research Directions. *IEEE Communications Surveys and Tutorials*, *24*(4), 1957–1996. DOI: 10.1109/COMST.2022.3205505

Sergiou, C., Lestas, M., Antoniou, P., Liaskos, C., & Pitsillides, A. (2020). Complex Systems: A Communication Networks Perspective towards 6G. *IEEE Access : Practical Innovations, Open Solutions*, *8*, 89007–89030. DOI: 10.1109/ACCESS.2020.2993527

Shafay, M., Ahmad, R. W., Salah, K., Yaqoob, I., Jayaraman, R., & Omar, M. (2023). Blockchain for deep learning: Review and open challenges. *Cluster Computing*, *26*(1), 197–221. DOI: 10.1007/s10586-022-03582-7 PMID: 35309043

Shafik, W. (2023). Introduction to ChatGPT. In *Advanced Applications of Generative AI and Natural Language Processing Models*. DOI: 10.4018/979-8-3693-0502-7.ch001

Shafik, W. (2024d). Generative AI for Social Good and Sustainable Development. In *Generative AI: Current Trends and Applications* (pp. 185–217). Springer. DOI: 10.1007/978-981-97-8460-8_10

Shafik, W. (2024g). Sustainable Development Goal 14: Explainable AI (XAI) for Ocean Health. In *Artificial Intelligence and Edge Computing for Sustainable Ocean Health* (pp. 167–198). Springer. DOI: 10.1007/978-3-031-64642-3_8

Shafik, W. (2024h). Towards Trustworthy and Explainable AI Educational Systems. In *Explainable AI for Education: Recent Trends and Challenges* (pp. 17–41). Springer. DOI: 10.1007/978-3-031-72410-7_2

Shafik, W. (2025a). Quantum Computing and Generative Adversarial Networks (GANs): Ethics, Privacy, and Security. In *Quantum AI and its Applications in Blockchain Technology* (pp. 111–156). IGI Global Scientific Publishing.

Shafik, W. (2025b). *SDG 4: Quality Education—Digital Platforms for Inclusive Learning* (pp. 163–193). DOI: 10.1007/978-981-96-7299-8_6

Shafik, W. (2025c). *SDG 5: Gender Equality—Bridging the Digital Gender Divide* (pp. 195–222). DOI: 10.1007/978-981-96-7299-8_7

Shafik, W. (2025f). *SDG 8: Decent Work and Economic Growth—Technology for Employment and Economic Opportunities* (pp. 277–301). DOI: 10.1007/978-981-96-7299-8_10

Shafik, W. (2025h). *SDG 11: Sustainable Cities and Communities—Smart Cities and Urban Sustainability* (pp. 333–363). DOI: 10.1007/978-981-96-7299-8_12

Shafik, W. (2025i). *SDG 12: Responsible Consumption and Production—The Circular Economy* (pp. 365–390). DOI: 10.1007/978-981-96-7299-8_13

Shafik, W. (2025j). *Technology as a Catalyst for Achieving the Sustainable Development Goals (SDGs)* (pp. 3–39). DOI: 10.1007/978-981-96-7299-8_1

Shafik, W. (2025k). *The Interplay Between Global Sustainable Development Goals (SDGs) and Inclusivity* (pp. 69–95). DOI: 10.1007/978-981-96-6557-0_3

Shafik, W., Mojtaba Matinkhah, S., & Sanda, M. N. (2020). Network Resource Management Drives Machine Learning: A Survey and Future Research Direction. *Journal of Communications Technology, Electronics and Computer Science, 2020*(0). https://doi.org/http://dx.doi.org/10.22385/jctecs.v30i0.312

Shafik, W. (2024a). Agile Security Strategies. In *Smart and Agile Cybersecurity for IoT and IIoT Environments* (pp. 82–101). IGI Global., DOI: 10.4018/979-8-3693-3451-5.ch004

Shafik, W. (2024b). Artificial intelligence and internet of things roles in sustainable next-generation manufacturing: An overview of emerging trends in Industry 6.0. *Advances in Business Information Systems and Analytics*, *6*(0), 207–239. DOI: 10.4018/979-8-3693-3140-8.ch012

Shafik, W. (2024c). Deep Learning Impacts in the Field of Artificial Intelligence. In *Deep Learning Concepts in Operations Research* (pp. 9–26). Auerbach Publications., DOI: 10.1201/9781003433309-2

Shafik, W. (2024e). Machine Learning for Advanced Wireless Communication. In *Microwave Devices and Circuits for Advanced Wireless Communication* (pp. 252–278). CRC Press., DOI: 10.1201/9781032656021-13

Shafik, W. (2024f). Navigating Emerging Challenges in Robotics and Artificial Intelligence in Africa. In *Examining the rapid advance of digital technology in Africa* (pp. 126–146). IGI Global., DOI: 10.4018/978-1-6684-9962-7.ch007

Shafik, W. (2025d). SDG 6: Clean Water and Sanitation—Smart. *Water Management*, •••, 223–248. DOI: 10.1007/978-981-96-7299-8_8

Shafik, W. (2025e). SDG 7: Affordable and Clean Energy—Renewable. *Energy Technology (Weinheim)*, •••, 249–275. DOI: 10.1007/978-981-96-7299-8_9

Shafik, W. (2025g). *SDG 9: Industry*. Innovation, and Infrastructure—Smart Technologies for Sustainable Industry., DOI: 10.1007/978-981-96-7299-8_11

Shafik, W. (2025l). *The Intersection of Technology*. Sustainability, and the Sustainable Development Goals., DOI: 10.1007/978-981-96-7299-8_2

Shafik, W., Kalinaki, K., Fahim, K. E., & Adam, M. (2024). Safeguarding Data Privacy and Security in Federated Learning Systems. In *Federated Deep Learning for Healthcare* (pp. 170–190). CRC Press., DOI: 10.1201/9781032694870-13

Shafik, W., Matinkhah, S. M., & Ghasemzadeh, M. (2019). A fast machine learning for 5g beam selection for unmanned aerial vehicle applications. *Journal of Information Systems and Telecommunication*, *7*(4). https://doi.org/https://doi.org/10.7508/jist.2019.04.003

Shafik, W., Singh, R., & Kumar, V. (2025). Artificial Intelligence Transparency and Explainability in Sustainable Healthcare. In *Transforming Healthcare Sector Through Artificial Intelligence and Environmental Sustainability* (pp. 165–191). Springer.

Shah, A. F. M. S., Karabulut, M. A., & Rabie, K. (2023). Mission-critical Internet of Things on the 6G network: Services and apps with networking architecture. *TechRxiv Preprint*. DOI: 10.36227/techrxiv.24115869.v1

Shangguan, Z. (2021). The impacts of 5G technology and cloud computing on the gaming accessories industry. *International Conference on Electronics and Information Engineering*. https://www.semanticscholar.org/paper/30bf71c20b552ac4767be36220bb065a3b5e8012

Sharma, M., Sehrawat, R., Luthra, S., Daim, T., & Bakry, D. (2024). Moving towards Industry 5.0 in the pharmaceutical manufacturing sector: Challenges and solutions for Germany. *IEEE Transactions on Engineering Management*, *71*, 13757–13774. DOI: 10.1109/TEM.2022.3143466

Sheemar, C. K., ... (2025). Joint communications and sensing for 6G satellite networks: Use cases and challenges. *arXiv Preprint*, arXiv:2501.05243.

Shen, L. H., Ten Feng, K., & Hanzo, L. (2023). Five Facets of 6G: Research Challenges and Opportunities. *ACM Computing Surveys*, *55*(11), 1–39. Advance online publication. DOI: 10.1145/3571072

Shokoor, F., Shafik, W., & Matinkhah, S. M. (2022). Overview of 5G & Beyond Security. *EAI Endorsed Transactions on Internet of Things*, *8*(30), e2. Advance online publication. DOI: 10.4108/eetiot.v8i30.1624

Singh, A., Sharma, R., & Gupta, P. (2023). Automation of surveillance systems using deep learning and facial recognition. *International Journal of System Assurance Engineering and Management*, *14*(1), 236–245. https://journals.sagepub.com/doi/10.1177/20319525241306327. DOI: 10.1007/s13198-022-01844-6

Singh, R., Srivastav, G., Kashyap, R., & Vats, S. (2023). Study on zero-trust architecture, application areas & challenges of 6g technology in future. *International Conference on Database Theory*. DOI: 10.1109/ICDT57929.2023.10150745

Siriwardhana, Y., & Porambage, P. (2021). *AI and 6G security: Opportunities and challenges*. https://ieeexplore.ieee.org/abstract/document/9482503/

Smith, A., Johnson, B., & Williams, L. (2021). Personality changes associated with 5G adoption. *Cyberpsychology, Behavior, and Social Networking*, *24*(3), 167–174.

Software, R. S. T. (2022). Understanding the impact of 5G vs 6G on mobile app development. Retrieved from https://www.rst.software/blog/5g-vs-6g-mobile-app-development

Solat, S., Calvez, P., & Naït-Abdesselam, F. (2021). Permissioned vs. Permissionless Blockchain: How and Why There Is Only One Right Choice. *Journal of Software*, •••, 95–106. DOI: 10.17706/jsw.16.3.95-106

Soldani, D. (2021). 6g fundamentals: Vision and enabling technologies. *Journal of Telecommunications and the Digital Economy*, *9*(3), 58–86. DOI: 10.18080/jtde.v9n3.418

Soni, M., & Singh, D. K. (2023). Blockchain-based group authentication scheme for 6G communication network. *Physical Communication*, *57*, 102005. Advance online publication. DOI: 10.1016/j.phycom.2023.102005

Sourjah, S. (2022). The 6 Impacts of Agile on Mental Health. Better Programming. Retrieved from https://betterprogramming.pub/the-6-impacts-of-agile-on-mental-health-6adcf0f1785b

Spiceworks. (2023). What Is a 6G Network? Working and Benefits. Retrieved from https://www.spiceworks.com/tech/networking/articles/what-is-6g/

Su, X., Larangeira, M., & Tanaka, K. 2023. "Provably Secure Blockchain Protocols From Distributed Proof-of-Deep-Learning." IACR Cryptology ePrint Archive. July 6, 2023. https://eprint.iacr.org/2023/1059

Suraci, C., Pizzi, S., Molinaro, A., & Araniti, G. (2022). A Trust-Based Selection Mechanism for the Support of 6G eHealth Multimedia Services. *2022 IEEE International Symposium on Broadband Multimedia Systems and Broadcasting (BMSB)*. https://www.semanticscholar.org/paper/413ba65910928aab46ddb463dbe4c32d927ae55c

Susandhika, M., & Edward, S. (2023). A Comprehensive Review and Comparative analysis of 5G and 6G based MIMO Channel Estimation Techniques. *2023 International Conference on Recent Trends in Electronics and Communication (ICRTEC)*. https://www.semanticscholar.org/paper/9eb59c508fd94d7100d6decaf8ae829091528df9

Sverko, M., Grbac, T. G., & Mikuc, M. (2022). SCADA systems with focus on continuous manufacturing and steel industry: A survey on architectures, standards, challenges and Industry 5.0. *IEEE Access : Practical Innovations, Open Solutions*, *10*, 109395–109430. DOI: 10.1109/ACCESS.2022.3211288

Swathi, S., Chakaravarthy, S. P., Wilson, A. J., & Bharathi, A. P. (2022). An Effective Addressal of Traffic using Tensor Flow. *2022 1st International Conference on Computer, Power and Communications, ICCPC 2022 - Proceedings*. https://doi.org/DOI: 10.1109/ICCPC55978.2022.10072253

Tallat, R., Hawbani, A., Wang, X., Al-Dubai, A., Zhao, L., Liu, Z., Min, G., Zomaya, A. Y., & Alsamhi, S. H. (2024). Navigating Industry 5.0: A survey of key enabling technologies, trends, challenges, and opportunities. *IEEE Communications Surveys and Tutorials*, *26*(2), 1080–1126. DOI: 10.1109/COMST.2023.3329472

Tataria, H., Shafi, M., Molisch, A. F., Dohler, M., Sjoland, H., & Tufvesson, F. (2021). 6G Wireless Systems: Vision, Requirements, Challenges, Insights, and Opportunities. *Proceedings of the IEEE*, *109*(7), 1166–1199. DOI: 10.1109/JPROC.2021.3061701

TechRepublic. (2022). 5G vs 6G: What's the Difference? Retrieved from https://www.techrepublic.com/article/5g-vs-6g/

TechTarget. (2022). What are the features and benefits of 5G technology for businesses? https://www.techtarget.com/searchnetworking/tip/What-are-the-features-and-benefits-of-5G-technology-for-businesses

Thakkar, P., Nathan, S., & Viswanathan, B. "Performance Benchmarking and Optimizing Hyperledger Fabric Blockchain Platform." 2018. IEEE Conference Publication | IEEE Xplore. September 1, 2018. https://doi.org/DOI: 10.1109/MASCOTS.2018.00034

Thilakavathy, P., Jayachitra, S., Aeron, A., Kumar, N., Ali, S. S., & Malathy, M. (2023). Investigating Blockchain Security Mechanisms for Tamper-Proof Data Storage. *2023 International Conference on Communication, Security and Artificial Intelligence, ICCSAI 2023*. https://doi.org/DOI: 10.1109/ICCSAI59793.2023.10421006

Tomaszewski, L., & Kołakowski, R. (2023). Mobile Services for Smart Agriculture and Forestry, Biodiversity Monitoring, and Water Management: Challenges for 5G/6G Networks. *Telecom*. https://www.mdpi.com/2673-4001/4/1/6

Torrens, S. A., Petrov, V., & Jornet, J. M. (2024). Modeling interference from millimeter wave and terahertz bands cross-links in low Earth orbit satellite networks for 6G and beyond. *IEEE Journal on Selected Areas in Communications*, *42*(5), 1371–1386. DOI: 10.1109/JSAC.2024.3365894

Tripwire (2025, March 6). 6 potential security concerns with the eventual rollout of 6G. State of Security. https://www.tripwire.com/state-of-security/potential-security-concerns-eventual-rollout-6g

Ukommi, U., Ubom, E., & Ikpaya, I. (2021). Ground station design for satellite and space technology development. [AJER]. *American Journal of Engineering Research*, *10*(8), 12–19.

Uusitalo, M. A., Rugeland, P., Boldi, M. R., Strinati, E. C., Demestichas, P., Ericson, M., Fettweis, G. P., Filippou, M. C., Gati, A., Hamon, M. H., Hoffmann, M., Latva-Aho, M., Parssinen, A., Richerzhagen, B., Schotten, H., Svensson, T., Wikstrom, G., Wymeersch, H., Ziegler, V., & Zou, Y. (2021). 6G Vision, Value, Use Cases and Technologies from European 6G Flagship Project Hexa-X. *IEEE Access : Practical Innovations, Open Solutions*, *9*, 160004–160020. DOI: 10.1109/ACCESS.2021.3130030

Vajiram & Ravi. (2024). 6G Technology: Revolutionizing the Future of Wireless Communication. Retrieved from https://www.vajiramandravi.com/6g-technology-revolutionizing-the-future-of-wireless-communication/

Vajiramandravi. (2023). 5G Technology - Features, Advantages, and Limitations. https://vajiramandravi.com/quest-upsc-notes/5g-technology/

Vujošević, D., Bojović, P. D., Šuh, J., Martic, G., & Bojović, Ž. (2022). The course on modern 5G/6G networks: A step toward understanding a flexible network core. *Computer Applications in Engineering Education*. https://www.semanticscholar.org/paper/ea12581946a831cb82e6daebeb269035556521dd

Wachter, S., Mittelstadt, B., & Russell, C. (2017). Counterfactual explanations without opening the black box: Automated decisions and the GDPR. *SSRN*, *31*(2), 841–887. DOI: 10.2139/ssrn.3063289

Wang, J., Ling, X., Le, Y., Huang, Y., & You, X. (2021). Blockchain-enabled wireless communications: a new paradigm towards 6G. In *National Science Review* (Vol. 8, Issue 9). https://doi.org/DOI: 10.1093/nsr/nwab069

Wang, C.-X., You, X., Gao, X., Zhu, X., Li, Z., Zhang, C., Wang, H., Huang, Y., Chen, Y., Haas, H., Thompson, J. S., Larsson, E. G., Di Renzo, M., Tong, W., Zhu, P., Shen, X., Poor, H. V., & Hanzo, L. (2023). On the road to 6G: Visions, requirements, key technologies, and testbeds. *IEEE Communications Surveys and Tutorials, 25*(2), 905–974. DOI: 10.1109/COMST.2023.3249835

Wang, C., You, X., Gao, X., Zhu, X., Li, Z., Zhang, C., Wang, H., Huang, Y., Chen, Y., Haas, H., Thompson, J., Larsson, E. G., Renzo, M. D., Tong, W., Zhu, P., Shen, X., Poor, H. V., & Hanzo, L. (2023). *On the road to 6g: visions, requirements, key technologies, and testbeds*. Institute of Electrical and Electronics Engineers.

Wang, J., Tang, W., Han, Y., Jin, S., Li, X., Wen, C.-K., Cheng, Q., & Cui, T. J. (2021). Interplay between RIS and AI in wireless communications: Fundamentals, architectures, applications, and open research problems. *IEEE Journal on Selected Areas in Communications, 39*(8), 2271–2288. DOI: 10.1109/JSAC.2021.3087259

Wang, L. (2022). Edge-core XAI for 6G network optimization. *IEEE Communications Magazine*.

Wang, Q., Yu, J., Chen, S., & Xiang, Y. (2023). SoK: DAG-based Blockchain Systems. *ACM Computing Surveys, 55*(12), 1–38. Advance online publication. DOI: 10.1145/3576899

Wang, X. (2022). AI-driven predictive maintenance for 6G networks: A comprehensive review. *IEEE Communications Magazine, 60*(2), 78–84. DOI: 10.1109/MCOM.2016.7402265

Wang, X., & Chen, Y. (2024). Transparency and explainability in AI algorithms: Building trust and fairness. *Journal of Artificial Intelligence Ethics, 12*(1), 45–60. DOI: 10.1234/jaie.2024.012345

Wenhua, Z., Qamar, F., Abdali, T. A. N., Hassan, R., Jafri, S. T. A., & Nguyen, Q. N. (2023). Blockchain Technology: Security Issues, Healthcare Applications, Challenges and Future Trends. In *Electronics (Switzerland)* (Vol. 12, Issue 3). https://doi.org/DOI: 10.3390/electronics12030546

Winfield, A. F. T. (2019). Ethical governance is essential to building trust in robotics and artificial intelligence systems. *Philosophical Transactions of the Royal Society A, 377*(2153), 20180085. PMID: 30323000

Wu, Y., Song, P., & Wang, F. (2020). Hybrid Consensus Algorithm Optimization: A Mathematical Method Based on POS and PBFT and Its Application in Blockchain. *Mathematical Problems in Engineering, 2020*(April), 1–13. DOI: 10.1155/2020/7270624

Xu, Z., & Zhang, Y. (2021). Potential carcinogenic effects of 5G frequencies: A review. *Environmental Research, 195*, 110863.

Yang, B., & Gupta, L. (2022). AI-augmented intrusion response system for dynamic 6G wireless networks using GAN and Bayesian classifiers. *IEEE Transactions on Cognitive Communications and Networking, 8*(1), 112–123. DOI: 10.1109/TCCN.2021.3112456

Yang, J., Geng, Y., Mao, H., Xiao, Z., Han, Z., & Wu, D. O. (2023). *Satellite-terrestrial integrated network architecture towards 6G with user plane function trimming. In 2023 IEEE Globecom Workshops*. GC Wkshps., DOI: 10.1109/GCWkshps58843.2023.10465214

Yang, M., Qu, Y., Ranbaduge, T., Thapa, C., Sultan, N., Ding, M., Suzuki, H., Ni, W., Abuadbba, S., Smith, D., Tyler, P., Pieprzyk, J., Rakotoarivelo, T., Guan, X., & M'rabet, S. (2024). *From 5G to 6G: A Survey on Security, Privacy, and Standardization Pathways*. http://arxiv.org/abs/2410.21986

Yapa, C., de Alwis, C., Liyanage, M., & Ekanayake, J. (2021). Survey on blockchain for future smart grids: Technical aspects, applications, integration challenges and future research. In *Energy Reports* (Vol. 7). https://doi.org/DOI: 10.1016/j.egyr.2021.09.112

Yap, K. Y., Chin, H. H., & Klemeš, J. J. (2023). Blockchain technology for distributed generation: A review of current development, challenges and future prospect. *Renewable & Sustainable Energy Reviews, 175*, 113170. Advance online publication. DOI: 10.1016/j.rser.2023.113170

You, L., Zhu, Y., Qiang, X., Tsinos, C. G., Wang, W., Gao, X., & Ottersten, B. (2024). Ubiquitous integrated sensing and communications for massive MIMO LEO satellite systems. *IEEE Internet of Things Magazine, 7*(4), 30–35. DOI: 10.1109/IOTM.001.2300201

Yue, Y., & Shyu, J. Z. (2024). A paradigm shift in crisis management: The nexus of AGI-driven intelligence fusion networks and blockchain trustworthiness. *Journal of Contingencies and Crisis Management, 32*(1), e12541. Advance online publication. DOI: 10.1111/1468-5973.12541

Zawish, M., Dharejo, F. A., Khowaja, S. A., Raza, S., Davy, S., Dev, K., & Bellavista, P. (2024). AI and 6G Into the Metaverse: Fundamentals, Challenges and Future Research Trends. *IEEE Open Journal of the Communications Society, 5*(January), 730–778. DOI: 10.1109/OJCOMS.2024.3349465

Zeebaree, M. Z. M., Zeebaree, M. A. M., & Aqel, M. A. M. (2023). Challenges facing E-government implementation and adoption in the Era of 5G, 6G. . https://www.semanticscholar.org/paper/35fd3d2397c05c271726fb69b89873e9f41ec5ce

Zhang, R. (2023). Privacy-preserving XAI in federated 6G networks. Journal of AI Research.

Zhang, J. (2022). Artificial intelligence for 6G: Enabling technologies and future directions. *Nature Electronics*, *5*(1), 1–15.

Zhang, J., Zheng, D., Zhang, Z., Charnas, A., Lin, Z., & Ye, P. D. (2023). Ultrathin InGaO thin film transistors by atomic layer deposition. *IEEE Electron Device Letters*, *44*(2), 273–276. DOI: 10.1109/LED.2022.3233080

Zhang, W., Yang, Y. T., & Liang, H. G. (2023). A bibliometric analysis of enterprise social media in the digital economy: Research hotspots and trends. *Sustainability (Basel)*, *15*(1), 12545. DOI: 10.3390/su151612545

Zhang, Y. (2021). Personalized edge intelligence in 6G networks: Architectures, challenges, and opportunities. *IEEE Internet of Things Journal*, *8*(10), 7905–7920.

Zhang, Z., Xiao, Y., Ma, Z., Xiao, M., Ding, Z., Lei, X., Karagiannidis, G. K., & Fan, P. (2019). 6G Wireless Networks: Vision, Requirements, Architecture, and Key Technologies. *IEEE Vehicular Technology Magazine*, *14*(3), 28–41. DOI: 10.1109/MVT.2019.2921208

Zhao, L., Zhu, D., Shafik, W., Matinkhah, S. M., Ahmad, Z., Sharif, L., & Craig, A. (2022). Artificial intelligence analysis in cyber domain: A review. In *International Journal of Distributed Sensor Networks* (Vol. 18, Issue 4). DOI: 10.1177/15501329221084882

Zhao, W., Qi, Q., Zhou, J., & Luo, X. (2023). Blockchain-Based Applications for Smart Grids: An Umbrella Review. In *Energies* (Vol. 16, Issue 17). https://doi.org/ DOI: 10.3390/en16176147

Zhao, D. (2024). Big data-driven digital economic industry based on innovation path of manufacturing. *IEEE Access : Practical Innovations, Open Solutions*, *12*, 24104–24115. DOI: 10.1109/ACCESS.2024.3365716

Zhao, D., Ding, R., & Song, B. (2025). Satellite-assisted 6G wide-area edge intelligence: Dynamics-aware task offloading and resource allocation for remote IoT services. *Science China. Information Sciences*, *68*(2), 122303. DOI: 10.1007/s11432-024-4258-x

Zhaofeng, M., Xiaochang, W., Jain, D. K., Khan, H., Hongmin, G., & Zhen, W. (2020). 013_Only abstract_Zhaofeng_A Blockchain-based Trusted Data Management Scheme in Edge Computing. *IEEE Transactions on Industrial Informatics*, *16*(3), 2013–2021. DOI: 10.1109/TII.2019.2933482

Zhou, S., Li, K., Xiao, L., Cai, J., Liang, W., & Castiglione, A. (2023). A Systematic Review of Consensus Mechanisms in Blockchain. In *Mathematics* (Vol. 11, Issue 10). https://doi.org/DOI: 10.3390/math11102248

Zong, B. (2021). 6G wireless networks: Vision, requirements, architecture, and key technologies. *IEEE Communications Surveys and Tutorials*, *23*(4), 2209–2247.

Zuo, Y., Guo, J., Gao, N., Zhu, Y., Jin, S., & Li, X. (2023). A Survey of Blockchain and Artificial Intelligence for 6G Wireless Communications. *IEEE Communications Surveys and Tutorials*, *25*(4), 2494–2528. DOI: 10.1109/COMST.2023.3315374

About The Contributors

Riaz Ahmed Shaikh received his Ph.D. degree from the Computer Engineering Department of Kyung Hee University, South Korea, in 2009. Between October 2009 and January 2012, he served as a postdoctoral fellow at the Computer Security Research Lab at the University of Quebec in Outaouais, Canada. In 2012, he was hired as an Assistant Professor at the Computer Science Department of King Abdulaziz University, Saudi Arabia. Since August 2022, he has been an Associate Professor at the School of Computing Sciences, University of East Anglia, UK. His research interests include privacy, security, trust management, risk estimation, sensor networks, vehicular networks, and the IoT. He wrote more than 50 research articles published in peer-reviewed journals and conferences. Two U.S. and one Korean patents have been issued to him. He also served as a technical program committee member for more than 35 international conferences. He is also the editor of the book entitled 'Secure Cyber-Physical Systems for Smart Cities' published by IGI Global.

***

Sridevi, Professor, Department of Computer Science, Karnatak University, Dharwad. Obtained her PhD from Mangalore University, Mangalore in 2017. Her research interests are Advanced Computer Networks, Mobile and Wireless Communication, Network Security, Cloud Computing, and the Internet of Things. At present, she is guiding four research scholars and One M.Phil. is awarded. She is a reviewer for the Journal of Advances in Mathematics and Computer Science. She has published more than 30 research papers in national and international journals.

A. Thamodharan, an Assistant professor in the department of Computer Science and Engineering-R at Koneru Lakshmaiah Education Foundation (KLEF), Guntur, Andhra Pradesh, India. Having very good Academic records and have 10+ years of experience in Teaching and Research and 1 year of Industry experience.

Have significant contributions to both the academic and research aspects of the field of computer science and engineering. I actively participate in the member of Counselling, Academic and other related activities. I collaborate effectively with my colleagues in preparing teaching materials through SRP for Video lecturing etc. in the department level. I served in different positions like Committee members, Program organizer etc. in the department. I am doing my Doctorate studies in the field of Artificial Intelligence (AI) particular Medical domain, where the early detection and prediction of cancer and how it is affecting the other organs in the human body. I am trying to make the decision systems through AI concepts, which can be useful to the doctors as an expert system for a quick diagnosis. Overall, my role as an Assistant Professor in the CSE department has been characterized by dedication to excellence in both teaching and research, with the aim of cultivating the next generation of skilled and forward-thinking computer scientists.

Leena Arya is working as a Professor at the Department of Computer Science and Engineering at Koneru Lakshmaiah Education Foundation Deemed to be University, Vaddeswaram, 22nd NIRF Ranking University, Guntur, AP, India. She completed her Ph.D. from IIT Roorkee in 2012. She has published over 55 research papers in Scopus and SCI-indexed international journals. She handled a research project for the Department of Science and Technology, DST, New Delhi, as Principal Investigator under the Women Scientists Scheme (WOS-A). She has been granted a UK design and Australian Government Innovation patents. She has been a reviewer of many prestigious international journals and conferences. Her research area includes wireless communication, the Internet of Things (IoT), network security, and artificial intelligence.

Mourad Elloumi received an Undergraduate Degree in Mathematics and Physics in 1984, and a Master's Degree in Computer Engineering in 1988, from the Faculty of Sciences of Tunis, Tunisia. He also received a Master's Degree in Computer Science in 1989, and a PhD Degree in Computer Science in 1994, from the University of Aix-Marseilles III, France. Then, he received a Habilitation for conducting research in Computer Science in 2003, from the National School of Computer Science, Tunis, Tunisia. He is currently a Full Professor in Computer Science, College of Computing and Information Technology, University of Bisha, Saudi Arabia. Professor Mourad Elloumi is the author/co-author of more than 80 publications in international journals, books and conference proceedings. He was a Guest Editor of a special issue on biological knowledge discovery and data mining, Knowledge Based Systems Journal (Elsevier 2002), a Guest Editor of a special issue on pattern finding in Computational Molecular Biology, Recent Patents on DNA and Gene Sequence Journal (Bentham Science 2012), a Co-Editor of the proceedings of two international conferences and Editor/Co-Editor of five books, respectively, on Algorithms in Computational Molecular Biology (Wiley 2011), Biological Knowledge Discovery (Wiley 2014), Pattern Recognition in Computational Molecular Biology (Wiley 2015), Algorithms for Next-Generation Sequencing Data (Springer 2017), Deep Learning for Biomedical Data Analysis (Springer 2021). His research interests include Algorithmics, Computational Molecular Biology, Knowledge Discovery and Data Mining, and Deep Learning.

MPJ Santosh Kumar is an Associate Professor in the Department of Computer Science and Engineering (Honors) at KL Deemed University, where he has been since 2023. From 2021 to 2023 he served as an Assistant Professor in the Department of Computer Science at GITAM Deemed University. During 2005 to 2021 he was served as an Assistant Professor in the Department of Computer Science and Engineering at Gayatri Vidya Parishad College of Engineer (Autonomous). He received a M.Tech. in Computer Science and Engineering with Specialization in Computer Networks & M.Sc. in Computer Science from Andhra University. He received his Ph.D. in Computer Science and Engineering from the Acharya Nagarjuna University in 2023. His research interests span both computer networking and network science. Much of his work has been on improving the understanding, design, and performance of parallel and networked computer systems, Cryptanalysis and Blockchain Technologies mainly through the application of data mining, statistics, and performance evaluation. In the networking arena, he has worked on characterizing the Internet and the World Wide Web. He has explored the presence and implications of self-similarity and heavy-tailed distributions in network traffic and Web workloads. He has also investigated the implications of Web workloads for the design of scalable and cost-effective Web servers. In addition he has made numerous contributions to Internet measurement and modeling; and he has examined the impact of network properties on the design of protocols and the construction of statistical models. In the network science arena, he has focused on the analysis of social, biological, and data networks.

Sooraj Nair is a passionate B.Tech graduate in Electronics and Computer Engineering, skilled in python and C, interested in areas of ML, Computer Vision and innovative, data-driven solutions.

Bala Namasivayam, an Assistant Professor in the Department of Computer Science and Engineering-R at Koneru Lakshmaiah Education Foundation (KLEF), Guntur, Andhra Pradesh, India. I have 15+ years of experience in Teaching and Research and 3 years of Industry experience. I significantly contribute to both the academic and research aspects of computer science and engineering. I actively participate in the member of Counselling, Academic and other related activities. I collaborate effectively with my colleagues in preparing teaching materials through SRP for Video lecturing etc. in the department level. I served in different positions like Committee members, Program organizer etc. in the department. I am doing my Doctorate studies in the field of Artificial Intelligence (AI) particular Medical domain, where the early detection and prediction of cancer and how it affects the other organs in the human body. I am trying to make decision systems through AI concepts, which can be useful to doctors as an expert system for a quick diagnosis. Overall, my role as an Assistant Professor in the CSE department has been characterized by dedication to excellence in both teaching and research, to cultivate the next generation of skilled and forward-thinking computer scientists.

Thamizh Thendral P M has completed her M.E. in Mobile and Pervasive Computing from the Department of Electronics and Communication Engineering, University College of Engineering, Bharathidasan Institute of Technology Campus, Anna University, Tiruchirappalli. She is currently working as an Assistant Professor in the Department of Electronics and Communication Engineering, A.K.T Memorial college of Engineering and Technology. Her research interests are Wireless networks, Digital systems, Mobile Networks.

Priyadharshini R has completed her Ph.D. in optical heterogeneous networks from the Department of Electronics and Communication Engineering, College of Engineering Guindy, Anna University. She is currently working as an Assistant Professor in the Department of Electronics and Communication Engineering, School of Electrical and Electronics Engineering, College of Engineering and Technology, SRM Institute of Science and Technology, Kattankulathur. Her research interests are Heterogeneous networks (Fiber-Wireless), Radio over Fiber, RF system design, Wireless Networks (5G/6G).

R. Rajeshkanna is an accomplished academic with over 16 years of experience in the field of computer science and information technology. He holds a Ph.D. from Bharathiar University, Coimbatore, and an M.Phil from Vinayaka Missions University, Salem. He also earned his MCA from Periyar University, Salem. Currently, Dr. Rajeshkanna serves as an Assistant Professor in the Department of Computer Science at CHRIST (Deemed to be University), Bangalore, a position he has held since July 2022. Prior to this, he was the Professor and Head of the Department of Information Technology at Dr. N.G.P Arts & Science College (Autonomous), Coimbatore. His tenure at this institution, spanning from January 2020 to June 2022, followed a series of progressive roles, including Associate Professor and Head of the Department, and earlier, as an Assistant Professor. Dr.

Rajeshkanna has made significant academic contributions through his research and scholarly activities. He has published 35 papers in reputed international journals with high impact factors and has contributed 16 book chapters through IGI Global Publications.

Eda Raju, Bachelor Degree in Swarnandhra Institute of Engineering and Technology, under JNTU Kakinada in May 2013, Seetharamapuram, Andhra Pradesh 534275. I done my Masters Degree in Dantuluri Narayana Raju College of Engineering and Technology, under JNTU Kakinada in December 2015, Bhimavaram, Andhra Pradesh 534202. Pursuing mine Ph.D. in KL Deemed University, Vaddeswaram, Vijayawada, Andhra Pradesh 522302 . I worked as Assistant Professor in CSE Department at Swarnandhra College of Engineering and Technology from January 2016- May 2023, Seetharampuram, Narsapur, Andhra Pradesh 534280. Currently Working in Malla Reddy University as Assistant Professor in CSE Department from June 2023 to Present, Maisammaguda, Hyderabad, Telangana 500043.

Ravi Rastogi received his Ph.D. in Computer Science and Engineering in December 2011 from Uttarakhand Technical University, Dehradun, Uttarakhand, India. MS in Computer Science degree in September 2005 from Fairleigh Dickinson University, Teaneck, New Jersey, USA. He is working as a Professor in the Department of Computer Science and Engineering (Honors) at Koneru Lakshmaiah Education Foundation Deemed to be a university. He was a database developer for Microsoft, Seattle, USA, and ING, Philadelphia, USA. His research interests are interconnection networks, stable matching problems, data mining and intelligence in systems, the Internet of Things, and cloud computing. Refereed International Journal publications are 22 and Refereed International Conference Publications are 8.

MMS Rauthan is working as Head of the department and professor in HNB Garhwal University in computer science and engineering department with 30 years of teaching experience. He has done M.Tech in 1987 from Roorkee University and has done his Ph.D. from Kumaon University in 2013. He has written a several research paper as well as 5 books in computer science. He is a core member of research committees, visiting committees.

Poorana Senthilkumar S, received his Bachelor of Science degree in Computer Science from Bharathiar University, Coimbatore, in 2004 and his Master of Computer Applications degree from Anna University, Chennai, in 2008. He successfully completed his Ph.D. from Bharathiar University and served as an Assistant Professor in the Department of Computer Applications at Dr. N.G.P. Arts and Science College, Coimbatore, Tamil Nadu, India. A lifetime member of IAENG, he has authored over 10 research articles in esteemed National/International

Journals. His extensive experience spans 15 years in teaching and 12 years in research, with a focus on Internet of Things, LLNs, VANET, Cloud Computing, Artificial Intelligence, Machine Learning, and WSN Networks.

S. B. Mahalakshmi is working as an Assistant Professor in the Department of Computing – Artificial Intelligence and Machine Learning at Coimbatore Institute of Technology, Coimbatore. With 18 years of experience, she has published many technical papers in National and International conferences and journals, and has acted as a resource person in various workshops, FDPs, and conferences. She is a member of various professional bodies like CSI, IAEng etc., She received a Best paper award during the year 2019 at Asia Pacific University of Technology and Innovation, Malaysia. She specializes in the fields of Machine learning, Deep learning, operating systems, and natural language processing.

M. Vanish Santosh, Bachelor Degree in Hi-Tech College of Engineering and Technology, under JNTU Hyderabad in May 2010, Himayath Nagar, Moinabad,Telangana.500047. I done my Masters Degree in Geethanjali College of Engineering and Technology, under JNTU Hyderabad in January 2013, Keesara, Telangana.500047. Pursuing mine Ph.D. in LPU, Jalandhar-Delhi, G.T. Road, Phagwara, Punjab (INDIA) -144411. I worked as Assistant Professor in ECE Department at Nalla Malla Reddy Engineering College from April 2015 - November 2018, Narapally, Hyderabad, Telangana. 500047. I worked as Assistant Professor in ECE Department at Siddartha Institute of Engineering and Technology from November 2018- December 2022,Narapally, Hyderabad, Telangana. 500047. Currently Working in Malla Reddy University as Assistant Professor in CSE Department from March 2023 to Present, Maisamma Guda, Dulapally, Hyderabad, Telangana 500043.

Wasswa Shafik (Member, IEEE) received a Bachelor of Science degree in information technology from Ndejje University, Uganda, a Master of Engineering degree in Information Technology (Computer and Communication Networks) from Yazd University, Iran, and a PhD in Computer Science with the School of Digital Science, Universiti Brunei Darussalam, Brunei Darussalam. He is also the Founder and Research Director of the Dig Connectivity Research Laboratory (DCRLab) after serving as a Research Associate at the Network Interconnectivity Research Laboratory at Yazd University. Prior to this, he worked as a Community Data Analyst at Population Services International (PSI-Uganda), a Community Data Officer at the Programme for Accessible Health Communication (PACE-Uganda), a Research Assistant at the Socio-Economic Data Centre (SEDC-Uganda), Uganda, an Assistant Data Officer at TechnoServe, Kampala, Uganda, and Asmaah Charity Organization as Cheif Executive Officer. He has hundreds of publications with renowned publishers. His research interests include Artificial Intelligence, Neural Networks, Computer Vision, Smart Agriculture, Digital Health, and Green Computing.

Mohana Priya T is Assistant Professor at CHRIST(Deemed to be University), Bangalore, India. She Holds a PhD degree in Computer Science in Machine learning at Bharathiar University, Coimbatore, India. Her research areas are Machine Learing and medical image analysis. She is acted as Coordinator for curriculum development cell and Software development cell. She published 10 Journal articles in various international peer reviewed journals, 2 Book publications and 15 presentations in various international level conference held in India and abroad. She can be contacted at email: drtmohanapriya @gmail.com

Index

Symbols

A

B

C

E

F

I

L

M

N

O

Q

S

T

U

W

www.ingramcontent.com/pod-product-compliance
Lightning Source LLC
LaVergne TN
LVHW080559300926
849162LV00005B/993